THE GLOBAL GOSPEL

"For I am not ashamed of the gospel,
for it is the power of God for salvation to everyone who believes,
to the Jew first and also to the Greek."
–*Romans 1:16*

THE
GLOBAL GOSPEL

Achieving Missional Impact in Our Multicultural World

WERNER MISCHKE

"Biblically based and well researched, *The Global Gospel* is a compelling read that helps frame the gospel in the unique social dynamics of honor and shame—something we in the West so often miss. This is more than a book. It is a full-fledged course on biblically based cross-cultural communication containing graphics, charts and diagrams which forcefully illustrate Mischke's insightful principles of sharing the gospel cross culturally."

Marvin J. Newell, D.Miss.
Senior Vice President
Missio Nexus

Mission ONE®
R E S O U R C E S

The Global Gospel: Achieving Missional Impact in Our Multicultural World
by Werner Mischke

Copyright © 2015 by Mission ONE

Published by: Mission ONE
                PO Box 5960
                Scottsdale, Arizona 85261
                U.S.A.
                mission1.org

Printed in the United States of America

Professional publishing services provided by Dan Wright Publisher Services LLC

Cover design by Larry Taylor, Dan Wright, and Werner Mischke

Interior design by Larry Taylor and Werner Mischke

Produced with the assistance of Livingstone, the Publishing Services Division of Barton-Veerman Company. Project staff includes: Bruce Barton, Linda Taylor, and Tom Shumaker.

Unless otherwise noted, Scripture quotations are from The Holy Bible, English Standard Version ® (ESV®), copyright © 2001 by Crossway, a publishing ministry of Good News Publishers. Used by permission. All rights reserved.

Hardback ISBN: 978-0-9848128-6-8
Paperback ISBN: 978-0-9848128-5-1
eBook ISBN: 978-0-9848128-7-5

"With magnificent, dominant, life changing themes invisible to Western eyes, *The Global Gospel* will enrich our understanding of who God is and change the way we do cross cultural mission forever."
Terry Dalrymple, Coordinator, Global CHE Network

"The first word that comes to my mind is *incredible.* Werner has reviewed a broad array of literature and a multitude of Scripture passages to establish this premise: Western theology has given the world a presentation of the gospel unwittingly influenced by its own Western values; in so doing, the culture of the Bible and the culture of the recipient peoples have often both been marginalized, resulting in unnecessary obstacles to faith in Christ. The value of the material and paradigm contained in *The Global Gospel* is immeasurable."
Paul R. Gupta, Ph.D., President, Hindustan Bible Institute & College, India

"We have much to learn from our brothers and sisters in honor-and-shame cultures, and in this wise and instructive book, Werner Mischke guides us along on that necessary journey of spiritual learning!"
Richard J. Mouw, Ph.D., Professor of Faith and Public Life,
Fuller Theological Seminary

"Thorough, targeted, touching, timely, theologically sound while demanding some theological turns, and teeming with applications, therefore it becomes required reading."
Tom Steffen, D.Miss., Professor Emeritus, Cook School of Intercultural Studies, Biola University

"It will be crucial that we allow this 'aha' wisdom to shape the way we reach the last and the least within the Majority World."
Pat Murdock, Executive Director, Issachar Initiative

"The Global Gospel provides an in-depth yet eminently practical analysis of the crucial topic of honor and shame that makes it indispensable reading for both biblical scholars and cross-cultural practitioners."
Mwana Hadisi, Ph.D., Assistant Professor of Intercultural Studies, Phoenix Seminary

"The Global Gospel is an essential contribution to missiology. Werner's understanding and experience of the dynamic of honor and shame should be read by anyone who truly wants to understand missions."
Dr. Bobby Brewer, Pastor of Spiritual Formation, City of Grace Church

"In our small church representing 21 nations, getting to grips with honor/shame dynamics has been so important. Through *The Global Gospel,* I began to grasp God's Word with the honor/shame lens and my mind was blown with really how big the grace of God is."
Pastor Andy Moyle, The Gateway Church, King's Lynn, United Kingdom

"This is a much needed resource for the global church. Werner Mischke provides a road map for anyone doing ministry in an honor/shame culture. I expect *The Global Gospel* will spur the kind of theological conversations that lead to practical solutions for many missiological challenges."
Jackson Wu, Ph.D., author of *Saving God's Face: A Chinese Contextualization of Salvation through Honor and Shame*

"*The Global Gospel* is a much needed book that provides deep insight into cultures of honor and shame and how this impacts the gospel and our mission. After reading this book I can't but read the Scriptures through a different lens. Werner helps us understand God's grace and our mission all the better."
Michelle Tessendorf, Executive Director, Orchard: Africa

"*The Global Gospel* demonstrates conclusively that understanding honor and shame is critical to a proper biblical hermeneutic. More than a book to be read once and then discarded, *The Global Gospel* is a manual for church leaders and missionaries to use as a reference for understanding honor and shame in the biblical context and how to apply the principles of honor and shame in cross-cultural engagement today."
Philip Bustrum, Ph.D., Former Chair Bible, Religion, Ministry Division, Professor of Intercultural Studies, Cornerstone University

"Werner Mischke offers an invaluable tool to better understand our Bible and most people. *The Global Gospel* shows how biblical writers communicated in an honor/shame culture, presenting Jesus as the one who took our shame to restore humanity's honor. From this scholarly grounding, he offers practical, specific ways to increase our missional impact in the global village."
John DelHousaye, Ph.D., Associate Professor, New Testament, Phoenix Seminary

"What Werner has done is this: He has gathered Scripture, missiology and biblical scholarship on shame and honor, he has offered it to us in a clear and cogent book, and, in this, he has blessed the church."
Edward T. Welch, Ph.D., Faculty and Counselor, CCEF, author of *Shame Interrupted: How God Lifts the Pain of Worthlessness and Rejection*

"We live in rapidly changing times where our audience for the gospel is growing in its diversity both where we live and in missions. This requires a better grasp of the world view of those we interact with, and *The Global Gospel* addresses this in a very helpful manner. The concepts of honor and shame are central to that understanding. I highly recommend this volume to all who have a passion to reach those who don't know Jesus."
T.J. Addington, Senior Vice President, EFCA, Leader, ReachGlobal

"*The Global Gospel* teaches us to see the world through the lens of honor and shame—so that our Great Commission ministry might be transformed."
Ben McGinnis, Mission mobilizer, Nashville, Tennessee

"*The Global Gospel* fills a significant hole in Western missiology and theology. Werner's insights and lucid diagrams will tremendously bless all those serving the global church."
Jayson Georges, Missionary and author of *The 3D Gospel*

"Werner does a superb job in peeling back the blinders that hinder our effectiveness in communicating the gospel. The insights he presents are crucial to avoid cultural collisions. Do yourself a favor—devour this book!"
Edward M. Smith, Ph.D., President, Williamson College

"In *The Global Gospel,* Werner Mischke has punched through to a world of honor and shame from a world that rarely talks in those terms much less thinks in those ways. In doing so he opens up not only the opportunity to understand each other better but the Scriptures as well. *The Global Gospel* is a fresh perspective of what it means to be citizens of heaven on earth."
Daniel Rickett, Ph.D., Executive Vice President, She Is Safe

"*The Global Gospel* feels like fresh cool wind in the desert. Millennial hybrid-cultures—present in every metro-urban region—require new biblical insight from the ancient biblical revelation. *The Global Gospel* gives us both wisdom and ways to deal with these emerging millennial realities that will see God honored and our shame covered. This book is a must read for these days."
Rev. Dr. Byron Spradlin, President, Artists in Christian Testimony Int'l.

"*The Global Gospel* is a thorough treatise and hands-on workbook for understanding the gospel's power to transform shame into honor. I am eager to see its impact in the lives of women we serve in Africa, Asia, and the Middle East as they gain insight into their infinite value in the eyes of God."
Kim Kerr, Executive Director, Women in the Window International

"We in the West have much to learn about honor and shame, which the New Testament world (and Majority World today), lived with on a daily basis. This book has influenced my understanding of the gospel and missions."
J. D. Payne, Ph.D., Pastor of Church Multiplication,
The Church at Brook Hills

"You cannot read *The Global Gospel* and not develop a better appreciation of God's rich wisdom in creating diversity and the challenges we face as we engage people of other cultures. It is a landmark contribution to global missiology and theology."
Emmanuel Ogunyemi, Ph.D., President, Life Builders Ministries Int'l.,
Lagos, Nigeria

"I have been teaching the Bible as a pastor and professor for over 50 years, and I am seeing things in the Bible I never saw until I read *The Global Gospel.*"
Joe Martin, Ph.D., Professor of Christian Ministries, Belhaven University

"The Global Gospel is an easy-to-read scholarly rendition of the importance of 'honor and shame' for a large segment of the world's population ... a must-read book for every Christian concerned to be an effective witness for the gospel."
Dr. Ravi I. Jayakaran, Vice President, Global Programs, MAP International

"The Global Gospel will give you a new lens in reading the Bible and new insights for the practice of missions."
Joel L. Hogan, Director of International Ministries,
Christian Reformed World Missions

"The Global Gospel points the way for all readers to encounter in Scripture a gospel that is better news than they had been taught. This book makes a significant and practical contribution to the global mission conversation."
David Bochman, Ph.D., International–Organizational Development,
Aphesis Group Ministries, Paraclete Mission Group

"The Global Gospel addresses what could be the greatest blind spot in the theology and missiology of Western and Western-influenced Christians around the world—namely, that a deep understanding of honor/shame is not only essential for effective mission work, but also for understanding the Bible."
Chris Clayman, Director, Global Gates Network, author of *ethNYcity:*
The Nations, Tongues, and Faiths of Metropolitan New York

"The Global Gospel is a very welcome, well-written, well-researched, biblically-rooted contribution to Christian ministry and mission in our 21st century multicultural world."
Rev. Dr. John A. Forrester, Author of *Grace for Shame: The Forgotten Gospel*

"Drawing on scholarship from across the globe, the reader is given the theological implications of honor and shame, and practical applications for more effective ministry. This is a much needed book."
Andrew & Sandra Freeman, Missionaries, Botswana, Africa

"The Global Gospel will expand your mind, heal your soul, and empower your witness for Jesus Christ."
Donald Mills, Financial Adviser, Associate Vice President, Ameriprise Financial, Inc., M. Div. and D. Min., Fuller Theological Seminary

"The Global Gospel serves as a primer; it introduces the subject and reviews much of the previous conversation. Werner also creatively links together several motifs (for example, the connection of purity with shame and honor) that will provoke the review of scholarship for some time to come. Also he aptly shows the importance of shame and honor for understanding the setting and culture of the Bible and the mission field. Take and read."
R. L. Hatchett, Ph.D., Professor of Theology and Philosophy, Houston Baptist University

To my father, Guenther Mischke,
who gave me the gift only he could give—his blessing.

And to my wife, Daphne, whose friendship
has been immovable in our long journey together and
whose love has been a treasure.

Your journey through this book—in four sections

1 It's a multicultural world, and it's hard to understand

Intro	
1.1	A longing for honor, a shadow of shame
1.2	Unreached people across the street and around the world
1.3	The Bible: It's not your book!
1.4	Why our blind spot about honor and shame?
1.5	The canopy of biblical truth
1.6	Does it hurt or does it heal?

Length of bar corresponds to length of chapter

1.6 The pathology of shame in our world

2 Hidden in plain sight— dynamics of honor and shame in the Bible

	Intro
Love of honor	2.1
Two sources of honor	2.2
Image of limited good	2.3
Challenge and riposte	2.4
Concept of face	2.5
Body language	2.6
Patronage	2.7
Name / kinship / blood	2.8
Purity	2.9
Honor-status reversal	2.10

3 A global gospel for our multicultural world

Intro	
3.1	Love of honor
3.2	Two sources of honor
3.3	Image of limited good
3.4	Challenge and riposte
3.5	Concept of face
3.6	Body language
3.7	Patronage
3.8	Name / kinship / blood
3.9	Purity
3.10	Honor-status reversal

How the gospel can be articulated using any of the honor/shame dynamics

4 Honor/shame dynamics in the world Christian movement

	Intro
Honor/shame dynamics in our purpose	4.1
... in our training	4.2
... in our practice	4.3
Summary: Believers have no honor deficit	4.4

CONTENTS

ACKNOWLEDGMENTS

İT HAS BEEN A JOURNEY OF MORE THAN FIVE YEARS to conduct the research and to eventually write this book. It would not have been possible without the support of so many.

My dear friend Bob Schindler (Mission ONE founder and president) was not only supportive but also a wise counselor. How grateful I am to have served at Mission ONE *with Bob* and *under his leadership* since 1992. His godly example and friendship have been foundational. Bob provided me the opportunity and space to learn, create, and thrive. How can one even begin to place a value on the treasure of this friendship? *Thank you, Bob.*

The members of the Mission ONE board of directors graciously empowered me to do this work. They have honored me by their trust. *Thank you, Mission ONE board members.*

My ministry with Mission ONE has been made possible by many through regular financial support as well as special project investments. I am indebted to the faithful giving and prayers of several churches and many individuals. *Thank you, all, for your support.*

Missionaries Philip and Bonnie Bustrum invited Bob Schindler to visit Kenya in 1988 to teach on the subject of evangelism to students at Moffat Bible College. Philip's advice to Bob was this: *Yes, you've come to be a blessing. But also, listen … and learn what it is like to be an African.* When Bob founded Mission ONE in 1991, this listening ethic was a core value. Philip, now a professor at Cornerstone University, has been a friend to Mission ONE for many years. He was one of the first to read a partial manuscript of this book and offered valuable counsel at that early stage of the project. Philip has been a wise, gracious, encouraging friend. *Thank you, Philip.*

This book was built on the foundational work of numerous scholars. The phrase, "Standing on the shoulders of giants," certainly applies here. The most influential scholars for this book were David deSilva, Dean Flemming, Jerome Neyrey, Timothy Tennent, and Jackson Wu. *Thank you, Drs. deSilva, Flemming, Neyrey, Tennent, and Wu.*

Dr. Steven Hawthorne is the scholar whose ministry, writings, friendship, and passion for God's glory among the nations has meant so much to me since the mid-1990s. His influence is deeply felt in this book. *Thank you, Steve.*

Dan Wright served as the publishing advisor for this book. His patient and wise counsel, based on decades in the Christian publishing industry, was invaluable for creating a professionally published book. Dan provided frequent encouragement.

He gave us crucial advice on the title as well as all other aspects of the publishing process. *Thank you, Dan.*

Jill Maher volunteered numerous hours over a span of more than a year to conduct valuable research. This has added nuance and richness to the book. *Thank you, Jill.*

Robby Butler provided nuanced editorial work as well as expert proofreading in the final stage of preprint production. Robby also effectively promoted the book among his network of mission professionals. His collaboration and encouragement was invaluable. *Thank you, Robby.*

Pauly Heller created the Scripture index and provided an added round of expert editing and proofreading at the final stage. *Thank you, Pauly.*

Marilyn Nasman was perhaps my biggest cheerleader for this project. Marilyn read my work all along the way, sponsored an honor/shame training event in her local church in Friday Harbor, Washington, and shared the material through her network of relationships. Many times Marilyn lifted my spirit and encouraged me to press on in this long writing journey. *Thank you, Marilyn.*

Samuel Chiang recognized the potential of the book long before it was done. He encouraged me to "keep writing." The addition of Part 4 is largely due to his influence. *Thank you, Samuel.*

Pastor Issam leads a ministry with his wife in the Middle East; their ministry organization is one of Mission ONE's partners. I learned so much through Issam's wisdom and relationship-building skills. His brotherly love and his passion to bless others through Jesus Christ was an inspiration. My ministry experiences with Issam in the Middle East—more than any other single thing— launched me on this learning journey about honor and shame. *Thank you, habibi.*

Every good gift and every perfect gift is from above,
coming down from the Father of lights ...
–James 1:17

FOREWORD BY
SAMUEL CHIANG (Q&A)

How will this book help believers communicate the gospel of Christ across the street and around the world?
Our neighborhoods, communities and cities are rapidly increasing in cultural diversity. With the arrival of immigrants, international students, refugees, expats, imported laborers, tourists, and sadly even with those who are trafficked, this generation of *people on the move* has morphed cities and societies into an unprecedented cultural mix. I believe that the basic social values, the worldview, of this generation is different from the dominant Western worldview of the previous five centuries. This presents an enormous challenge to the Church. How must we adjust in living out and presenting the gospel in this cultural melting pot?

The content of the gospel of Jesus Christ is timeless, but the way we communicate the gospel requires a deep reset. For generations we have counted on a legal framework for the gospel; this generally works when the worldview of our neighbors and colleagues is that of *guilt and innocence*—with a binary thinking process of "yes and no" or "right and wrong." But what happens when the worldview is more concerned with *honor and shame?*

The Global Gospel helps us to thoroughly examine and even redeem the cultural value of honor and shame, which we see both in Scripture and more and more in our own cities and communities.

Why should Christian leaders read *The Global Gospel*?
Christianity is no longer predominately in the West. The majority of Christians are now in the Majority World—Africa, Asia, and Latin America. In fact, within a few short years, by 2020, 65 percent of the global Christian community will be outside of North America and Europe. Plus, the vast majority of unreached and unengaged peoples are in the Majority World. *Should we not better understand how the gospel speaks within the honor/shame values of these cultures?*

What would you tell a pastor about why this book is important?
Your audience is changing! Drastically! The new generation, the *postmoderns,* receive, process, and pass on gospel messages differently. They generally do not belong to the *rule-centered* generation. They are a *relationship-centered* generation. This places them into an honor/shame worldview—with all the behaviors that go along with that. *The Global Gospel* helps you understand the values of this generation in order to better connect with and serve them.

Why would teachers and professors of intercultural studies use this book?
For a long time, we have had excellent material about honor and shame from the studies and writings of cultural anthropology. However, we have been massively underserved by the dearth of biblical and theological writings concerning honor and shame. *The Global Gospel* plays a small but a significant and catalytic role toward diminishing that vacuum. It will be an enduring resource to help students develop a biblically sound worldview. It will help students better understand the Majority World and many unreached peoples for whom honor and shame is vital.

Why would a missionary team read *The Global Gospel*?
A missionary team may suspect that their methods are not working well. What can be done? *The Global Gospel* provides a license to experiment. This book can be that field manual to stimulate conversations about new approaches, to reflect on how to do things differently—and trust God for the resulting, multiplying, and lasting fruit.

At one point in the writing process, Werner thought he was nearly finished with the manuscript. But you encouraged him to keep writing. Why?
When I first read this wonderful manuscript, I was left thinking of the implications. When I stepped back, I thought, *The reader must be encouraged to move from reflection to action.* So I encouraged Werner to expand the material for application and practice. Furthermore, since little exists in Christian literature that deals with honor and shame from a biblical and theological perspective, I thought that with additional material, this could truly be a survey book with a shelf life beyond just a few years. In fact, I believe the richness in this book will journey with the postmodern generation.

How might *The Global Gospel* influence the world Christian movement?
The Global Gospel is a necessary torch on our learning and practices. If we can glean just some of the many nuggets of gold that this book offers, and put them into practice, we might just become much more relevant as living servants of the gospel. This book is rich in dimensions to help us share the gospel across many cultures—from the colleague in the next cubicle, to the campuses across the world, to the unreached people group among whom we are serving, and into the mega-cities that are upon us in this century.

I believe this book is a *tour de force*. I surmise that many practitioners of various aspects of the Christian faith—whether discipleship, pastoral ministry, hermeneutics and preaching, missions, counseling, and other domains—will find great value in *The Global Gospel,* and for many years to come!

Samuel Chiang
Executive Director, International Orality Network
Hong Kong, April 2014

FOREWORD BY
STEVEN C. HAWTHORNE

THIS BOOK IS WELCOME AT THIS JUNCTURE OF MISSION HISTORY. It has become obvious that the world is changing. The tectonic plates of political alliance and culture affinity have been colliding, setting off tsunamis of migration and marketing, so that every city is now a globalized soup of different ethnicities and economies. Instead of being dissolved into a homogenized Internet sameness, the ethnic compression has brought an unprecedented yearning for identity—for a kind of collective respect—among the scattered peoples. Perhaps we shouldn't say that this yearning is unprecedented. Ever since the uniculture of Babel, we have sought to "make a name for ourselves" (Gen 11:4).

In this cauldron of competing identities, we are now seeing God's people becoming the long-promised fulfillment of the Abrahamic covenant, a people of blessing amidst all peoples, with a God-granted name (Genesis 12:2–3). This is God's answer to Babel. Like never before in history, we are seeing God's people sent and positioned to bring blessing. To serve this purpose, we must have wisdom in his ways. This book—about honor and shame in Scripture and culture—will help form that needed wisdom. Here is why we need this book:

- **To see new movements flourish.** Almost all of the remaining unreached peoples—those lacking a Christ-following movement—have sturdy family bonds that make it seem impossible for individuals to follow Christ without bringing great disgrace on themselves and their families. Missionaries who work alongside such incipient movements must be conversant with the struggle to sustain family honor.

- **To endure persecution.** More people suffer for the name of Christ than at any other time, and the persecution is increasing. Many who have endured well speak of identifying with Christ in his suffering, and of finding joy in anticipating honor with Christ. To find the resources to remain vulnerable and to embrace a fellowship in Christ's sufferings, our eyes must be open to God's ways of reversing shame and rewarding faithfulness in suffering with lasting glory.

- **To sustain fruitful partnerships.** The global church is learning to walk and work together. Of course, understanding honor/shame dynamics can help anyone to mind one's manners and avoid embarrassing cultural blunders. But we must do more than avoid embarrassment. Our best partnerships flourish where there is steady willingness to serve with honor, creating an environment of reciprocal respect that is deepened with celebration.

- **To contextualize the gospel message.** Don't underestimate the significance of articulating the great story that is culminated by Christ and for Christ. It is a story of God reversing the shame of the nations to bring us near to him in celebratory honor. The hermeneutic of honor reversing shame with Christ may do more than give you new lenses to read the Bible. It could well trigger your imagination to find fresh ways to present the message so that it is retold easily and effectively.

- **To mobilize in hope.** The world may be as evangelized as it will ever get if we attempt to complete the remaining task with a motivation built around the fleeting feelings of compassion. Mercy can strike a match, but we need emissaries from many lands who are ablaze with the inexhaustible fuel of jealousy for God's glory.

The reason this book has value in so many different ways is that Werner identifies the core of the drama that impels all things: God's great honor reverses deep shame. This story will and must culminate in God's reception—with honor—of the beautified worship of every people. This global glory is God's love accomplished. This is certainly the story of *His* glory. And yet it is also the story of *our* glory in and with Christ. The fulfillment of all things is Christ exalted and loved amidst the nations, the hope of *their* glory (Colossians 1:27). Only an announcement of the fulfillment of the all-encompassing drama of God's love can be called the *gospel*.

Werner may be audacious to title this book as *The Global Gospel*, but he is not wrong to do so.

Steven C. Hawthorne, Ph.D.
Austin, Texas
April 2014

AUTHOR'S PREFACE

THIS BOOK IS ABOUT THE GOOD NEWS OF JESUS CHRIST. It speaks to how followers of Christ *contextualize* and make known this magnificent and glorious gospel.

The book is also about the *pivotal cultural value of honor and shame* in Bible societies. You'll gain new "tools" to better understand the ancient Scriptures—and discover ways that honor/shame dynamics can enhance your ministry in today's globalized world.

You'll soon realize this material is widely applicable. Not only is this book about blessing your neighbors across the street, it is also about blessing unreached and unengaged peoples—whether they are in distant lands or close by in your own community.

You may also be surprised how this Christ-centered material can help that person you know who has struggled with toxic shame for years and can't seem to get past it.

So the singular issue that this book addresses may be defined by posing this question:

> *How can the honor/shame dynamics common to the Bible and many*
> *Majority World societies be used to contextualize the Christian faith*
> *in order to make it more widely understood and accepted?*

May countless conversations be started and new creative efforts launched to make known the good news of Jesus. May the gospel be understood in fresh ways that resonate deeply in your own heart—and that better resonate with many peoples, tribes, and nations.

God bless you in your learning journey through *The Global Gospel: Achieving Missional Impact in Our Multicultural World.*

INTRODUCTION

A longing for honor, a shadow of shame

The longing for honor and the struggle to avoid shame are universal. Individuals and families, kinship groups and communities, peoples and nations—all endure the pathologies of shame and the struggle for honor. Whether the issue is sexual abuse and trafficking, HIV-AIDS, racism or slavery, mental illness, disabilities of various kinds, ethnic cleansing, the identity challenges of refugees and immigrants, the perpetual passions of tribalism or nationalism, or simply the ubiquitous competitive pursuit for greater social status ... honor and shame are central to the human condition. Below is the author's own story of a longing for honor and a shadow of shame.

"GO FOR IT, SON; YOU HAVE MY BLESSING." These were the words I wanted to hear. A son always looks for the approval and blessing of his father, and I was no different. But this is not what happened to me when I tried to earn a place on our high school baseball team.

I remember as a boy going to bed at night and secretly listening to the radio broadcasts of the Rochester "Red Wings" baseball team. The announcers painted a picture of the game, the players, the drama. *Would he get the big hit? Would my team win? Winning feels wonderful.* I did not want my parents to know that I was doing things like this. My affection for baseball was a secret. My parents didn't care about the American sport of baseball. They were German.

When I was in tenth grade, I decided to go out for my high school baseball team. I wanted *to go for it,* and try to make the team.

The process was to stay after school and meet somewhere outside. It was called "tryouts." You would practice and you would do your best. If you were good enough, you made the team.

Of course, I had to have my baseball glove along for tryouts. But I remember on the first day of tryouts, I forgot my glove! How could I do that? It was so new—bringing my glove to school. This glove that I nurtured had always represented a non-school activity. Now I was connecting love for a game with school. Plus bringing my glove to school meant explaining to my mom or pop, German-born Americans with no appreciation for baseball, that I was bringing the equivalent of a toy to school.

That was an obstacle right there—bringing my glove to school. What would I tell them? Something like, *This is what I'm doing—and I don't much care what you think.* It feels a little dangerous, risky, unsettling—even today.

I don't remember exactly what I told them. In any case, I was out there. I was trying. I had my baseball glove. I felt unsure of myself; this was all so new, but I was asserting myself to prove I could do it.

My dream was to play and score and be on a winning team. *Would I succeed? Would I make the team? Would other guys want me on their team? Would I be good enough?* My little manhood was at stake.

My "Pop"—German father with an illness

My father, Guenther Mischke, was born in Germany in 1925. He died in January 1992 at age 67. I called him *Papi* as a little boy, and *Pop* as I became a teenager.

Pop was tall, about 6-feet 2-inches tall. He was warm and had a good sense of humor. I remember him laughing, and I loved it when he laughed. He deeply loved my mom and his three children. He loved me and I loved him. With his family, he attended Latta Road Baptist Church. He and my mom took us to church every Sunday.

I believe that one of the defining things about Pop was that he saw himself as a failure. Although I loved him, as a teenager I saw him as a failure, too.

As a little boy, until I was in my early teens, Papi gave me affection and discipline. When I needed to be spanked, he occasionally did so. He kissed me once in a while, maybe every night at bedtime. He pretended to be Santa Claus at Christmastime. Sometimes, he was fun and laughed very hard.

Pop became mentally ill when I was 14 years old or so. He lost his job taking care of the tools at a tool-and-die company where he had worked all the years that I remember. He never had another full-time job.

I remember my mother gathering my two sisters and me in a little sharing time. Mom said something like this: "Pop is sick. He has *manic depressive psychosis.*" This disease is now sometimes called by another name: bipolar disorder.

This is why he lost his job. This is why my mother had a nervous breakdown. This is why there were so many heated arguments between my mom and pop in our home. This is why I would go to bed at night and pray, *Lord, please give me wisdom to say the right things so that there isn't so much anger and conflict and yelling.* I felt this crazy responsibility to behave in such a way that I could bring a modicum of healing to my family.

This is why Pop embarrassed me and made me feel ashamed.

The hurtful event—embarrassed and ashamed

It was springtime, probably March of 1971. I remember going out for the baseball team at Greece Olympia High School. I was in tenth grade. I had not yet made a growth spurt because I entered puberty later in my teen years. I think of myself as being skinny with moderate height. Nothing impressive physically.

We were outside on the front grounds of the school—not on a baseball diamond. The varsity high school team was out on the real baseball diamonds in the back of the high school.

The drills were simple. The coach would hit a ground ball and I would gather it in my glove and throw it back. We had begun doing this drill. I remember I was not fielding the ball very well, always hoping to do better the next time.

Then I saw my father nearby.

I'm thinking: *Oh no! What is Pop doing here? My mentally ill father showing up here? Why? This is so embarrassing.*

Pop said to me in strong words, with his German accent, "Werner, let's go. Come home."

I don't want to.

"You must come home." Pop was looking angry. I could see he was not going to lose this showdown with his son. He was emotionally intense with a dogmatic sternness. He tilted his head a little, "Come home!"

"Why?"

"We have spring cleaning to do. Mom wants you to come home."

I knew all the other guys were watching what I would do. I imagine the coach saw it all, as well. I didn't want to look at any of them.

My heart sank. Here was sickness personified in my father bringing sickness and shame into my life. Reflecting on it now, I wonder: *Was Pop being sadistic? Was his behavior involuntary? Did my mother tell him to go and get me? Why would he do this?* I didn't know.

Reluctantly, I walked off the field with Pop following me into the boy's locker room where I had my regular clothes and school stuff. Even that was weird—that he would follow me into the locker room. Maybe he was afraid I would run away and hide. Looking back, I feel like I was controlled by a force that was unkind, strange, and diseased.

I gathered my stuff and walked back out with Pop to the parking lot. *Get me outta here before anyone else sees me.* We got in our car and drove home. It was a ten-minute drive from Greece Olympia High School to 194 Rosecroft Drive.

While riding home, what was I thinking? What did I say to Pop, if anything? I probably just looked out the window. *Unbelievable.* Did I cry? I don't think so. Maybe I just felt numb. Like, *Did this really just happen?*

The next day, I loathed going back to school. Walking down the school hallway, I was asked by one or two boys, "How was spring cleaning?"

If, because of prior weirdnesses in Pop's behavior, there was the onset of a shame-sickness in my soul, then this event (on the baseball practice field) lodged that shadow of shame firmly inside of me. I, along with my sisters and mother, was destined to live with feelings of shame concerning the man who was supposed to love me, but at times, just couldn't.

The father who supposedly loved me made me look like an idiot. Instead of encouraging me to take up a challenge and pursue my dream, he extracted me from my dream and joy. He yanked it from me in front of my friends—other teenage boys who were trying to make the team.

I looked like a weak mama's boy from a weird family, whose weird old man without a job comes out on the practice field and calls his only son home. *And for what?* To do spring cleaning.

Are you kidding me? It was awful. In this event he was deeply unloving and uncaring. The exact opposite of what a father was supposed to be.

No other moment in my youth had the depth of shame that this moment had. Looking back now, I remember it painfully. But I also laugh about it because it was so irrational, so weird. It created a *shadow of shame* which affected my life in many ways.

The healing event—he gave me his blessing

Fast-forward to 1991. I had been married for fourteen years. My wife Daphne and I along with our two sons were living in Lee, Massachusetts, serving as members of a small Baptist church. And I was *in transition*—from being a small business owner to taking a step of faith into the world of global missions.

I wanted to leave my graphic design business and work with evangelist Bob Schindler, who had just founded a cross-cultural partnership ministry called Mission ONE. I had to tell my parents what I was planning to do. My decision required moving from Massachusetts to Tennessee—1500 miles away—with Daphne and two boys. A drastic move like this meant I would not see my parents as often.

In the fall of '91, Daphne and I were visiting my parents in Rochester, New York. My dad was still mentally disabled, and he had begun kidney dialysis treatments. I knew I had to share my plans with him individually. He was proud of me for owning my own business, and he loved the periodic visits we made to see them, so I honestly did not know how he would react to my announcement. Would he be disappointed? Mad? Confused?

Daphne had gone shopping with my mother. So there we were, just Pop and me, in the small living room in their apartment. I presented my plans and why I wanted to make such a radical change in our lives. The financial outlook was uncertain. I wasn't completely sure how I would support my family. But I was undeterred. I said something like this, "This is my desire—to serve with Bob Schindler in the ministry of Mission ONE—and I think somehow it will all work out. We are trusting God."

I explained the big move my family and I were planning to make. Then I asked, "So Pop, what do you think?" I waited for his response.

"Werner, we are behind you 100 percent, whatever you do."

Immediately, my eyes filled with tears. I got up from the couch and hugged him. Pop kissed me. We embraced. My tears took me by surprise.

Despite Pop's bipolar illness, he loved me. Despite my constant need to compensate for his weaknesses, he gave me his blessing.

A few months later, in January of 1992, Pop passed away. I was honored to give his eulogy at his memorial service.

There is much that I wish I could have received from Pop—counsel, friendship, financial assistance, spiritual encouragement. I had decided not to ask for what I knew he was unable to give.

But the one thing I needed most I did receive—the honor of *his blessing*. I am grateful.

Hurt and healing

In thinking about, on the one hand, my shame-trauma as a teenager, and on the other hand, my emotional response of deep joy and tears when my father gave me his blessing—I ask myself what ties these two events together? There are two things.

The first is obvious. Both of these events are between my father and me. The first event was hurtful; the second event was healing.

The second thing that ties these events together is less obvious. It is that both events were disconnected from my faith. My "umbrella of belief" in Jesus Christ was not nearly broad enough to provide answers to the deep emotional impact that these events had on my life. In response to the traumatic first event, the teachings and social dynamics of the church failed to address the hurtful shame I had experienced. And in the healing event, I never expected to experience the joy and honor of my father's blessing. I never heard about the power of *blessing* (until much later in my Christian life).

What I didn't know then but do know today is this: Concerning the hurtful event, the Bible speaks volumes to the shame that people experience both as agents and victims of sin. Concerning the healing event, the Bible gives many examples of the love, honor and power of *blessing.* In this book I am addressing both of these issues, as well as a host of other things.

A long journey for learning about honor and shame

When I was a boy, my family went to church every Sunday. So I heard a weekly sermon—many on Jesus forgiving our *sin and guilt.* I received Jesus as my Savior as a ten-year-old boy, wanting to have my sins forgiven after watching Billy Graham on TV with my parents.

But I remember almost nothing about Jesus cleansing our *sin and shame.* In fact, to this day (I am 58), having heard hundreds of sermons, I can only recall one time when the preacher's message touched on the cure for one's sin and *shame.* I think the year was 1979. It was a message about Jesus healing the man with the withered hand (Luke 6:6–11).

In the spring of 2009, I traveled to Lebanon to visit our Mission ONE ministry partner. We had agreed to conduct a one-day Bible "conference" for a small group of first-generation believers from the Druze religious background.[1] The pastor and I had agreed on going through Philippians, and to do so through the lens of honor and shame. It was a study that had a profound impact on one young lady, Maya, a mature believer. She told me a few days later how this study about honor and shame in Philippians had freed her from fear.

My experience in Lebanon was a watershed moment. I returned home and started reading everything I could concerning honor and shame in the Bible and in cross-cultural ministry. To this day, in my own regular personal Bible readings, I find that being alert to the honor/shame dynamics in Scripture is a great help in making the Word of God *come alive.*

Since 2009, I have been on a journey of reading, writing, training, and speaking about the dynamics of honor and shame in Scripture and in cultures. I've discovered a treasure trove of grace and truth in Jesus Christ that has helped bring healing for my shame.

---

1. The Druze are a religious and social community located in Syria, Lebanon, Israel, and Jordan.

Perhaps more importantly, I've become convinced that the cultural dynamic of *honor and shame*—in understanding, communicating, and living out the gospel of Christ—is an important strategic issue for world missions. Hence, *The Global Gospel: Achieving Missional Impact in Our Multicultural World.*

"So the honor is for you who believe ... " (1 Pet 2:7). "For from him and through him and to him are all things. To him be glory forever. Amen" (Rom 11:36).

Werner Mischke
Scottsdale, Arizona
May 2014

SECTION 1

It's a Multicultural World and It's Hard to Understand

Unreached People Across the Street and Around the World

I POSTED THIS ON MY FACEBOOK PAGE, July 20, 2013:

> Well, I missed my nonstop flight to Tampa. (Forgot to bring my backpack with my laptop.) Went into crisis mode. Where's that bag? Did I leave it on the SuperShuttle? Nope. Did I leave it outside the office door? Nope. So I called a cab that took me back to our office ... About a 40-mile roundtrip. Of course, the cab driver was from Somalia via Kenya ... his name ... Abdullah. We had the best conversation about family and stuff, and laughed together. Knowing a tiny bit of Arabic helps ("habibi" means friend). So I am planning to meet him at the Juba Restaurant (a gathering place for Somali men) on McDowell Rd in Phoenix next Thursday night. I told him I want to hear his story, and then I said I want to tell him the best story Isa (Jesus) ever told.

Unfortunately, I didn't return home in time for that Thursday evening get-together at the Juba Red Sea Restaurant. But I *did* show up the following Thursday evening, and the Thursday evening after that. Although Abdullah wasn't there, I did end up talking with Bashir, the owner of the restaurant. It was a friendly, positive connection. Bashir told me that about fifteen thousand Somalis live in the Phoenix area. *Amazing*, I thought. A huge number of people from an unreached Muslim people group live just a short drive from my home in Arizona. My friendship with Bashir has continued.

Ours is a multicultural world

The world has always been comprised of thousands of ethnicities, languages, and cultures. But "the world" of our own lives—our own cities, communities, schools, workplaces, and neighborhoods—is vastly more multicultural than a generation ago. Plus, through the Internet and social media, our connections internationally and multiculturally have also multiplied.

In one recent 24-hour period: I had an extensive chat session on Facebook with our ministry partner, Pastor Severino, in Torit, South Sudan ... I chatted on Skype with Pastor Issam, my dear friend in Lebanon ... I did a video call over the Internet with Bishop Bhatti in Karachi, Pakistan ... my wife and I enjoyed an afternoon getting to know a young Chinese woman who is studying architecture at a university nearby ... and I had a wonderful conversation over the Internet with my aunt and uncle in Germany.

The world *really is* right next door.

- *The New York Times* reported, "While there is no precise count, some experts believe New York is home to as many as 800 languages—far more than the 176 spoken by students in the city's public schools or the 138 that residents of Queens, New York's most diverse borough, listed on their 2000 census forms."[1]

- "Los Angeles' population consists 57% of multilingual residents. The city has some of the nation's largest cultural enclaves including Historic Filipinotown, Koreatown, Little Armenia, Little Ethiopia, Tehrangeles, and Thai Town."[2]

- Increasing cultural and ethnic diversity also characterizes smaller cities and communities. In the city in which I was born, Rochester, New York (population about 210,000), a local non-profit organization provides English instruction for immigrants: "The Maplewood Library ESL program has met every Saturday since June 2008. Over 400 students, including refugees and immigrants from Burma, Nepal, Bhutan, Burundi, Somalia, Sudan, the Congo, Cuba, Colombia, Peru, Russia, Azerbaijan, Afghanistan, Iraq, Yemen, Syria, China, Korea, Vietnam, and Laos have attended."[3]

- Patrick Johnstone states, "By 2050, Caucasians will probably be a minority in North America."[4]

- The Brookings Institution reported that, based on the 2010 U.S. Census, there were stunning demographic changes in America's child population between 2000 and 2010:[5]

  o **"New minorities—Hispanics, Asians, and other groups apart from whites, blacks, and American Indians—account for all of the growth among the nation's child population.** From 2000 to 2010, the population of white children nationwide declined by 4.3 million, while the population of Hispanic and Asian children grew by 5.5 million.

  o **"In almost half of states and nearly one-third of large metro areas, child populations declined in the 2000s.** White child populations dropped in 46 states and 86 of the 100 largest metro areas, but gains of new minority children forestalled more widespread overall declines in youth.

---

1. Sam Roberts, "Listening to (and Saving) the World's Languages," *The New York Times, 28* April 2010, accessed 18 September 2013, http://www.nytimes.com/2010/04/29/nyregion/29lost.html?_r=0.
2. Daniel Echevarria, "Top Multilingual U. S. Cities," *Beyond Words—Language Blog*, 3 March 2010, accessed 18 September 2013, http://www.altalang.com/beyond-words/2010/03/03/top-multilingual-u-s-cities/. Alta's website has a good overview of the most diverse cities in the United States.
3. "Learn English as a Second Language," *ESOL Associates of Rochester, NY*, accessed 18 September 2013, http://www.livingonweekends.com/EAR.html#.
4. Patrick Johnstone, *The Future of the Global Church: History, Trends and Possibilities* (Downers Grove, IL: InterVarsity Press, 2011), 5.
5. William H. Frey, "America's Diverse Future: Initial Glimpses at the U.S. Child Population from the 2010 Census," *The Brookings Institution*, 6 April 2011, accessed 18 September 2013, http://www.brookings.edu/research/papers/2011/04/06-census-diversity-frey.

- "**In areas of the country gaining children, Hispanics accounted for most of that growth.** Fully 95 percent of Texas's child population growth occurred among Hispanics. Los Angeles was the only major metropolitan area to witness a decline in Hispanic children from 2000 to 2010.

- "**Ten states and 35 large metro areas now have minority white child populations.** Child populations in the Atlanta, Dallas, Orlando, and Phoenix metro areas flipped to 'majority minority' by 2010."

J. D. Payne's book, *Strangers Next Door: Immigration, Migration and Mission,* is an excellent resource for getting our minds and hearts around the mega-trend of peoples on the move in our world. Payne introduced me to a new term—*diaspora missiology*—which is defined by the Lausanne Movement as "a missiological framework for understanding and participating in God's redemptive mission among people living outside their place of origin."[6]

Below is a tiny sampling of highlights from Payne's rich resource book.

- As of 2006, "Toronto is the country's largest migrant-receiving area, with the 2006 census noting 2,320,200 foreign-born people. The foreign-born population is now at 45.7% of the census metropolitan area's total population of 5,072,100, with India and the People's Republic of China as the two major-source countries for recent immigrants."[7]

- From 2000 to 2007, the number of international students more than doubled to over 2 million. The main destination countries were the United States, the United Kingdom, Germany, France, and Australia. The greatest percentage increases occurred in New Zealand, Korea, the Netherlands, Greece, Spain, Italy, and Ireland.

- In 2010, migrants comprised 14.2 percent of the total population in North America, 12.4 percent in Western Europe, 22 percent in Australia, 21.3 percent in Canada, 13.5 percent in the United States, and 10.4 percent in the United Kingdom.

Robert Schreiter is a widely respected expert in the area of intercultural understanding and what it means for the church. He writes of the *unprecedented* migration of peoples and the resulting clash of cultures.

The spread of global market capitalism, creating new centers of wealth and communication in the world, has also fostered a worldwide migration of peoples, either seeking some share in the wealth in the burgeoning cities or fleeing the poverty created by the widening gap between rich and poor. In some areas this has led to conflicts as cultures clash and peoples compete for the same scarce resources. ... This churning of peoples and

---

6. Sadiri Joy Tira, "Diaspora Missiology," *The Lausanne Movement* (blog), 6 October 2010, accessed 20 September 2013, http://conversation.lausanne.org/en/conversations/detail/11103#.UjuI9hbM7o4.

7. J. D. Payne, *Strangers Next Door: Immigration, Migration and Mission* (Downers Grove, IL: InterVarsity Press, 2012), Kindle edition. Payne cites as his source, "Census snapshot—Immigration in Canada: A portrait of the foreign-born population, 2006 Census," *Government of Canada,* accessed 19 September 2013, http://www.statcan.gc.ca/pub/11-008-x/2008001/article/10556-eng.pdf.

cultures is unprecedented in world history. Frequently in the past, regions of the world would experience such demographic flow. But never has it been on such a worldwide scale.[8]

How is the church responding? Soong-Chan Ray is an Asian American Christian leader who is Professor of Church Growth and Evangelism at North Park Theological Seminary in Chicago. Born into a Korean family and raised in America, he has written about the ethnic changes that the American evangelical church is undergoing:

> The American church needs to face the inevitable and prepare for the next stage of her history—we are looking at a nonwhite majority, multiethnic American Christianity in the immediate future. Unfortunately, despite these drastic demographic changes, American evangelicalism remains enamored with an ecclesiology and a value system that reflect a dated and increasingly irrelevant cultural captivity and are disconnected from both a global and a local reality.[9]

Multicultural world, multi-ethnic global church

In the literature of Christian world missions over the last ten years, it has been clearly stated again and again that Westerners no longer live in a world of missions that is from "the West to the rest."[10] The gospel is now, more than ever, going "from everywhere to everyone," as Samuel Escobar says.[11]

The *Atlas of Global Christianity* has a remarkable study on the change of the location of "Christianity's centre of gravity."

> Sometime after 1980, Christians from the Global South outnumbered Northern Christians for the first time since the 10th century. The most vigorous growth was in Africa, exploding from 10 million Christians in 1900 to 360 million in 2000. In the second half of the century, however, the fastest-growing portion of the global church was in Asia. For the first time in over 1,300 years the centre of global Christianity was again moving towards the east.[12]

In his book *The Next Christendom,* Philip Jenkins reflects on the massive demographic changes which the global church is undergoing. "If we are to live in a world where only one Christian in five is a non-Hispanic White, then the views of that small minority are ever less likely to claim mainstream status, however

8. Robert J. Schreiter, "Reconciliation as a Model of Mission," in *Landmark Essays in Mission and World Christianity,* eds. Robert L. Gallagher and Paul Hertig (Maryknoll, NY: Orbis Books, 2009), Kindle edition locations 1458–64.

9. Soong-Chan Rah, *The Next Evangelicalism: Freeing the Church from Western Cultural Captivity* (Downers Grove, IL: InterVarsity Press, 2009), Kindle edition locations 114–17.

10. See for example: Todd M. Johnson and Kenneth R. Ross, eds., *Atlas of Global Christianity* (Edinburgh: Edinburgh University Press, 2009); Philip Jenkins, *The Next Christendom: The Coming of Global Christianity* (New York: Oxford University Press, 2002, 2011); Mark Noll, *The New Shape of World Christianity: How American Experience Reflects Global Faith* (Downers Grove, IL: InterVarsity Press, 2009).

11. Samuel Escobar, *The New Global Mission: The Gospel from Everywhere to Everyone* (Downers Grove, IL: InterVarsity Press, 2003).

12. Johnson and Ross, 52.

desperately the Old World Order clings to its hegemony over the control of information and opinion."[13]

Citing the scholarship of Philip Jenkins and speaking from his own extensive career in serving the world Christian movement, Paul Borthwick states, "Even though the Western world has dominated Christianity for much of Christian history, Christianity is now primarily a nonwhite, non-western, non-wealthy religion."[14]

Scottish missiologist Andrew Walls has written much about major trends in world Christianity:

> What has changed most over the course of my lifetime is the demography of the Christian church, the southward movement of its center. Europe and, to a lesser extent, North America have seen recession, while Latin America, some parts of Asia-Pacific, and especially Africa have seen growth, and all present evidence suggests that these trends will continue. The corollary is that African, Asian, and Latin American Christianity will become more and more important within the church as a whole and Western Christianity less and less so. Neither the churches of the North nor those of the South have yet taken in the full implications of this major movement of the Christian heartland, the theological academy perhaps least of all.[15]

The southward movement of the Christian faith into such a broad myriad of languages, cultures and ethnicities contributes mightily to the credibility of the gospel in those cultures, where Western values are viewed with suspicion. Tite Tiénou rightly says, "The shift of Christianity's center of gravity is good news because it means that, as a global reality, the Christian faith is increasingly at home in many cultures and will not be imprisoned by any single culture."[16]

Having given examples of outstanding mission efforts from people in Majority World nations, Samuel Escobar writes, "There is an element of mystery when the dynamism of mission does not come from people in positions of power or privilege, or from the extensive dynamism of a superior civilization, but from below—from the little ones, those who have few material, financial or technical resources but who are open to the prompting of the Spirit."[17]

Yes, the growth of the number of Christ-followers in the past one hundred years is amazing. But there is still *so much* unfinished work to fulfill our Lord's Great Commission.

The persistence of large numbers of unreached and unengaged peoples

What is an unreached people group? What is an unengaged people group? According to the Joshua Project website:

---

13. Jenkins, 108.

14. Paul Borthwick, *Western Christians in Global Mission: What's the Role of the North American Church?* (Downers Grove, IL: InterVarsity Press, 2012), Kindle edition locations 355–56.

15. Andrew Walls, "Globalization and the Study of Christian History" in *Globalizing Theology: Belief and Practice in an Era of World Christianity*, eds. Craig Ott and Harold A. Netland (Grand Rapids, MI: Baker Publishing Group, 2006), Kindle edition locations 1410–15.

16. Tite Tiénou, "Christian Theology in an Era of World Christianity" in *Globalizing Theology: Belief and Practice in an Era of World Christianity*, Kindle edition locations 692–93.

17. Escobar, 19.

An unreached or least-reached people is a people group among which there is no indigenous community of believing Christians with adequate numbers and resources to evangelize this people group. The original Joshua Project editorial committee selected the criteria less than 2 percent Evangelical Christian and less than 5 percent Christian Adherents.[18]

An unengaged people group is one that has no active church planting underway. According to the IMB Global Research Office, "A people group is engaged when a church planting strategy, consistent with evangelical faith and practice, is under implementation. In this respect, a people group is not engaged when it has been merely adopted, is the object of focused prayer, or is part of an advocacy strategy."

At least four essential elements constitute effective engagement:

(1) apostolic effort in residence;
(2) commitment to work in the local language and culture;
(3) commitment to long-term ministry;
(4) sowing in a manner consistent with the goal of seeing a Church Planting Movement (CPM) emerge.[19]

The Joshua Project website has a searchable database. I did four searches. My variables were unengaged, religious bloc (Buddhist, Hindu, Muslim, tribal), and population greater than 100,000. Here are the results:

- There are 17 unengaged Buddhist people groups, each with a population of over 100,000. Together these peoples comprise 19,032,000 individuals.
- There are 272 unengaged Hindu people groups over 100,000 with a population totaling 246,557,000.
- There are 285 unengaged Muslim people groups over 100,000 with a population totaling 372,513,000.
- There are 35 unengaged tribal people groups over 100,000 with a population totaling 23,651,000.
- When the population of the group is not a factor, there are a total of 4,793 people groups who are unengaged, with a total population of 735,046,000 individuals.

These numbers are hard to grasp. My friend Mike Latsko has a special passion for mobilizing the church for the unengaged peoples of the world. "The term 'unengaged,'" he says, "is the most offensive in missionary terminology. ... It is offensive to the LORD of hosts. ... It is offensive to Christ Himself. ... It is offensive to the Holy Spirit. ... It is offensive to the church. ... It is offensive to the missionary community." ... As of 2013, "34% of all unreached Hindu peoples ... are also

---

18. "Definitions," *Joshua Project*, accessed 19 September 2013, http://www.joshuaproject.net/definitions.php?term=26.
19. Ibid.

unengaged, as are 43% of all Buddhist unreached and 59% of all Muslim unreached. Enough. No more."[20]

We can also recognize that the thousands of unreached and unengaged Buddhist, Hindu, Muslim, and tribal peoples are very non-Western in their culture. Our Western culture, characterized by individualism and pluralism, is culturally distant from the Buddhist, Hindu, Muslim, or tribal world. Non-Western societies are usually *collectivistic*—group-oriented—rather than *individualistic*; thus, they are much more motivated by honor/shame dynamics than Western peoples. We will thoroughly explain what this means as we go forward.

Do we have good news for our multicultural world?

Of course we do. We have *the* good news, the gospel of Jesus Christ. But what if ...

- *What if* ... the gospel as we know it contained some Western assumptions that make the good news of Jesus less appealing to peoples from Majority World cultures?

- *What if* ... we could read the Bible in a new light—the light of the cultural values in which the Scriptures were originally written?

- *What if* ... we could overcome certain theological blind spots? What if we could shift from a gospel articulated exclusively through a legal framework?

- *What if* ... we could share a more comprehensive *global* gospel which, by God's grace, would better resonate with our multicultural neighbors— across the street and around the world?

- *What if* ... we discovered that the societies of the Old and New Testament had the pivotal cultural value of *honor and shame*, and found that this is a lot closer to the values of our multicultural neighbors than we as Westerners ever realized?

That's what the next chapter is all about.

---

20. Mike Latsko, "The Most Abominable Word," *Mission Frontiers* 35, no. 1 (Jan/Feb 2013): 12. This entire edition of *Mission Frontiers* is devoted to the issue of the unengaged peoples and has a variety of experienced voices contributing to the discussion. Alas, not one word is devoted to the significance of contextualizing the gospel.

The Bible: It's Not Your Book!

"We can easily forget that Scripture is a foreign land and that reading the Bible is a cross-cultural experience." [1]

Discomfort and "otherness"

THE BIBLE IS FULL OF STRANGE CUSTOMS, strange names, strange lands. You can use a Bible dictionary or a concordance to gain insight on the significance of these customs, names and lands.

The Bible is also full of *values* that are strange to Westerners—the cultural values of the ancient Middle East: Mesopotamia, Egypt, Palestine, Arabia, Syria, the Roman Empire, the Mediterranean basin. But the meaning and significance of these cultural values are largely hidden. Like the 90 percent of an iceberg that is underwater, *values are below the surface.* Values are implicit rather than explicit. The "otherness" of Bible cultures is located in the 90 percent that's hidden underwater.

Bruce Malina is known for his classic work, *The New Testament World: Insights from Cultural Anthropology.* He writes, "The words we use to say and speak do in fact embody meaning, but the meaning does not come from the words. Meaning inevitably derives from the general social system of the speakers of the language." [2]

In the book, *Misreading Scripture with Western Eyes: Removing Cultural Blinders to Better Understand the Bible,* authors Randolph Richards and Brandon O'Brien help us understand how easy it is to misinterpret and misunderstand Scripture—simply because the societies we read about in the Bible have cultural values vastly different from those of modern-day Western Christians.

Many pastors interpret the Bible and then preach sermons through their Western cultural mindset. Richards and O'Brien write, "... it is a better method to speak of what the passage meant to the original hearers, and *then* to ask how that applies to us." [3] Plus, the challenge of knowing what *the passage meant to the original hearers* is made worse when ...

---

1. E. Randolph Richards and Brandon J. O'Brien, *Misreading Scripture with Western Eyes: Removing Cultural Blinders to Better Understand the Bible* (Downers Grove, IL: InterVarsity Press, 2012), Kindle edition locations 74–75.

2. Bruce J. Malina, *The New Testament World: Insights from Cultural Anthropology,* rev. ed. (Louisville, KY: Westminster John Knox Press, 1993), 2.

3. Richards and O'Brien, Kindle edition locations 80–81.

... the most powerful cultural values are those that go without being said. It is very hard to know what goes without being said in another culture. But often we are not even aware of what goes without being said in our own culture. This is why misunderstanding and misinterpretation happen. When a passage of Scripture appears to leave out a piece of the puzzle because something went without being said, we instinctively fill in the gap with a piece from our own culture—usually a piece that goes without being said. *When we miss what went without being said for them and substitute what goes without being said for us, we are at risk of misreading Scripture.*[4] (Emphasis mine.)

If we are to take seriously the cultural component for interpreting the New Testament, then would not the study of the social dynamics of the Roman Empire be essential? One book that explains the social and political dynamics of the Roman Empire—and thus reveals the degree to which honor and shame was woven into every aspect of its social and political life—is J. E. Lendon's *Empire of Honour: The Art of Government in the Roman World.* It is a work of scholarship that demonstrates how honor and shame affected every aspect of the Empire. Of course, the Roman Empire is the sociopolitical reality into which Jesus Christ was born and inside of which the New Testament was written.

Commenting on the way *honor* trumped *obedience* in the Empire, Lendon states:

> The marked perception, therefore, is not of subjects, officials, and emperor dealing with each other in terms of obedience. Rather, the subject paid "honour" to his rulers as individuals deserving of it in themselves, and, in turn, the rulers are seen to relate to their subjects by "honouring" them. Subject and official were linked by a great network of honouring, and obedience was an aspect of that honouring. Moreover, it was very largely in terms of honour that relations between individuals in the government were described. ... And at the very centre of this network stood the Roman emperor, relentlessly honoured by the men and cities of his world, and busily honouring them in return, or augmenting the honours they had bestowed upon others. This focus on the business of honouring in no way set the relations of subject and official, or official and official, apart from relations within society at large. ... [T]here was nothing specifically governmental in honouring people: it was an everyday social function, the constant expectation of a man in any respect distinguished.[5]

New Testament scholar Jerome Neyrey emphasizes that understanding the social system of an ancient culture is vital for interpreting its literature. This applies to the Bible, which is, of course, an ancient book. Neyrey says it this way:

> Words take their meaning from a social system, not from a lexicon. Our dictionaries translate words such as father, mother and household, but they cannot tell us their meanings in Greco-Roman culture. Despite our

---

4. Ibid., 89–92.
5. J. E. Lendon, *Empire of Honour: The Art of Government in the Roman World* (New York: Oxford University Press, 1997), Kindle edition locations 312–17.

temptation to take the easy road and think that those words meant *then* what we mean by them *now,* social-science reading alerts us to the fact that proper reading requires that we learn the ancient cultural system that filled those words with distinctive meaning.[6] (Emphasis mine.)

The *English Standard Version Study Bible,* in its chapter on Scripture interpretation, sums up this point nicely: "Wise interpreters still locate every verse in its context and ask how the original audience understood it."[7] The problem is that the majority of "modern students of the Bible have not focused on the significantly different social world and dynamics of Bible times."[8]

This challenge is a big part of what this book is about.

Is it helpful to apply social science to the interpretation of the Bible?

The application of honor/shame dynamics for interpreting the Bible falls into the category of "social-scientific approaches to Scripture." But many followers of Jesus Christ and students of the Bible are not familiar with social science as a tool for interpreting Scripture. They are right to be cautious as they endeavor to be "rightly handling the word of truth" (2 Tim 2:15).

According to Klein, Blomberg, and Hubbard, "... social-scientific studies fall into two broad categories: (1) research that illuminates the social history of the biblical world and (2) the application of modern theories of human behavior to scriptural texts."[9]

This book is written with the understanding of primarily the first category—"research that illuminates the social history of the biblical world"—thus, a tool for faithful *exegesis* of God's Word. My goal is to interpret the Word of God according to its original cultural context.[10]

Klein, Blomberg and Hubbard ask, "What kind of 'meaning' ought to be the goal of interpretation?" I agree with their answer wholeheartedly:

---

6. Jerome H. Neyrey and Eric C. Stewart, eds., *The Social World of the New Testament: Insights and Models* (Peabody, MA: Hendrickson, 2008), *xxi.*

7. *The ESV Study Bible* (Wheaton, IL: Crossway, 2007), 2564.

8. William W. Klein, Craig L. Blomberg, and Robert I. Hubbard Jr., *Introduction to Biblical Interpretation, Revised ed.* (Nashville, TN: Thomas Nelson, 2004), 79.

9. Klein, Blomberg and Hubbard, 78. This is one small part of their extensive treatment of the subject.

10. This author believes that the reader of this book will find that social science research into the ancient cultures of the Bible has a profoundly positive impact. It is positive for our understanding of the Bible—and thus, for our faithfulness to the God of the Bible. But it should be noted that sometimes, theological liberalism is associated with social science research relative to biblical studies. For example, an association of scholars called The Context Group is the forerunner for much of the material about honor/shame dynamics in biblical studies. Even though their contribution has been significant, The Context Group is considered liberal by some evangelicals because some participants in The Context Group do not hold to as high a view of Scripture. Nevertheless, a standard textbook on hermeneutics by Klein, Blomberg, and Hubbard (cited above) proclaims the use of social science as an important resource for faithful biblical interpretation. Moreover, it should be noted that two authors quoted in this book—Bruce Malina and Jerome Neyrey—were both founding members of The Context Group. The fact that Malina, Neyrey and others who have participated in The Context Group are quoted in this book does not imply that this author or Mission ONE agree with all that they say in their writings. There is obviously a certain tolerance for ambiguity necessary to learn from others with whom you may not agree in every respect. This author agrees with conservative theological scholars such as David deSilva, Timothy Tennent, and Jackson Wu whose writings demonstrate that social science research makes valuable contributions to our understanding and application of the Bible. For more information about The Context Group, see <http://en.wikipedia.org/wiki/The_Context_Group>, accessed 23 April 2014.

We believe God intended the Bible to function not as a mirror reflecting the readers and their meanings, but as a window into the worlds and meanings of the authors and the texts they produced. Therefore we posit the following: *the author-encoded historical meaning of these texts remains the central objective of hermeneutics.*[11] (Emphasis in original.)

In other words, Bible interpretation is the process to understand what the authors intended and what the original hearers understood. "It is the meaning those words would have conveyed to the readers at the time they were written by the author or editor."[12]

Benefits of this book

By reading this book you will discover:

The primary social value of the ancient Middle East in the Bible is *the pivotal cultural value of honor and shame*; knowing this will provide a new perspective to:

- enrich your personal relationship with Jesus Christ by discovering the God of honor revealed in Scripture,
- better understand and communicate God's story from Genesis to Revelation so that more lost and hurting people will respond to the gospel of Jesus Christ,
- give you new ways to understand and communicate the gospel of Christ, and
- enhance the impact of your church or mission team locally and globally.

Understanding the ancient dynamics of honor and shame in Scripture is a *catalyst* to help you and your church be more faithful to God's Word now for more effective ministry in our multi-ethnic, multicultural world.

Definitions: Honor and Shame

Our definitions come from expert researchers.

Our definition of *honor* comes from the aforementioned Jerome Neyrey, Professor Emeritus of New Testament Studies at the University of Notre Dame. Our definition of *shame* comes from Brené Brown, a research professor at the University of Houston Graduate College of Social Work. She identifies herself as a "shame researcher."[13]

- **HONOR** is "the worth or value of persons both in their eyes and in the eyes of their village, neighborhood, or society." ... "The critical item is the public nature of respect and reputation."[14]

---

11. Klein, Blomberg and Hubbard, 184.
12. Ibid., 186.
13. Brené Brown, *Daring Greatly: How the Courage to Be Vulnerable Transforms the Way We Live, Love, Parent, and Lead* (New York: Gotham, 2012), 59. Later in this book we will explore some of Brown's concepts about "shame resilience" in relation to the Christian life and to cross-cultural ministry.
14. Jerome H. Neyrey, *Honor and Shame in the Gospel of Matthew* (Louisville, KY: Westminster John Knox Press, 1998), 15.

- **SHAME** is "the intensely painful feeling or experience of believing that we are flawed and therefore unworthy of love and belonging" ... "the fear of disconnection."[15]

What these two definitions reveal is the *social, relational,* or *public* aspect. J. E. Lendon references the first-century Roman philosopher Seneca (ca. 4 B.C.–A.D. 65); the public nature of honor in the ancient Roman world is obvious:

> In Seneca's words, honour is "the favourable opinion of good men; for just as good reputation does not consist of one man's remarks, and bad of another's ill opinion, distinction is not simply a matter of pleasing a single individual." A man's honour was a *public verdict* on his qualities and standing, *established publicly;* and, among those who (in Cicero's words) "are in such a position of life ... that men will talk about us all the time", life was lived under the constant, withering gaze of opinion, everyone constantly reckoning up the honour of others. ... [T]he court of prestige met many times a day, wherever men gathered, in the baths or where wine flowed.[16] (Emphasis mine.)

Zeba Crook points out the distinction between shame as an emotion and shame as a social dynamic in the ancient cultures of the Bible:

> [H]onour had to do with a public claim of worth, one's reputation; shame, on the other hand, was a demotion in one's reputation, or depreciation in the eyes of the public court of reputation. Shame among the males with honor, thus, was not an *emotion,* but a *demotion.*[17] (Emphasis in original.)

In cultures characterized by the pivotal cultural value of honor and shame, one's concept of the "self" is established primarily by one's family and community.[18] This is called the *dyadic personality*, and it is completely different from the individualistic personality by which Westerners view the world. Bruce Malina asks, "What sort of personality sees life nearly exclusively in terms of honor? For starters, such a person would always see himself or herself through the eyes of others."[19]

African theologian Andrew Mbuvi has used the dictum made famous by Descartes, "I think, therefore, I am" and modified it to describe people in honor/shame cultures: "I am, because we are; and since we are, therefore I am."[20] This reveals a complete immersion—*the individual inside the group*—in honor/shame cultures. For the introspective, individualistic, self-reliant person of the Western world—this can be difficult to grasp.

---

15. Brown, 69.

16. Lendon, Kindle edition locations 477–82.

17. Zeba A. Crook, *Reconceptualizing Conversion: Patronage, Loyalty, and Conversion in the Religions of the Ancient Mediterranean* (Berlin: Walter de Gruyter, 2004), 45.

18. This is in stark contrast to the Western value of the "self" which is much more self-determined. The question often asked of children in an American family, "What do you want to be when you grow up?" is unthinkable in many honor/shame cultures.

19. Malina, 63.

20. Jackson Wu, *Saving God's Face: A Chinese Contextualization of Salvation through Honor and Shame* in EMS Dissertation Series (Pasadena, CA: William Carey International University Press, 2012), 190. Wu quotes Andrew M. Mbuvi, "African Theology from the Perspective of Honor and Shame," in *The Urban Face of Mission: Ministering the Gospel in a Diverse and Changing World,* eds. Manuel Ortiz and Susan S. Baker (Phillipsburg, NJ: P & R Publishing, 2002), 288–89.

Individualism is related more to guilt than shame. Guilt is a negative emotion often tied to the individual's conscience, thus it is more internally derived. One need not be in a social setting in order to feel guilt. Evangelical scholar Timothy Tennent writes that shame is different:

> In contrast, shame leaves us with a sense of humiliation, defeat, and ridicule and is intricately tied to our exposure and loss of honor or status before our peers and those in authority within our social network. Shame is not inherently individualistic or private, but corporate and public; it cannot be experienced apart from the larger social context.[21]

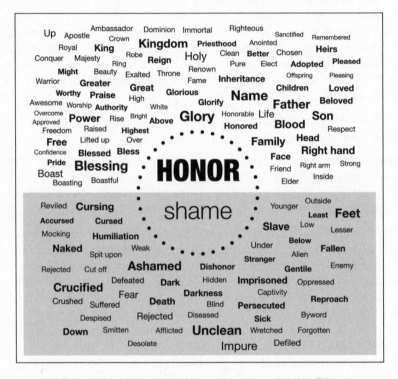

Figure 1.01: A taxonomy of honor/shame words in the Bible

Moreover, we have to go way beyond the definitions of two words, *honor* and *shame*. Since a major purpose of this book is to explore *honor* and *shame* in the Bible, it is important to recognize that, in a large number of other words in Scripture, honor/shame dynamics are *implicit,* just below the surface. One cannot limit the dynamics of honor/shame merely to those places in the Bible where the words *honor* and *shame* are found. Figure 1.01: "A taxonomy of honor/ shame words in the Bible," helps to make this clear. This will sink in as we journey through this book.

---

21. Timothy C. Tennent, *Theology in the Context of World Christianity: How the Global Church Is Influencing the Way We Think About and Discuss Theology* (Grand Rapids, MI: Zondervan, 2007), 79.

Geography and values: The West versus Majority World

In this book, we will frequently talk about "the West" (generally the culture of North America, Northern Europe, Australia and New Zealand) in contrast with "the East," or "Middle East." Sometimes we will contrast the Western World with the Majority World or Global South—which refers to Africa, Asia, the Middle East, and Latin America. Below is a chart of broad generalizations between the guilt/innocence values of the Western World and the honor/shame values of the Majority World.

Guilt/Innocence World (primarily the West)	Honor/Shame World (primarily Majority World)
North America, Northern Europe, Australia, and New Zealand	Africa, Asia, Latin America, Middle East, Southern and Eastern Europe
Generalizations about culture: What societies tend to value	
More guilt-based	More shame-based
EQUALITY More likely to measure worth of a person based on individual merits and performance	**HIERARCHY** More likely to measure worth of a person based on age, position, title, rank, or tradition
DIRECT More likely to communicate in a direct manner, face to face—to "cut to the chase"	**INDIRECT** More likely to communicate indirectly (especially in conflicts) through stories or a mediator in order to "save face"
INDIVIDUAL More likely to value the uniqueness of each person, individual human rights, "my own destiny"	**GROUP** More likely to value the opinion of the family, harmony in the community, welfare of the group
TASK More likely to value work accomplished, efficiency in "getting the job done"	**RELATIONSHIP** More likely to value personal relationships; social harmony trumps efficiency
RISK More likely to venture forth rapidly, experiment with new ideas, not knowing how things will work out	**CAUTION** More likely to proceed cautiously, slowly, to keep what one has gained, even though it may be small

Figure 1.02: Guilt/Innocence World and Honor/Shame World— generalizations about honor/shame and the "five basic culture scales"

These generalizations about culture are taken from what is called the "five basic culture scales."[22] They offer a glimpse at the dramatic, often unseen, differences that exist between cultures.

And because we are making broad generalizations, a few comments are in order:

- **It's a matter of degree.** All cultures, all societies are affected by shame and guilt, as well as fear. Tennent writes, "Virtually every culture in the world contains concepts of both guilt and shame, including the pressure to conform to certain group expectations as well as some kind of internalized

---

22. See Brooks Peterson, *Cultural Intelligence: A Guide to Working with People from Other Cultures* (Boston: Intercultural Press, 2004).

ideas about what is right or wrong."[23] What differentiates one culture from another is not *whether* shame, guilt, or fear exist, but the *degree* to which they occur, the *degree* to which they influence behavior.[24]

- **Still, honor/shame is king.** The cultural value of honor and shame is nevertheless *paramount* in Scripture and in most Majority World societies. The basis and value of making this claim will become increasingly apparent as you journey through this book.

Honor/shame, the Middle East, and the Bible

Since the pivotal cultural value of honor and shame is characteristic of the Middle East, and since the Bible grew out of Middle Eastern culture, then it follows that the pivotal cultural value of the Bible is also: *honor and shame.* It's a simple "equation":

The ancient Middle East was characterized by the pivotal cultural value of honor and shame. **+** The Bible grew out of ancient Middle Eastern culture. **=** **The Bible's pivotal cultural value is honor and shame.**

Figure 1.03: A simple equation—why the Bible is an honor/shame book

Why emphasize this? Here's why: If you are a Christian from North America (or Northern Europe and Australia or elsewhere)—and you consider yourself influenced primarily by Western values, please consider this:

**Culturally speaking, the Bible does not
"belong" to you; it's not your book.**

As we go forward on this journey together, would you kindly suspend your sense of familiarity with the Bible?

- It was the people of the ancient Middle East—characterized not by the

---

23. Tennent, 80.

24. "Although assigning cultures to either a guilt or shame category remains a common practice in contemporary Christian writing, and particularly in missiological literature, it is now clear that such strong dichotomies are naïve and simplistic. Every culture experiences both shame and guilt. ... Granted, either shame or guilt may indeed predominate in certain cultural contexts, yet no culture requires or precludes either experience to the exclusion of the other. It is more helpful to learn how each culture has a particular integrative hierarchy that involves both these two internal controls." William A. Dyrness and Veli-Matti Kärkkäinen, eds., *Global Dictionary of Theology* (Downers Grove, IL: InterVarsity Press, 2008), 814.

individualistic guilt-based values of contemporary Northern Europe and North America, but by the group-oriented values of honor and shame—to whom this book was originally written.

- It was in the culture of the ancient Middle East—characterized not by the equality-oriented values of the West, but by the hierarchical values of honor and shame—that men inspired by the Holy Spirit authored the sixty-six books of the Bible.

- It was the ancient Middle East—characterized not by the direct communication style of the USA and Northern Europe, but by the indirect communication style of honor/shame cultures—where God chose to call out for himself a man named Abraham, so that through his descendants all the peoples of the earth would be blessed.

- It was into Greco-Roman culture at the height of the Roman Empire— characterized not by the individualistic values of the West, but by the family-based, hierarchical values of honor and shame—that Jesus Christ was born and grew up, worked and lived, proclaimed the gospel of his kingdom, called and taught his disciples, suffered a humiliating death, and victoriously rose again.

- It was through the kingdom and story of Israel—characterized not by the fast-paced lifestyle and risk-oriented values of urban America, but by the slow lifestyle, the cautionary traditional values of honor and shame—that Christ called his newly formed people, the church, to extend his gospel of the kingdom to the ends of the earth.

Let's face it. *Honor* is largely alien to the modern mentality. J. E. Lendon describes our modern remoteness from the Roman Empire's (and I would add, the New Testament's) culture of honor this way:

> That a government making broad and systematic use of appeals to honour seems odd and alien to us, that the concept of honour itself seems impossibly distant and romantic, is a consequence of the particular outlook of the late twentieth century; a sign of our removal from the ancient rhythms of rulership and subjection. ... Historically, government by honour is usual; it is we who are strange.[25]

Therefore, if what I am saying is true, it would follow that:

- The dynamics of honor and shame would be woven into the entire fabric of Scripture from Genesis to Revelation.

- It would make sense that many of Jesus' actions and teachings would be permeated with the dynamics of honor and shame.

- It would be evident that the books of the New Testament would have multiple messages specifically addressed to people and communities whose motivation was to (1) gain or maintain honor and (2) avoid shame.

---

25. Lendon, Kindle edition locations 360–63.

- It would be possible to communicate the gospel of Jesus Christ in a way that harnesses the honor/shame dynamics in Scripture.

I believe you will discover that all these things are true.

Is it possible to remove our Western reading lenses?

People and *peoples* are dying to know how the Bible, and specifically the life and kingdom of Jesus Christ, speaks healing to their shame.

Our cities and communities are in the midst of cultural transformations, lifestyle clashes, and new stress points as a result of dramatic increases in ethnic diversity. (We'll be looking at this in more depth later on.) The majority of this diversity is a result of people living among us from societies, which, you guessed it, have *honor and shame* as their primary cultural value.

I will argue that Christian pastors, leaders, and cross-cultural workers who explore this *otherness*—the *strange honor/shame dynamics* in the Bible—will have more effective ministries in our world.

Honor and shame. Perhaps you've never encountered the phrase as it relates to the Bible. Or perhaps the phrase is brand new to you. If so, you're not alone! Truth is, there's a glaring blind spot about this in the Western church. That's what the next chapter is all about.

Why Our Blind Spot about Honor and Shame?

WE WILL EXPLORE THREE REASONS WHY it is so easy to miss the pivotal cultural value of honor and shame in the Scriptures. Why this blind spot?

Theologically ignored. The first reason is that, compared to *innocence/guilt*, the matter of *honor/shame* has been largely ignored as a matter of theological inquiry.

New area of study. The second reason is related; it's a relatively new area of study. In the fields of anthropology, theology, and missiology, shame and honor have only recently been understood as significant for understanding peoples from the Majority World or for understanding and interpreting the Scriptures.

Blind spots are common. The third reason is that blind spots are common—they're a part of the human condition. Christians in every society and every culture, no matter how mature, have theological blind spots.[1]

Let's explore these three reasons one by one.

Honor/shame is ignored by pastors and theologians

John Forrester writes as a pastor about this blind spot:

> We Western pastors have a blind spot. In a word, that blind spot is shame. We don't learn about shame in seminary. We don't find it in our theological reading. We don't recognize it on the pages of Scripture. We don't see it in our people. Shame is just not part of our pastoral perspective.[2]

But why do so many pastors have this blind spot? Because *shame* has not been a subject of theological inquiry.

One way to ascertain the degree of theological importance of a particular word is by looking at theological dictionaries. I went to Phoenix Seminary here in Arizona and did a little research at the library. My question was simple: In the available theological dictionaries, is there an entry for *guilt* and also an entry for *shame?* Here's what I found. The dictionaries are listed in order of the year they were published.

---

1. A fourth reason for this blind spot (but not one explored in this book) is that *shame is taboo*. This reason is more subjective. To study honor and shame implies a personal willingness to explore shame in one's own life and one's own church community. All too often, chronic shame is unintentionally promulgated in the church. It can be uncomfortable for Christian leaders to address these things—causing resistance in studying the matter. See Stephen Pattison, "Shame and the Unwanted Self" in *The Shame Factor: How Shame Shapes Society,* eds. Robert Jewett, Wayne L. Alloway, and John G. Lacey (Eugene, OR: Wipf & Stock Publishers, 2010), 9–10.

2. John A. Forrester, *Grace for Shame: The Forgotten Gospel* (Toronto: Pastor's Attic Press, 2010), 9.

Title / Editor / Publisher	Year Published	Entry for	
		Guilt	Shame
The Westminster Dictionary of Christian Theology, Alan Richardson and John Bowden, eds. (Philadelphia, PA: The Westminster Press).	1983	✓	
Evangelical Dictionary of Theology, Walter A. Elwell, ed. (Grand Rapids, MI: Baker Book House).	1984	✓	
Dictionary of Christian Theology, Peter A. Angeles (San Francisco, CA: Harper).	1985	✓	
Baker Theological Dictionary of the Bible, Walter A. Elwell, ed. (Grand Rapids, MI: Baker Book House).	1996	✓	✓
New Dictionary of Biblical Theology, Exploring the Unity and Diversity of Scripture, T. Desmond Alexander, Brian S. Rosner, D. A. Carson, Graeme Goldsworthy, eds. (Downers Grove, IL: InterVarsity Press).	2000	✓	
The Theological Wordbook: The 200 Most Important Theological Terms and Their Relevance for Today, Donald K. Campbell . . . [et al.]; Charles R. Swindoll, general ed. (Nashville, TN: Word Publishing).	2000	✓	
Global Dictionary of Theology, William A. Dyrness, Veli-Matti Kärkkäinen, eds. (Downers Grove, IL: InterVarsity Press).	2008	Entry for "Guilt" under "Sin"	✓

Figure 1.04: Entries for "guilt" and "shame" in theological dictionaries

This survey shows that it was 1996 when *shame* appeared as an entry in Elwell's redo of his 1984 version. Interestingly, neither of the dictionaries published in 2000 had an entry for shame. The massive *Global Dictionary of Theology* by Dyrness and Kärkkäinen has an extensive entry for *shame*. But (sadly) the vast majority of Western pastors would not likely use a theological dictionary with a global scope.

Perhaps a more profound reason for the blind spot about honor and shame has to do with the study of systematic theology. Most seminary students preparing for the pastorate study systematic theology. Take a look at whatever systematic theology book you may have: When one compares the amount of material concerning sin and *guilt* compared to sin and *shame*—one discovers that sin and *shame* is almost completely ignored.

Evangelical scholar Timothy Tennent has written about this blind spot in the Western church concerning honor and shame. I offer an extensive quote below:

> Since Western systematic theology has been almost exclusively written by theologians from cultures framed primarily by the values of guilt and innocence, there has been a corresponding failure to fully appreciate the importance of the pivotal values of honor and shame in understanding Scripture and the doctrine of sin ... .

> Bruce Nicholls, the founder of the *Evangelical Review of Theology*, has acknowledged this problem, noting that Christian theologians have "rarely if ever stressed salvation as honoring God, exposure of sin as shame, and the need for acceptance as the restoration of honor."[3] In

---

3. Tennent cites Bruce Nicholls, "The Role of Shame and Guilt in a Theology of Cross-Cultural Mission," *Evangelical Review of Theology* 25, no. 3, (2001): 232.

fact, a survey of all of the leading textbooks used in teaching systematic theology across the major theological traditions reveals that although the indexes are filled with references to guilt, the word "shame" appears in the index of only one of these textbooks.[4] This omission continues to persist despite the fact that the term guilt and its various derivatives occur 145 times in the Old Testament and 10 times in the New Testament, whereas the term shame and its derivatives occur nearly 300 times in the Old Testament and 45 times in the New Testament.

Figure 1.05: Words in the Bible derived from "guilt"—versus "shame"

This is clearly an area where systematic theology must be challenged to reflect more adequately the testimony of Scripture. I am confident that a more biblical understanding of human identity outside of Christ that is framed by guilt, fear, and shame will, in turn, stimulate a more profound and comprehensive appreciation for the work of Christ on the cross. This approach will also greatly help peoples in the Majority World to understand the significance and power of Christ's work, which has heretofore been told primarily from only one perspective.[5]

Honor/shame is a relatively new field of exploration

The second reason for our blind spot has to do with the newness of this field of study. Our awareness of the fundamental differences between guilt-based and shame-based cultures is a recent phenomenon. According to Timothy Tennent, "Ruth Benedict was the first anthropologist to categorize Western cultures as guilt-based and Eastern cultures as a shame-based."[6] Benedict's book was written in 1946. In addition:

- Bruce Malina is credited with being a pioneer in understanding the pivotal cultural value of honor and shame as it applies to the interpretation of Scripture. His book *The New Testament World: Insights from Cultural Anthropology* was first published in 1993.

---

4. Tennent includes the following citation: "See L. Berkhof, *Systematic Theology* (Grand Rapids: Eerdmans, 1941); Henry Thiessen, *Lectures in Systematic Theology*, rev. ed. (Grand Rapids: Eerdmans, 1977); Alan Gomes, ed., *Dogmatic Theology by William T. Shedd*, 3rd ed. (Phillipsburg, NJ: Presbyterian & Reformed, 2003); Helmut Thielicke, *The Evangelical Faith* (Grand Rapids: Eerdmans, 1974); Wolfhart Pannenberg, *Systematic Theology*, vols. 1–3 (Grand Rapids: Eerdmans, 1991–1997); Millard J. Erickson, *Christian Theology*, 2nd ed. (Grand Rapids: Baker, 1998); James Leo Garrett Jr., *Systematic Theology: Biblical, Historical and Evangelical*, 2 vols., (Grand Rapids: Eerdmans, 1990–1995); Wayne Grudem, *Systematic Theology* (Grand Rapids: Zondervan, 1994). The only systematic theology I found with a reference to shame is a single line in volume 3 of Norman Giesler's *Systematic Theology* (Minneapolis: Bethany, 2002), which acknowledges that Adam's sin 'brought on him guilt, as well as the shame he expressed in view of it' (Gen. 3:7)."

5. Tennent, 92–93.

6. Ibid., 79.

- Jerome Neyrey's *Honor and Shame in the Gospel of Matthew*[7] is a book that I consider a classic in describing both the honor/shame dynamics of ancient Greco-Roman culture—and in explaining how the various features of an honor/shame social system are woven into the structure and fabric of Matthew's Gospel. The book was published in 1998.

- Roland Muller is a cross-cultural church planter who has served extensively in the Middle East. His *Honor & Shame: Unlocking the Door* is a good introduction concerning the vital role of honor and shame in Middle Eastern culture. Muller wrote another book, *The Messenger, The Message, The Community: Three Critical Issues for the Cross-Cultural Church Planter,* which incorporates the former book and provides a comparison of three worldviews: *guilt/innocence, honor/shame,* and *fear/power.* It is a useful handbook for missionaries. These two books were published in 2000 and 2013 respectively.[8]

- David A. deSilva has made major contributions in using social science scholarship to understand the New Testament. His books on the subject include *Honor, Patronage, Kinship & Purity: Unlocking New Testament Culture,* published in 2000.[9]

- Robert Jewett's massive commentary on the book of Romans, which includes extensive references to the pivotal cultural value of honor and shame, was published in 2007.[10]

- John A. Forrester's *Grace for Shame: The Forgotten Gospel* is both scholarly and useful, especially for pastors.[11] It was published in 2010.

- Robin Stockitt's *Restoring the Shamed: Towards a Theology of Shame* was published in 2012.[12] He writes from a European pastor's perspective.

- Edward Welch's *Shame Interrupted: How God Lifts the Pain of Worthlessness and Rejection* is written from the perspective of the Christian counselor. It was published in 2012.[13]

- Timothy Tennent's, *Theology in the Context of World Christianity: How the Global Church Is Influencing the Way We Think about and Discuss Theology* (quoted above), was published in 2007. His chapter 4, "Anthropology: Human Identity in Shame-Based Cultures of the Far East" is a brilliant exploration of the theological issues of honor and shame, especially with regard to the atonement.

---

7. Jerome H. Neyrey, *Honor and Shame in the Gospel of Matthew* (Louisville, KY: Westminster John Knox Press, 1998).

8. Roland Muller, *Honor & Shame: Unlocking the Door* (Bloomington, IN: Xlibris Corporation, 2000); *The Messenger, The Message, The Community: Three Critical Issues for the Cross-Cultural Church Planter* (Saskatchewan, Canada: CanBooks, 2013).

9. David deSilva, *Honor, Patronage, Kinship & Purity: Unlocking New Testament Culture* (Downers Grove, IL: InterVarsity Press, 2000) 159.

10. Jewett writes in the introduction, "In the shameful cross, Christ overturned the honor system that dominated the Greco Roman and Jewish world, resulting in discrimination and exploitation of barbarians as well as in poisoning the relations between the congregations in Rome. The gospel offered grace to every group in equal measure, shattering the imperial premise of exceptionalism in virtue and honor." Robert Jewett, *Romans: A Commentary* (Minneapolis: Fortress Press, 2007), 1.

11. John A. Forrester, *Grace for Shame: The Forgotten Gospel* (Toronto: Pastor's Attic Press, 2010).

12. Robin Stockitt, *Restoring the Shamed: Towards a Theology of Shame* (Eugene, OR: Cascade Books, 2012).

13. Edward Welch, *Shame Interrupted: How God Lifts the Pain of Worthlessness and Rejection* (Greensboro, NC: New Growth Press, 2012).

- Jackson Wu's groundbreaking book, *Saving God's Face: A Chinese Contextualization of Salvation through Honor and Shame* (EMS Dissertation Series),[14] integrates Reformed theology with the honor/shame dynamics of Scripture. It was published in 2012.
- Zeba Crook's book, *Reconceptualizing Conversion: Patronage, Loyalty, and Conversion in the Religions of the Ancient Mediterranean* was published in 2004.[15] The book is a definitive study on the honor/shame practice of patronage as it relates to the conversion and ministry of Apostle Paul.
- Brené Brown calls herself a "shame-and-vulnerability researcher." Brown does not write as a Christian scholar, but as a mother, educator and social science researcher; nevertheless, I believe her work concerning shame resilience is broadly applicable to Christian ministry. Her last two books, published in 2010 and 2012, have popularized the study of shame as a serious field of study.[16] Her two "TED Talks" have been viewed more than 13 million times.[17]

The point here is that the insights and research that these scholars offer is obviously very recent—only since the 1990s—in the overall history of the church.

Theological blind spots are common

The third reason for our blind spot about honor and shame is that blind spots are part of human nature. How can people with all their limitations— spiritually, intellectually and culturally— completely understand an infinite holy God? *Impossible.* I reference Jackson Wu to explain.

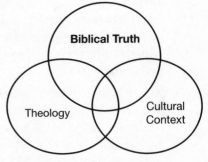

In Wu's book, *Saving God's Face: A Chinese Contextualization of Salvation through Honor and Shame,* he offers a diagram to help describe the process of

Figure 1.06: Jackson Wu's Figure 1 concerning contextualization

contextualization. In doing so, Wu also explains how blind spots occur.[18] Let's consider the various components of this diagram.

The top oval represents *biblical truth*. The left oval represents *theology*. The right oval represents the *cultural context* in which followers of Christ endeavor to communicate the gospel.

14. Wu, *Saving God's Face.*
15. Zeba A. Crook, *Reconceptualizing Conversion: Patronage, Loyalty, and Conversion in the Religions of the Ancient Mediterranean* (Berlin: Walter de Gruyter, 2004).
16. Brené Brown, *Daring Greatly: How the Courage to Be Vulnerable Transforms the Way We Live, Love, Parent, and Lead* (New York: Gotham Books, 2012); *The Gifts of Imperfection: Let Go of Who You Think You're Supposed to be and Embrace Who You Are* (Center City, MN: Hazelden, 2010).
17. Brené Brown, *Ted Talks,* accessed 9 August 2013, http://www.ted.com/search?cat=ss_all&q=brene+brown.
18. Wu, *Saving God's Face,* 52–53.

Notice this important aspect of the diagram: *Biblical truth* is larger and higher than *theology;* this is because no matter how refined one's theology may be, it can never be as comprehensive as the totality of biblical truth. Humans have limited knowledge, but God is omniscient; humanity is fallen and fallible, but God's Word is holy and infallible. It follows that every theology is smaller than the totality of biblical truth.

The esteemed missiologist Paul Hiebert addressed the distinction between the totality of biblical truth—*revelation*—and *theology:*

> The former is God-given revelation; the latter is human understandings of that revelation and cannot be fully equated with it. Human knowledge is always partial and schematic, and it does not correspond one to one with reality. Our theology is our understanding of Scripture in our contexts; it may be true, but it is always partial and subject to our own perspectives. It seeks to answer the questions we raise.[19]

Now let's consider the numbered spaces in the diagram and what they represent.[20]

- Area 1 is where matters of truth in one's *theology* overlap with *biblical truth,* but they are outside of, or inconsistent with, the *cultural context;* these biblical matters confront the culture.

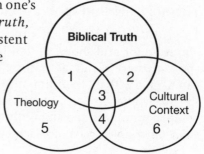

Figure 1.07: Jackson Wu's Figure 1 with numbered areas

- Area 2 is where the "culture has accepted biblical categories and values (perhaps unknowingly),"[21] but are outside of one's *theology.* This is the area where blind spots occur, which is explained below.

- Area 3 is where values and beliefs are consistent with *biblical truth,* one's *theology* and the *cultural context.*

- Area 4 is where specific values in one's *theology* are accepted by the *cultural context,* but are outside of *biblical truth.*[22]

---

19. Paul Hiebert, "The Gospel in Human Contexts: Changing Perceptions of Contextualization" in *MissionShift: Global Mission Issues in the Third Millennium,* eds. Ed Stetzer and David Hesselgrave (Nashville, TN: B&H Publishing, 2010), 93.

20. The following bulleted items 1–6 have been slightly reworded from Jackson Wu. The concept is entirely his.

21. Wu, *Saving God's Face,* 53.

22. Two examples of Area 4 are offered here. The first example is the so-called "Prosperity Gospel," which overlaps with American consumerism but is inconsistent with the overall testimony of Scripture. A second example (and one that is much more extreme) comes from the work of liberal German theologians prior to and during World War II. So-called scholars from the "German Christian Movement" actually created theology to support the holocaust against the Jews. This group supported the philosophy and goals of Germany's Nazi government but was obviously completely unfaithful to God's revelation in Scripture. See Susannah Heschel's meticulously researched book, *The Aryan Jesus: Christian Theologians and the Bible in Nazi Germany* (Princeton, NJ: Princeton University Press, 2008).

- Area 5 is where beliefs are part of one's *theology,* but are neither *biblical* nor overlap with the *cultural context.*
- Area 6 is where beliefs and values in the *cultural context* are neither *biblical* nor a part of one's *theology.*

Wu explains that proper contextualization of the gospel requires a dialog or conversation—as indicated by the diagram—between the overarching *biblical truth,* one's *theology,* and the *cultural context.* He calls this conversation a "dialogical model" of contextualization.[23] He writes that all theology is necessarily already contextualized. Wu quotes Lesslie Newbigin: "We must start with the basic fact that there is no such thing as a pure gospel if by that is meant something which is not embodied in a culture. ... Every interpretation of the gospel is embodied in some cultural form."[24]

Mark Noll makes the same point, "The contrast between the West and the non-West is never between culture-free Christianity and culturally embedded Christianity, but between varieties of culturally embedded Christianity."[25]

Area 2 is where blind spots occur. Wu writes:

In area 2, the culture has accepted biblical categories and values (perhaps unknowingly). General revelation makes this possible. Nevertheless, the temptation remains for missionaries to reject the culture and press hard the truths expressed in area 1, or in 5 (where one's theology is neither biblical nor intersects the local culture). ... For example, personal bias may cause him or her to deny uncritically the legitimacy of the culture's insights.[26]

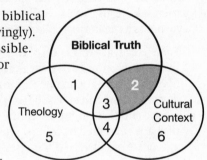

Figure 1.08: Jackson Wu's Figure 1; area 2 is where blind spots occur

The theological and cultural matter of honor and shame is, therefore, one example that fits into Area 2. We have demonstrated its biblical prominence. Honor/shame is likewise prominent in the majority of cultures of our world. An estimated 70 to 80 percent of the world's peoples are collectivistic rather than individualistic,[27] and therefore have honor and shame as a more dominant cultural

23. Wu, *Saving God's Face,* 52.
24. Lesslie Newbigin, *The Gospel in a Pluralistic Society* (Grand Rapids, MI: Eerdmans, 1989), 144.
25. Noll, Kindle edition locations 399–400.
26. Wu, *Saving God's Face,* 53.
27. "How prevalent are collectivistic societies? In today's world, Triandis (1989, 48) observes, 70 percent of the world's population remain collectivistic while 30 percent are individualistic. As a matter of fact, individualism seems totally strange, esoteric, incomprehensible, and even vicious to observers from collectivistic societies. Again, Triandis (1989, 50) notes that what is most important in the United States—individualism—is of least importance to the rest of the world." Bruce J. Malina and Jerome H. Neyrey, SJ, "Ancient Mediterranean Persons in Cultural Perspective: Portrait of Paul," in *The Social World of the New Testament: Insights and Models,* eds. Malina and Neyrey (Peabody, MA: Hendrickson, 2008), 258. They reference Henry C. Triandis, "Cross-Cultural Studies of Individualism and Collectivism" in *Nebraska Symposium on Motivation 1989: Cross-Cultural Perspectives,* eds. Richard A. Diensbar and John J. Berman (Lincoln, NE: University of Nebraska Press, 1989), 41–133. Malina estimates that 80 percent of the world's peoples are collectivistic in "Anachronism, Ethnocentrism, and Shame: The Envy of the Chief Priests" in eds. Jewett, Alloway, and Lacey, 148.

value than do Western peoples. But honor/shame has been ignored by a majority of Western theologians. The systematic theologies disregard the matter of honor and shame altogether.

Wu adds: "From a Chinese perspective, Western theologians under-stress biblical ideas such as HS [honor/shame], group-identity, idolatry, and familial piety."[28]

Concerning African issues, Andrew Walls writes that Western theology is "too small" for African realities of life.

> The truth is that Western models of theology are too small for Africa. Most of them reflect the worldview of the Enlightenment, and that is a small-scale worldview, one cut and shaved to fit a small-scale universe. ... They have nothing useful to say on issues involving such things as witchcraft or sorcery, since these do not exist in an Enlightenment universe. Nor can Western theology usefully discuss ancestors, since the West does not have the family structures that raise the questions.[29]

But the fact that theological blind spots occur does not merely point to a deficit of theological knowledge. It ultimately points to the possibility of a fuller, maturing experience of Jesus Christ. Walls writes about the cross-cultural proliferation of the gospel as a means to a fuller knowledge of Christ:

> Each [cultural expression of Christian faith] is to have, like Jew and Greek in the early church, its own converted lifestyle as the distinctive features of each culture are turned toward Christ. The representation of Christ by any one group can at best be only partial. At best it reflects the conversion of one small segment of reality, and it needs to be complemented and perhaps corrected by others. The fullness of humanity lies in Christ; the aggregate of converted lifestyles points toward his full stature.[30]

So to unmask theological blind spots can be a most valuable exploration, for it can lead us to a fuller expression of the life of Jesus in our own lives, our own families, churches, and communities. Moreover, to unmask a theological blind spot can be critically important for making Christians more effective in cross-cultural ministry.[31]

In order to better grasp the reality of theological blind spots which are connected to cultural differences, we need to see a paradox: *God's Word stands in authority above all cultures, but at the same time, God's Word can embrace varying cultural ideas and styles, which on the surface seem contradictory.*

We will therefore move to the next chapter, where we will explore this paradox in something called the *canopy of biblical truth*. Let's take a look.

---

28. Wu, *Saving God's Face*, 54.

29. Walls, Kindle edition locations 1379–85.

30. Walls, Kindle edition locations 1342–45.

31. One of the most famous examples of an unmasked blind spot is represented by an article by missiologist Paul Hiebert. Craig Ott writes: "Hiebert's landmark article 'The Flaw of the Excluded Middle' (1982) is an example of how the worldview of Western theologians led to a blind spot regarding the biblical teaching on unseen powers, a teaching desperately needed especially in animistic contexts." *Globalizing Theology: Belief and Practice in an Era of World Christianity*, eds. Craig Ott and Harold A. Netland (Grand Rapids, MI: Baker Publishing Group, 2006), Kindle edition locations 6595–97. The Hiebert article referenced is "The Flaw of the Excluded Middle" *Missiology* 10, no. 1 (January, 1982): 35–47. For more on Hiebert's article and how it relates to the dynamics of honor and shame, see Section 3, Chapter 4 of this book. Hiebert's article was originally published in Missiology 10, no. 1 (January, 1982): 35–47.

The Canopy of Biblical Truth

A s CHRISTIANS, WE BELIEVE THE BIBLE IS GOD'S WORD. God created the universe (Gen 1:1); therefore, he is not a mere tribal god. He is the one God who rules over all nations and peoples. Nevertheless, God has revealed himself inside a particular culture and history, that of the ancient Middle East and of his people, the Jews. We believe Jesus Christ is the fulfillment of the story of God's people. As God, Jesus became a man (John 1:14) in a particular historical situation and culture (Gal 4:4).

We believe that God will save and transform at least some from all peoples and cultures into the image of Christ, for we read in Revelation that in eternity future God's people will comprise the diversity of all tribes, tongues, and nations (Rev 5:9; 21:24–26). This means that there is a sense in which God affirms all cultures, for the cultural diversity of the *peoples* is somehow preserved in heaven. We also see from Scripture that he stands in confrontation and judgment over all peoples and cultures. It is with this dual dynamic in mind—affirmation and confrontation (or celebration and judgment)—that we can consider the idea of a *canopy of biblical truth.*

Consider the diagram on the next page: "Canopy of Biblical Truth." The idea of *canopy* may be seen in this Scripture: "The LORD is high above all nations, and his glory above the heavens!" (Ps 113:4). Like a canopy, God is above all nations, peoples and cultures. His righteousness is *above all nations.* Although his Word is rooted in specific histories and cultures, it is likewise *supra-cultural.* The diagram contains a sample list of contrasts reflected in Scripture. The list consists of ideas, truths, cultural values, or areas of emphasis. The list of twelve "dualities" is by no means comprehensive; it is truly a mere sampling.

Let's explore in a little more detail these thirteen contrasts or "dualities."

1. **Narrative/oral—and propositional/written:** God's Word contains *narrative* truth in the form of histories, stories, and parables. Sometimes God's Word and mission are referred to as God's *story.* Jesus told many *stories.* Moreover, the people in the Bible were primarily *oral* peoples whose access to books and writing instruments was extremely limited. The stories of Scripture can be read aloud and memorized in order to fit the cultures of oral peoples. In contrast, the Bible also contains *propositional* truth. It is the Book of books— the *written* Word of God. Scripture is rich with *propositional* truth—in the form of declarations, proverbs, and principles, laws, prophetic revelations of the future, or letters explaining theological truth.

Canopy of Biblical Truth

"The Lord is high above all nations,
and his glory above the heavens!" (Psalm 113:4)

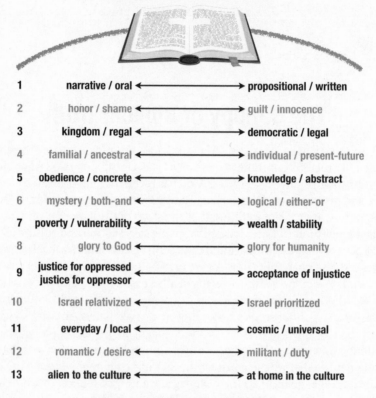

1	narrative / oral	←————————→	propositional / written
2	honor / shame	←————————→	guilt / innocence
3	kingdom / regal	←————————→	democratic / legal
4	familial / ancestral	←————————→	individual / present-future
5	obedience / concrete	←————————→	knowledge / abstract
6	mystery / both-and	←————————→	logical / either-or
7	poverty / vulnerability	←————————→	wealth / stability
8	glory to God	←————————→	glory for humanity
9	justice for oppressed / justice for oppressor	←————————→	acceptance of injustice
10	Israel relativized	←————————→	Israel prioritized
11	everyday / local	←————————→	cosmic / universal
12	romantic / desire	←————————→	militant / duty
13	alien to the culture	←————————→	at home in the culture

Figure 1.09: Canopy of Biblical Truth

2. **Honor/shame—and innocence/guilt:** God's Word is loaded with material about the *honor* or *shame* of humanity as well as the *guilt* or *innocence* of humanity. Scripture reveals that the gospel of Christ is the remedy for sin/guilt (Lev 5:19; Rom 3:23–25; 1 Cor 15:1–3). The gospel is also revealed as the remedy for sin/shame (Luke 15:11–32; Eph 1:3–11; Heb 12:2).[1]

3. **Kingdom/regal—and democratic/legal:** God's Word has enormous material about *kings* and *kingdoms* beginning in the Old Testament and continuing into the New; Jesus Christ is the Son of David (Mat 1:1)—the King of kings whose *regal kingdom* is forever (1 Tim 6:15). In contrast, Scripture is sometimes cited as the foundation for democracy, limitations on the absolute power of kings, as well as human rights, and freedom. Moreover, the laws of God—the *legal* aspects of God's truth—are widely present in both Old and New Testaments, although generally inside of a relational or covenantal framework.

---

1. The diagram suggests that according to the spectrum of *honor/shame vs. Innocence/guilt*, the only two results of sin are *shame* and *guilt*. Roland Muller points to another negative dynamic, that of *power/fear*, which is also a result of sin. This can be seen in the Genesis 3 account of the Fall of Humanity. See Muller, 107–12.

4. **Familial/ancestral—and individual/present-future:** God's Word has a huge amount of material about his working through *family* and offspring on behalf of other *families* (Gen 12:1). There is also much about remembering the past and having regard for one's *ancestors* (Mat 1:1–17). This may be contrasted with all the material in which God works through *individuals,* and where the orientation is the *present* or *future.* Scripture presents the gospel of salvation as being offered both to *families* and *individuals* (Acts 16:30–31).

5. **Obedience/concrete—and knowledge/abstract:** God's Word emphasizes the necessity of *obedience* to God and *concrete* action; knowledge apart from obedience results in pride. At the same time, God's people are commanded to "love the Lord your God ... with all your mind" (Mark 12:30) and are warned that they will be destroyed for lack of *knowledge* (Isa 5:13; Hos 4:6).

6. **Mystery/both-and—and logical/either-or:** God's Word teaches the *mystery* of the Trinity; God is *both* One God, *and* a community of Three Persons. The paradox of God's sovereignty and human responsibility (both are biblical truths) is also a *both-and mystery.* However, God's Word also teaches in abundance many truths which are *logical* and *either-or.* "No, I tell you; but unless you repent, you will all likewise perish" (Luke 13:3). *Either* repent and be saved *or* do not repent and perish.

7. **Poverty/vulnerability—and wealth/stability.** "Blessed are you who are poor, for yours is the kingdom of God" (Luke 6:20; cf. Mat 5:3). God's Word speaks favorably to his people in *poverty* and in *vulnerable* conditions. In contrast, God's Word contains a "development ethic" that produces *wealth* for individuals and nations—along with social *stability.*[2] The book of Proverbs contains many principles for gaining *wealth.*

8. **Glory to God—and glory for humanity:** God's Word teaches that the glory of God is the crux of all reality (Rom 11:36). At the same time, God's Word teaches that human beings are made in the image of a good and glorious God (Gen 1:27), and God shares his glory with those who believe and follow Jesus Christ (John 17:22).

9. **Justice for the oppressed/justice for the oppressor—and acceptance of injustice:** God's Word teaches the good news that God will bring liberty to the *oppressed* (Luke 4:18) and that God will harshly judge the *oppressor* (Isa 14:3–6; Mat 23:1–36; Luke 6:24–28; Rev 18:19–24). However, God also calls his people to *accept* and endure *injustice* and persecution (Mat 5:10–12; 1 Pet 3:9), following the example of Jesus (1 Pet 2:23).

10. **Israel relativized—and Israel prioritized:** God's Word teaches that "There is neither Jew nor Greek, there is neither slave nor free, there is no male and female, for you are all one in Christ Jesus" (Gal 3:28). The laws and traditions of God's people Israel are to be *relativized* under the Lordship of Christ. At

---

2. For more about the "development ethic" contained in the Bible see Darrow Miller and Stan Guthrie, *Discipling Nations: The Power of Truth to Transform Cultures* (Seattle, WA: YWAM Publishing, 1998).

the same time, we see in Paul's letter to the Romans that the gospel is "to the Jew first and also to the Greek" (Rom 1:16). Paul writes that God's people Israel are, in a sense, *prioritized* (Rom 4:16–18; 9:1–5) because the promise of the *all-nations blessing in Christ* came through God's people Israel, whose father is Abraham.

11. **Everyday/local—and cosmic/universal:** God's Word teaches that obedience to God is for the benefit of people right now in the immediate *everyday* and *local* situation. The second half of the Ten Commandments deals with society and the realm of family and human relationships (Ex 20:12–17). The kingdom of God is for today, right here, right now (Mat 6:10). But God's Word also teaches that he is reconciling together *all things* in Christ; this is the *cosmic* and *universal* level (Eph 1:10; Col 1:19–20).

12. **Romantic/desire—and militant/duty:** The Bible presents God as a husband and the people of God as his bride in the Old Testament (Eze 16:1–8; Is 54:5; 62:4–5; Hos 1:2–3) and also in the New Testament (Eph 5:25, 31–32; Rev 19:6–9). This shows that the nature of the relationship between God and his people is characterized by deep affection and *desire.* There is, indeed, a kind of *romance* between Christ and his bride. At the same time, God's Word reveals that his people are under the command of an all-powerful King whose mission is to destroy the works of the devil (1 John 3:8). God's people are called in *militant duty* to engage with their Lord through prayer in a battle "against the cosmic powers over this present darkness, against the spiritual forces of evil" (Eph 6:12).

13. **Alien to the culture/at home in the culture:** The church is an alien community, standing against the idolatries of any political or social status quo (Rev 13) that is a rival to Almighty God.[3] At the same time, the New Testament also provides support for working within the church's socio-political environment (Rom 13:1–7; 1 Pet 2:13–17) and identifying foreign cultural signposts as entry points for the gospel (Acts 17:22–34; cf. 1 Cor 9:19–23).

The point in reflecting on this sampling of contrasts is that God's Word covers a very wide spectrum of human ideas, social situations and cultural styles. Richard Bauckham writes, "The Bible does, in some sense, tell an overall story that encompasses all its other contents, but this story is not a sort of straitjacket that reduces all else to a narrowly defined uniformity. It is a story that is hospitable to considerable diversity and to tensions, challenges and even seeming contradictions of its own claims."[4] This contributes to our awareness that although the Bible

---

3. Dean Flemming does an excellent job exploring the paradox of the church being both *for* and *against* the socio-cultural environment in which it exists. He writes, "Perhaps most striking of all is the tension between Revelation and other New Testament writings in their respective attitudes toward the Roman 'powers-that-be.' Revelation's call for Christians to 'come out' of oppressive Babylon seems to be a far cry, say, from Peter's advice to 'accept the authority of every human institution' and to 'honor the emperor' (1 Pet 2:13, 17). And John's parody of Roman power as a diabolical beast (Rev 13) cuts a bold contrast with Paul's teaching that Roman authorities are 'instituted by God' (Rom 13:1) and function as 'God's servants' for the church's good (Rom 13:4, 6)." See Dean Flemming, *Contextualization in the New Testament: Patterns for Theology and Mission* (Downers Grove, IL: IVP Academic, 2009), Kindle edition locations 288–89.

4. Richard Bauckham, *Bible and Mission: Christian Witness in a Postmodern World* (Grand Rapids, MI: Baker Academic, 2004), 93–94.

was written in the specific cultural milieu of the ancient Middle East and Roman Empire—and thus reflects the pivotal cultural values of the time—the Bible as God's Word nevertheless stands above all cultures and reveals God's righteousness for *all peoples.*

This also reinforces to us that whatever our own expression of Christianity, the way we communicate the gospel of Christ is by necessity embodied in our own set of values and our own cultural style. As N. T. Wright says in the foreword to Scot McKnight's book *The King Jesus Gospel:* "The Christian faith is kaleidoscopic, and most of us are color-blind. It is multidimensional, and most of us manage to hold at most two dimensions in our heads at any one time. It is symphonic, and we can just about whistle one of the tunes."[5]

Let's take a look

The quote from Lesslie Newbigin bears repeating: *"Every interpretation of the gospel is embodied in some cultural form."* I was able to observe this more clearly when I prepared a presentation for a conference hosted by ACMI (Association of Christians Ministering among Internationals). My presentation compared the cultural assumptions of two different presentations of the gospel. The first example is "The Four Spiritual Laws" produced by CRU (formerly known as Campus Crusade for Christ);[6] the second is "The Father's Love Gospel Booklet," produced by Mission ONE (and designed by this author).[7] A free download from this workshop presentation is available on the Internet.[8]

"The Four Spiritual Laws" contains laws (or principles) ... propositional truth concerning the problem of sin ... verses about the gift of salvation through Christ ... abstract diagrams intended to clarify for individuals how their sin/guilt problem can be solved through Christ ... and what it means to have Christ on the "throne" of one's heart for a "Christ-directed life."

"The Father's Love Booklet" contains the Parable of the Prodigal Son (Luke 15:11–32) accompanied by drawings to illustrate the story. It has the parable Jesus told about a family, the descent into shame of the younger of two sons, and a father's radical love. Rather than using abstract diagrams, it has pictures illustrating the story; the story's surprising drama sets the stage for a gospel message that highlights sin-*shame* rather than sin-*guilt.* The booklet shows how to have one's shame covered and one's honor restored through Christ. "The Father's Love Booklet" does contain propositional truth, but it comes after the presentation of the deeply compelling story.

Let's explore how "The Four Spiritual Laws" is *embodied* in the cultural values of Western evangelicalism:

---

5. Scot McKnight, *The King Jesus Gospel: The Original Good News Revisited* (Grand Rapids, MI: Zondervan, 2011), Kindle edition location, 11.

6. "The Four Spiritual Laws" has been renamed "How to Know God Personally." The "laws" have been renamed as "principles." See "How to Know God Personally," *Cru,* accessed 14 September 2013, http://www.cru.org/how-to-know-god/would-you-like-to-know-god-personally/index.htm.

7. Werner Mischke, "The Father's Love Gospel Booklet," *Mission One,* accessed 26 September 2013, http://thefatherslovebooklet.org.

8. Werner Mischke, "Knowing and sharing the gospel of Christ in the language of honor and shame," accessed 26 September 2013, http://www.slideshare.net/WernerMischke/contextualization-acmi. Presentation was made at the ACMI Conference, May 2013.

Western gospel presentation: "The Four Spiritual Laws" ("How to Know God Personally")				
Cultural factors (generally non-Western)	✓	Cultural factors (generally Western)	✓	Comment
narrative / oral		propositional / written	✓	• No narrative or story • No mention of Christ as fulfillment of Jewish prophecy • Content is entirely propositional
honor / shame		guilt / innocence	✓	• Focused exclusively on forgiveness of "sins" • No mention of a gospel that addresses sin/shame
kingdom / regal		democratic / legal	✓	• Content entirely based on "laws" or "principles" from Scripture • Legal, rather than regal framework • No mention of a King or "gospel of the kingdom"
familial / ancestral		individual / present-future	✓	• Message for individuals to receive Christ • No mention of the possibility of families or communities receiving Christ together • No value placed on ancestors
obedience / concrete	✓	knowledge / abstract	✓	• Emphasis on follow-through (obedience) • Has abstract diagrams: bridge over chasm symbolizing Christ as the bridge between God and humanity; chair diagram symbolizing 'throne' of human heart
mystery / both-and		logical / either-or	✓	• Nothing mysterious, presented in highly logical approach
poverty / vulnerability		wealth / stability	✓	• Assumes reader in economically stable situation • Assumes no poverty or oppression

Figure 1.10: Comparing cultural factors in a Western presentation of the gospel

In the simple exercise above concerning the cultural assumptions of a typical Western presentation of the gospel, we have brought to the surface what otherwise is hidden. Paul Hiebert writes about cultural assumptions as being a part of a culture's worldview, and that these assumptions must be examined in order for genuine transformation to occur: "One way to transform worldviews is to 'surface them'—to consciously examine the deep, unexamined assumptions we have and thereby make explicit what is implicit."[9]

Hiebert quotes Dean Arnold:

Cultural assumptions are insidious, not necessarily because they are wrong, but because they are hidden and affect the way members of a culture see and interpret the world. Cultural assumptions affect what we see and what we believe is true, right, and proper without question. They are so obvious to us that they seem to be universal and are seldom questioned unless they come in conflict with a set of assumptions from

---

9. Paul G. Hiebert, *Transforming Worldviews: An Anthropological Understanding of How People Change* (Grand Rapids, MI: Baker Academic, 2008), Kindle edition locations 6845–46.

another culture. More frequently than not, we fail to recognize that the values and assumptions that drive our culture are not in the Bible.[10]

Of course, the gospel presentation known as "The Four Spiritual Laws" is not unique in being influenced by Western cultural assumptions.[11] Every presentation of the gospel—by default—is expressed with its own cultural influences or assumptions. We acknowledge, of course, that God has used "The Four Spiritual Laws" and other presentations like it. God only knows the multitudes who have made professions of faith through the Spirit-empowered witness of believers who have used and are using these resources.

Referencing "The Four Spiritual Laws" and "The Romans Road" plan of salvation, Timothy Tennent writes, "Both of them are based on scriptural passages and are simple enough for any believer to use. The question is whether this basic approach is adequate for evangelism in the Majority World and whether the gospel story can also be approached from a shame perspective, while yet remaining fully scriptural."[12]

Roland Muller writes as a seasoned missionary who worked for decades among peoples in the Middle East. Speaking of "The Four Spiritual Laws," Muller writes:

> Once again, this method of sharing the gospel is based on a legal interpretation of the gospel message and works well with people who have an understanding of guilt and innocence. I believe that this plan, like The Romans Road, has severe limitations for hearers in a shame-based culture. It requires an understanding of the concept of sin and guilt, and it fails to address the life of the believer after he confesses and believes.[13]

In the quote below, Jackson Wu explains the main contours of Western theology, not to say that it is wrong or unbiblical, but simply to recognize that Western theology is itself influenced by Western culture.

> A few features generally typify Western theology. First, typical Western constructions of the gospel are oriented on law, guilt, justification, and judgment. Second, gospel content tends to focus narrowly on the life, death, and resurrection of Jesus wherein people find forgiveness from sin and eternal life. This book does not use the term "Western" in a derogatory manner. Using this word does not imply that Western Christianity has been mistaken in its primary forms of theologizing. Instead, this label is used because certain patterns and emphases are especially prominent in Western theology.[14]

---

10. Dean Arnold, Foreword to *The Fall of Patriarchy: Its Broken Legacy Judged by Jesus and the Apostolic House Church Communities*, ed. Dell Birkey (Tucson, AZ: Fenestra Books, 2005), viii. As quoted in Hiebert, *Transforming Worldviews*, Kindle edition locations 6846–50.

11. The organization Evangelism Explosion has an evangelistic presentation called "Steps to Life." The organization E3 Partners has a tool called the "Evangecube." Not surprisingly, these resources share the same Western cultural influences as "The Four Spiritual Laws" of CRU.

12. Tennent, 82.

13. Muller, *The Message, The Messenger, The Community*, 128.

14. Wu, *Saving God's Face*, 14. Wu does an extremely thorough job of showing how Western presentations of the gospel contain the assumptions of Western culture, in his Chapter Two: "Theological Contextualization in Practice," 10–69.

Hiebert writes about the negative impact of the West's secular worldview (often called "modernity") on the church and theology of the West:

> In modernity the gospel increasingly was defined in terms of abstract doctrinal truths, not everyday living. The result was the development of systematic theology as a kind of science based on positivist presuppositions, a grand unified theory that explained everything. ... Truth was to be determined by rational argument and encoded in propositional statements linked by reason. This work of experts assumed that human rationality is based on universal, transcultural, and transhistorical laws of thought.[15]

"Truth was to be determined by rational argument and encoded in propositional statements linked by reason."

"What could possibly be wrong with that?" I might ask.

As a Christian raised and trained in the West and as one who values logic and propositional truth, it can be deeply challenging (even disturbing) to entertain the idea that my Western assumptions influence—and may actually *limit*—the way I think about and communicate the gospel.

We must come to terms with the fact that the West's typical rendition of the gospel of Jesus Christ is *not* without theological blind spots, *not* neutral in its cultural assumptions, *not* universal in its appeal. Rather, the West's typical rendition of the gospel represents a truncated version of God's *comprehensive* glorious good news for all peoples, tribes, cultures, and nations.

Therefore, I am proposing in this book:

If a Christian's theology is Western while his or her cultural context is Majority World—Asian, African, Middle Eastern, Latin American (or other honor/shame culture)—then to ignore the theological/ cultural matter of honor and shame comprises a blind spot which hinders the missional impact of the gospel.

Blind spots in the West are more problematic

Again, the problem of "blind spots" is not unique to Western Christians. All Christians everywhere face this problem. Every expression of the Christian faith has its theological omissions or blind spots, whether Western, Latin American, East Asian, African, or Middle Eastern.

However, it is important to recognize that the Western expression of the faith has great influence in many parts of the world, and the West continues to hold a leadership role in the enterprise of Christian missions. The wealth of the Christian West also remains dominant relative to the church in the Majority World, and this accrues to undue influence.

---

15. Hiebert, *Transforming Worldviews*, Kindle edition locations 4032–36.

But that's not all. Many Christians in the Majority World have been or are being trained in a Western theological tradition, so unwittingly, they often carry forward in their ministries the theological biases of the West.[16]

This often results in Majority World Christians sharing the gospel in a way that the gospel itself carries Western values to peoples whose pivotal cultural values (frequently, including honor and shame) are quite different from the West's. It's a strange and unfortunate situation, indeed. This is one of the symptoms of what Jackson Wu calls "assuming the gospel."[17]

To compound this problem, many theological students in the West receive no training concerning the fact that the church's center of gravity has shifted from the West to the Global South. These students are thus unwittingly deprived—both academically and spiritually. Andrew Walls writes:

> All over the Western world, ministers are being trained and future theo-
> logical scholars are being identified and taken to doctoral level and beyond
> without any idea of what the church of today, in which they are called to
> serve, is really like. The way that Christian thought is presented to them
> implies that it is a Western religion, or at least, if it did not start that way,
> it has now become one.[18]

> ... More seriously, nothing in their theological education has prepared
> them for intelligent participation in a church that is principally African,
> Asian, and Latin American in composition or enabled them to realize the
> changed place of Western believers within that church.[19]

It therefore behooves us to try to recognize the blind spots inherent in Western Christianity—and I contend that *honor/shame* is a major one. It also requires that we look again at Scripture with a greater awareness about *its* culture and the way it intersects with the multicultural complexities of our world. Finally, we need to see afresh how the gospel of Jesus Christ can be communicated with greater impact for greater receptivity. Section 3 of this book explores a variety of approaches.

Having considered the problem of theological blind spots relative to honor and shame, let us now turn to another problem. That problem is the *pathological nature of shame.*

---

16. Darrell Whiteman writes about the negative aspects of globalization relative to cross-cultural theological dialog: "The bad news [about globalization] is that people are likely to try to dominate the conversation from a position of power, which in turn creates a new form of ecclesiastical and theological hegemony. Once again, it will look like the West is trying to dominate the world, not with economic structural adjustment policies that create poverty but with theological arrogance." See Darrell Whiteman, "Anthropological Reflections on Contextualizing Theology in a Globalizing World" in *Globalizing Theology: Belief and Practice in an Era of World Christianity*, eds. Ott, Netland, and Shenk (Grand Rapids, MI: Baker Academic, 2006), Kindle edition locations 1182–86.

17. Wu, *Saving God's Face,* 51.

18. Walls, Kindle edition locations 1442–44.

19. Ibid., 1459–60.

Does It Hurt or Does It Heal?

THE BOOK *SHAME AND GUILT,* by social scientists June Price Tangney and Ronda L. Dearing, provides compelling insights that relate to Christian ministry, including global missions.

Below is material quoted from Tangney and Dearing that summarizes their research comparing the emotion of guilt to the emotion of shame and how they affect society.[1] Of course, from the Christian eternal perspective, guilt also refers to humanity's legal standing before God apart from salvation in Christ. But here we are looking at the varying emotional and social impacts of guilt and shame on everyday life.

Features shared by shame and guilt
- Both fall into the class of "moral" emotions
- Both are "self-conscious," self-referential emotions
- Both are negatively balanced emotions
- Both involve internal attributions of one sort or another
- Both are typically experienced in interpersonal conflicts

The negative events that give rise to shame and guilt are highly similar (frequently involving moral failures or transgressions).

Key dimensions on which shame and guilt differ:

	SHAME	GUILT
Focus of evaluation	Global self: "*I* did that horrible thing"	Specific behavior: "I *did* that horrible *thing*"
Degree of distress	Generally more painful than guilt	Generally less painful than shame
Phenomenological experience	Shrinking, feeling small, feeling worthless, powerless	Tension, remorse, regret
Operation of "self"	Self "split" into observing and observed "selves"	Unified self intact
Impact on "self"	Self impaired by global devaluation	Self unimpaired by global devaluation

---

1. June Tangney and Ronda Dearing, *Shame and Guilt* (New York: Guilford Press, 2002), 25. The book makes a compelling case from citing more than forty years of quantitative research that, generally speaking, *guilt* is more likely to lead to *healing* behavior, whereas *shame* is more likely to lead to *hurtful* behavior.

	SHAME	GUILT
Concern vis-à-vis the "other"	Concern for others' evaluation of self	Concern with one's effect on others
Counterfactual processes	Mentally undoing some aspect of self	Mentally undoing some aspect of behavior
Motivational features	Desire to hide, escape, or strike back	Desire to confess, apologize, or repair

Figure 1.11: Key dimensions on which shame and guilt differ according to Tangney and Dearing[2]

What does this imply for Christian ministry?

There are many implications for students and teachers of the Bible, pastors, cross-cultural workers, counselors—everyone involved in Christian ministry.

Shame tells us: *"I* did that horrible thing," whereas guilt tells us: "I ***did*** that horrible ***thing***."

Dyrness and Kärkkäinen agree. "[S]hame points to a much deeper reality. It is not only behavior that is wrong, but the person as well. The shamed self is a damaged, deficient self and falls short of some good goal or standard of excellence. It is fundamentally flawed."[3]

Simply stated, shame is about *who I am;* guilt is about *what I've done.* It follows, as stated above, that shame is generally more painful than guilt. Tangney and Dearing clearly describe the contrast between the effects of *guilt* versus the effects of *shame:*

Figure 1.12: Guilt is about "what I've done;" shame is about "who I am"

The tension, remorse, and regret of guilt causes us to stop and rethink, and it offers a way out, pressing us to confess, apologize, and make amends. We become better people, and the world becomes a better place.

In contrast, shame appears to be the less "moral" emotion in several important regards. When people feel ashamed of themselves, they are not particularly motivated to apologize and attempt to repair the situation. This is not an emotion that leads people to responsibly own up to their failures, mistakes, or transgressions and make things right. Instead, they are inclined to engage in all sorts of defensive maneuvers. They may withdraw and avoid the people around them. They may deny responsibility and blame others for the shame-eliciting situation. They may become downright hostile and angry at a world that has made them feel so small. In short, shamed individuals are inclined to assume a defensive posture rather than take a constructive, reparative stance in their relationships.[4]

2. Ibid., 25.
3. Dyrness and Kärkkäinen, 815.
4. Tangney and Dearing, 180.

Of course, our need for the forgiveness for our *sin and guilt* is urgent. Jesus said, "Whoever believes in him is not condemned, but whoever does not believe is condemned already, because he has not believed in the name of the only Son of God" (John 3:18). But when it comes to the emotional and social dimensions, the cure for our shame *is also urgent*. Could it be that when we teach God's Word with a focus on guilt while ignoring the sin-pathology of shame, we are ignoring an aspect of the gospel with great power to heal and transform the human soul?

The data presented by Tangney and Dearing indicate that shame has far more negative and sick effects on people than does guilt. Their research found that shame generally motivates people to "hide, escape, or strike back." In striking contrast, guilt generally motivates people to "confess, apologize, or repair." According to Tangney and Dearing, these results have been affirmed again and again over a period of more than forty years of conducting research by various universities.

Simply stated, *shame* is more likely to lead to *hurtful* behavior, whereas *guilt* is more likely to lead to *healing* behavior.

Many mission and culture leaders recognize that Majority World peoples have honor and shame as their pivotal cultural value. Could it be that when Christians present the gospel of Christ to Majority World peoples in a way that only addresses humanity's *guilt* before God, that resistance to the message of Christ's gospel may be easier to understand?

Consider what it would be to have as your constant, everyday drama the avoidance of shame, along with the pursuit of honor. This is what deeply motivates your life in every pursuit. Your life is moving in a deep, powerful river whose current is *honor and shame*. Consider how David Pryce-Jones expresses the dominance of honor/shame values in the Arab world:

> Honor is what makes life worthwhile: shame is a living death, not to be endured, requiring that it be avenged. Honor involves recognition, the openly acknowledged esteem of others which renders a person secure and important in his or her own eyes and in front of everyone else.[5]

> Between the poles of honor and shame stretches an uncharted field where everyone walks perilously all the time, trying as best he can to interpret the actions and words of others, on the watch for any incipient power-challenging response that might throw up winners and losers, honor and shame.[6]

Imagine if the atonement of Jesus Christ was not only presented as the solution to the problem of guilt and condemnation from God, but also as the covering of our shame and the restoration of our honor before God. Is not this the basic message of the Parable of the Prodigal Son?[7] Wouldn't this be more attractive? For persons and peoples who are saturated by the cultural value of honor and shame, wouldn't this more likely be a treasure worth dying for?

---

5. David Pryce-Jones, *The Closed Circle: An Interpretation of the Arabs* (Chicago: Ivan R. Dee, 1989, 2009), 35.
6. Ibid., 40–41.
7. Luke 15:11–32. See "The Father's Love Booklet" for a concise understanding of the honor/shame dynamics in the prodigal son parable and how it can be used to convey the message of the gospel: http://thefatherslovebooklet.org.

A missing piece in Reformed theology?

One of the key doctrines in Reformed theology is known as "total depravity."

> Total depravity (also called total inability or total corruption) is a biblical doctrine closely linked with the doctrine of original sin as formalized by Augustine and advocated in many Protestant confessions of faith and catechisms, especially in Calvinism. The doctrine understands the Bible to teach that, as a consequence of the Fall of man, every person born into the world is morally corrupt, enslaved to sin and is, apart from the grace of God, utterly unable to choose to follow God or choose to turn to Christ in faith for salvation.[8]

Consider this problem:

- One, the doctrine of total depravity affirms the utter fallenness of humanity not only in our *behavior* ("I *did* that horrible *thing"*)—but also in our *being* ("*I* did that horrible thing").

- Two, because of a blind spot about honor and shame in Western theology, there is a tendency to focus on the atonement of Christ as the means by which sinners are justified and absolved of their sin and *guilt,* while generally being silent about sin and *shame.*

- Three, could it be, therefore, that a theology that tends to address the *guilt and behavior* of our sins to the exclusion of the *shame and being* of our sinfulness is problematic? Is it possible to believe in *total depravity,* while missing a vital part of the *total gospel?*

I submit that communicating the gospel of Christ in such a way that the message includes both the removal of our guilt—*and* the covering of our shame—comprises a more "global" gospel. It is more theologically coherent, reflecting a broader witness of Scripture; plus, it is more congruous to the whole need of deeply depraved humanity—our guilt *and shame.* Therefore, it is more likely to lead to transformation in the Christian life.

Moreover, it is especially wise and vital when communicating the gospel with people whose pivotal cultural value is honor and shame. Whether this refers to people from Majority World cultures or Westerners like myself who have struggled with a persistent shadow of shame (see Figure 1.13 on the next page), there is a widespread need for a more "global gospel."

Christian leaders, pastors, and missionaries should be asking themselves: *When is the last time I communicated a message about overcoming shame through the cross of Jesus Christ?*

Shame is experienced in different ways

Shame is complex. Whether you look at it emotionally, socially, psychologically, or spiritually, it is a multifaceted dynamic. Shame is experienced in different ways

---

8. "Total depravity," *Theopedia.com*, accessed 8 October 2013, http://www.theopedia.com/Total_depravity#note-0.

Pre-Fall	**Fallen Humanity**	**Salvation from Guilt**	**Salvation from Guilt & Shame**
Made in God's image	Depravity: sin permeates both the external and internal…	Western-oriented gospel addresses sin/guilt but ignores sin/shame	Global gospel addresses sin/guilt and sin/shame
Naked and not ashamed			
No sin, therefore no guilt / no shame	1) *External behavior*—**guilt** for my behavior which violates God's laws, and	Positional salvation (guilt forgiven)— but shame persists in experience	Positional and experiential salvation; guilt forgiven and shame covered for greater wholeness
Innocence	2) *Internal being*—**shame** for who I am, falling short of God's glory and dishonoring God's Person; moreover, this can be the result of being a victim of the sin of others, creating additional layers of shame	Limited shame resilience; honor deficit	Strong shame resilience; honor surplus from knowing Christ as King; being God's beloved children in his family
Unbroken fellowship with the Lord; honor in walking with God		Little transformation in being conformed to the image of Christ	Transformed from glory to glory in the image of Christ

Figure 1.13: Salvation is a remedy for both guilt and shame

among different cultures. So as you make your way through this book, you may discover a paradox. Let me explain.

The focus of this book is cross-cultural ministry and the goal of Christian missions is to bless all peoples of the world. I often write about how a particular honor/shame dynamic relates to ministry among Majority World peoples. While reading, you may think to yourself, *Wow, this isn't just for cross-cultural ministry; this has great application to Western people as well.*

The diagram and chart on the next page (Figure 1.14) may help resolve the tension of this paradox.

A careful look at Figure 1.14 demonstrates why this book relates to a broad audience—not just people involved in cross-cultural ministry. It is for pastors, Bible teachers and other leaders who want to discover how the Bible addresses sin/guilt *and* sin/shame. It is for all Christians who want to see how the gospel of Jesus Christ speaks to persons and peoples who struggle with the problem of shame, whether it is expressed as an *external behavior* or a *hidden emotion.*

Let me give you an example of how this material about honor and shame relates more broadly than one might think. In 2013, I was preaching about honor and shame at a church in Tempe, Arizona as part of their missions-emphasis week. My text was Luke 15:11–32. We gave each person a copy of "The Father's Love Booklet" (see chapter 3.1). With Majority World peoples in mind, this booklet illustrates The Parable of the Prodigal Son, and shows how the language of honor and shame can be used to present the gospel. I also briefly shared a story from my teenage years about how I was affected by a shadow of shame (see Introduction).

Primarily Western	Comments	Primarily Eastern or Majority World
Shame is more internal, hidden	• Since shame is the result of sin, it affects all peoples and all persons.	Shame is more external, obvious
Shame is more about feelings	• Honor competition—shame leading to revenge, and the pursuit of honor gains—frequently expresses itself in international affairs. It has often been the fuel for war. This is a powerful dynamic in both Majority World and Western nations.	Shame is more about behavior
Shame is more about the individual's affect *(emotion)*	• Shame affects both Majority World peoples and Western peoples, but the impact tends to differ. • No individual or people group is to the far extreme of one side, to the total exclusion of the other. Every person or people can be placed somewhere on this continuum. • The Bible's vast material about honor and shame comes from an Eastern cultural view that is more about external behavior and is group-oriented. • Some of the Bible's material about shame may nonetheless be applied to Westerners for whom shame is more often hidden—or often expressed through internal feelings and emotions.	Shame is more about the social group *(demotion)*

Figure 1.14: East-West shame continuum

When the service ended, a Caucasian American woman around seventy years old with a joyful countenance came over to me and said something like this:

> You know, when I was a little girl, something happened to me, and it has troubled me ever since. I have been a Christian for a long time, but in all my years, not once did I hear a message on shame. But today, God did something in my heart which has set me free. Thank you so much for your sermon!

"Not once did I hear a message on shame." Only God knows how many people in churches all over the world—regardless of ethnicity or social status—would sadly agree with this sentiment.

The need to cure both guilt and shame

Later in the book, we will consider views of the atonement of Christ and how a balanced view incorporates a cure for both *guilt* and *shame*, as well as the hope for both *righteousness* and *honor*. But for now, here is an introductory chart. Specific Scripture verses are not included here. These concepts will be unpacked scripturally in Sections 2 and 3 of this book.

The gospel of Christ as cure for both guilt and shame		
	GUILT ("I *did* that horrible *thing*")	SHAME ("*I* did that horrible thing")
Problem question	How can my sins and guilt be forgiven?	How can my sin and shame be covered and my honor restored?
Atonement cure	Christ satisfied the wrath of God against humanity's guilt by his sacrificial death for my sins.	Christ vindicated the honor of God and absorbed humanity's shame whereby we were reconciled to God —and to one another—by his death for our sins.
Salvation statement	The divine Judge forgives guilty sinners who by faith accept the death of Christ as the payment for their sins.	The divine King rescues shameful sinners who by faith believe that their King is a suffering servant to represent and rescue shameful humanity. First, he himself absorbs on the cross all evil and sin, guilt and shame; then, he conquers all evil through his own honor-status reversal of: life lived in perfect service, humiliating death, burial, resurrection, and exaltation in glory.
Main benefit to believers	Christ's righteousness imputed to the believer satisfies the legal demands of the righteousness of God, thereby neutralizing the wrath of God. Believers are innocent before Holy God.	Believers have a new source of honor—Christ himself— by which their shame is covered. Christ shares his honor with believers (1) through the Holy Spirit, (2) as they are adopted into God's family, and (3) by identifying with Christ's honor-status reversal.

Figure 1.15: The gospel of Christ as cure for both guilt and shame

The key discovery in this chapter has been that shame is perhaps a bigger problem than we ever realized. Shame is more likely to lead to *hurtful* behavior, whereas guilt is more likely to lead to *healing* behavior. This leads us to the next chapter, in which we will explore just how massive a problem, and how pathological a sin-sickness, *shame* really is.

The Pathology of Shame in Our World

WE HAVE SEEN THAT SHAME IS MORE LIKELY to lead to *hurtful* behavior, whereas guilt is more likely to lead to *healing* behavior. The pathology of shame for individuals and families can be terrible and impact generations. But when the pathology of shame impacts whole societies and nations, it becomes truly horrendous. James W. Jones writes,

> The two greatest group humiliations of the modern age produced the two greatest movements of genocide and terrorism in the modern world: the collapse of the Ottoman Empire along with the imposition of European colonialism on the Arab world leading to the rise of the jihad; and the Treaty of Versailles at the end of the First World War and the appeal of Nazism in Germany.[1]

So let's look at these "two greatest group humiliations" in a little more detail. We'll begin with Nazi Germany and then look at the Arab/Muslim example.

Shame as fuel for genocide in Nazi Germany

Concerning the humiliation—the *shaming*—of Germany following World War One, Jones writes:

> The Treaty of Versailles removed all of Germany's colonies from its control, laid on Germany the worst sanctions that decimated the economy, and demanded its disarmament. All of these had been sources of pride and their loss was a total humiliation for the Germans. These humiliations along with the virtual collapse of the weak Weimar government and the German economy laid the groundwork for Hitler's rise to power. German veterans returning to a defeated and destabilized nation reported "as a Front-fighter, the collapse of the Fatherland in November 1918 was to me completely incomprehensible," or "I had believed adamantly in Germany's invincibility and now I only saw the country in its deepest humiliation—the entire world fell to the ground."[2] People holding such sentiments became the core of the Nazi movement. National humiliation

---

1. James W. Jones, "Shame, Humiliation, and Religious Violence: A Self-Psychological Investigation," in eds. Jewett, Alloway, and Lacey, 41.
2. Jones quotes an article by David Redles, "Ordering Chaos: Nazi Millennialism and the Quest for Meaning," in *The Fundamentalist Mindset: Psychological Perspectives on Religion, Violence, and History*, ed. Charles B. Strozier et al., (New York: Oxford University Press, 2010), 156–74.

caused by military defeat, internal political weakness, and economic collapse had at least two disastrous results for Germany and for the rest of the world: it set off a furious search for scapegoats, for someone or some group to blame and to punish for all this suffering; and it unleashed a ferocious drive to undo the humiliation by defeating those who had humiliated Germany. Many citizens were vulnerable to someone who could explain which group was to blame and could offer a way to overcome the humiliation. That person was obviously Adolf Hitler who pointed the finger of responsibility at Jews and other "non-Arians" and had a plan to restore German prominence through military conquest.[3]

It is ironic that the national shame that fueled World War Two and the Holocaust ended up giving Germany the reputation as the most barbaric of civilized nations—shaming the German people for generations for their descent into such horrible evil. As a first-generation American from a German family, this shame has touched my life and other members of my extended family in deep and enduring ways.

Shame as fuel for terrorism in the Muslim world

The last century has not been favorable to the Muslim world.

- The Ottoman Empire lasted more than six hundred years, from 1299 to 1922. When it was defeated by Western powers, European colonialism took the reins, humiliating the Arab and Muslim world (as well as the Arab Christian world).[4]

- Israel became an official nation in 1948. The gaining of Jewish sovereignty over the majority of Palestine—partly a result of failed negotiations with Arab leaders, plus the Arab League's unsuccessful military response to the newly formed Jewish state—was a profound indignity.[5]

- Israel's resounding military defeat of Egypt in 1967 remains a disgrace on Arab pride.

"These collective humiliations still cast a shadow over the Muslim world and are an important background for the rise of militant and violent Islamic groups who seek to restore the ancient caliphate and with it the pride and power of the Muslim civilization."[6]

---

3. Jones, 41.

4. In a broad-ranging comment concerning the end of the Ottoman Empire and World War I, Marc Aronson writes, "The Ottomans lost; England, France, and America won. The winners got to decide what would happen in the Middle East. And they did. If the Jews did better at convincing those powers to back them than the Muslims did, that is hardball politics. Too many Arabs either kept their eyes on their clans and families, or held onto the losing idea that all the Arab people could be unified and not divided up into separate nations. That was unfortunate for them. But that is what happens in conflicts: if you back the wrong horse, you lose. The Arabs may feel frustrated, resentful, even furious about that outcome. But that anger does nothing to change political facts." Marc Aronson, *Unsettled: The Problem of Loving Israel* (New York: Atheneum, 2008), 32–33.

5. Allis Radosh and Ronald Radosh, *A Safe Haven: Harry S. Truman and the Founding of Israel* (New York: HarperCollins, 2009) describes with meticulous documentation the story of how Israel became a nation and that the Arab position about Jewish statehood was non-negotiable: "The Arabs made it clear they would accept nothing less than an Arab Palestine, with a Jewish minority living under its laws" (203). This refusal to compromise one iota doomed the Arab position with regard to the United Nations Special Committee on Palestine (UNSCOP), which ultimately recommended to the United Nations General Assembly that Palestine be "partitioned" to allow for a Jewish sovereign state. The chapters "UNSCOP: Prelude to Partition" and "The Fight Over Partition: 'A Line of Fire and Blood'" (207–76) tell the story. See especially pages 227, 244, and 260.

6. Jones, 41.

Below is a short excerpt from Osama bin Laden's article, written in 2002, in response to questions about why Al Qaeda flew planes into the World Trade Center and the Pentagon. (Note: By quoting bin Laden, *we are in no way expressing sympathy for the actions of Al Qaeda or any other terrorist organization. We simply want to gain a better understanding of how the dynamics of honor and shame fuel violence.*) Central to bin Laden's argument for violence against America is the mistreatment of Palestinians ever since they were forcibly removed in 1948 when Israel became a nation: "The blood pouring out of Palestine must be equally revenged. You must know that the Palestinians do not cry alone; their women are not widowed alone; their sons are not orphaned alone." At the end of his diatribe, bin Laden writes:

> The Islamic Nation that was able to dismiss and destroy the previous evil Empires like yourself; the Nation that rejects your attacks, wishes to remove your evils, and is prepared to fight you. You are well aware that the Islamic Nation, from the very core of its soul, despises your haughtiness and arrogance.
>
> If the Americans refuse to listen to our advice and the goodness, guidance and righteousness that we call them to, then be aware that you will lose this Crusade Bush began, just like the other previous Crusades in which you were humiliated by the hands of the Mujahideen, fleeing to your home in great silence and disgrace. If the Americans do not respond, then their fate will be that of the Soviets who fled from Afghanistan to deal with their military defeat, political breakup, ideological downfall, and economic bankruptcy.[7]

Observe the key words, "the Islamic Nation, from the very core of its soul, despises your *haughtiness and arrogance.*" Notice also the sentence, "[B]e aware that you will lose this Crusade [which] Bush began, just like the other previous Crusades in which you were *humiliated* by the hands of the Mujahideen, fleeing to your home in great silence and disgrace."

The key dynamic underlying the Muslim reaction to "American imperialism" is honor and shame. *Make no mistake about it:* Honor and shame—honor competition—is the underlying dynamic of the events of September 11, 2001. The Muslim world had been shamed by the West, America and Israel—*and Al Qaeda is taking revenge.* Honor competition is the most combustible fuel for war; this is as true today as it has been for millennia.

But honor competition is not only at the crux of conflict between the "house of Islam" and the "imperial West." Honor competition is also the fuel for bloodshed *within* the "house of Islam"—and it has been so for centuries. As this book is being

---

7. From "Full text: bin Laden's 'letter to America'." *The Guardian,* Sunday 24 November 2002, http://www. theguardian.com/world/2002/nov/24/theobserver, accessed 15 September 2013. It is enlightening to read the perspective of a radical Muslim leader concerning America. The letter is argued from a moral position consistent with the absolutes of Islamic Sharia law. He criticizes America's separation of religion from politics, the use of interest (usury) as oppressive to the poor, and America's laws permitting intoxicants and drugs. Plus, America is "a nation that permits acts of immorality, and you consider them to be pillars of personal freedom." This is just a sampling of the wrongs levied against America that form the logical basis for the war waged by Al Qaeda against America.

written, more than 150,000 people have been killed in the civil war in Syria[8]—between the Sunni rebels and the government forces who are Shiite or Alawite.[9]

Caution: Don't generalize

Having said this, it is wise to remember that only a minority of Muslims actually believe that the Quran supports the use of violence. An even smaller minority are actually engaged in violence.[10] Islam comprises over 1.6 billion people—about 26 percent of the world's population. And there is great diversity of views among them.

Moreover, the dynamics of honor and shame existed in the Arab region prior to the birth of Islam's Prophet Muhammed.

> Like other peoples in the Mediterranean basin, the Arabs use concepts of shame and honor to sanction their conduct. This shame-honor ranking—to borrow a term from the social sciences—stems from the ancient tribalism of the region and predates Islam, though in the course of time merging with it in some respects. Acquisition of honor, pride, dignity, respect and the converse avoidance of shame, disgrace, and humiliation are keys to Arab motivation, clarifying and illuminating behavior in the past as well as in the present.[11]

Honor-based violence in the family unit

Since the year 2000, there has been a significant increase in the *awareness* among westerners concerning honor-based violence. Many North Americans and residents of Europe have begun to hear news about "honor killings" that have been occurring more frequently in Western cities.

Perhaps the most famous honor-killing is the murder of the provocative filmmaker Theo van Gogh in Amsterdam, The Netherlands on November 2, 2004. Theo's great grandfather was the brother of the world-famous painter Vincent van Gogh. The article for Theo van Gogh on Wikipedia records the murder as follows:

> Van Gogh was murdered by Mohammed Bouyeri as he was cycling to work on 2 November 2004 at about 9 o'clock in the morning. The killer shot Van Gogh eight times with an HS 2000 handgun. Initially from his bicycle, Bouyeri fired several bullets at Van Gogh, who was hit, as were two bystanders. Wounded, Van Gogh ran to the other side of the road and fell to the ground on the cycle lane. According to eyewitnesses, Van Gogh's last words were: "Mercy, mercy! We can talk about it, can't we?" Bouyeri then walked up to Van Gogh, who was still lying down, and calmly shot him several more times at close range. Bouyeri then cut Van Gogh's throat, and tried to decapitate him with a large knife, after which he stabbed the knife deep into Van Gogh's chest, reaching his spinal cord. He then

8. "Death toll in Syria's civil war above 150,000: monitor." *Reuters*, 1 April 2014, http://www.reuters.com/article/2014/04/01/us-syria-crisis-toll-idUSBREA300YX20140401, accessed 12 July 2014.

9. Pryce-Jones writes convincingly about a culture of violence across multiple generations and a variety of Arab nations which is fueled by honor and shame. See Pryce-Jones, 108–21.

10. For a nuanced and thorough article on the subject of Islamic terrorism, see Colin Chapman, "Christian responses to Islam, Islamism and 'Islamic terrorism,'" *Jubilee Centre*, Cambridge Papers, Vol. 16 No 2, June 2007, http://www.jubilee-centre.org/document.php?id=55, accessed 16 September 2013.

11. Pryce-Jones, 34.

attached a note to the body with a smaller knife. Van Gogh died on the spot. The two knives were left implanted.[12]

The note that was attached by knife to van Gogh's body was written by Mohammed Bouyeri, an Islamist Muslim. The note was addressed, not to van Gogh, but to a woman from Somalia who had become part of the Dutch government. Her name: Ayaan Hirshi Ali, an outspoken critic of radical Islam. The note includes the following words:

Dear Mrs Hirshi Ali,

Since your appearance in the Dutch political arena you have been constantly busy criticizing Muslims and terrorizing Islam with your statements. You are hereby not the first and not the last and also won't be the last to have joined the crusade against Islam.

With your attacks you have not only turned your back on the Truth, but you are also marching along the ranks of the soldiers of evil. U [You] are not putting your hostility towards Islam under chairs and benches and therefore your masters have rewarded you with a seat in parliament. They have found in you an ally who gives them all the "powder" so that they don't have to dirty their own hands. It appears that you are blinded by your burning unbelief and in your rage you are not able to see that your [sic] are just an instrument of the real enemies of Islam … .

Mrs. Hirshi Ali, I don't blame you for all of this, as a soldier of evil you are just doing your work.

This letter is Inshallah (God willing) an attempt to stop your evil and silence you forever. These writings will Inshallah cause your mask to fall off.[13]

Hirshi Ali and Theo van Gogh had been collaborating. "Working from a script written by Ayaan Hirshi Ali, Van Gogh created the ten-minute short film *Submission*. The movie deals with violence against women in some Islamic societies; it tells the stories, using visual shock tactics, of four abused Muslim women."[14]

After the gruesome murder of van Gogh, Hirshi Ali went into hiding and ultimately moved to the United States where she became the founder in 2007 of the AHA Foundation. The purpose of the foundation is "to help protect and defend the rights of women in the US from religiously and culturally instigated oppression."[15]

Honor violence is a form of violence against women committed with the motive of protecting or regaining the honor of the perpetrator, family, or community. Victims of honor violence are targeted because their actual or perceived behavior is deemed to be shameful or to violate cultural or religious norms. Conduct such as resisting an arranged marriage, seeking

12. "Theo van Gogh," *Wikipedia*, http://en.wikipedia.org/wiki/Theo_van_Gogh_(film_director), accessed 17 September 2013.
13. See http://www.militantislammonitor.org/article/id/312, accessed 17 September 2013.
14. "Theo van Gogh," *Wikipedia*, accessed 17 September 2013.
15. AHA Foundation, http://theahafoundation.org/about/, accessed 23 August 2014.

a divorce, adopting a Western lifestyle and wearing Western clothing, and having friends of the opposite sex have resulted in honor violence.

Honor violence involves systematic control of the victim that escalates over a period of time and may begin at a young age. Honor violence can be perpetrated by one individual or can be a group campaign of harassment and violence committed by an entire family or community. It can take many forms, including verbal/emotional abuse, threats, stalking, harassment, false imprisonment, physical violence, sexual abuse, and homicide.[16]

The AHA Foundation addresses three primary problems: honor violence, forced marriage, and female genital mutilation (FGM). AHA estimates that each year, there are approximately five thousand honor-killings in the world.

The rise of immigrants from Hindu and Muslim religious backgrounds to Western cities has increased the awareness of the problem among North Americans. In response to the question, "Does this happen in the United States?" the AHA website states the following:

Yes. There are numerous recent examples of honor violence and honor killings in the U.S., a few of which are described below.

Aiya Altameemi: In Arizona in February 2012, 19-year-old Aiya Altameemi was physically assaulted by her mother, father, and younger sister because she was seen talking to a boy. Her father put a knife to her throat and threatened to kill her, while her mother and sister tied her to a bed, taped her mouth shut, and beat her. This incident followed a previous incident in November 2011 when Aiya's mother burned her on the face with a hot spoon because she refused to consent to an arranged marriage with a man twice her age. During an interview with police, Aiya's parents stated that they had abused their daughter because her behavior violated "Iraqi culture." Aiya's mother, father, and sister are all facing charges related to these incidents.

Sarah and Amina Said: In Texas in January 2008, Yaser Said shot and killed his teenage daughters, Sarah and Amina, because he was enraged by their Western lifestyle, particularly that they each had boyfriends. During a vigil held for the girls after their deaths, their brother took the microphone and suggested that his sisters were responsible for what had happened to them, saying, "They pulled the trigger, not my dad." Said fled after the murders and has not yet been apprehended.

Noor Almaleki: In Arizona in October 2009, Faleh Almaleki murdered his 20-year-old daughter, Noor, by running her down with his vehicle because he believed that she had shamed the family by becoming too Western and refusing to marry a man he had selected for her in Iraq. In February 2011, Almaleki was convicted of murder and sentenced to 34½ years in prison.

---

16. "Honor Violence," *AHA Foundation*, http://theahafoundation.org/issues/honor-violence/, accessed 27 September 2013.

Fauzia A. Mohammad: In May 2008, Waheed Allah Mohammad stabbed his 19-year-old sister, Fauzia, outside of their home in Henrietta, New York. The stabbing occurred during a heated argument between Fauzia and a number of family members over Fauzia's plan to move to New York City with a friend. Mohammad told investigators that he had stabbed his sister because she had disgraced their family by going to clubs and wearing immodest clothing and was a "bad Muslim girl." Mohammad pleaded guilty to attempted murder and assault and was sentenced to 10 years in prison.[17]

Our office conducted a search of all articles in *The New York Times* by "honor killing." The survey and related research yielded the following graph:

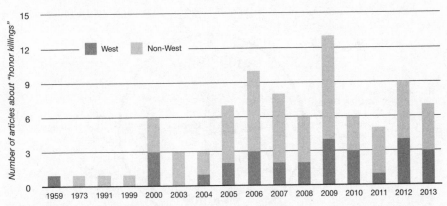

Western nations mentioned in NYT articles: Italy, United States, Australia, Germany, Denmark, United Kingdom
Non-Western nations mentioned in NYT articles: Lebanon, Brazil, Jordan, Dominican Republic, Turkey, Pakistan, Iraq, Japan, China, Afghanistan, Syria, India, Mali, Saudi Arabia

Figure 1.16: Articles in The New York Times under search for "honor-killings"

The purpose of conducting this small research project is to simply point out that in the West, the strange practice of "honor killings" has emerged as a criminal phenomena in our own cities and communities—due in part to ever-increasing cultural diversity.[18] If you doubt such a problem exists in your city, I suggest you go to the website of the newspaper of your city, or of the large city closest to where you live, and conduct your own search for "honor killing." You may be surprised at what you discover.

Is all shame bad?

In exploring these extreme examples of honor-based violence, we might conclude that all shame is harmful, all shame is bad. However, Lewis Smedes makes a strong case for the distinction between healthy and unhealthy shame. Not all shame is

---

17. Ibid.
18. Gang violence may also be considered honor-based violence because "gang culture" reflects a hierarchical community based on loyalty and honor/shame rather than ethics. To add the number of killings resulting from gang violence would, of course, magnify these numbers enormously.

bad; not all shame causes harm. In his chapter titled, "Healthy Shame: A Voice from Our True Self," he writes, "There is a nice irony in shame: our feelings of inferiority are a sure sign of our superiority, and our feelings of unworthiness testify to our great worth. Only a very noble being can feel shame. ... If we never feel shame, we may have lost contact with the person we most truly are."[19]

The subsequent chapter in Smedes's book is, "Unhealthy Shame: A Voice from Our False Self." He lists the sources of unhealthy shame as *culture, religion,* and *parents.*[20] John Forrester also speaks of the contrast between *good shame,* which he calls "discretionary shame"—and *bad shame,* which he calls "disgrace shame."[21] For the purposes of this book, when we refer to shame, we are generally referring to the latter—*unhealthy/disgrace shame* or *toxic shame.*

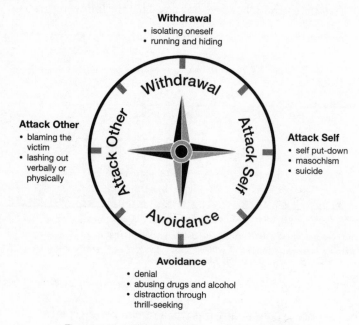

Withdrawal
- isolating oneself
- running and hiding

Attack Other
- blaming the victim
- lashing out verbally or physically

Attack Self
- self put-down
- masochism
- suicide

Avoidance
- denial
- abusing drugs and alcohol
- distraction through thrill-seeking

Figure 1.17: Nathansan's Compass of Shame

The Compass of Shame

Dr. Donald Nathansan has developed a way of understanding the pathological effects of shame using something he calls, "The Compass of Shame." He contends that "at each pole is a library of responses or scripts for things to say and do when shame strikes and we don't know how to deal with it honestly."[22]

---

19. Lewis B. Smedes, *Shame and Grace: Healing the Shame We Don't Deserve* (New York: HarperCollins, 1993), 38. A portrayal of healthy shame or appropriate dishonor is found in Jeremiah: "But from our youth the shameful thing has devoured all for which our fathers labored, their flocks and their herds, their sons and their daughters. Let us lie down in our shame, and let our dishonor cover us. For we have sinned against the LORD our God, we and our fathers, from our youth even to this day, and we have not obeyed the voice of the LORD our God" (Jer 3:24–25). See also Jer 6:15; 8:12.

20. Smedes, 31.

21. Forrester, 23.

22. Dr. Donald Nathansan, *The Compass of Shame,* YouTube video, accessed 17 September 2013, http://www.youtube.com/watch?v=LZ1fSW7zevE. Also see his *The Many Faces of Shame* (New York: Guilford Press, 1987).

We can easily see in these four poles that this is consistent with the principle we explored earlier in this section: Whereas guilt is more likely to lead to *healing* behavior, shame is more likely to lead to *hurtful* behavior.

Some interesting questions may be asked based on this diagram. All the various "scripts" of the Compass of Shame may be observed to varying degrees in all cultures. But one wonders whether there are some major contours:

- **Contour #1.** *Shame in East Asia—eastern pole—"Attack Self."* Could it be that the "eastern pole" located at the right of the compass is generally consistent with East Asian culture in which social harmony is more highly valued? One thinks of China, Japan, Korea, or Thailand—where the "fear of losing face" may lead to suicide—an "attack on the self." The *Bangkok Post* reported on September 3, 2013: "Fear of losing face and an inability to express emotion are contributing factors behind Northern Thailand's status as the country's suicide capital, a mental health expert said on Tuesday. The North has had the highest suicide rate in Thailand for 10 consecutive years, with Chiang Mai, home to almost two million people, reporting a suicide rate of 14 for every 100,000 people, the highest in the region."[23]

- **Contour #2.** *Shame in Western Asia and Mediterranean Basin—western pole—"Attack Others."* In Western Asia and the Mediterranean Basin, could it be that in the response to shame there is less of the "Attack Self" dynamic and more of the dynamic of the "western pole"— "Attack Others"—hence the propensity toward bloodshed and terrorism? Malina believes that peoples who are from the region of the Mediterranean Basin and Middle East "are anti-introspective and not psychologically minded." He shares an anecdote both funny and tragic: "As I was recently told by a Mediterranean informant after we both witnessed an incident of public shaming, 'If I was shamed and felt the urge to commit suicide, I would kill somebody.' This, in a nutshell, is a typical anti-introspective, collectivistic reaction to being shamed."[24]

- **Contour #3.** *Shame in the West—all four poles.* The West has experienced a deterioration of the family and community ... increasing loneliness ... widespread alcoholism and drug abuse ... the postmodern loss of meaning ... rampant materialism and greed ... a crisis of confidence in social institutions ... along with the rise of multiculturalism due to globalization and the migration of peoples. Could it be that the characteristics of the Compass of Shame at all four poles—*Withdrawal, Avoidance, Attack Others, Attack Self*—are on the rise in the West?

In the above three "contours," we tread lightly because of the broad generalizations involved. However, taken in the context of this entire first section of the book, a clear and compelling problem may be summarized by this question:

---

23. "Suicide linked with fear of 'losing face,'" *Bangkok Post*, http://www.bangkokpost.com/breakingnews/367783/fear-of-losing-face-leads-to-suicide-in-northern-thailand, accessed 17 September 2013.
24. Bruce Malina, "Anachronism, Ethnocentrism, and Shame" in eds. Jewett, Alloway, and Lacey, 149–50.

**Considering the pervasive sinful pathology of shame in our world,
is the gospel of Jesus Christ robust enough, comprehensive
enough, *global enough*—to provide the cure?**

The purpose of this book is to answer this question with a resounding *YES!* But we won't see how the gospel of Christ addresses the sinful pathology of shame if we do not first understand the varied honor/shame dynamics in the Bible; we need to identify these features in the panorama of Scripture. To be sure, we will see in the Bible the *dark side* of honor and shame. But we will also explore an extensive, glorious *bright side*, as well.

And so we continue now to Section 2, where we will discover that the dynamics of honor and shame in the Bible are literally *hidden in plain sight*.

Hidden in Plain Sight— Dynamics of Honor and Shame in the Bible

Figure 2.00: The honor/shame wheel

Hidden in Plain Sight—
Honor/Shame Dynamics in the Bible

IN THIS SECTION WE WILL EXPLORE NINE DYNAMICS of honor/shame in Scripture, and one overarching motif. The dynamics are: (1) Love of honor, (2) Two sources of honor, (3) Image of limited good, (4) Challenge and riposte, (5) Concept of face, (6) Body language, (7) Patronage, (8) Name / Kinship / Blood, and (9) Purity. The biblical motif we will explore is called *Honor-Status Reversal;* this is the tenth honor/shame dynamic explored in this book.

Progressive levels of awareness of honor/shame

Some people involved in cross-cultural ministry are aware of the negative aspects of honor/shame cultures. They readily point out honor/shame dynamics as being ethically negative. Statements like this (by Westerners) are common: *"You cannot really trust them because when they talk to you they only tell you what you want to hear; they are just trying to 'save face.'"* Sometimes new believers are shamed, ostracized, or even killed by their families and communities when they become Christians—evidence of the unethical nature of an honor/shame culture. As already discussed in this book, honor-killings are sometimes condoned when an individual brings shame on one's family. We are right in exposing and condemning such sinful behavior.

But while it is true that there is a dark side to honor/shame cultures—evidenced in both the ancient cultures of the Bible and in today's honor/shame cultures[1]— there is nevertheless a bright (even glorious!) side to honor and shame that we behold in the Scriptures. It is this *positive* dimension of honor/shame about which many Christians lack awareness and which is a symptom of the theological blind spot discussed in the prior section of this book.

Figure 2.01, below, represents varying levels of awareness regarding honor and shame. (The full chart is found in Appendix 2.)

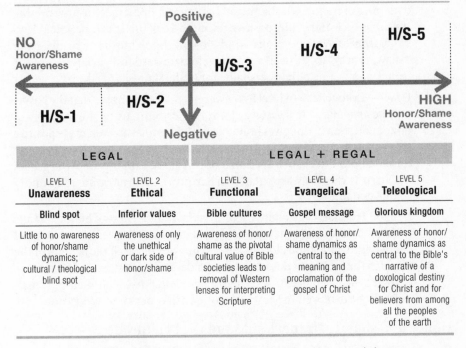

LEGAL		LEGAL + REGAL		
LEVEL 1 **Unawareness**	LEVEL 2 **Ethical**	LEVEL 3 **Functional**	LEVEL 4 **Evangelical**	LEVEL 5 **Teleological**
Blind spot	Inferior values	Bible cultures	Gospel message	Glorious kingdom
Little to no awareness of honor/shame dynamics; cultural / theological blind spot	Awareness of only the unethical or dark side of honor/shame	Awareness of honor/ shame as the pivotal cultural value of Bible societies leads to removal of Western lenses for interpreting Scripture	Awareness of honor/ shame dynamics as central to the meaning and proclamation of the gospel of Christ	Awareness of honor/ shame dynamics as central to the Bible's narrative of a doxological destiny for Christ and for believers from among all the peoples of the earth

Figure 2.01: H/S-1 to H/S-5: Levels of awareness of honor and shame
(for full chart see Appendix 2)

---

1. Missionaries have historically viewed the honor/shame dynamic of *face* as a negative trait of Thai culture. Concerning this negative attribution, Christopher Flanders writes, "Some might object that since face is essentially a negative cultural trait, a disconnect with Thai culture is actually proper. Though face can indeed be negative, I will argue that face is something all of us do all the time. Face forms a critical and necessary dimension of the human self and all social relations. There is room to explore not only negative dimensions of face but also potentially positive and healthy dimensions as well." See Christopher L. Flanders, *About Face: Rethinking Face for 21st Century Mission* (Eugene, OR: Wipf and Stock, 2011), 8.

Levels of awareness of honor and shame. As I have done research for this book and conducted training about honor and shame in various settings (including cross-cultural environments), I have observed that there are varying levels of awareness concerning the dynamics of honor and shame in cross-cultural ministry. This diagram proposes that two levels are negative and three levels are positive. Let's begin with the two *negative* levels:

- **H/S-1—Unawareness:** Level one refers to the *absence of understanding* of honor/shame dynamics; it is called "unawareness."

- **H/S-2—Ethical:** Level two is called the "ethical" level. Some Christians have an awareness of honor and shame but it is altogether negative, seeing exclusively an immoral quality to the honor/shame dynamics of a culture. I call this the "ethical" level of awareness because it sees primarily the *unethical* aspects of honor/shame.

Three additional levels are *positive:*

- **H/S-3—Functional:** In level three awareness, Christians understand that the dynamics of honor and shame can be a most helpful *tool* for interpreting the Bible—a wonderfully positive resource. I call this the "functional" level of awareness. *Note:* Sections 1 and 2 of this book move the reader from "unawareness," to "ethical" awareness, and upward to an awareness of the "functional" value of honor/shame for understanding Scripture.

- **H/S-4—Evangelical:** In level four awareness, Christians see that the gospel may be articulated in a variety of ways in Scripture using the language of honor and shame; this gives honor/shame dynamics an even more positive role in Christian ministry. This is called the "evangelical" level because it is all about the gospel. Section 3 of this book explores how the gospel of Christ is variously articulated in Scripture incorporating ten honor/shame dynamics.

- **H/S-5—Teleological:** Finally, there is level five awareness of honor/shame. Seeing that God's ultimate purpose of gathering worshipers from among all peoples is to honor and glorify Christ, while honoring all the peoples of the world in the process—this is what I consider the highest level of awareness. I call this the "teleological" level (teleology has to do with ultimate purpose). This will be explored in Section 4 along with other summary points.

Honor and shame: The dark side and the bright side

One of the signature aspects of this book is to explore both the dark side and bright side of the pivotal cultural value of honor and shame in the Bible. Therefore, in Section 2 you will see a comparison chart that is near the conclusion of each of the first nine chapters in this section.

Each comparison chart has three parts, as indicated in the template on the next page. First, the particular honor/shame dynamic is represented graphically by an icon in the first column. Second, the middle column—representing the *dark side* of the honor/shame dynamic under consideration—is categorized as "kingdom of this world." And third, a column representing the *bright side* of the honor/shame dynamic under consideration is categorized as "kingdom-reign of God."

A kingdom summary—dark side and bright side (template)

Honor/shame dynamic—kingdom of this world vs. kingdom-reign of God		
H/S (honor/shame graphic icon)	**Kingdom of this world**	**Kingdom-reign of God**
	• Feature #1 of dark side of the honor/shame dynamic as informed by Scripture and lived out in the kingdom of this world • Feature #2 of dark side • Feature #3 of dark side • Feature #4 of dark side	• Feature #1 of the bright side of the honor/shame dynamic as informed by Scripture lived out in the kingdom-reign of God • Feature #2 of bright side • Feature #3 of bright side • Feature #4 of bright side

Figure 2.02: Template of comparison chart—
dark side and bright side of honor/shame dynamic

We turn now to the first chapter in Section 2, "Honor/Shame Dynamic #1: Love of Honor."

Honor/Shame Dynamic #1: Love of Honor

Why is this important?

- Demonstrates from Scripture that the love of honor can be rooted in both evil and good motivations.

- Helps explain stories in the Bible in which people appear strangely "selfish."

The epic film *Gladiator* depicts the violence and values of the Roman Empire. When the hero Maximus inspires the other gladiators to fight, he cries, "For the glory of Rome!" And the Romans' love of honor and glory is on full display.

In the ancient Middle East, including the Roman Empire, the *love of honor* was a core value; it was simply *understood.* We know this because men wrote this down before, during, and after the Roman Empire.

For example, before the Roman Empire came into existence, the Greek philosopher Aristotle said:

> Now the greatest external good we should assume to be the thing which we offer as a tribute to the gods and which is most coveted by men of high station, and is the prize awarded for the noblest deeds; and such a thing is honour, for *honour is clearly the greatest of external goods ... it is honour above all else which great men claim and deserve.*[1] (Emphasis mine.)

J. E. Lendon references the Roman lawyer, author, and magistrate, Pliny the Younger, who lived in the first century (c. 61–112). "Pliny wrote hundreds of letters, many of which still survive, that are regarded as a historical source for the time

---

1. As quoted in Neyrey, *Honor and Shame in the Gospel of Matthew,* 5.

period."[2] Lendon comments on the typical affection for honor, glory and fame among the Romans:

> How little surprising, then, the sentiments of Pliny the Younger: "Men differ in their views, but I deem that man happiest of all who enjoys the anticipation of good and abiding *fame,* and who, assured of posterity's judgement, *lives now in possession of the glory* that he will then have." To the historian, it was naturally the *pursuit of renown* that raised man above the animal. And the orator took it for granted that *honour stood at the root of human motivation* and human institutions."[3] (Emphasis mine.)

The great Christian leader Augustine of Hippo (354–430) lived during the latter part of the Roman Empire. He said, "For the glory that the Romans burned to possess, be it known, is the favourable judgment of men who think well of other men."[4]

Love of honor: Zeba Crook points out that the Greeks even had a word for it—*philotimia.*[5] Jerome Neyrey simply states, "The ancients name love of honor and praise as their premier value."[6]

Examples

Consider the blatant pursuit of honor we find among the disciples:

> And they came to Capernaum. And when he was in the house he [Jesus] asked them, "What were you discussing on the way?" But they kept silent, for on the way they had argued with one another about *who was the greatest"* (Mark 9:33–34). (Emphasis mine.)

Jesus caught them in the act. "What were you discussing on the way?" (As though Jesus didn't know.) The disciples were arguing about who was the greatest, who had the most honor, prestige, or power in their group. They were engaging in honor competition. The Bible calls it *rivalry.*[7] Here's how Jesus responded.

> And he sat down and called the twelve. And he said to them, "If anyone would be first, he must be last of all and servant of all" (v. 35).

Jesus called his disciples. What he said would be opposite their social, religious, and cultural ways. This was hard to grasp. Jesus said, in effect: *I understand your love of honor. I get it. Like you, I'm also very interested in honor and glory. So in my kingdom, here's how you gain honor. It's simple. If you want to be first—if you want to have the most honor—you must be the servant of all.*

This is upside-down—a reversal of our normal ways. But it is God's way.

In the next chapter, Mark 10:35–45, this theme is amplified. The disciples James and John, the sons of Zebedee, tell Jesus, "Teacher, we want you to do for us

---

2. "Pliny the Younger," *Wikipedia,* http://en.wikipedia.org/wiki/Pliny_the_Younger, accessed 2 December 2013.

3. Lendon, Kindle edition locations 465–68.

4. Neyrey, *Honor and Shame in the Gospel of Matthew,* 17.

5. Crook, 63.

6. Neyrey, *Honor and Shame in the Gospel of Matthew,* 17.

7. Philippians 1:15

whatever we ask of you." This was bold. If I was Jesus, I would have said, *Get real. Come back to me when you have a more reasonable request.*

Surprisingly, Jesus said, "What do you want me to do for you?" (v. 36).

And they said to him, "Grant us to sit, one at your right hand and one at your left, in your glory" (v. 37).

This is nothing less than audacious to my Western mindset. What a blatant request for a favor from Jesus. What were James and John displaying? *Love of honor!*

Did Jesus rebuke James and John for their seemingly selfish request? No. Interestingly, Jesus ended up *endorsing* their pursuit of honor, although he turned it upside-down.

And Jesus called them [all of his disciples] to him and said to them, "You know that those who are considered rulers of the Gentiles lord it over them, and their great ones exercise authority over them. But it shall not be so among you. But whoever would be great among you must be your servant, and whoever would be first among you must be slave of all. For even the Son of Man came not to be served but to serve, and to give his life as a ransom for many" (vv. 42–45).

Jesus was teaching: *In God's kingdom, you gain honor in a way that's backward from the ways of the world. Here's how: If you want to be first—if you want to have the most honor—you must be the slave of all. And here's the proof of the principle: The very one who has and deserves the most honor—the Son of Man—is one who humbles himself by giving his life "as a ransom for many."*

Honor and shame: A kingdom summary—dark side and bright side

The interaction between Jesus and the disciples concerning the desire of honor raises a question: *Is the pursuit of honor, the love of honor, the longing for honor—always sinful?* It appears that Jesus tells us, *No, there is an appropriate pursuit for honor.*

However, first let's delve into the dark and sinful side of the *love of honor* that the Bible clearly reveals. Let's consider first some select passages in Genesis in the light of honor and shame.

We discover first of all that before sin there was no shame (Gen 2:25). Lewis Smedes describes it beautifully: "Adam and Eve walked naked with God in the cool of the garden and felt no shame. ... They felt no shame because they felt perfect trust. When they lost trust they felt shame. And so it was that 'the Lord God made for Adam and his wife garments of skin and clothed them.'"[8] God provided a covering for their nakedness (Gen 3:21) through "garments of skins," thereby alleviating some of their shame and restoring some of their honor.[9]

---

8. Smedes, 63.

9. The *ESV Study Bible* notes: "Because God provides garments to clothe Adam and Eve, thus requiring the death of an animal to cover their nakedness, many see a parallel here related to (1) the system of animal sacrifices to atone for sin later instituted by God through the leadership of Moses in Israel, and (2) the eventual sacrificial death of Christ as an atonement for sin" (from *ESV Study Bible*, 57). This author agrees that these verses describe how humanity's sin problem of nakedness and shame (3:10–11) is solved by God's mercy through sacrifice (Gen 3:21). It follows that as blood was shed in Gen 3:21 for the sin and shame of Adam and Eve, so also Christ's blood was shed for the sin and shame of all humanity. Do these foundational verses in Genesis suggest that the meaning of Christ's atonement may be understood, in part, as the covering of shame? Could it be that humanity's need for the covering of shame is just as *theologically basic* as humanity's need for the forgiveness of guilt?

Origins of shame in Genesis—how the sinful "love of honor" leads to shame	
Passage	Honor/shame dynamic
Adam and Eve / The Fall	
And the man and his wife were both naked and were not ashamed (Gen 2:25).	• Adam and Eve lived in the honor of God's presence in the beatific Garden. • Their condition is described as the absence of shame (not the absence of guilt nor the absence of fear).
He said to the woman, "Did God actually say, 'You shall not eat of any tree in the garden'?" (Gen 3:1).	• Satan challenges God's honor by questioning God's Word and integrity.
For God knows that when you eat of it your eyes will be opened, and you will be like God ... (Gen 3:5)	• "You will be like God" is an appeal to pride, the sinful love of honor.
So when the woman saw that the tree was good for food, and that it was a delight to the eyes, and that the tree was to be desired to make one wise, she took of its fruit and ate, and she also gave some to her husband who was with her, and he ate (Gen 3:6).	• The desire for increased honor (love of honor) is inherent in saying "the tree was to be desired to make one wise." • Living in God's presence was not enough, a dishonor to God.
But the Lord God called to the man and said to him, "Where are you?"And he said, "I heard the sound of you in the garden, and I was afraid, because I was naked, and I hid myself." He said, "Who told you that you were naked? Have you eaten of the tree of which I commanded you not to eat?" (Gen 3:9–11).	• The sinful love of honor led to the Fall. • Disobedience to God is equivalent to dishonoring God. • Self-awareness about one's nakedness means shame. • Shame leads to hiding because of fear.
. . . cursed is the ground because of you; in pain you shall eat of it all the days of your life (Gen 3:17).	• The ground is cursed; their work will require pain—both of which connote shame
Cain and Abel	
In the course of time Cain brought to the Lord an offering of the fruit of the ground, and Abel also brought of the firstborn of his flock and of their fat portions. And the Lord had regard for Abel and his offering, but for Cain and his offering he had no regard. So Cain was very angry, and his face fell (Gen 4:3–5).	• It is likely that giving the firstborn of his flock, as Abel did, was a more sacrificial offering than what Cain offered, expressing more gratitude and greater honor to God. • God "had regard" for Abel's offering, but "he had no regard" for Cain's. The jealousy of Cain (love of honor/ honor competition) led to the murder of Abel.
Tower of Babel	
Then they said, "Come, let us build ourselves a city and a tower with its top in the heavens, and let us make a name for ourselves, lest we be dispersed over the face of the whole earth" (Gen 11:4).	• A clear expression of the love honor is contained in the phrase, "and let us make a name for ourselves." This is human-derived honor, a stark contrast to God-derived honor given Abraham when God promised him: "I will ... make your name great" (Gen 12:2). • God disallowed it, confusing their languages to disperse them across the earth (Gen 11:9).

Figure 2.03: Select examples in Genesis—the love of honor leads to shame

Shame, as the result of the evil pursuit of honor, is at the very origin of humanity's sin in Genesis. "There is a prominent contrast in the Garden of Eden account (Gen 2:25; 3:7–10) between the pre-sin lack of shame, and the shame-related experiences (hiding, awareness of nakedness) after Eve and Adam ate the fruit. Thus the initial experience after sin entered the world seems to have been shame."[10]

---

10. Dyrness and Kärkkäinen, 815.

Another clear expression of the sinful dimension of the love of honor is expressed in Isaiah 14 in the account of the fall of the King of Babylon (Is 14:12–14).[11] "You said in your heart, 'I will ascend to heaven; ... I will set my throne on high; I will sit on the mount of assembly ... I will ascend above the heights of the clouds; I will make myself like the Most High.'"

Of course, God condemns the King of Babylon for his arrogant pursuit of honor. God says through Isaiah, "But you are brought down to Sheol, to the far reaches of the pit" (Isa 14:15).

From the Fall of humanity ... to the first murder ... to the origin of language ... and the fall of the King of Babylon ... there is clearly a very dark side to the love of honor as revealed in Scripture. The prideful love of honor is *so dark* that it brought destruction, pain, oppression, confusion, death—to the full spectrum of humanity.

However, this book will demonstrate that honor and shame has a bright and glorious side as well. In fact, you may be surprised to discover that we'll spend as much or more time on the *bright side* of honor and shame as on the dark side. But for now, here is the point:

> Whether we observe *love of honor* as a value in the kingdom of darkness— or *love of honor* as a value in the kingdom of God—you will discover honor and shame as a pervasive, pivotal cultural value and emotional dynamic in Scripture.

Love of honor—the bright side

We have seen the origins of the dark side of honor and shame in Genesis—how the sinful love of honor led to shame. We now turn to the *bright side, the glorious side* of the love of honor. From the Old Testament, I'll begin with two examples. The first example involves Moses; the second involves David:

"Show me your glory"

> And the Lord said to Moses, "This very thing that you have spoken I will do, for you have found favor in my sight, and I know you by name." Moses said, "Please show me your glory." And he said, "I will make all my goodness pass before you and will proclaim before you my name 'The Lord.' And I will be gracious to whom I will be gracious, and will show mercy on whom I will show mercy. But," he said, "you cannot see my face, for man shall not see me and live" (Ex 33:17–20).

"Please show me your glory." What a bold request! Moses wanted to behold the glory of God. His love of glory was expressed as the desire to essentially see God. Curiously, God did not chastise Moses for his desire. However, God could only partially grant Moses's request.

"Awake, my glory"

The second Old Testament example involves David when he was fleeing from Saul in the cave (Ps 57; 1 Sam 22). Here we find a magnificent expression of faith

---

11. In the immediate historical context, Isaiah 14:12–15 refers to the King of Babylon. This passage is sometimes described as the fall of Satan; this is because Satan is the leader of the kingdom of darkness, which in Revelation 18 is called Babylon.

in God. David laments his vulnerability and the darkness of this cave experience (Ps 57:1–4); he acknowledges the anxiety and fear he feels because Saul and his army are out to kill him. Remarkably, David then calls for God to be exalted and glorified "above the heavens" and "over all the earth" (v. 5).

Next, David speaks to his own soul—and to God:

> My heart is steadfast, O God, my heart is steadfast! I will sing and make melody! Awake, my glory! Awake, O harp and lyre! I will awake the dawn! I will give thanks to you, O Lord, among the peoples; I will sing praises to you among the nations (Ps 57:7–9).

"Awake, my glory!" David is expressing his *longing for glory.* What is the Bible telling us? David had been anointed king by Samuel some years before (1 Sam 16:1–13), but he was still not king. In fact, here he was in a cave, afraid for his life! Would he ever become king and experience the honor and glory of his regal destiny?

In the midst of this dark cave, David envisions his regal identity being fully expressed—and having international, if not *global,* influence.[12] David describes what this global influence will look like: *"I will give thanks to you, O Lord, among the peoples; I will sing praises to you among the nations."*

Is there a God-honoring way to love honor and seek glory?

Consider Paul's words to the Romans:

> He will render to each one according to his works: to those who by patience in well-doing *seek for glory and honor and immortality,* he will give eternal life; but for those who are self-seeking and do not obey the truth, but obey unrighteousness, there will be wrath and fury (Rom 2:6–8). (Emphasis mine).

Notice Paul's description of believers: They are people "who by patience in well-doing seek for glory and honor and immortality;" it is to *them* that God "will give eternal life." And this is contrasted with "those who are self-seeking and do not obey the truth." How can that be? How can seeking "glory and honor and immortality" be the opposite of "self-seeking"? To our Western Christian sensibilities, this seems dissonant, weird.

Consider also in John 5 (a chapter loaded with references to honor and glory) what Jesus said to the Pharisees:

> How can you believe, when you receive glory from one another and do not seek the glory that comes from the only God? (John 5:44).

Here we see the unbelief of the Pharisees described as *not seeking glory*—the failure to "seek the glory that comes from the only God."

Another Scripture in the same vein is John 12:42–43. Jesus is speaking of "the authorities [who] believed in him, but for fear of the Pharisees they did not confess it ... for they loved the glory that comes from man more than the glory that comes from God."

---

12. "I will awake the dawn" (Ps 57:8) is poetic speech for "I will make the sun rise"—an indirect way of saying "I will have influence beyond the horizon," i.e. global influence.

Jesus is making a comparison: He is comparing the love of *honor which comes from man*—to another kind of honor—*the honor which has its source in God himself.* Jesus is saying that there is a right and proper seeking of honor and glory from God. It's a reflection of honor/shame dynamic #1—love of honor.

Glory to God and glory for humanity

As Christians, when we think of the word *glory* in the Bible, we rightly think of God. As Christians we believe that the glory of God is paramount in all of life. The Westminster Shorter Catechism begins this way:

> Q. 1. What is the chief end of man? A. Man's chief end is to glorify God, and to enjoy him forever.

Perhaps the most concise statements about the crux of God's glory were written by Apostle Paul:

> For from him and through him and to him are all things. To him be glory forever. Amen (Rom 11:36). ... So, whether you eat or drink, or whatever you do, do all to the glory of God (1 Cor 10:31). ... To him be glory in the church and in Christ Jesus throughout all generations, forever and ever. Amen (Eph 3:21).

But there is an aspect about this word *glory* in Scripture that is frequently ignored. It is this: *the many Scriptures in which "glory" refers to humanity.* In fact, of the 470 cases in which the words *glory, glorify, glorified,* or *glorious* appear in the English Standard Version of the Holy Bible, 139 refer to humanity.

My research yielded these results: Of the English words in the Bible[13] translated as *glory, glorify, glorified,* and *glorious* ...

- 65% relate to God and his domain.
- 29% relate to humanity.[14]
- 6% relate to "other"—neither God nor humanity.

For me, the surprise is that nearly one-third of the "glory verses" relate to humanity. Here's a short selection:

> Yet you have made him a little lower than the heavenly beings and crowned him with glory and honor (Ps 8:5).

> On God rests my salvation and my glory; my mighty rock, my refuge is God (Ps 62:7).

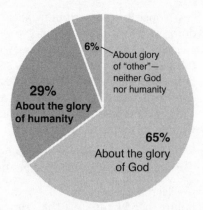

Figure 2.04: Usage of the word "glory" and its derivatives in the Bible— 29% refers to humanity

---

13. This analysis was done using the *Holy Bible, English Standard Version*® (ESV®), copyright © 2001 by Crossway Bibles, a publishing ministry of Good News Publishers.

14. There are eleven cases in which humanity's glory is embedded in the glory of Christ, so the "case" is counted twice. Some examples are 2 Cor 3:18; Col 1:27; 2 Thes 1:10, 12; 2:14; 2 Tim 2:10.

Behold, you shall call a nation that you do not know, and a nation that did not know you shall run to you, because of the LORD your God, and of the Holy One of Israel, for he has glorified you (Isa 55:5).

How can you believe, when you receive glory from one another and do not seek the glory that comes from the only God? (John 5:44).

... for they loved the glory that comes from man more than the glory that comes from God (John 12:43).

The glory that you have given me I have given to them, that they may be one even as we are one (John 17:22).

To those who by patience in well-doing seek for glory and honor and immortality, he will give eternal life (Rom 2:7).[15]

... that the creation itself will be set free from its bondage to corruption and obtain the freedom of the glory of the children of God (Rom 8:21).

But we impart a secret and hidden wisdom of God, which God decreed before the ages for our glory (1 Cor 2:7).

Yet in like manner these people also, relying on their dreams, defile the flesh, reject authority, and blaspheme the glorious ones (Jude 1:8).

What are we to make of all these references to the glory of humanity—the psalmist David praying, "Awake, my glory" ... believers seeking "the glory that comes from the only God" ... Jesus telling the Father about the glory "I have given to them" ... creation being set free and obtaining the "glory of the children of God" ... and believers being called the "glorious ones"?

All this biblical "glory and honor" about humanity is first of all attributable to all humans (despite the Fall) having been made in the image of a good and glorious God (Gen 1:27). It is then magnified by the believer's faith and identity in Christ.

Peter writes to believers in exile in Asia Minor, "So the honor is for you to believe" (1 Pet 2:7). This *longing for honor* relates to what it means to follow Jesus. This is an answer to humanity's struggle with shame—*and longing for honor.*

Let's observe the contrast in the chart on the next page between honor/shame dynamics in the kingdom of this world versus the honor/shame dynamics in the kingdom-reign of God.

When you read the Bible with an awareness of this *emotional* landscape—the love of/longing for honor and fear of shame—God's Word simply makes more sense and it has more impact. I contend that by incorporating the emotional variable in Scripture interpretation, you will come closer to understanding how the original authors and hearers of the Scriptures would have experienced God's Word. And remember, this is

---

15. Jewett comments on Rom 2:7: "Paul is deliberately employing honorific categories to appeal to his audience. ... Both glory and honor are central motivations in the culture of the ancient Mediterranean world, where young people were taught to emulate the behavior of ideal prototypes. ... That one should seek honor and glory was simply assumed in Rome. ... Later in Romans, Paul will link 'eternal life' more closely with grace in Christ (Rom 5:21; 6:21–22), thus removing it from the framework of a reward for good behavior. But there is no hint of this clarification in 2:7, which simply conforms to what Paul perceives to be the orientation of his audience." See Jewett, *Romans*, 205–6.

one of the goals of hermeneutics: Get as close as possible to how the original hearers and readers would have understood God's revelation—to try to stand in their shoes.

A kingdom summary—dark side and bright side

Love of honor—kingdom of this world vs. kingdom-reign of God		
HONOR	**Kingdom of this world**	**Kingdom-reign of God**
	Honor is self-derived: "Let us make a name for ourselves" (Gen 11:4)	Honor is God-derived: God says, "I will bless you and make your name great" (Gen 12:2)
	Honor is located exclusively in human-based family, institutions, achievement	Honor is located in the kingdom of God and Christ the King
	Shame is the loss of honor, and the fear of disconnection from one's family, people or other group	No shame for God's people when living in obedience under God's loving reign
	Violence, exclusion, oppression, death	Peace, harmony, social progress, abundance
	Destructive honor competition is inevitable	Destructive honor competition is avoidable

Figure 2.05: Love of honor—kingdom of this world vs. kingdom-reign of God

Action points

- *Fast-forward:* To explore ways that the *love of honor* can shape a contextualized presentation of the gospel of Christ, turn to Section 3, Chapter 1.

- *Reflect:* Consider the location of your honor. (1) To what extent is your honor—the honor you actually *experience*—located in your family, job, wealth, sports team, ministry, education, or appearance? (2) To what extent is your honor—the honor you actually *experience*—located in Jesus Christ, his church, and his kingdom? How do (1) and (2) compare?

- *Bible study:* Do a word study in the Psalms on the word *glory* and of the related words *glorify, glorified,* and *glorious.* Examine how many refer to the glory of God and how many refer to the glory of humanity. What conclusions can you make from this comparison?

- *Teaching:* Develop a lesson about salvation incorporating the longing for honor and the covering of shame based on 1 Peter. (Alternatively, base your message on Romans 3:23, Romans 2:7–8, or John 5:44.)

- *Mission:* Some mission leaders and cross-cultural workers recognize the dark side of honor and shame (e.g., ethical compromise, honor-based violence). This can lead to looking down on honor/shame societies as culturally inferior. Can we also see the *bright side* of honor/shame as revealed in Scripture? In what ways might this impact your church or mission team?

Honor/Shame Dynamic #2: Two Sources of Honor—Ascribed and Achieved

Why is this important?

- Shows how honor-status is attached to title, rank, family name, and social position (ascribed honor)—compared to status and respect gained by competition or aggression (achieved honor).

- Helps the Bible reader see the dramatic attention given by Scripture's authors to the ascribed and achieved honor of Jesus Christ.

- Helps pastors, teachers and counselors better communicate that the believer's immense *ascribed* honor in Jesus Christ finds expression in words such as *adoption, child of God, heir*—and *member* of the body of Christ.

Definition

According to Jerome Neyrey, "Worth and value are either *ascribed* to individuals by others, or they are *achieved* by them."[1]

There are two sources of honor—*ascribed* and *achieved*.[2]

- **Ascribed honor** "refers to the granting of respect and given to a person from members of the two basic institutions of antiquity, namely: family/kinship or state/politics."[3]

---

1. Neyrey, *Honor and Shame in the Gospel of Matthew*, 15.
2. This point is true for honor/shame societies, but is also true in general. People in all societies—whether they have honor and shame as their pivotal cultural value or not—have only two sources of honor: ascribed and achieved.
3. Neyrey, *Honor and Shame in the Gospel of Matthew*, 15.

- **Achieved honor** refers to honor gained by "competition, aggression, and envy: ... Some scholars of the ancient world describe it as an 'agonistic society,' by which they point to its intensely competitive nature and the common envy shown successful persons."[4]

It is clear; *ascribed honor* is more about one's *being*—derived from family, kinship, tribe, place of birth, or title, regardless of individual merit. On the other hand, *achieved honor* is more about one's *behavior*—achieved honor is gained by action through honor competition in the arenas of education, sport, politics, warfare, or simply the daily "social game of push-and-shove." The diagrams used in Section 1 to describe the difference between shame and guilt can now also be extended to describe the difference between ascribed and achieved honor.

Figure 2.06: Ascribed honor relates more to one's being—"who I am;" achieved honor relates more to one's behavior—"what I do"

Examples

Let's begin with verses about the *ascribed* honor of Jesus Christ. First ...

The book of the genealogy of Jesus Christ, the son of David, the son of Abraham (Mat 1:1).

The entire first chapter of Matthew is given to establish the honor of Christ's identity by recording the Jewish family line through which Jesus came. This was extremely important to the Jewish people, and it makes perfect sense that it appears in Matthew's gospel, since this gospel more than any other was written to the Jewish audience.

Secondly ...

and behold, a voice from heaven said, "This is my beloved Son, with whom I am well pleased" (Mat 3:17).

Following the baptism of Jesus, God the Father declares the honor of his Son by publicly stating his divine love and pleasure toward him. Now add to that the understanding that *family*—also referred to as *kinship*—is the starting point of each person's ascribed honor.

Speaking of the importance of family and kinship, New Testament scholar David deSilva says,

In the ancient world, people are not just taken on their "merits." Instead, their merits begin with the merits (or debits) of their lineage,

---

4. Ibid., 16. Agonistic behavior is defined as "any social behavior related to fighting. The term has broader meaning than aggressive behavior because it includes threats, displays, retreats, placating aggressors, and conciliation." See "Agonistic behaviour," *Wikipedia,* http://en.wikipedia.org/wiki/Agonistic_behavior, accessed 29 April 2014.

the reputation of their ancestral house. Greeks and Romans receive a basic identity from their larger family: for Romans this takes the form of including the clan name in the name of each individual.[5]

Suddenly, one begins to grasp that this public, divine declaration of the Father's love for his Son is intended to amplify Christ's ascribed honor for everyone watching and listening. For people in honor/shame societies, the force of this cannot be overstated.

Now let's turn to a classic passage about the *achieved* honor of Jesus Christ:

And being found in human form, he humbled himself by becoming obedient to the point of death, even death on a cross. Therefore God has highly exalted him and bestowed on him the name that is above every name, so that at the name of Jesus every knee should bow, in heaven and on earth and under the earth, and every tongue confess that Jesus Christ is Lord, to the glory of God the Father (Phil 2:8–11).

Note the word, "Therefore." This word is a conjunction, linking the super-exaltation of the Lord Jesus Christ with what he achieved on the cross. Christ's honor was, in this sense, earned or achieved, because of the humiliation he suffered and the work he accomplished ("It is finished," John 19:30)—through his shameful death by crucifixion and subsequent resurrection.

Below is a passage that combines both the ascribed honor and achieved honor of Jesus Christ—Hebrews 1:1–5, 8–9:

Long ago, at many times and in many ways, God spoke to our fathers by the prophets,

but in these last days he has spoken to us by his Son, whom he appointed the heir of all things, *[ascribed honor]* through whom also he created the world.

He is the radiance of the glory of God and the exact imprint of his nature *[ascribed honor]*, and he upholds the universe by the word of his power *[achieved honor]*. After making purification for sins, he sat down at the right hand of the Majesty on high *[achieved honor]*,

having become as much superior to angels as the name he has inherited is more excellent than theirs *[ascribed honor]*.

For to which of the angels did God ever say, "You are my Son, today I have begotten you"? *[ascribed honor]*

Or again, "I will be to him a father, and he shall be to me a son"? *[ascribed honor]*

... But of the Son he says, "Your throne, O God, is forever and ever, *[ascribed honor]* the scepter of uprightness is the scepter of your kingdom. You have loved righteousness and hated wickedness; therefore God, your God, has anointed you with the oil of gladness beyond your companions." *[achieved honor]*

---

5. deSilva, 159.

The first chapter of Hebrews is all about the honor of one Person. The author is making an irrefutable case for the exalted honor of the Son of God, the Lord Jesus Christ. I contend that the author of Hebrews wants the reader to not just *know* something about Christ, but to *feel* something, to *emote* with obedience, to obey with emotion—in response to our highly exalted Savior. The author *feels astounded, amazed, terrified with delight* concerning the utterly supreme honor, authority, power and glory of Jesus Christ—and he wants the reader to have the same experience.

A Western Christian may observe the opening chapter of Hebrews in a detached, logical way—while the Eastern Christian from an honor/shame culture may perceive this with far more relevance and impact.

For the Western Christian, it would be like looking at a map called the Bible and seeing on that map a river called "The Honor and Glory of the Son of God." The Western believer says, "Ah, yes, there it is; that is a very big river, indeed."

Christians from an honor/shame culture—where the value of honor and shame dominates life—would be more likely to receive this passage of Scripture with deep emotional and life-impacting significance. Because of the significance for them of honor and shame, it is *unlike* seeing the name of the river on a map; it is more like *swimming* in that river of truth, being influenced by the strong current of the river, terrified by its depth while enjoying its life-giving vitality. The believer from an honor/shame culture cannot compartmentalize honor and shame as a facet of truth to be acknowledged, but swims in this honor and shame reality every hour of every day of his or her life.

A kingdom summary—dark side and bright side

Ascribed and achieved honor—kingdom of this world vs. kingdom-reign of God		
	Kingdom of this world	Kingdom-reign of God
Ascribed Honor **Achieved Honor** ✓	Ascribed and achieved honor become corrupt and destructive when isolated from God's kingdom—leading to arrogance, pride, and competitive praise-seeking from others apart from God's praise.	ASCRIBED HONOR • Jesus has ascribed honor as Son of God, loved by the Father • People gain a new source of honor by being born again, becoming children of God ACHIEVED HONOR • Jesus has achieved honor as Savior of the world, conquering sin and shame, death and the devil • Believers gain honor by serving and loving others • Believers experience honor by abiding in a life-long cruciform journey of loving obedience in Christ • God's people involved in athletic, educational, professional, or artistic accomplishment—performed for the glory of God

Figure 2.07: Ascribed and achieved honor—kingdom of this world vs. kingdom-reign of God

Action points

- *Fast-forward:* To explore ways that the *two sources of honor, ascribed and achieved*, can shape a contextualized presentation of the gospel of Christ, turn to Section 3, Chapter 2.

- *Reflect:* How can the first chapter of Hebrews—describing the ascribed and achieved honor of Jesus Christ—be used in your personal devotional life to worship God? How might this be used in a small group worship experience?

- *Bible study:* When studying Scripture, attach more significance to names and titles. Since ancient Middle Eastern cultures were very hierarchical (not egalitarian), the ascribed honor inherent in titles carried real power and emotional weight—conveying respect and fear. Names and titles carry much more honorific meaning in the East than in the West.

- *Teaching:* How can you best portray the exalted wonder—the ascribed and achieved honor—of Jesus Christ, the Son of God? Suggested passages: Philippians 2:5–11, Hebrews 1:1–14.

- *Mission:* When conducting your mission trips, cross-cultural partnerships, or other cross-cultural ministry, consider what impact your efforts are having on the ascribed *honor* of the people involved. How does this affect the honor or dignity of your partners? Of the community that your partners are serving?

Honor/Shame Dynamic #3: Image of Limited Good

Why is this important?

- Emphasizes a strongly held value of honor/shame societies that is contrary to Western ideals.

- Contributes to an understanding of why honor competition is a continuous dynamic in the drama of Scripture.

- Jesus and the Jewish religious leaders were in constant honor competition; this helps explain—from a social science perspective—why this led to violence and why the Jews conspired to have Jesus crucified.

- Contributes to a rationale for the seemingly unending cycle of conflict and violence in some honor/shame societies, i.e., the Middle East.

Definition

The image of limited good is "the belief that everything in the social, economic, natural universe ... everything desired in life: land, wealth, respect and status, power and influence ... exist in finite quantity and are in short supply."[1] If you gain, I lose ... it's a "zero-sum game."

---

1. Neyrey, *Honor and Shame in the Gospel of Matthew,* 18. Scholars call this the *"image* of limited good," because, in fact, "good" is not necessarily limited. This author considered calling this honor/shame principle "limited good" for the sake of simplicity, but rejected the idea. While *land* may be correctly considered finite and limited—wealth and power, honor and glory—may or may not be limited. The limitations are real only in the mind of the person or society, thus the description is apt: "the *image* of limited good." The Bible teaches that in Christ there is no "limited good."

All people do not view the world similarly. The industrialized West considers the world to be a limitless source of resources for an ever expanding economy that benefits all. A rising tide lifts all boats. But anthropologists who study other cultures, modern and ancient, inform us that other people see the world as a fixed and limited source of just so much grain, water, fertility, and honor. For them, this supply will never expand, and the benefits must be divided out between all people. Thus, one person or group's share increases only because it is being taken away from others. When people operating under the presumption that everyone is born into a family with only so much wealth, grain, siblings, and respect perceive others apparently getting more of the limited goods, the scene is set for conflict.[2]

Saul and David

Consider this account from the life of David—following his victory over the Philistine Goliath. The honor/shame dynamic of King Saul in relation to David is revealing:

> As they were coming home, when David returned from striking down the Philistine, the women came out of all the cities of Israel, singing and dancing, to meet King Saul, with tambourines, with songs of joy, and with musical instruments. And the women sang to one another as they celebrated, "Saul has struck down his thousands, and David his ten thousands." And Saul was very angry, and this saying displeased him. He said, "They have ascribed to David ten thousands, and to me they have ascribed thousands, and what more can he have but the kingdom?" And Saul eyed David from that day on (1 Sam 18:6–9).

It is easy for us to recognize Saul's jealousy. But when you add to this the understanding that in an honor/shame culture, honor is a "limited good" (a zero-sum game), the power of this value to influence behavior—particularly to *generate conflict*—is raised to another order of magnitude.

From an honor/shame perspective, King Saul saw that his honor as king was threatened by the *achieved* honor of David. Saul's very personhood, his total identity, was threatened by David. As David's honor rose in the hearts of the people of Israel, Saul's own honor fell—even though he was still king. Saul's honor was at stake, and David's dramatic increase in honor was to Saul the equivalent of a mortal threat. Therefore, Saul became obsessed with finding a way to kill David.

Contrary to the idea that Saul was perhaps mentally disturbed, his reaction was only logical. Since Saul believed in the concept of "limited good," it was inconceivable for him to celebrate David's victory with the people.

---

2. Neyrey and Stewart, 235. Of course, not everyone in the "industrialized West" has the view that "an ever expanding economy ... benefits all." Neyrey is broadly generalizing. In fact, the reader will note that a few pages further into this chapter, a chart by Darrow Miller characterizes the secular worldview of the West to reflect a "limited good" worldview.

Paul in prison

In the New Testament, consider this passage from the first chapter of Paul's letter to the Philippians. Observe the honor/shame dynamics, and in particular, how Paul completely overturns "the image of limited good."

> What then? Only that in every way, whether in pretense or in truth, Christ is proclaimed, and in that I rejoice. Yes, and I will rejoice, for I know that through your prayers and the help of the Spirit of Jesus Christ this will turn out for my deliverance, as it is my eager expectation and hope that I will not be at all *ashamed,* but that with full courage now as always Christ will be *honored* in my body, whether by life or by death. For to me to live is Christ, and to die is gain. If I am to live in the flesh, that means fruitful labor for me. Yet which I shall choose I cannot tell. I am hard pressed between the two. My desire is to depart and be with Christ, for that is far better. But to remain in the flesh is more necessary on your account (Phil 1:18–24). (Emphasis mine.)

Paul was an apostle of Jesus Christ and a Roman citizen—both great honors. However, Paul was in prison as he wrote this letter, which would normally be considered a low and shameful condition. But Paul wrote with great faith, "It is my eager expectation and hope that I will not be at all ashamed" (1:20).

How does Paul's relationship with Jesus Christ give him the means to overturn "the image of limited good" ... turning "win-lose" into "win-win?"

At the crux of this dynamic shift is Paul's life in Christ. His expectation is that, rather than being ashamed of imprisonment or death, he will trust in Christ. Rather than being ashamed by disloyalty or dishonor toward God, Paul will "with full courage" allow "Christ [to] be honored" in his body, "whether by life or by death." How can Paul do this?

Here's how: "For to me to live is Christ, and to die is gain."

The win-lose drama of Paul's imprisonment and possible execution is turned into a sublime declaration of irrepressible victory in Jesus Christ. It overturns the dynamics of *win-lose* and the "image of limited good"—through the *win-win* of a life totally immersed in the resurrection life and supreme honor of Jesus Christ. Paul did not locate his honor in his achievements, his family, title, or circumstances. Paul located his honor in *the most honorable One,* Jesus Christ.

Paul goes on in other parts of his joy-filled letter to demonstrate how this works—not just for him during his imprisonment—but for all believers, regardless of their circumstances. In the latter part of his letter he writes, "And my God will supply every need of yours according to his riches in glory in Christ Jesus" (Phil 4:19). Paul was directly challenging this widespread belief of the "image of limited good." He revealed that for all Christians, there is no "limited good" in Christ. There is, in fact, an unlimited storehouse of provision for physical needs, for blessing, and for honor through Christ. Paul calls it God's "riches in glory in Christ Jesus"— potentially available by faith to all persons who follow Jesus as their Lord and Savior.

Reinforcing the cycle of poverty

In *Discipling Nations: The Power of Truth to Transform Cultures,* Miller and Guthrie describe how societies can perpetuate a culture of poverty primarily because of their basic worldview. The *image of limited good* is completely at odds with what Miller calls the "development ethic" that is contained in the "transforming story" of the Bible.[3]

Throughout the book, Miller and Guthrie compare three basic worldviews: *animism, theism,* and *secularism.* These basic three worldviews have drastically different perspectives about nature. One of the society-transforming ideas that comes from the Bible is a view of nature called the "open system."[4] Below is a chart, "The Nature of Nature,"[5] which shows the contrasts:

	Animism	Theism	Secularism
Ruler	Nature	GOD	Man
Perspective	Biocentric	Theocentric	Anthropocentric
Nature	Capricious	Open System (Created)	Closed System
Man	A Spirit	A Mind, The Image of God (A living soul)	A Mouth, The Highest Animal
Resources	Limited Good	Positive Sum	Zero Sum
Man's Role	Worshiper / Victim	Steward / Regent	Consumer / Miner

Figure 2.08: Miller's "The Nature of Nature"

In a closed system, everyone competes for the same resources. As stated above, "Everything desired in life: land, wealth, respect and status, power and influence ... exist in finite quantity and are in short supply."

But those who believe in an "open system" are not bound by the *image of limited good.* Miller writes, "Development is thus more about discovering and exploring God's world than merely trying to help people survive. It is about creating new resources, not redistributing scarce ones."

Secularists, and those influenced by their teaching, have a hard time with this. They are locked into a worldview that takes as an article of faith the idea that "spaceship earth" is headed for a crash. Like all pessimists, the ecological glass for them is always half empty. They believe we live in a closed system. Their brothers in the mindset of poverty, the animists, do not believe in natural laws, which cuts at the knees any kind of scientific progress. Those who look at the world as God's creation, however, have a radically different outlook. They see a world of potentialities limited only by their own creativity and moral stewardship.[6]

---

3. Miller and Guthrie, 243–79.
4. Ibid., 147.
5. Ibid., 149. Figure 7.2.
6. Ibid., 148.

Miller is drawing broad generalizations, to be sure, but in the context of his book's multifaceted overall theme, it is valid. There are many reasons for chronic poverty, some of which are oppressive *external* social or political forces. But among the *internal* dynamics that contribute to chronic poverty is a worldview that clings to the *image of limited good*.[7]

In the economic development or relative prosperity of nations, *ideas matter,* including whether a nation clings to the "idea" of *limited good.* Former Harvard economics and history professor David S. Landes wrote a landmark book, *The Wealth and Poverty of Nations: Why Some Are So Rich and Some So Poor.* In his summary he stated, "If we learned anything from the history of economic development, it is that culture makes all the difference."[8]

A kingdom summary—dark side and bright side

Image of limited good—kingdom of this world vs. kingdom-reign of God		
	Kingdom of this world	Kingdom-reign of God
WIN / LOSE	• Contributes to the onset of violence toward self and others • Reinforces culture of poverty and a mindset of despair	• There is no limited good in Jesus Christ and the riches of his glory • Abundance for all is the mindset of God's kingdom; this generates hope and transformation in families, communities, peoples, nations

Figure 2.09: *Image of limited good—kingdom of this world vs. kingdom-reign of God*

We will further explore the dynamics of violence in relation to honor/shame later in this book.

Action points

- *Fast-forward:* To explore how the *image of limited good* can shape a contextualized presentation of the gospel of Christ, turn to Section 3, Chapter 3.

- *Reflect:* In what ways has God's "riches in glory in Christ Jesus" (Phil 4:19) helped you overcome a sense of inadequacy or satisfied your longing for honor?

- *Bible study:* Read through the Gospel of Mark in one sitting, keeping in mind how the honor/shame variables worked together in a dark symmetry of religious and political powers to generate violence and crucify the Son of God.

---

7. See Wayne Grudem and Barry Asmus, *The Poverty of Nations: A Sustainable Solution* (Wheaton, IL: Crossway, 2013). The book offers a multitude of historical evidences and Scripture-based principles that support my contention that some honor/shame dynamics such as the *image of limited good* inhibit economic development, and thus perpetuate poverty. See especially pages 275–307; as I read these pages, I discovered that many of the principles of economic growth are antithetical to some of the values of honor/shame cultures.

8. David S. Landes, *The Wealth and Poverty of Nations: Why Some Are So Rich and Some So Poor* (New York: W. W. Norton, 1999), 516, as quoted in Grudem and Asmus, 317.

- *Teaching:* In the story of Jesus feeding the five thousand (Luke 9:10–17), explore how the image of limited good is overturned by the miracle of Jesus.
- *Mission:* In ministering to the poor and oppressed, to what degree does your ministry sometimes have the attitude of the "image of limited good"? This would be reflected in thinking, "They cannot help themselves, we must do it for them." How can you explore together with your ministry partners their *assets and blessings,* rather than their deficits and limitations, pursuing together the *unlimited good* and abundance of the reign of God?

Honor/Shame Dynamic #4: Challenge and Riposte

Why is this important?

- Reveals honor competition as an ever-present dynamic in the drama of Scripture.

- Gives a specific four-part structure to the honor competition characterizing the confrontations between Jesus and the Jewish religious leaders.

- Magnifies the extent of Christ's victories—along with his superior intelligence and humanity—in his honor competition with the religious leaders.

- Contributes to an explanation for the seemingly unending cycle of conflict and violence in some honor/shame societies, such as the Middle East.

- Gives insight to the radical nature of Jesus' upside-down honor code.

Definition

"Riposte" is a term used in the sport of fencing, meaning "a quick return thrust following a parry." Socially it means, "a quick clever reply to an insult or criticism." There are four steps to this protocol or social code of challenge and riposte—or "push-and-shove."

- Claim of worth or value
- Challenge to that claim or refusal to acknowledge the claim
- Riposte or defense of the claim
- Public verdict of success awarded to either claimant or challenger[1]

---

1. Neyrey, *Honor and Shame in the Gospel of Matthew*, 20.

When I first learned about this honor/shame dynamic, it placed a whole new light on the many encounters between Jesus and the Pharisees. Most if not all of the interactions recorded in the Gospels between Jesus and the Pharisees were conducted in public. These interactions, when seen through the cultural lens of honor and shame, follow the rules of the "honor game," also known as *challenge and riposte*.

Examples

In Matthew 12, you'll see ... Jesus' claim of worth or value ... the challenge by the Pharisees to Jesus' honor ... the riposte by Jesus in defense of his claim ... and the public verdict. You will also observe that the riposte by Jesus consisted of both direct and indirect communication, in addition to a miracle.

[8] "For the Son of Man is Lord of the Sabbath."

[9] He went on from there and entered their synagogue.

[10] And a man was there with a withered hand. And they asked him, "Is it lawful to heal on the Sabbath?"—so that they might accuse him.

[11] He said to them, "Which one of you who has a sheep, if it falls into a pit on the Sabbath, will not take hold of it and lift it out?

[12] "Of how much more value is a man than a sheep! So it is lawful to do good on the Sabbath."

[13] Then he said to the man, "Stretch out your hand." And the man stretched it out, and it was restored, healthy like the other.

[14] But the Pharisees went out and conspired against him, how to destroy him.

[15] Jesus, aware of this, withdrew from there. And many followed him, and he healed them all

[16] and ordered them not to make him known ... .

[23] And all the people were amazed, and said, "Can this be the Son of David?" (Mat 12:8–16, 23).

1. Claim of worth or value: Matthew 12:8 is a claim by Jesus concerning his worth and value. Verses 1–7 of this chapter describe the confrontation between Jesus and the Pharisees concerning the disciples plucking and eating grain on the Sabbath. Verse 8 is the verdict—"For the Son of Man is Lord of the Sabbath."

2. Challenge to that claim or refusal to acknowledge the claim: Verse 10 displays the challenge by the Pharisees to Jesus' claim. "And they asked him, 'Is it lawful to heal on the Sabbath?'—so that they might accuse him."

3. Riposte or defense of the claim: Jesus' riposte, or defense, is in three powerful parts.

First, Jesus uses indirect communication. "He said to them, 'Which one of you who has a sheep, if it falls into a pit on the Sabbath, will not take hold of it and lift it out? Of how much more value is a man than a sheep!" (vv. 11–12).[2] Jesus describes a sheep in desperate need being rescued by its shepherd—a word-picture that goes beyond reason to connect heart-to-heart. Jesus answers their challenge indirectly.

Second, Jesus adds a declarative direct response. Jesus says straightforwardly, "So it is lawful to do good on the Sabbath" (v. 12). The statement is dripping with irony. As I imagine the crowd watching, I can almost hear them laughing with Jesus at the Pharisees.

Third, Jesus adds to his words an action—he performs a miracle: "Then he said to the man, 'Stretch out your hand.' And the man stretched it out, and it was restored, healthy like the other" (v. 13).

This three-part riposte to the Pharisees' challenge was so powerful that "the Pharisees went out and conspired against him, how to destroy him" (v. 14). Why were they so enraged? Because their honor and standing in the public sphere took a huge hit, while at the same time, the honor and renown of Jesus was skyrocketing. This led to:

4. Public verdict of success awarded to either claimant or challenger. "And many followed him, and he healed them all and ordered them not to make him known. ... And all the people were amazed, and said, 'Can this be the Son of David?' (vv. 15, 23). The public verdict of increased honor for Jesus is represented by the words, "And many followed him" and "all the people were amazed."[3]

On the facing page is another example of *challenge and riposte;* it is contained in Luke 13:10–17.

As you read through the gospels, you can see these steps unfold time and again. Keep in mind that step four—*public verdict of success awarded to either claimant or challenger*—is not always explicitly stated. Since Jesus won every honor competition between himself and the religious leaders, it was not always necessary for the gospel writers to state the obvious.

Jerome Neyrey puts it this way:

This peer game of push-and-shove can be played in any of the typical forums of social life: marketplace, gymnasium, synagogue, banquet with one's male companions, and the like. From our reading of the Gospels, it seems to have occurred whenever Jesus stepped into the public space. The very pervasiveness of this challenge-riposte game indicates that Jesus was both claiming prestige and worth (as God's agent) and achieving a splendid reputation as prophet, teacher, and healer. The fact that he was so regularly challenged ... indicates that he was a very honorable person who was worthy of allegiance and loyalty. It is to his credit that he was both envied (Matt. 27:18) and challenged.[4]

---

2. Jesus is pointing out the hypocrisy of the Pharisees, causing them a loss of honor or "face."

3. In honor/shame cultures the social "game" of challenge-riposte can readily escalate to violence, and we shall see that Jesus teaches us to abandon this game of oneupmanship. Jesus engaged in *challenge and riposte* not so much as an example to believers, but because *he had to.* Because of Jesus' holiness as the Son of God and his very life purpose, it was by necessity that he challenged the status quo. Jesus engaged with his culture in such a way as to identify himself as the Messiah to provoke his own death in fulfillment of all that was written.

4. Neyrey, *Honor and Shame in the Gospel of Matthew,* 20.

Challenge & riposte: Four steps	Jesus heals a woman with a disabling spirit	Comment
1. Claim of worth or value	Now he was teaching in one of the synagogues on the Sabbath. And behold, there was a woman who had had a disabling spirit for eighteen years. She was bent over and could not fully straighten herself. When Jesus saw her, he called her over and said to her, "Woman, you are freed from your disability." And he laid his hands on her, and immediately she was made straight, and she glorified God. (Luke 13:10–12).	Note the public nature of the situation—in the synagogue with everyone watching. Jesus' claim of worth is that he is able to heal the woman and set her free—and to do so in violation of the Jewish Sabbath codes.
2. Challenge to that claim or refusal to acknowledge the claim	But the ruler of the synagogue, indignant because Jesus had healed on the Sabbath, said to the people, "There are six days in which work ought to be done. Come on those days and be healed, and not on the Sabbath day" (Luke 13:13–14).	Jesus undermined the honor of the synagogue ruler by challenging the Sabbath codes. In response, the "indignant" synagogue ruler challenged Jesus' right to heal on the Sabbath.
3. Riposte or defense of the claim	Then the Lord answered him, "You hypocrites! Does not each of you on the Sabbath untie his ox or his donkey from the manger and lead it away to water it? And ought not this woman, a daughter of Abraham whom Satan bound for eighteen years, be loosed from this bond on the Sabbath day?" (Luke 13:15–16).	Jesus reveals that compassion and mercy is at the heart of God's law. The phrase, *"Does not each of you,"* suggests that Jesus is not just speaking to the leader of the synagogue but also to the whole crowd.
4. Public verdict of success awarded to either claimant or challenger	As he said these things, all his adversaries were put to shame, and all the people rejoiced at all the glorious things that were done by him (Luke 13:17).	The crowd is delighted; the public verdict is that Jesus wins the honor competition. Moreover, "his adversaries were put to shame"—which ultimately fueled violence against Jesus.

Figure 2.10: Challenge and riposte in Luke 13:10–17

The cosmic challenge and riposte

The above examples of *challenge and riposte* are representative of all the interactions between Jesus and the Jewish religious leaders. Time after time, Jesus won each honor competition with these men. In doing so, two things resulted. First, he exposed their evil origins and motivations (John 8:44–47); second, by exposing them, he incurred their violence against him—a conspiracy that led to his death.

Notice the paradox: Jesus won every public "game" of *challenge and riposte* in conversation with the Pharisees. But winning these honor competitions created so much jealousy among the Pharisees that it led to his shameful death by crucifixion, an apparent final humiliation of Jesus. Christ's purposeful submission to all that the Father willed through the cross required that "when he was reviled, he did not revile in return" (1 Pet 2:23).

To human observers at the time of the crucifixion, the cross seemed to be the destruction of Christ, when in fact, the murder of God's Son was ordained by God (Acts 2:23)—and only led to a cosmic *riposte,* a conquest of much larger proportions. The death and resurrection of Christ comprised a victory over the ultimate enemy—*sin-and-death-and-the-kingdom-of-darkness*—the great adversary of the kingdom of God and all humanity.

Christians follow the example of Jesus

In the cross we see Christ's reaction to the violence against him: Submit to the will of God (Luke 22:42) in order to gain a much greater victory. He absorbed the shaming attacks of his human enemies rather than taking revenge. Retaliation was not in God's plan for Jesus. Likewise, the practice of retaliation is outside of God's will for Christians.

In the Sermon on the Mount, Jesus taught his disciples to abandon the culturally accepted practice of retaliation and defending one's honor through violence—or through playing the "game" of *challenge and riposte.*

> You have heard that it was said, "An eye for an eye and a tooth for a tooth." But I say to you, Do not resist the one who is evil. But if anyone slaps you on the right cheek, turn to him the other also. And if anyone would sue you and take your tunic, let him have your cloak as well. And if anyone forces you to go one mile, go with him two miles. Give to the one who begs from you, and do not refuse the one who would borrow from you. You have heard that it was said, "You shall love your neighbor and hate your enemy." But I say to you, Love your enemies and pray for those who persecute you (Mat 5:38–44).

Jerome Neyrey interprets this to mean that followers of Jesus are to simply "vacate the playing field"[5] of the honor/shame game of *challenge and riposte.*

During the episode of Christ's arrest, interrogation, flogging and crucifixion, Jesus did not respond with a *riposte*—despite the fact that he was insulted, shamed, and reviled. In the Garden of Gethsemane, Peter attempted to physically defend Jesus, cutting off the ear of Malchus, servant of the high priest (John 18:10). Jesus swiftly squashed this response: "Put your sword back into its place. For all who take the sword will perish by the sword. Do you think that I cannot appeal to my Father, and he will at once send me more than twelve legions of angels?" (Mat 26:52–53).

Jesus did not have to defend himself. He knew that, ultimately, his honor was eternally secure and would be vindicated when he rose from the dead (Mark 10:34, cf. Phil 2:9–11).

Peter got the message

The same Peter who had tried to defend Jesus learned his lesson. Many years later he wrote to Gentile believers that Jesus is an example for all Christians:

> When he was reviled, he did not revile in return; when he suffered, he did not threaten, but continued entrusting himself to him who judges justly (1 Pet 2:23).

> Finally, all of you, have unity of mind, sympathy, brotherly love, a tender heart, and a humble mind. Do not repay evil for evil or reviling for reviling,

---

5. This is the phrase Neyrey uses. He contends that Jesus is calling his followers, particularly males, to "vacate the playing field," so that rather than gaining honor in the traditional way through public game-playing, they are gaining honor by living in the kingdom of God in joyful obedience to their King. See Neyrey, *Honor and Shame in the Gospel of Matthew*, 214.

but on the contrary, bless, for to this you were called, that you may obtain a blessing (1 Pet 3:8–9).

When Christians are challenged by unbelievers concerning their life in Christ, the only acceptable *riposte* for a Christian is one that is infused by the gentle wisdom of Jesus:

But in your hearts honor Christ the Lord as holy, always being prepared to make a defense to anyone who asks you for a reason for the hope that is in you; yet do it with gentleness and respect (1 Pet 3:15).

David deSilva describes the passage in 1 Peter this way: "The Christian is challenged to answer the hostile challenge with generosity, the violent challenge with the courageous refusal to use violence, the challenge in the form of a curse with a blessing from God's inexhaustible resources of goodness and kindness."[6]

Is there any kind of rivalry that is acceptable for those who claim to be followers of Christ? *Yes.* It is a rivalry of affectionate honor: "Love one another with brotherly affection. Outdo one another in showing honor" (Rom 12:10).[7]

Before moving on to the next principle of honor/shame societies, let's briefly go back to the dark side of honor and shame. You will see how the dynamics of certain honor/shame features work together in a dangerous synergy which leads to a greater likelihood of violence.

Honor, shame, conflict

These three features of honor/shame societies— *love of honor,* the *image of limited good,* and *challenge and riposte*— may be considered variables in the equation of violence.

Broadly speaking, when these dynamics are present in individuals, families and peoples, the result is a greater propensity for violence.

As stated in Section 1, Chapter 5, there are two

Honor/shame arithmetic

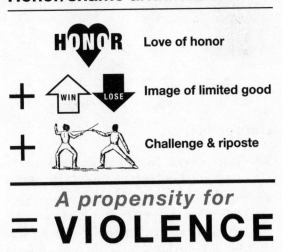

Figure 2.11: Honor/shame arithmetic which adds up to violence

---

6. See David deSilva's chapter, "Turning Shame into Honor: The Pastoral Strategy of 1 Peter" in *The Shame Factor: How Shame Shapes Society,* eds. Jewett, Alloway, and Lacey, 175.

7. The *no-retaliation-ethic* taught by Jesus is also re-articulated by Paul in Romans 12:14–21. Moreover, Paul instructed the church at Philippi, "Do nothing from selfish ambition or conceit, but in humility count others more significant than yourselves" (Phil 2:3). ESV 2002 uses "rivalry" in place of "selfish ambition." Rivalry is another word for honor competition, the "social game" of *challenge and riposte.*

attack modes in the "Compass of Shame" by which violence manifests itself in honor/shame societies:

- **"Attack self"**—violence directed internally—against oneself (depression, self-afflicted wounds, suicide). This is more common in societies where *social harmony* trumps violence against others.

- **"Attack other"**—violence directed externally—against others (honor-based violence such as honor killings, kidnapping, etc.). This is more common in societies where violence (such as honor killings) is an acceptable form of protest.

A kingdom summary—dark side and bright side

Challenge and riposte—kingdom of this world vs. kingdom-reign of God		
	Kingdom of this world	Kingdom-reign of God
	• Many forms of honor competition lead to conflict, revenge, violence, destruction, death • Cyclical win-lose competition magnifies the problem—between individuals, families, peoples, nations; making it seemingly endless • Some rivalry may be socially acceptable (athletic, educational, business), but still not glorify God	• As the only true king, Jesus rightfully reigns; he won every honor competition in the human arena (with religious and political leaders)—and cosmic arena (with the kingdom of darkness) • The cross, death, resurrection and ascension of Christ form a cosmic riposte against all evil • All rivalry between Christians is forbidden except outdoing one another in serving, showing honor • When Christians locate their honor in King Jesus, they have no honor deficit; this frees them from the need for honor competition and its destructive force

Figure 2.12: Challenge and riposte—kingdom of this world vs. kingdom-reign of God

Action points

- *Fast-forward:* To explore ways that *challenge and riposte* can shape a contextualized presentation of the gospel of Christ, turn to Section 3, Chapter 4.

- *Reflect:* When was the last time you were offended and tempted to defend yourself and engage in rivalry—but because of your deeply felt awareness of your own honor in Christ, you withheld from striking back by words or actions?

- *Bible study:* Read through one of the Gospels in your daily devotional time and make note of every conversation that occurs in public between Jesus and the Jewish leaders. Observe the degree to which the dynamics of challenge and riposte are present in each occurrence.

- *Teaching:* When teaching on the Gospels, don't miss the humor of Jesus when he responds to the challenges of the Jewish religious leaders. Emphasize the intelligence, irony and humor that Jesus uses in his various ripostes. For example, Luke 15:7 is loaded with irony, even humor.

- *Mission:* Rivalry can flourish among mission colleagues, mission teams, and on mission trips. To what extent is this part of your team? It is crucial for leaders to exhibit servanthood and humility. The only kind of honor competition befitting Christians is when they try to out-serve one another (Mark 10:43–44), or "Outdo one another in showing honor" (Rom 12:10).

Honor/Shame Dynamic #5: Concept of Face

Why is this important?

- Explains the concept of "face"—largely unknown in Western societies—as it is expressed in the honor/shame societies of the Bible.

- "God's turning away" from a person or a people means they are in shame. But when people turn to the Lord their shame is removed and honor restored.

- The "concept of face" is especially strong in the cultures of East and Southeast Asia (China, Korea, Japan, Indonesia, Thailand, etc.); what Scripture says about "face" should be incorporated into the process of contextualizing the gospel for them.

Definition

The concept of "face" in East Asian culture is aptly defined by Chris Flanders:

> By face, I do not mean the physical body part, but the use of the term as a metaphor representing a type of interpersonal social honor and identity projection—"the claimed sense of self-respect or self-dignity in an interactive situation."[1]

The concept of "face" in Scripture has two parts. First, humanity's shame before God is the result of sin and is expressed by *turning away* and *hiding from* the face of God. Second, humanity's redemption and healing from shame comes when people *turn to,* and are given peace *before,* the face of God.[2]

---

1. Christopher Flanders, *About Face*, 1. Flanders quotes Stella Ting-Toomey, "Face and Facework: An Introduction" in *The Challenge of Facework: Cross-Cultural and Interpersonal Issues,* Stella Ting-Toomey, ed. (Albany, NY: State University of New York Press, 1994), 1–14.
2. This definition is adapted from Stockitt, Kindle edition locations 2679–81.

Examples

The first example is from Genesis 3 regarding the Fall from innocence of Adam and Eve.

> And they heard the sound of the LORD God walking in the garden in the cool of the day, and the man and his wife hid themselves from the presence of the LORD God among the trees of the garden (Gen 3:8).

Robin Stockitt makes sense of the Genesis account:

> The notion of facing away in Gen 3:8 is captured poignantly in the original Hebrew, but lost altogether in the English translation, which renders the verse, "they hid from the LORD God among the trees of the garden." The Hebrew text depicts the couple as withdrawing away from the face (*pānîm*) of God. In the acuteness of their shame, their instinct was to turn immediately away from God's face. Here we observe the beginnings of a pattern of paired experiences; innocence, sinlessness, joy, and delight dwell together with an unashamed enjoyment in the face of God. By contrast, shame, guilt, and sin appear to be the natural consequences of a withdrawal from God's face.[3]

Consider also the account of Cain and Abel. As you read, watch for references to "face."

> And Abel also brought of the firstborn of his flock and of their fat portions. And the LORD had regard for Abel and his offering, but for Cain and his offering he had no regard. So Cain was very angry, *and his face fell.* The LORD said to Cain, "Why are you angry, and why has your *face fallen?* If you do well, will you not be accepted? And if you do not do well, sin is crouching at the door. Its desire is for you, but you must rule over it."
>
> Cain spoke to Abel his brother. And when they were in the field, Cain rose up against his brother Abel and killed him. Then the LORD said to Cain, "Where is Abel your brother?" He said, "I do not know; am I my brother's keeper?" And the LORD said, "What have you done? The voice of your brother's blood is crying to me from the ground. And now you are cursed from the ground, which has opened its mouth to receive your brother's blood from your hand. When you work the ground, it shall no longer yield to you its strength. You shall be a fugitive and a wanderer on the earth." Cain said to the LORD, "My punishment is greater than I can bear. Behold, you have driven me today away from the ground, and *from your face I shall be hidden.* I shall be a fugitive and a wanderer on the earth, and whoever finds me will kill me." Then the LORD said to him, "Not so! If anyone kills Cain, vengeance shall be taken on him sevenfold." And the LORD put a mark on Cain, lest any who found him should attack him. Then Cain went away from the presence of the LORD and settled in the land of Nod, east of Eden (Gen 4:4–16). (Emphasis mine.)

---

3. Stockitt, Kindle edition locations 370–81.

So it is clear that sin results in not just guilt, but also *shame*—as expressed in *turning away from the face of God*. A similar dynamic is found in Isaiah—God's face being hidden from his sinful people: "But your iniquities have made a separation between you and your God, and your sins have hidden his face from you so that he does not hear" (Isa 59:2).

Conversely, other passages of Scripture describe how the honor of God's people is expressed, in part, by *beholding the face of God*.

The LORD spoke to Moses, saying, "Speak to Aaron and his sons, saying, Thus you shall bless the people of Israel: you shall say to them, The LORD bless you and keep you the LORD make his face to shine upon you and be gracious to you; the LORD lift up his countenance upon you and give you peace. So shall they put my name upon the people of Israel, and I will bless them" (Num 6:22–27).

This is the "Aaronic Blessing." We see the clear link between God's people *beholding God's face* and *countenance*—and having God's "name" put "upon the people of Israel." The name of God represents the honor of God. *What a blessing*—God's honor was attached to his people!

Consider also these verses from the Psalms:

Those who look to him are radiant, and their faces shall never be ashamed (Ps 34:5).

May God be gracious to us and bless us and make his face to shine upon us (Ps 67:1).

What is revealed here is that the "face" of God's people—that is, their *honor*—is inextricably linked to the experience of beholding the face of God. It is assumed that intimacy with God is possible, intimacy as close as *face to face*. "Restore us, O God; let your face shine, that we may be saved!" (Ps 80:3). Evidently, for the Hebrew mind, even salvation is linked to "God's face."

In the New Testament, Paul makes the connection between the Old Testament *concept of face* and the life-transforming progressive honor gained by followers of Jesus Christ.

And we all, with unveiled face, beholding the glory of the Lord, are being transformed into the same image from one degree of glory to another. For this comes from the Lord who is the Spirit (2 Cor 3:18).

For God, who said, "Let light shine out of darkness," has shone in our hearts to give the light of the knowledge of the glory of God in the face of Jesus Christ (2 Cor 4:6).

With "unveiled face," Christians have the inestimable honor of beholding the glory of God "in the face of Jesus Christ." Within this brilliant relational intimacy, the glory and honor of God himself shines into human hearts to dispel every darkness and shame. Followers of Christ are "transformed into the same image from one degree of glory to another"—reflecting the very honor of God.

Concept of face in East Asia

Jackson Wu has written an important book called *Saving God's Face: A Chinese Contextualization of Salvation through Honor and Shame (EMS Dissertation Series)*.[4] Wu's book is his Ph.D. thesis. Wu explains the dynamics of "face" in Chinese society as part of an overall effort to merge a theological emphasis on the glory of God with the Bible's cultural dynamics of honor and shame.[5]

Below are some of Jackson Wu's observations concerning "face" in Chinese culture:

- "'Face' is a Chinese way of talking about HS [honor/shame]."[6]

- "Authors sometimes distinguish between two kinds of face, *mianzi* and *lian*. Hu describes *mianzi* as one's prestige or reputation due to 'high position, wealth, power, ability, through cleverly establishing ties to a number of prominent people.' ... *Mianzi* mainly concerns conformity to 'social conventions' rather than 'integrity of character.' On the other hand, *lian* 'is the respect of a group for a man with a good moral reputation.' Cheng adds that to lose *lian* '... means dishonor and disgrace, while to lose [*mianzi*] means merely that one's honor is not honored or honor is not recognized.'"[7]

- "*Mianzi* can simply mean one is well known or has impressed others, regardless of moral grounds (e.g. athletes, singers, CEOs). A poor person could have *lian* but little *mianzi*."[8]

- "There are many ways to lose face. Some are minor, like forgetting words to a song or tripping while walking. Any number of bad habits can make people lose face. Other reasons are more serious. One study shows having mental illness, disease, or getting tested for AIDS (not necessarily having it) can cause a loss of face leading to a loss of relationships, discrimination, even a denial of medical care."[9]

- "In summary, two aspects consistently appear in face/honor discourse. First, face/honor is social or public. Second, face/honor expresses worth or status."[10]

- "There are people in the world, like the Chinese, who define themselves not so much by what they do as who they know. In Chinese culture, *guanxi* [relationship] is the leading functional savior. Giving and receiving face is the way to enter, sustain, and strengthen relationships."[11]

---

4. Wu, *Saving God's Face*.

5. I am giving attention to the concept of face in the East Asian context and including some of Wu's observations here (about the concept of face) because cross-cultural workers more commonly understand the concept of "face" in East Asian societies than they understand "face" as a dynamic in Scripture. Therefore, I felt that at least some material about "face" in East Asia would be prudent to include in this book.

6. Wu, *Saving God's Face*, 151.

7. Wu, 156–157. Wu quotes Hsien Hu Chin, "The Chinese Concepts of 'Face,'" *American Anthropologist* 46, no. 1 (March 1994): 45, 61, and Yongtao Chen, "The Concept of Face and Its Confucian Roots," in Journal of Chinese Philosophy 13 (1986), 335.

8. Ibid., 157.

9. Ibid., 158. Wu cites Lawrence Hsin Yang and Arthur Kleinman, "'Face' and the Embodiment of Stigma in China—The Cases of Schizophrenia and AIDS," *Social Science and Medicine* 30 (2008): 1–11.

10. Ibid., 162.

11. Ibid., 176.

The main idea behind this exploration of the *concept of face* is that, in addition to the fact that "face" is a very prominent social and cultural dynamic among more than 2.1 billion people of East and Southeast Asia,[12] there is likewise abundant material about "face" in the Bible. Why this overlap? The contemporary societies of East Asia and the ancient societies of the Bible have this in common—*the pivotal cultural value of honor and shame.*

"Face" in the final chapter

In the final chapter of the Bible, Revelation 22, there is a beatific vision of the heavenly city, and a marvelous reference to seeing the "face" of God:

> No longer will there be anything accursed, but the throne of God and of the Lamb will be in it, and his servants will worship him. *They will see his face, and his name will be on their foreheads.* And night will be no more. They will need no light of lamp or sun, for the Lord God will be their light, *and they will reign forever and ever* (Rev 22:3–5). (Emphasis mine.)

Observe and be stunned: *"They will see his face, and his name will be on their foreheads. … and they will reign forever and ever"* (Rev 22:4–5). The royal honor of God will be shared with the redeemed peoples in eternity future. It is nearly beyond our imagination to conceive.

- **Intimate honor:** The compulsion to turn away from God's face because of sin and shame will have passed. *What honor belongs to God's people, what intimacy, in beholding the very face of the Lord!*

- **Exchanged honor:** Moreover, "his name will be on their foreheads"—God's name, that is, his *honor,* will forever be imprinted on the conscious identity of all the redeemed peoples.

- **Regal honor:** "And they will reign forever and ever." Who will reign? *They will.* And who are "they"? … The ones who are "his servants." The ones who "will see his face" … the ones who *"will need no light of lamp or sun, for the Lord God will be their light."*

Yes, the ones who reign are the people of God. The redeemed are co-regents with their Savior, King of the universe!

---

12. There are nearly 1.6 billion people in East Asia. "East Asia," *Wikipedia*, http://en.wikipedia.org/wiki/East_Asia, and over 600 million people in Southeast Asia, "Southeast Asia," *Wikipedia*, http://en.wikipedia.org/wiki/Southeast_Asia, accessed 20 June 2013.

A kingdom summary—dark side and bright side

Concept of face—kingdom of this world vs. kingdom-reign of God		
	Kingdom of this world	**Kingdom-reign of God**
	• To cover one's face is a universal reaction to shame • "Saving face" is often a means for preserving group harmony but can generate dishonesty in order to avoid embarrassment • Shaming techniques that cause another person to "lose face" can cause deep hurt that persists for decades, even generations, plus unwarranted discrimination and isolation • The "loss of face" can be so painful that it leads to suicide—or deadly violence against others	• To turn to the Lord in salvation is to have one's shame covered and honor restored; this is God's "face" shining upon us • Christians have intimacy with God—the honor of beholding with "unveiled face" the glory of God in the face of Jesus Christ • The Aaronic Blessing suggests that people can be the very agents of God's blessing, the mediators of God's "face" to other people and families • In the eternal city of the kingdom of Christ, the redeemed people of God will see his face and reign with him in honor forever and ever

Figure 2.13: Concept of face—kingdom of this world vs. kingdom-reign of God

Action points

- *Fast-forward:* To explore how the *concept of face* can shape a contextualized presentation of the gospel of Christ, turn to Section 3, Chapter 5.

- *Reflect:* How does a believer "behold the glory of the Lord ... in the face of Jesus Christ"? What is the mindset, the attitude, the behavior?

- *Bible study:* Explore the dynamic of "face" and "unveiled face" in 2 Corinthians 3.

- *Teaching:* Develop a lesson about how people are transformed by beholding the glory of the Lord (2 Cor 3:18)—based on God's Word and your own experience.

- *Mission:* Consider praying the Aaronic Blessing (Num 6:22–27) for families and people who may not be believers. You may be surprised at how open those being prayed for would be to this blessing.

Honor/Shame Dynamic #6: Body Language

Why is this important?

- Explains the "body language" of honor/shame societies in the Bible.
- Contributes to an understanding of why *right hand* and *feet* are woven into the drama God's story.
- Gives insight to and amplifies the dramatic nature of the conquest of Jesus Christ over sin and shame, death and hell.

Definition

In the social world of the Old and New Testaments, the most honorable parts of the body were considered to be the head, face and hands. One of the most shameful body parts was considered to be the feet.[1]

Examples

The foremost example in Scripture of the honor/shame dynamic of *body language* is contained in Psalm 110, a psalm of David. The verse is one of the most-quoted Old Testament verses in the New Testament.

> The LORD says to my Lord: "Sit at my right hand, until I make your enemies your footstool" (Ps 110:1).[2]

---

1. Timothy Tennent writes, "In the ancient world honor was tied to the physical body, which was understood as a microcosm of the larger social context. The head and face were the most honorable parts of the body, and the person was thereby honored by being crowned. In contrast, to slap someone in the face or spit on someone's face brought shame. The less honorable parts of the body, such as genitals and buttocks, must be covered if one's honor is to be preserved." See Tennent, 86. Tennent references the work of Julian Pitt-Rivers: "Honor and Shame," in *Honor and Shame, The Values of Mediterranean Society,* ed. J. G. Peristiany. (London: Weidenfeld & Nocholson, 1966), 21–77.

2. Concerning Psalm 110, The *ESV Study Bible* states, "This psalm is one of the most cited OT texts in the NT, with quotations or allusions appearing in the Gospels, Acts, the Pauline epistles, Hebrews, and the Petrine epistles. Christians sing this psalm to celebrate that Jesus has taken his Davidic kingship by his resurrection …, and that God is busy now subduing the Gentiles into the empire of Jesus." *Crossway Bibles (2009-04-09). ESV Study Bible (Kindle Locations 75504–75507). Good News Publishers/Crossway Books. Kindle Edition.*

There are two references to the human body: one, the *right hand,* and two, the *foot.* A comparable and related verse is from another psalm of David:

> You have given him dominion over the works of your hands; you have put all things under his feet (Ps 8:6).

Consider the many verses that refer to Christ sitting at the right hand of the Father, having put all enemies under his feet (emphasis mine in all the quoted verses).

The Gospels

> He said to them, "How is it then that David, in the Spirit, calls him Lord, saying, 'The Lord said to my Lord, "Sit at my *right hand,* until I put your enemies under your *feet*"'"? (Mat 22:43–44).

> Jesus said to him, "You have said so. But I tell you, from now on you will see the Son of Man seated at the *right hand* of Power and coming on the clouds of heaven" (Mat 26:64).

> David himself, in the Holy Spirit, declared, "The Lord said to my Lord, 'Sit at my *right hand,* until I put your enemies under your *feet*'" (Mark 12:36).

> So then the Lord Jesus, after he had spoken to them, was taken up into heaven and sat down at the *right hand* of God (Mark 16:19).

> But he said to them, "How can they say that the Christ is David's son? For David himself says in the Book of Psalms, 'The Lord said to my Lord, "Sit at my *right hand,* until I make your enemies your *footstool.*"' David thus calls him Lord, so how is he his son?" (Luke 20:41–44).

> But from now on the Son of Man shall be seated at the *right hand* of the power of God (Luke 22:69).

Acts

> Being therefore exalted at the *right hand* of God, and having received from the Father the promise of the Holy Spirit, he has poured out this that you yourselves are seeing and hearing. For David did not ascend into the heavens, but he himself says, "The Lord said to my Lord, 'Sit at my *right hand,* until I make your enemies your *footstool*'" (Acts 2:33–35).

> But he, full of the Holy Spirit, gazed into heaven and saw the glory of God, and Jesus standing at the *right hand* of God. And he said, "Behold, I see the heavens opened, and the Son of Man standing at the *right hand* of God" (Acts 7:55–56).

Paul's letters

> Then comes the end, when he delivers the kingdom to God the Father after destroying every rule and every authority and power. For he must

reign until he has put all his enemies under his *feet*. The last enemy to be destroyed is death. For "God has put all things in subjection under his *feet*" (1 Cor 15:24–27).

Who is to condemn? Christ Jesus is the one who died—more than that, who was raised—who is at the *right hand* of God, who indeed is interceding for us (Rom 8:34).

... that he worked in Christ when he raised him from the dead and seated him at his *right hand* in the heavenly places (Eph 1:20).

If then you have been raised with Christ, seek the things that are above, where Christ is, seated at the *right hand* of God (Col 3:1).

Hebrews

He is the radiance of the glory of God and the exact imprint of his nature, and he upholds the universe by the word of his power. After making purification for sins, he sat down at the *right hand* of the Majesty on high (Heb 1:3).

And to which of the angels has he ever said, "Sit at my *right hand* until I make your enemies a *footstool* for your *feet*"? (Heb 1:13).

Now the point in what we are saying is this: we have such a high priest, one who is seated at the *right hand* of the throne of the Majesty in heaven (Heb 8:1).

But when Christ had offered for all time a single sacrifice for sins, he sat down at the *right hand* of God (Heb 10:12).

Looking to Jesus, the founder and perfecter of our faith, who for the joy that was set before him endured the cross, despising the shame, and is seated at the *right hand* of the throne of God (Heb 12:2).

1 Peter

... who has gone into heaven and is at the *right hand* of God, with angels, authorities, and powers having been subjected to him (1 Pet 3:22).

What can we conclude from this panorama of verses? Over and over again, New Testament authors emphasize the honor of Jesus Christ by referring to his being seated in exalted honor at the right hand of the Father, with his "enemies a footstool" for his feet. New Testament believers understood the elevated honor of a sovereign ruler who had resoundingly conquered his enemies.

Naturally, this would prompt elevated honor, respect, and obedience to that sovereign king. It was this attitude and lifestyle of honor that Christians were to maintain in their relationship to the one Sovereign, our Lord Jesus Christ.

A kingdom summary—dark side and bright side

Body language—kingdom of this world vs. kingdom-reign of God		
	Kingdom of this world	Kingdom-reign of God
	• Shaming techniques involving the body are painful and powerful, creating oppression and hurt that can last decades and be transferred to the next generation. • Some shaming techniques involving the body consist of violence resulting in death (honor killings).	• Jesus is the one and only King who reigns forever and ever, seated at the right hand of God with his enemies under his feet. • Jesus Christ conquered all enemies of humanity, all enemies of God—sin and shame, death and hell.

Figure 2.14: Body language—kingdom of this world vs. kingdom-reign of God

Action points

- *Fast-forward:* To explore how the dynamic of *body language* can shape a contextualized presentation of the gospel of Christ, turn to Section 3, Chapter 6.

- *Reflect:* Do you ever use your body to shame others, causing hurt or oppression? How do you imagine Jesus setting you free from this sin?

- *Bible study:* Read Psalm 44 and identify each example of "body language." How does this help you connect with the psalmist's emotions?

- *Teaching:* Luke 6:6–11 has the story of Jesus healing the man "whose right hand was withered." Develop a lesson about the bold compassion of Jesus Christ in healing people whose honor is withered.

- *Mission:* Ask your cross-cultural ministry partners or friends from other cultures what *body language* they have in their societies. You might ask specifically about the meaning of *right hand* or *feet*. You may be surprised to discover how commonly significant this is.

Note: Beginning with this chapter, the length of the chapters through the end of this section (chapters 7–10) are considerably longer than the previous (chapters 1–6). This is due to the abundance of the material in the Bible under consideration, and the need for thorough explanation.

Honor/Shame Dynamic #7: Patronage

Why is this important?

- Helps explain the unequal status of persons in Bible societies as described in the *patron-client* relationship.

- Demonstrates that first-century Christians would have understood the gift of their salvation in light of the widespread social practice of patronage.

- Links the practice of patronage with the Abrahamic covenant by showing how being a *patron who blesses others* is likened to God's promise to Abraham that he and his descendants would be *co-benefactors with God in blessing all the families of the earth.*

Definition

"Patronage was the distinctive relationship in ancient Roman society between the …'patron' and his 'client.' The relationship was hierarchical, but obligations were mutual. The [patron] was the protector, sponsor, and benefactor of the client…. Although typically the client was of inferior social class, a patron and client might

even hold the same social rank, but the former would possess greater wealth, power, or prestige that enabled him to help or do favors for the client."[1]

J. E. Lendon's *Empire of Honour* is a scholarly book about the vital significance of honor and shame in the social and political life of the Roman Empire. Lendon writes about patronage as an intrinsic, essential practice.

> The emperor was the patron, the benefactor, of his every subject. The subjects, in turn, paid him back for his benefactions with their loyalty; this was the basis of his power. Thus, the empire was a single enormous spider's web of reciprocal favours.[2]

To understand the significance of patronage, it is essential to grasp the enormous social inequality that existed in Palestine during the time of Christ. Society consisted of a very small number of people at the top—while the vast majority of people lived with much lower status and power, and had a constant struggle to survive.[3] Observe the diagram below[4] and the chart on the next page.

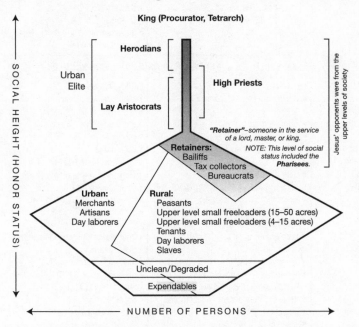

Figure 2.15: Social structure iwn first-century Palestine (adapted from Rohrbaugh)

1. This paragraph is taken from "Patronage in Ancient Rome," *Wikipedia*, http://en.wikipedia.org/wiki/Patronage_in_ancient_Rome, accessed 28 May 2013, citing Kenneth Quinn, "Poet and Audience in the Augustan Age," Aufstieg und Niedergang der römischen Welt II.30.1 (1982), 117.

2. Lendon, Kindle edition locations 170–73.

3. It is notable that Jesus' opposition came from high-status leaders occupying religious and political positions of power. Richard Rohrbaugh writes: "Given the prominent role of social conflict in Mark's narrative, we are not surprised to find that all of Jesus' opponents come from this group or its retainers. ... Recognition that Jesus' opponents come from a single social strata and act in genuine solidarity with each other is sufficient to demonstrate that the conflict is social as well as theological." Richard Rohrbaugh, "The Social Location of the Markan Audience," in *The Social World of the New Testament: Insights and Models* (Peabody, MA: Hendrickson, 2008), 147.

4. Adapted from Rohrbaugh, "The Social Location of the Markan Audience," 146. Rohrbaugh cites Dennis Duling, *The New Testament: An Introduction* (New York: Harcourt, Brace, Jovanovich, 1994).

URBAN ELITE		RETAINERS
• Caesar (12:14, 17) • Pontius Pilate (15:2, 8, 15) • Rulers of the Gentiles (10:42) • Herod (6:14; 8:15) • Herodias's daughter (6:22) • Philip (6:17) • Governors (13:9; 15:16) • High Priest (2:26; 14:47, 53, 54, 60, 61, 63, 66) • Chief priests (8:31; 10:33; 11:18, 27; 14:1, 10, 43, 53, 55; 15:1, 3, 10, 11, 31) • Scribes (1:22; 2:6, 16; 3:22; 7:1, 5; 8:31; 9:11, 14; 10:33; 11:18, 27; 12:28, 35, 38; 14:1, 43, 53; 15:1, 31)	• Strong man (3:27) • Those who have (4:25) • Elders (8:31; 11:27; 14:43, 53; 15:1) • Rich man (10:22) • Wealthy (10:23, 25) • Vineyard owner and son (12:1, 6) • Sadducees (12:18) • Family of seven brothers (12:20) • Rich people (12:41) • Kings (13:9) • Man going on a journey (13:34) • Owner of upper room (14:14) • Joseph of Arimathea (15:43) • Jairus and his family (5:22, 23, 40)	• Pharisees (2:16, 18, 24; 3:6; 7:1, 3, 5; 8:11, 15; 10:2; 12:13) • People from Jairus's house (5:35) • Men arresting John the Baptist (6:17) • Soldier of the guard (6:27) • Levi (2:14) • Those selling in the temple (11:15) • Servant girl of high priest (14:66) • Crowd sent from chief priests, scribes, and elders (14:43) • Physicians (2:17; 5:26) • Galilean priest (1:44) • Courtiers, officers (6:21) • Judas Iscariot (14:11) • Tax collectors (2:15, 16) • Moneychangers (11:15) • Doorkeeper (13:34) • Soldiers (15:16) • Centurion (15:39) • Slave/servant (1:20; 9:35; 10:43, 44; 12:2, 4; 13:34; 14:47)

URBAN NON-ELITE / PEASANTS / UNCLEAN / EXPENDABLES		
URBAN NON-ELITE	**PEASANTS**	**EXPENDABLES**
• Those buying in the temple (likely includes peasants) (11:15) • Widow (12:42) • Crowd/People (1:5; 11:18, 32; 12:12, 37, 41; 14:2, 43; 15:8, 11, 15)	• Those from the Judean countryside (1:5) • Peter, Andrew (1:16) • James, John, (1:19–20) • Simon's mother-in-law (1:30) • Jesus (6:3) • Mary (6:3) • James, Joses, Judas, Simon, and Jesus' sisters (6:3) • Seed scatterer (4:26) • Mary Magdalene, Mary the mother of James, Joses, Salome (15:40) • Little ones (9:42) • Children (10:13) • Bystanders in Bethpage (11:5) • Those buying in the temple (likely included urban poor as well) (11:15) • Tenants (12:1) • Simon of Cyrene (15:21) • Crowd (2:4, 13; 3:9, 20, 32; 4:1, 36; 5:21, 24, 27, 30, 31; 6:14, 17, 34, 39, 45; 7:14, 17, 33; 8:1, 2, 6, 34; 9:14, 15, 17, 25; 10:1, 46)	• Man with an unclean spirit (1:23) • The sick and demon possessed (1:32–34, 39; 6:9, 13, 55; 9:38) • Leper (1:40) • Paralytic (2:3) • Man with withered hand (3:1) • Those who have nothing (4:25) • Demoniac (5:2) • Hemorrhaging woman (5:25) • Syro-Phoenician woman and daughter (7:25–26) • Deaf man with speech impediment (7:32) • Blind man (8:22) • Boy with an unclean spirit (9:14) • Blind Bartimaeus (10:46) • Simon the Leper (14:3) • Swineherds (5:14) • Man carrying a jar (14:13)

Figure 2.16: Urban elite, retainers, urban non-elite, peasants, and expendables in the Gospel of Mark[5]

5. Adapted from Rohrbaugh, "The Social Location of the Markan Audience," 147–52.

Writing about a likely audience for the Gospel of Mark, Richard Rohrbaugh comments on the specific and unequal layers of social status in Jesus' time.[6]

Figure 2.15 shows a dramatic inequality in Palestine at the time of Christ. Below are just a few observations from Rohrbaugh.

- "As in most agrarian societies, between 1 and 3 percent of the population owned the majority of the arable land in Galilee, southern Syria, and Transjordan at the time Mark wrote."[7]

- " ... rural people, artisans, slaves, and women were mostly non-literate. Not only could very few people read or write, but also many could not use numbers either."[8]

- " ... the urban elite made up about 2% of the total population."[9]

- "In ever-increasing numbers during the first century, landless peasants worked the lands of the wealthy, to whom they paid significant portions of the produce for the opportunity."[10]

- "Rents for tenants could go as high as two-thirds of a crop, though rabbinic sources more commonly mentioned figures ranging from one-fourth to one-half."[11]

- "Many such landless people drifted to the cities and towns, which were in frequent need of new labor, not because of expanding opportunity but rather because of extremely high death rates among the urban non-elite."[12]

- "About 60% of those who survived their first year of life were dead by age sixteen, and in few families would both parents still be living when the youngest child reached puberty."[13]

- "For most lower-class people who did make it to adulthood, health would have been atrocious. By age 30, the majority suffered from internal parasites, rotting teeth, and bad eyesight."[14]

- " ... violence was also a regular part of village experience ... fraud, robbery, forced imprisonment for labor, beatings, inheritance disputes, enforceable removal of rents are all reflected in the village life in Mark's Gospel."[15]

Can you begin to see the extreme vulnerability that people endured in first-century Palestine, and why, as a result, patronage would have been widely practiced?

Patronage was a [prevalent] social framework in the ancient Mediterranean basin. Patrons were people with power who could provide goods and services not available to their clients. In return, clients provided

---

6. Richard Rohrbaugh in "The Social Location of the Markan Audience," in Neyrey and Stewart, 143–59.
7. Ibid., 146.
8. Ibid., 144.
9. Ibid., 145.
10. Ibid., 153.
11. Ibid., 153.
12. Ibid., 153.
13. Ibid., 154.
14. Ibid., 154.
15. Ibid., 154.

loyalty and honor to the patrons. Social inequality characterized these patronal relationships, and exploitation was a common feature of such relationships.[16]

In the West, we usually look at patronage as a morally inferior practice. It is viewed as being unethical, or perhaps a necessary evil. For example, if someone gets a job, promotion, or advancement on the basis of something *other* than his or her achievement, qualifications, and merits, then we believe this to be wrong, especially if it is at our expense.

But in ancient Greece and Rome, patronage was neither socially wrong nor exceptional:

> The world ... of the New Testament ... was one in which personal patronage was an essential means of acquiring access to goods, protection, or opportunities for employment and advancement. Not only was it essential—it was expected and publicized! The giving and receiving of favors was, according to a first-century participant, the "practice that constitutes the chief bond of human society."[17]

A *patron* was considered the benefactor, the *blesser*—the one who conferred blessing and grace on the one in need. The *client* was the *blessee*—the one receiving the gift, the blessing, the grace.

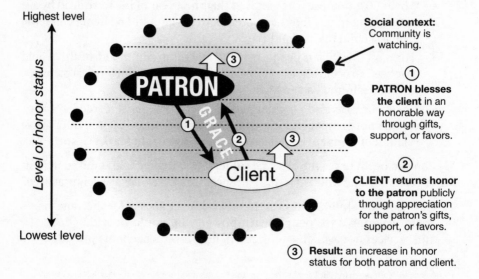

Figure 2.17: The patron blesses the client and the client returns praise to the patron; this can result in greater honor for both

16. Neyrey and Stewart, 47.

17. deSilva, citing (Seneca, Ben. 1.4.2), 96. His two chapters on patronage are titled "Patronage & Reciprocity" and "Patronage & Grace in the New Testament." DeSilva describes in detail how the practice of patronage in the Roman Empire informed the early church's understanding of the gift of God's grace in Christ.

The practice of patronage was widespread. According to deSilva, "Jesus and his first disciples moved among and within patronage and friendship networks, for patronage was as much at home on Palestinian soil as in Greece, Asia Minor, Egypt, Africa, and Rome."[18]

The patron-client relationship was characterized by three things: "1) It revolved around the reciprocal exchange of goods and services, 2) the relationship was personal and of some duration, and 3) it was not an equal relationship but rather was between parties of differing status."[19]

Patronage in the Bible

Patrons and benefactors are specifically mentioned in Scripture. Luke speaks of the centurion who built a synagogue for the Jews.

> Now a centurion had a servant who was sick and at the point of death. ...
> When the centurion heard about Jesus, he sent to him elders of the Jews,
> asking him to come and heal his servant. And when they came to Jesus, they
> pleaded with him ... "He is worthy to have you do this for him, for he loves
> our nation, and he is the one who built us our synagogue" (Luke 7:2–5).

Jesus speaks of the higher social status and authority of benefactors when teaching about servanthood in God's kingdom:

> And he said to them, "The kings of the Gentiles exercise lordship over them,
> and those in authority over them are called benefactors" (Luke 22:25).

Patronage is also found in Paul's letter to the Romans where he names a wealthy Christian woman named Phoebe as his patron:

> I commend to you our sister Phoebe, a servant of the church at Cenchreae,
> that you may welcome her in the Lord in a way worthy of the saints, and
> help her in whatever she may need from you, for she has been a patron
> of many and of myself as well (Rom 16:1–2).[20]

Finally, patronage is clearly implied in Luke 1:1 and Acts 1:1. Luke acknowledges Theophilus in the opening verse of each book. "To produce the Gospel and Acts, Luke needed the equivalent in today's currency of perhaps as much as four thousand US dollars for each text. It is no surprise he needed a benefactor."[21]

Patronage and grace

According to deSilva, first-century believers understood that "God's grace (*charis*) would not have been of a different kind than the grace with which they were

---

18. deSilva, 121.
19. Alicia Barrett, "God in the Letter of James: Patron or Benefactor?" in eds. Neyrey and Stewart, 50.
20. Richards estimates the cost of hiring a scribe to write Romans (identified as "Tertius" in Rom 16:22), as the equivalent of $2,275. See E. Randolph Richards, "Reading, Writing, and Manuscripts," in eds. Joel B. Green and Lee Martin McDonald, *The World of the New Testament: Cultural, Social, and Historical Contexts* (Grand Rapids, MI: Baker, 2013), 361. Jewett writes, "It would have required weeks of intensive work during which Tertius must have been made available on a full-time basis. This expense is most easily explained by the detail Paul reveals in 16:2, that Phoebe 'became a patroness to many and to myself as well.' This is the only time in Paul's letters that he acknowledges having received funding from a patron ... ." See Jewett, *Romans*, 22–23.
21. Richards, in Green and McDonald, 364.

already familiar; it would have been understood as different only in quality and degree."[22] So the social practice of patronage and benefaction would have related to the love and grace of God. "For God so loved the world, that he gave his only Son, that whoever believes in him should not perish but have eternal life" (John 3:16). Even the giving of God's Son would have been seen in the light of *patronage.* A highly honored, magnificent Benefactor is providing a great blessing—*the gift of his own Son* to many people.

There was a distinct honor code about how to give and receive. The *benefactor* was to be wise, not self-serving. Their gifts were to be given only to honorable people—and thus, examples of excellent stewardship. Reciprocally, the *client* was to show proper gratitude and honor to the benefactor or patron.

According to the ancient writer Seneca, the reciprocal relationship between patron and client was to be characterized by "three graces":

> Some would have it appear that there is one [grace] for bestowing a benefit, one for receiving it, and the third for returning it; others hold that there are three classes of benefactors—those who receive benefits, those who return them, and those who receive and return them at the same time.[23]

Seneca compared these three "graces" of *giving, receiving,* and *returning favor* to three sisters who dance "hand in hand ... in a ring which returns upon itself." Speaking of the word *grace* or *charis,* deSilva says it "encapsulated the entire ethos of the relationship."[24]

Blessing, honor, patronage

Our office conducted an analysis of the word *bless* and its derivatives in the Bible. I wanted to discover how frequently the occurrence of blessing was directed from *God to humanity,* from *humanity to God,* or from *humanity to humanity.* We counted each occurrence in the Bible of the words *blessed, bless,* and *blessing.* Then we categorized them accordingly.[25]

Our results show that a little less than two-thirds of the occurrences (62 percent) are of God blessing humanity. A little more than one-third of the occurrences (38 percent) are of humanity blessing others. Of these, blessing God was 20 percent, blessing other persons or peoples, 18 percent.

It is important to recognize that the word *blessing* overlaps in a significant way with *honor* (Gen 12:1–3; Rev 5:12–13). In fact, Neyrey argues that in the Beatitudes (Mat 5:3–12), the Greek word for blessed, *makarios,* is better translated as *honored,* citing a number of scholars.

Sometimes the Beatitudes are referred to by scholars as the "makarisms." Neyrey writes:

> Reading the makarisms in terms of honor and shame is compatible with current research on them. Commentators regularly point to parallels to the makarisms in both Jewish and Greek literature. ... And the pivotal value

---

22. deSilva, 122.
23. As quoted in deSilva, 106.
24. Ibid., 105.
25. We used the *Holy Bible: English Standard Version (ESV).*

of both Greek and Hebrew culture was honor. Moreover, some allege that typical makarisms have a close relationship to morality and ethics, which means that the praise or "blessing" constitutes a public acknowledgment of the worth and value of commonly held values and expected behavior. This, of course, is the basic meaning of honor, namely, public acknowledgment of worth grounded on local expectations of value.[26]

	God to humanity	Humanity to God	Humanity to humanity
Blessed	191	59	43
Bless	64	35	32
Blessing	64	6	17
Total	319	100	92

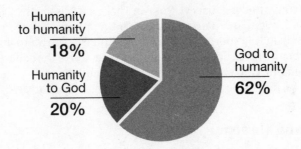

Figure 2.18: Various directions of blessing

So Neyrey recommends a more culturally appropriate translation. For example: *"Blessed* are the poor in spirit" becomes *"Honored* are the poor in spirit" ... *"Blessed* are those who mourn" becomes *"Honored* are those who mourn" ... *"Blessed* are those who hunger and thirst for righteousness" becomes *"Honored* are those who hunger and thirst for righteousness" ... and, *"Blessed* are you when others revile you and persecute you and utter all kinds of evil against you falsely" becomes *"Honored* are you when others revile you and persecute you and utter all kinds of evil against you falsely" (Mat 5:3, 4, 6, 11). Neyrey sums up the point of the Beatitudes:

[T]rue honor comes from living up to Jesus' new code and receiving the "reward" of praise of the heavenly Father. Jesus, then, changed the way the honor game was played and redefined the source of honor, namely, acknowledgment by God, not neighbor. As a result, by conforming to

---

26. Neyrey, *Honor and Shame in the Gospel of Matthew,* 166.

the image of the Master, disciples are shamed in the eyes of their peers and become least and last before their neighbors. But Jesus honors them himself with a grant of reputation and respect that far surpasses what could be hoped for in the public arena of the village.[27]

Therefore, in the context of the dynamics of patron-client relationships in the ancient world, we can draw some conclusions about *patronage and blessing:*

- **When God blesses humanity,** God may be understood as the divine Patron who gives grace to humanity as the client.

- **When humanity blesses God,** they are fulfilling the role of the loyal client, returning honor to God in public worship and praise.

- **When humanity blesses humanity,** the one blessing is the patron, and the one being blessed is the client.

One might ask, *Why is this detail about patronage, blessing, and honor important at all?* Here's why: Key passages of the Bible—passages related to God's purpose to bless the peoples of the earth—are conceptually framed in the language of patronage and blessing. And it becomes even more important when you realize that in many cultures of the Majority World, the ancient values of *patronage, blessing,* and *honor* are very much alive and well!

For example, in a trip to Thailand, the indigenous Christian leader with whom our agency partners told me that everyone in Thai society is involved in patronage. Everyone is both client and patron to someone. A father is a patron to a child. A sponsor is a patron to a sports team. A foundation is a patron to an orphan. An uncle is a patron to a niece or nephew. And God is patron to the believer. Patronage is deeply woven into the fabric of Southeast Asian culture.

Let's now further explore the honor/shame dynamic of patronage in the story of Abraham.[28]

Patronage and Abraham

The concept of *patronage* helps us understand the role of Abraham in God's story. Abraham experienced patronage in at least two ways: [29]

(1) as a "client" who was blessed/honored by the "benefactor" Melchizedek (Gen 14:17–20), and,

(2) as an honored "patron," chosen by and representing God, through whom all the families of the earth would be blessed (Gen 12:1–3).

Let's first explore how Abraham experienced patronage as a *client.* Here is the dynamic:

Abraham experienced patronage as a "client" who was blessed by the "benefactor" Melchizedek.

---

27. Ibid., 164–65.

28. God changed Abram's name to *Abraham* in Genesis 17:5. God changed Sarai's name to Sarah in Genesis 17:15. For the sake of clarity, we will use the names *Abraham* and *Sarah* throughout this book—except when *Abram* or *Sarai* is in the Scripture quotation.

29. It can also be said that Abraham "experienced patronage" when God called and blessed him (Gen 12:1–3); God could be considered the patron, and Abraham the client.

The unequal nature of the patron-client relationship may be observed in the relationship between Melchizedek and Abraham. It is recorded in Genesis 14 in which Abraham rescued his brother Lot, who had been taken captive by an alliance of kings that conquered Sodom and Gomorrah (Gen 14:1–16).

Abraham executed a daring and successful rescue of Lot[30]—along with a victory over King Chedorlaomer and his allies. In honor of Abraham's victory, an unusual figure—a person named Melchizedek—showed up to bless Abraham. (Remember this is while Abraham and his wife Sarah were still barren, without their promised offspring.)

> After his return from the defeat of Chedorlaomer and the kings who were with him, the king of Sodom went out to meet him at the Valley of Shaveh (that is, the King's Valley). And Melchizedek king of Salem brought out bread and wine. (He was priest of God Most High.) And he blessed him and said, "Blessed be Abram by God Most High, Possessor of heaven and earth; and blessed be God Most High, who has delivered your enemies into your hand!"And Abram gave him a tenth of everything (Gen 14:17–20).

More is said about the mysterious Melchizedek in Psalm 110, in which Christ's conquering kingship is prophesied (Ps 110:1–2, 4–6). And the author of Hebrews quotes Psalm 110:4 to describe Jesus Christ as a "priest forever, after the order of Melchizedek" (Heb 7:17).

But for the purpose of this chapter, I want you to see the nature of the unequal relationship—*the difference in honor-status*—between Melchizedek and Abraham. Curiously, it receives a significant comment in Hebrews 7.

> For this Melchizedek, king of Salem, priest of the Most High God, met Abraham returning from the slaughter of the kings and blessed him, and to him Abraham apportioned a tenth part of everything. He is first, by translation of his name, king of righteousness, and then he is also king of Salem, that is, king of peace. He is without father or mother or genealogy, having neither beginning of days nor end of life, but resembling the Son of God he continues a priest forever.

> See how great this man was to whom Abraham the patriarch gave a tenth of the spoils! And those descendants of Levi who receive the priestly office have a commandment in the law to take tithes from the people, that is, from their brothers, though these also are descended from Abraham. But this man who does not have his descent from them received tithes from Abraham and blessed him who had the promises. It is beyond dispute that the inferior is blessed by the superior (Heb 7:1–7).

It is beyond dispute that the inferior is blessed by the superior. This is a statement about relative honor-status. Melchizedek symbolizes the benefactor, the one with greater honor, because he blessed Abraham, father of our faith. No mortal human is accorded greater honor than Abraham, but Melchizedek is greater!

---

30. Abraham's little army consisted of "his trained men, born in his house, 318 of them" (Gen 14:14).

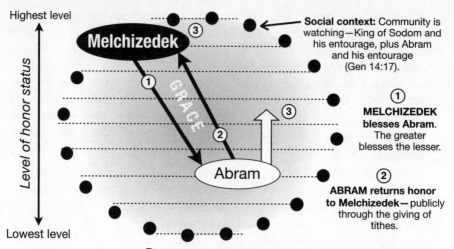

Figure 2.19: The benefactor Melchizedek blesses the client Abraham, who in turn, honors Melchizedek

It is clear Abraham experienced patronage as a "client" who was blessed by the "benefactor" Melchizedek, resulting in the elevation of his honor-status.

Let's now explore a second way by which Abraham experienced patronage. Here's the dynamic:

Abraham became an honored "benefactor" through whom all the families of the earth would be blessed.[31]

To see this clearly, it is worth reviewing God's Call of Abraham in Genesis 12:1–3.

> Now the LORD said to Abram, "Go from your country and your kindred and your father's house to the land that I will show you. And I will make of you a great nation, and I will bless you and make your name great, so that you will be a blessing. I will bless those who bless you, and him who dishonors you I will curse, and in you all the families of the earth shall be blessed."[32]

---

31. The reader may rightly ask: *Why use the Roman Empire's practice of patronage and apply it to Abraham, who lived some two thousand years before Christ? Abraham would have known nothing of the practice of Roman patronage.* Zeba Crook offers helpful insights about ancient cultures like that of Abraham's: "The idea or image of a god calling or commissioning a human and establishing a relationship of unequal status ... can be found in cultures without the patronage system, for example, ancient Israelite society." Crook demonstrates how Jewish authors around the time of Christ (such as Josephus) used the Greco-Roman concept of patron-client relations in their writings. They often described God's relationship with their own ancient leaders, such as Moses and David, using terms of client-patronage and benefaction. Crook states that "certain Jews found the Greco-Roman framework of divine patronage and benefaction a fruitful way of talking about their own God. ... God called Abram, offering him a benefaction from the outset (to be a father of a great nation), and he appeared to him frequently." Crook, 99–100.

32. Christopher Wright argues that the Hebrew word for "families" (*mišpāḥâ*) is better translated as "kinship groups." Wright says, "In Israelite tribal structure [*mišpāḥâ*] was the clan, the subgroup within the tribe. It can sometimes imply whole peoples, considered as related by kinship (as in Amos 3:1–2)." See Christopher J. H. Wright, *The Mission of God: Unlocking the Bible's Grand Narrative* (Downers Grove, IL: InterVarsity, 2006), 200.

I submit that contained in these verses is the concept of *patronage*. Here's why: God is promising that Abraham's honor will increase in an immense way: "I will ... make your name great." Contrast this with the intentions of the peoples in Genesis 11 to build the Tower of Babel: "Let us make a name for ourselves" (Gen 11:4). Christopher Wright contrasts the motivation of the Babel builders with God's promise to Abraham:

> [T]he builders of the city and tower wanted to "make a name" for themselves—that is, achieve their own renown and establish a permanent memorial to their cleverness or a citadel for their power. God put a stop to that ambition. To Abraham, however, God says, "I will make your name great" (v. 2). The echo is undoubtedly deliberate.[33]

And there is a purpose for this colossal accrual of name-greatness (honor). It is *"so that* you will be a blessing." *And to what extent will Abraham be a blessing?* The greatness of Abraham's being-a-blessing will correspond to the greatness of the global God who is making this promise. Abraham will be a blessing to all the families of the earth!

In fact, God is promising Abraham that the honor of his family and his descendants will be so great, that "in you all the families of the earth will be blessed." Abraham will be the co-progenitor with God, the co-benefactor with God for the whole world. Literally all the earth's families (or ethnic groups) will be blessed through Abraham.

Abraham could not have dreamed up such a vision. It would have been news too good to be true, news of *such grandeur*, a promise too wonderful, a pledge too large and expansive, a dream of name-greatness and honor only God could conceive. The very source of Abraham's family and the very source of Abraham's immense honor accrual could only be God himself.

Let's review. Abraham experienced patronage in two ways:

(1) as a "client" who was blessed/honored by the "benefactor" Melchizedek, and

(2) as an honored "patron," chosen by and representing God, through whom all the families of the earth would be blessed.

Now let's fast forward to the New Testament and the writings of Paul.

Abraham, the gospel, and patronage

The purpose of this last segment of this chapter is to show how *patronage*—as expressed in the relationship between God and Abraham—is built into the gospel.[34] This segment is in three parts.

- We will explore the broad biblical witness about how *Abraham* relates to the *gospel*.

---

33. Ibid., 202. Christopher Wright's excellent chapter 6 is about Abraham, blessing and mission. It is titled, "God's Elect People: Chosen for Blessing" (191–221). However, Wright makes no comment concerning this significant fact: In an honor/shame society like that of the ancient Middle East, "name greatness" would have been a significant motivational factor for Abraham to leave his country, kindred, and father's house as he obeyed God. Wright largely ignores the honor/shame dynamics of the passage.

34. I am grateful to Jackson Wu for several insightful suggestions for some of the material in this final segment of the chapter.

- We will look at the staggering honorific rewards for Abraham's obedience to God's promise.
- We will discover how the honor/shame dynamic of *patronage*—expressed in the relationship between God, Abraham, and the nations—is a part of the gospel.

Abraham and the gospel

Let's begin by considering these words in Galatians 3:

> Know then that it is those of faith who are the sons of Abraham. And the Scripture, foreseeing that God would justify the Gentiles by faith, *preached the gospel beforehand to Abraham,* saying, "In you shall all the nations be blessed." So then, those who are of faith are blessed along with Abraham, the man of faith (Gal 3:7–9). (Emphasis mine.)

Without a doubt the context of this passage is the justification by faith of believers from all the nations/people groups. In the book of Galatians, one of Paul's strategies is to use the doctrine of justification to expose the ethnocentric values of the Jews. According to Jackson Wu, "The doctrine of justification explains *who can be justified* by explaining how one is justified. 'All nations' is the specific locus of the Abrahamic covenant. Faith simply explains how God undermines ethnic exclusivism and so keeps his promise."[35]

The *faith* of the Gentiles, like the *faith* of Abraham, was the sole basis of their being counted righteous before God—no need to comply with all the Jewish laws, most notably circumcision (Gal 2:7–9; 6:15). Moreover, for the Jews, there was now no basis for boasting that they were favored by God according to their law-keeping.[36] Paul struck at the heart of the problem of ethnocentrism and boasting near the end of his letter to the Galatians: "For neither circumcision counts for anything, nor uncircumcision, but a new creation" (Gal 6:15).

Christopher Wright nicely summarizes the significance of Galatians 3:8 concerning the gospel and Abraham. Recalling that God's promise to Abraham of global blessing was proclaimed five times in Genesis (Gen 12:1–3; 17:1–8; 18:18; 22:17–18; 26:3–5), Wright says:

> Finally, we stand amazed at the universal thrust (repeated five times) of the Abrahamic promise—that ultimately people of all nations will find blessing through Abraham. And we confess, with Paul, that it is of the essence of the biblical gospel, first announced to Abraham, that God has indeed made such a blessing for all nations available through the Messiah, Jesus of Nazareth, the seed of Abraham. In Christ alone, through the gospel of his death and resurrection, stands the hope of blessing for all nations.[37]

---

35. Wu, 270.

36. Ibid., 274–75. Wu writes, "As Rom 4:14, 17 suggest, God's promise is at stake since he promised Abraham 'all nations,' not simply one, namely Israel. At the heart of the Abrahamic covenant is the justification of Gentiles (cf. Gal 3: 8). Ethnicity plays a central role in Paul's gospel. Paul particularly aims to nullify the Jewish boast, regardless of how one defines 'works.'"

37. Christopher Wright, 221.

The full-orbed gospel

What is a full-orbed biblical view of the gospel? Here are some highlights. You will observe in the following bullet points that I am making the biblical overlap in a selection of Scriptures between *the gospel* and *God's original promise to Abraham*.

- **Galatians 3:8.** The gospel was "preached" or announced to Abraham. The gospel's multi-generational trajectory across two millennia (from Abraham to the time of Christ) is essentially the story-mission of God's covenant with Abraham's family, Israel. The good news, the gospel to Abraham, was that the one-and-only covenant-keeping God would extend his blessing to all the peoples of the earth—and use *his family* to accomplish this purpose. *Abraham was chosen with universal intent.* Yes, the promise seemed like it was virtually forgotten. But the long Abrahamic family drama was punctuated with prophetic hints of the promise being realized (1 Ki 8:60; Ps 67:3-4; Is 66:18-24; Dan 7:14; Mal 1:11). One day, all the peoples will worship Abraham's God, the only true and living God, the King of all creation.

- **The Gospel According to Matthew (Mat 1:1).** The gospel's King is Jesus Christ, and he has arrived! Jesus embodies the *regal* identity of the "son of David" (Mat 1:1; cf. 1 Ki 2-8; Is 9:7; Rom 1:3). He also embodies the *sacrificial* identity of the "son of Abraham" (Mat 1:1; cf. Gen 22:1-18; Gal 3:16). The gospel is altogether wrapped up in the fulfillment of God's promise to his people Israel. N. T. Wright puts it this way: "'The gospel' is the story of Jesus of Nazareth told as the climax of the long story of Israel, which in turn is the story of how the one true God is rescuing the world."[38]

- **Luke 4:18.** God's eternal kingdom was inaugurated on earth through Christ's life and ministry. He lived out and proclaimed the gospel of the kingdom (Luke 4:18-20, 43; 8:1; 9:1-6). Jesus declared himself as the fulfillment of the "good news" (4:18) which was promised in Isaiah 61:1-2.

- **1 Corinthians 15:1.** The "gospel" (1 Cor 15:1) that Paul summarized is "that Christ died for our sins in accordance with the Scriptures, that he was buried, that he was raised on the third day in accordance with the Scriptures" (vv. 3-4). The phrase *in accordance with the Scriptures* refers to the same "Scripture" that "preached the gospel beforehand to Abraham" (Gal 3:8).

- **Romans 1:1.** The Lord of "the gospel of God" (Rom 1:1) is Jesus Christ. He is the one-and-only resurrected King and Ruler of all. He calls for "the obedience of faith for the sake of his name among all the nations" (v. 5)—in fulfillment of God's promise to Abraham (Gen 12:3). This fulfillment of the promise through the gospel is the means by which God's glory and honor are vindicated (John 12:28; Rom 4:16).

- **Romans 1:16.** The gospel "is the power of God for salvation to everyone who believes" (Rom 1:16). The gospel's power is fueled in part by God's ancient promise to Abraham that all the kinship groups of the earth will be blessed (Gen 12:3).

---

38. N.T. Wright's comments are in the introduction to McKnight, 12.

- **Romans 4:16.** The gospel is the dynamic that propels the fulfillment of God's all-nations promise to Abraham (Gen 12:3). The promise "depends on faith, in order that the promise may rest on grace [herein is the gospel] and be guaranteed to all his offspring—not only to the adherent of the law but also to the one who shares the faith of Abraham, who is the father of us all" (Rom 4:16).

- **Matthew 24:14.** Jesus said, "And this gospel of the kingdom will be proclaimed throughout the whole world as a testimony to all nations, and then the end will come" (Mat 24:14). This grand culmination will be a cosmic echo of God's promise to honor Abraham by using Abraham's offspring to bless all the peoples of the earth (Gen 12:3).

- **Revelation 14:6–7.** Finally, the "eternal gospel" will have been proclaimed to "every nation and tribe and language and people" so that they will "fear God and give him glory ... and worship him who made heaven and earth" (Rev 14:6–7). Their worship will reverberate throughout eternity—recalling God's original promise to Abraham that all the kinship groups of the earth would be blessed (Gen 12:3).

The above highlights represent the trajectory of the good news—the divinely powerful *eternal gospel* of Jesus Christ. The blessing-for-all-nations gospel was "preached" to Abraham; this is the primary meaning of Galatians 3:8.

We have observed that the *global promise* of God to ancient Abraham is tethered to the universal scope of the *global gospel*. We'll expand on this below as we explore how the honor/shame dynamic of patronage relates to the gospel.

Staggering honorific rewards for Abraham's obedience

We have observed that according to Galatians 3:8, when the Scripture "preached the gospel beforehand to Abraham," the gospel—the good news—is that "in you shall all the nations be blessed."

God's global promise and command to Abraham to "Go ... and be a blessing"[39] is certainly something that Abraham needed to dutifully heed and obey. Christians rightly embrace the need for "obedience of faith ... among all the nations" (Rom 1:5) toward the gospel (10:16).

Obedience to the gospel: yes, it is required of Christians today. Likewise, it was required of Abraham in God's call, God's global promise and command. But would Abraham have understood God's global promise—along with all the necessary sacrificial obedience—*as also good news for himself?*

Let's keep digging; there is more gold to mine in this vein. The promise to Abraham was, "In you shall all the nations be blessed" (Gal 3:8). Let's emphasize what this would have meant to Abraham ... "In you" ... *in YOU!* ... "shall all the nations

---

39. Christopher Wright summarizes Genesis 12:1–3 as "Go ... and be a blessing." See Christopher Wright, 208.

be blessed." There is immense honor implicit in God's promise-command.[40] That's what I want to focus on here.

Let's also recall the other honorific elements of God's call on Abraham in Genesis 12:1–3. Abraham's obedience required him to leave the very source of his honor: *country, kindred,* and *father's house* (Gen 12:1). But consider the manifold honorific rewards:

- God will give Abraham a new land, ensuring a new source of land-based honor.
- God will make of Abraham "a great nation," ensuring that Abraham will have an heir with many descendants.
- God "will bless" Abraham, promising that Abraham will enjoy God's divine favor.
- God will make Abraham's "name great," ensuring Abraham's renown in the larger community.
- God commands Abraham, "you will be a blessing," promising him that he will acquire the honor of being a patron who will, in turn, bless many others.
- God will "bless those who bless" Abraham, ensuring Abraham's favor in his community.
- God will protect Abraham's honor: "and him who dishonors you I will curse."
- God promises Abraham: "in you all the families of the earth shall be blessed."

What did all this mean to Abraham? Yes, God required obedience from Abraham. But how can we miss the immense, lasting honor promised by God to the previously pagan but now obedient and faith-full Abraham?[41] How can we miss the staggering *good news* this must have been to Abraham?

God the Patron, Abraham the co-patron

Let's now consider the honor/shame dynamic of patronage. It is represented here in two forms.

First, God is the great Patron who confers an astounding scope of blessings on Abraham. Second, as stated in the fifth bullet above, God promised that *Abraham will be a blessing.* God promised Abraham that he will receive the honor of being a patron, and that together with God, Abraham and his family will have the honor of blessing many others; in fact, the blessing is to go to all the peoples of the earth.

I submit that, based on the *concept* of patronage woven into the ancient cultural context and life of Abraham, the *good news to Abraham* was this truth:

---

40. Zechariah 8:13 confirms the principle that *being a blessing* is a great honor: "And as you have been a byword of cursing among the nations, O house of Judah and house of Israel, so will I save you, *and you shall be a blessing ...*" (emphasis mine). Zechariah sets up a contrast between shame and honor. The profound shame of being "a byword of cursing among the nations" is contrasted with an immense honor. What is that great honor? It is God's promise, "and you shall be a blessing." Interestingly, the nexus between (1) the *shame* of God's people among the nations and (2) the *honor* of God's people blessing the nations is God's sovereign work of salvation— "so will I save you."

41. The great honor that Abraham gained by his faith-obedience toward God is also expressed in Romans 4:13. Remarkably, Abraham is called "heir of the world," a title of breathtaking honor.

God, as the ultimate source of all honor and glory is sovereignly including Abraham in the honor-laden role of *co-benefactor*—to bless all nations through his family.[42]

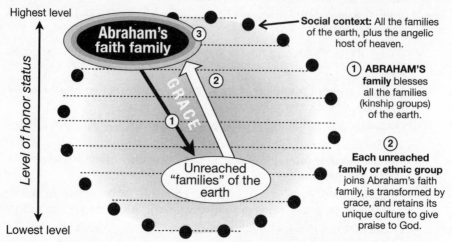

(3) **Results:** a) The Abrahamic faith family grows ever larger; b) as each family or ethnic group of the earth receives the blessing of the gospel of Christ, it gains honor in becoming part of the universal body of Christ, and c) joins in the honor of being a co-benefactor with God in Christ—to bless the rest of the families of the earth.

Figure 2.20: Abraham's faith family serves as co-benefactor with God to bless the rest of the unreached families on earth who are yet to be discipled into the kingdom of Christ

Restated here, then, is the good news—*the gospel*—to Abraham:

God will bless all nations. And God will do this through Abraham and his spiritual family, giving him and us the honor of being co-patrons, co-benefactors with God to be a blessing to all the other peoples of the earth.

Why am I spending so much time on this? Here's why:

- **Spiritually, our "grandfather" is Abraham.** As Christians we are saved by grace through faith. As sons and daughters of God, our faith is our badge of membership in God's ancient family: "... it is those of faith who are the sons of Abraham" (Gal 3:7).

- **Abraham's family is equivalent to God's people.** In the New Testament and in our present-tense new covenant period of grace, Abraham's family is equivalent to the Lord's church. This all-ethnicities family of believers whose head is Jesus Christ has some of its original DNA in Abraham. This DNA is a missional, all-cultures, international DNA! The story is still moving

---

42. I contend that the practice of *blessing* is related to the practice of *benefaction and patronage*. As blessing from a superior person conveyed honor to the weaker, lower-status person—so also patronage conveyed *honor* to the weaker or lower-status person. The practice of blessing preceded Roman patronage, but both conveyed honor from the strong to the weak. The *blessee* (the weaker, lower-status person) would give public recognition and praise to the *blesser* (the strong, higher-status person). *Patronage and benefaction* may therefore be considered a derivative of the more basic and ancient practice of *blessing*.

forward to its glorious fulfillment of God's original promise to Abraham—that all the families of the earth *will be blessed!*

- **If Abraham's honor was raised by being a co-benefactor with God to the nations, then so is our honor raised as we bless the peoples of the earth.** God is sovereignly inviting and choosing people to recognize that they and their *faith-family* are co-benefactors with God to bless the rest of the families of the earth. This honorific good news is part of the gospel.

- **Would this resonate with unengaged, unreached peoples of the Majority World?** One wonders whether hearkening back to an ancient ancestor could provide a key to the discipling of the nations. The 'hearkening-back' to this one ancestor, Abraham ... the plain honor/shame dynamics of the story ... the richness and humor of Abraham's life ... the emotionally draining drama of the *long anticipation*—and then later—the *sacrifice* of his son Isaac ... and the immense, global significance of *family* ... could not these elements attract peoples to the offspring of Abraham, Jesus Christ?

A kingdom summary—dark side and bright side

Patronage—kingdom of this world vs. kingdom-reign of God	
Kingdom of this world	**Kingdom-reign of God**
• Ideally, patronage consisted of three "graces"—giving, receiving, and returning favor, resulting in a rise in honor-status for both benefactor and client. • Practically, patronage was often a means of controlling and abusing people of lower status, perpetuating poverty, causing dependency and making them obligated without hope of ever being released from their obligations.	• The gift of salvation as expressed by John 3:16 was likely understood by the early church as an act of divine benefaction. • God is sovereignly inviting and choosing people to recognize that they and their faith-family are co-benefactors with God to bless the rest of the families of the earth. • Being co-benefactors with God is part of the gospel; it is good news because it promises a rise in honor-status for God's family of peoples and greater worship for God.

Figure 2.21: Patronage—kingdom of this world vs. kingdom-reign of God

Action points

- *Fast-forward:* To explore how the *dynamic of patronage* can shape a contextualized presentation of the gospel of Christ, turn to Section 3, Chapter 7.

- *Reflect:* To what extent do you and your church family view the mission of the church as a burden of responsibility? To what extent do you see it also as a massive *joy* (Ps 96), the eternal *honor* of being co-benefactors with God and ambassadors for Christ (2 Cor 5:20) to the nations?

- *Bible study:* "And the Scripture, foreseeing that God would justify the Gentiles by faith, preached the gospel beforehand to Abraham, saying, 'In you shall all the nations be blessed'" (Gal 3:8). What was the content or essence of God's "gospel message" to Abraham?

- *Teaching:* Genesis 12:1–3 is one of the most foundational Old Testament passages for the mission of the church. Develop a teaching about the honorific blessings given by God to Abraham in these three brief, but loaded, verses.

- *Mission:* Do you serve among people who have high regard for *family*, *ancestors*, and *honor?* If so, how would you communicate the story of Abraham and its connection to the family of God in Galatians 3:7–9, 25–29?

Honor/Shame Dynamic #8:
Name / Kinship / Blood

Why is this important?

- Describes how family *honor* is replicated by the family *name* and family *blood*—just as God's *honor* is replicated by God's *name* and Christ's *blood*.

- Unpacks the importance of Abraham as the progenitor of a *family*—a kinship group, Israel—by whom all the families of the earth would be blessed.

- Shows how the criteria for membership in the people/family of God is both narrowed and broadened from one that is primarily based on God's covenant with the Jews—to one that is based on a new covenant for a new community of *all ethnicities*—based solely on faith in Jesus Christ.

- Shows that blood and honor in the kingdom of this world often generates violence—whereas the blood and honor of Christ in the kingdom of God generates peace.

Definition

New Testament scholar David deSilva explains the honor attached to one's "kinship" or family.

> In the ancient world, people are not just taken on their "merits." Honor "begins with the merits (or debits) of their lineage, the reputation of their ancestral house. Greeks and Romans receive a basic identity from their larger family: for Romans this takes the form of including the clan name in the name of each individual."[1]

---

1. deSilva, 158.

The honor carried by kinship and family are represented by the family *name*, as well as the blood (or bloodline) of the family. The Bible uses the word "name" to convey the *honor* and *reputation* of a family—or of God himself. There are overlaps of honorific meaning—all related to *family*—between *name, kinship* and *blood*.

Commenting on the honor of kinship and blood in the Roman Empire, J. E. Lendon states, "Although honour was a personal quality, its aura extended over household and connections by blood and marriage: a man's family was part and parcel of his social persona."[2]

"NAME" AND HONOR

In Scripture, the word *name* is laden with the connotation of honor or glory. Consider this verse from Malachi:

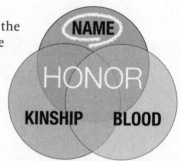

> A son honors his father, and a servant his master. If then I am a father, where is my *honor*? And if I am a master, where is my fear? says the LORD of hosts to you, O priests, who despise my *name*. But you say, "How have we despised your name?" (Mal 1:6). (Emphasis mine.)

Consider also these verses from the Psalms:

> Ascribe to the LORD the glory due his *name*; bring an offering, and come into his courts! (Ps 96:8). (Emphasis mine.)

> Nations will fear the *name* of the LORD, and all the kings of the earth will fear your *glory* (Ps 102:15). (Emphasis mine.)

And these verses from Isaiah:

> I am the LORD; that is my *name*; my *glory* I give to no other, nor my praise to carved idols (Isa 42:8). (Emphasis mine.)

> ... everyone who is called by my *name*, whom I created for my *glory*, whom I formed and made" (Isa 43:7). (Emphasis mine.)

Consider also the following verse where the salvation of God's people, including the atonement for their sins, is contingent on God's commitment to the *glory of his name*—in other words, his *honor*...

> Help us, O God of our salvation, for the *glory* of your *name*; deliver us, and atone for our sins, for your name's sake! (Ps 79:9). (Emphasis mine.)

---

2. Lendon, Kindle edition locations 576–77.

A similar salvation theme related to God's name/honor is contained here: "For your name's sake, O LORD, pardon my guilt, for it is great" (Ps 25:11), and in the New Testament: "I am writing to you, little children, because your sins are forgiven for his name's sake (1 John 2:12).

"Name" and honor in the Gospel of John

In John's Gospel, the relationship between God's *name* and God's *honor/glory* is a major theme. For example, Jesus said:

> I have come in my Father's name, and you do not receive me. If another comes in his own name, you will receive him (John 5:43).

Jesus came in his "Father's name." It is plain that the word *name* refers to honor. Here's why: In that culture, if someone came to you in their *own name* (that is, their *own honor*), it would not be nearly as weighty as if they came in their *father's name* (that is, their *father's honor*).

So Jesus is creating an outrageous contrast. He came in his "Father's name," but he was not received. The outrage of this is magnified by the fact that the Pharisees *do* receive people coming to them in their "own name," that is, their *own honor*. How astounding that God's people Israel would receive people coming on the basis of their own name with far less honor, but reject the One whose Father is their very own covenant-making God. What an insult!

A similar dynamic of honor and shame is contained in John chapter 1:

> He came to his own, and his own people did not receive him. But to all who did receive him, who believed in his name, he gave the right to become children of God (John 1:11–12).

In effect, John is saying, *Jesus came to his very own people, the Hebrews, the nation of Israel—and believe it or not, they rejected him. How insulting! But there are some who did receive him (this gave Jesus his due honor), and—get this!—to them he gave the honor of becoming the very children of God!* Amazing.

"Name" = reputation, character, story ... honor!

What does it mean to believe in the *name* of Jesus Christ? It means to believe in the reputation, the character, the entire Person, the whole story of Jesus Christ. At the risk of sounding ludicrous, believing in Jesus' *name* is not about believing in the way it is spelled ... J–E–S–U–S. It means embracing his *honor* and *glory*.

Just before Christ went to the cross, he was praying in agony to the Father.

> Now is my soul troubled. And what shall I say? "Father, save me from this hour"? But for this purpose I have come to this hour (John 12:27).

When Jesus refers to "this purpose" he is referring to his approaching Passion—the horrifying, humiliating series of events he is about to endure: *betrayal, arrest, interrogation, flogging, crucifixion, and burial*—followed by *his resurrection unto exalted glory.*

It was a purpose of breathtaking proportions: be "pierced for our transgressions," "crushed for our iniquities," and receive the "chastisement that brought us peace" (Is 53:5) ... have "laid on him the iniquity of us all" (Is 53:6) ... endure the "wounds" by which we "are healed" (Is 53:5) ... "give his life as a ransom for many" (Mat 20:28; Mark 10:45; cf. 1 Tim 2:6) ... inaugurate a new kingdom that reigns over all (Acts 8:12) ... obtain a new community, the people of God, the church (Acts 20:28) ... atone for the sins of the world (Rom 3:25) ... vindicate the righteousness of God (Rom 3:26) ... be "delivered up for our trespasses and raised for our justification" (Rom 4:25) ... justify us "by his blood" to save us "from the wrath of God" (Rom 5:9) ... condemn sin in the flesh (Rom 8:3) ... redeem people from the bondage of sin (Eph 1:7; Rev 1:5) ... be the archetypal representative by which "in Christ shall all be made alive" (1 Cor 15:21–22) ... justify all those who place their faith in Christ (Gal 2:16) ... redeem believers "from the curse of the law by becoming a curse for us" (Gal 3:13) "so that we might receive adoption as sons" of God (Gal 4:5) ... initiate the process of uniting "all things in him" (Eph 1:10) ... create a new reconciling community (Eph 2:14–15) by killing the hostility between peoples (Eph 2:16) ... "reconcile to himself all things" (Col 1:20) ... make believers honorable before God, covering their shame to make them "holy and blameless and above reproach before him" (Col 1:22) ... cancel "the record of debt that stood against us with its legal demands" (Col 2:14) ... shame all his enemies in overwhelming triumphant victory (Col 2:15) ... be the "mediator between God and men" (1 Tim 2:5) ... abolish death (2 Tim 1:10) ... "redeem us from all lawlessness and to purify for himself a people" (Titus 2:14) ... make "purification for sins" (Heb 1:3) ... "taste death for everyone" (Heb 2:9) ... "purify our conscience from dead works" (Heb 9:14) ... "put away sin" (Heb 9:26) ... make "a single sacrifice for sins" (Heb 10:12) ... make clean and holy those who believe in him—"sanctify the people" (Heb 13:12) ... ransom us from "the futile ways inherited from [our] forefathers" (1 Pet 1:18) ... bear "our sins in his body on the tree, that we might die to sin and live to righteousness" (1 Pet 2:24) ... heal our wounds (1 Pet 2:24) ... "bring us to God" (1 Pet 3:18) ... establish his glorious kingdom (Rev 2:6; 5:10) ... ransom people for God "from every tribe and language and people and nation" (Rev 5:9) ... and provide a means for believers to overcome the devil, "the accuser" of believers (Rev 12:10).

In John 12:27, Jesus is referring to the entire purpose for the cross as he concluded his life on earth as the Son of God. How did Jesus describe *this purpose?* One might anticipate that he might have said *the love of God for the peoples of the world*—or, *the mercy of God for sinners.* Or simply, *to atone for sin.* But none of these true aspects of the cross are mentioned by Jesus when he said "this purpose."

Here is what Jesus said:

Father, glorify your name (John 12:28).

The glory of God's name—the reputation of God, the honor of God—was put to the ultimate test as Jesus endured the torture, defilement and shame of the cross. And yet, somehow in the infinite wisdom of God, it proved to be the highest expression of God's honor!

How can this be? How can something so dark, so shocking and shameful, be so sublimely, gloriously wise and honorable?

God was being faithful to his promise made to Abraham some two thousand years prior, that through Abraham's offspring all the families of the earth would be blessed (Gen 12:3; 22:18). He demonstrated his honor by showing that his Word is true. For it was through Abraham's seed, or offspring, that all the families of the earth would be blessed (Gen 12:3; Gal 3:16, 29). Christ was that seed, that offspring! God's *integrity* was at stake. God's *honor* hung in the balance ... *this* was the purpose for Christ's Passion.

Then a voice came from heaven: "I have glorified it, and I will glorify it again" (John 12:28).

The Father confirmed *this purpose* with a thunderous Amen! (John 12:29). Steve Hawthorne writes in his classic article, "The Story of His Glory":

What purpose was this? The purpose bursts forth from his heart in his next statement. It becomes the prayer of his death and his life: "Father! Glorify your name!" And then, to the bewildered amazement of those standing near him, God the Father himself answered Jesus from heaven: "I have both glorified it (my name), and will glorify it again." God's answer from heaven thunders, if you can hear it. It is God's answer to anyone who yields their life to the Father for the greater glory of his name. Jesus said that the answer didn't come for him, but for his followers who would come to similar moments of choosing to follow him (12:30) in accordance with God's ancient purpose. How would Jesus' death glorify God's name? "If I be lifted up, I will draw all people to Myself" (12:32).[3]

Jackson Wu writes:

The atonement is necessary and not merely for the sake of human salvation. This claim says more than just God wants to glorify himself. Rather, it states that if Christ did not die, God would not be righteous. In that case, God lacks honor. God is shameful. The atonement is a God-centered act. It is true that Christ's death vindicates God's justice so that he is able to save his people. Yet, one must not get the order backwards. God's glory is not an obstacle to his main goal, i.e. saving sinners. Saving sinners is a means to his main goal. Therefore, atonement theology does not terminate simply on human salvation. That is not the end for which God does all things.[4]

God's love for the peoples of the world—demonstrated through the life, death and resurrection of Jesus Christ—has been inextricably woven into the divine tapestry of God's passion for his own glory.[5]

---

3. I am indebted to Steve Hawthorne for being the first to introduce me to the beautiful drama of the glory of God. See his article in "The Story of His Glory," in eds. Ralph D. Winter and Steven C. Hawthorne, *Perspectives on the World Christian Movement* (Pasadena, CA: William Carey Library Publishers, 1999).

4. Wu, 197–98.

5. See John Piper, *God's Passion for His Glory: Living the Vision of Jonathan Edwards (With the Complete Text of The End for Which God Created the World)* (Wheaton, IL: Crossway Books, 1996), and *The Pleasures of God: Meditations on God's Delight in Being God* (Sisters, OR: Multnomah, 1991, 2000).

Name, honor, glory!

The significant thing here is the very close proximity between name, honor, and glory. When the Lord complains, *"O priests, who despise my name"* (Mal 1:6), God's honor is being despised. When nations *"fear the name of the Lord"* (Ps 102:15; Isa 59:19), they are respecting God's glory and honor. When Isaiah prophesies of *"everyone who is called by my name"* (Isa 43:7), he is referring to his people being summoned by his honor.

When Jesus prayed just hours before going to the cross, "Father, glorify your name" (John 12:28), he was passionately pleading for the honor of God to be vindicated.

When God says, "I am the LORD; that is my name; my glory I give to no other" (Is 42:8), one senses the mirror-like quality between *name* and *glory,* between *name* and *honor.*

It is one important truth to keep in mind when reading Scripture: the *name* of God is nearly synonymous with the *honor* of God and the *glory* of God.

We move on now to the aspect of *kinship* in honor and shame. ... Let's talk about *family.*

KINSHIP AND HONOR

Kinship: The example of Abraham and his family

Throughout Scripture, there are many examples of family, kinship, and blood conveying the honor of people and peoples in the Bible. The story of Abraham's kinship group is one such example, and it is foundational. In fact, one can say that the story of Abraham's family—how his own honor is gained ... how Abraham's honor is extended through his blood descendants ... and how this family blessing, this extended family honor rooted in God himself, is extended to all the families of the earth—is the essence of the story of the Bible.

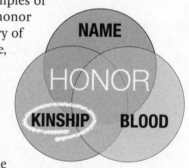

Let's trace the beginning of this family and the way honor and shame is woven into its forming.

> Now the LORD said to Abram, "Go from your country and your kindred and your father's house to the land that I will show you" (Gen 12:1).

When God told Abraham to leave *his country, his kindred, and his father's house,* God was telling him to leave his core identity—to abandon his very source of honor—in exchange for another. All of the wealth and honor of a man in the ancient Near East consisted of land and family: *land,* because their wealth would be based largely on the number of livestock they would have (camels, sheep, goats, etc.); and *family,* because it was through family (that is, blood relations, father to son) that wealth and honor was passed from one generation to another.

Here are the specific promises of God to Abraham regarding family and kinship. In God's original call of Abraham, he said:

And I will make of you a great nation ... (Gen 12:2).

God made this promise to a man whose wife Sarah was barren. Barrenness represented a condition of vulnerability for the family name and legacy. Abraham's wife Sarah is the first of several key women in the Bible who were barren and suffered shame as a result. God made an astounding promise to the old man Abraham: *not only would his wife give birth to an heir, God promised that Abraham's offspring would ultimately be innumerable!*

I will make your offspring as the dust of the earth, so that if one can count the dust of the earth, your offspring also can be counted (Gen 13:16).

God established his covenant with Abraham in Genesis 15. It involved the shedding of the blood of animals—"He said to him, 'Bring me a heifer three years old, a female goat three years old, a ram three years old, a turtledove, and a young pigeon'" (Gen 15:9). Here is the promise:

And he brought him outside and said, "Look toward heaven, and number the stars, if you are able to number them." Then he said to him, "So shall your offspring be" (Gen 15:5).

However, Abraham and Sarah did not have the patience to wait on God. In a self-directed honor pursuit saturated with unbelief, Abraham followed Sarah's desperate suggestion to "go in to" and impregnate her servant girl Hagar in Genesis 16:2. Hagar conceived and bore a son who was named Ishmael. Despite the fact that Ishmael was born out of disobedience, God nevertheless blessed both Hagar and Ishmael. God said to Abraham: "As for Ishmael, I have heard you; behold, I have blessed him and will make him fruitful and multiply him greatly. He shall father twelve princes, and I will make him into a great nation" (Gen 17:20).

Then, Genesis 17 describes God's covenant with Abraham as one ratified by circumcision. This time it is not a ritual by which mere animal blood is shed; this time, human blood is shed—beginning with Abraham and extending to his entire household. God calls for circumcision, the cutting of the foreskin of every male, for a sign of God's covenant with them (Gen 17:9–14). This is the seal of the binding sacred relationship between God and Abraham and the extended family that will be formed from Abraham's descendants.

Through circumcision—the sign of Abraham's manhood—his organ of reproductive honor would be cut and marked for God's global family and purpose. This cutting marked by blood would be unforgettable for Abraham and all of his descendants.

When Abram was ninety-nine years old the LORD appeared to Abram and said to him, "I am God Almighty; walk before me, and be blameless, that I may make my covenant between me and you, and may multiply you greatly." Then Abram fell on his face. And God said to him, *"Behold, my covenant is with you, and you shall be the father of a multitude of nations. No longer shall your name be called Abram, but your name shall be Abraham, for I have made you the father of a multitude of nations. I will make you exceedingly fruitful, and I will make you into nations, and kings shall come from you.* And I will establish my covenant between me and you and your offspring after you throughout their generations for an everlasting covenant, to be God to you and to your offspring after you" (Gen 17:1–7). (Emphasis mine.)

By the grace of God, Abraham and Sarah miraculously conceived and gave birth to Isaac. And when Isaac was a teenager, God asked Abraham to do *the unthinkable*— offer his beloved son Isaac as a burnt offering in worship to God. Abraham obeyed God ... God intervened to provide a ram in the place of Isaac ... and Abraham was rewarded for his faith:

And the angel of the LORD called to Abraham a second time from heaven and said, "By myself I have sworn, declares the LORD, because you have done this and have not withheld your son, your only son, *I will surely bless you, and I will surely multiply your offspring as the stars of heaven and as the sand that is on the seashore. And your offspring shall possess the gate of his enemies, and in your offspring shall all the nations of the earth be blessed,* because you have obeyed my voice" (Gen 22:15–18). (Emphasis mine.)

God's promise extended to Isaac and Jacob

After Abraham died, God made the same promise of *offspring-for-the-purpose-of-blessing-the-nations* to Abraham's son Isaac:

Sojourn in this land, and I will be with you and will bless you, for to you and to your offspring I will give all these lands, and I will establish the oath that I swore to Abraham your father. I will multiply your offspring as the stars of heaven and will give to your offspring all these lands. *And in your offspring all the nations of the earth shall be blessed,* because Abraham obeyed my voice and kept my charge, my commandments, my statutes, and my laws" (Gen 26:3–5). (Emphasis mine.)

Years later, God also made the same promise to Isaac's son Jacob:

And behold, the LORD stood above it and said, "I am the LORD, the God of Abraham your father and the God of Isaac. The land on which you lie I will give to you and to your offspring. Your offspring shall be like the dust of the earth, and you shall spread abroad to the west and to the east and to the north and to the south, *and in you and your offspring shall all the families of the earth be blessed*" (Gen 28:13–14). (Emphasis mine.)

The main discovery of this exploration in Genesis of the beginning of Abraham's family is this:

God miraculously created a large extended *family* of people who became known as "God's people," Israel ...

whose father is Abraham,

who became a family, a kinship group called the Jews,

whose sacred honor is located in God himself and his purposes—

in order to bring God's blessing and honor to all the other *families* (or clans, or ethnic groups) of the earth.

The Romans 4 "family bridge" between old and new covenant

In Romans 4, Paul writes extensively about the key role of Abraham's faith and what that means for establishing the new community of believers under the new covenant in Christ. It links God's original global purpose—to bless all the families/peoples of the earth (Gen 12:3)—with the new reality, the new covenant that God had put into motion through the life, death, and resurrection of Christ.

Romans 4:1–9 establishes that Abraham's faith was "counted to him as righteousness" (Rom 4:3, 9), and that this occurred *before* the giving of the Jewish law, which included circumcision for males (4:10). Then Paul writes:

He received the sign of circumcision as a seal of the righteousness that he had by faith while he was still uncircumcised. The purpose was to make him the father of all who believe without being circumcised, so that righteousness would be counted to them as well, and to make him the father of the circumcised who are not merely circumcised but who also walk in the footsteps of the faith that our father Abraham had before he was circumcised (Rom 4:11–12).

So let's note these three crucial principles about circumcision:

- The first purpose of circumcision was *not* to make Abraham righteous, but to be a *sign* of the faith that had *already* made him righteous.
- This allows for the second purpose of circumcision to be realized: "to make him the father of all who believe without being circumcised." *God wants to make sure that the faith will go global!* This is true, because circumcision would be an insurmountable obstacle to the faith being received by all peoples.
- The third purpose of circumcision—it ensures that those who are of the Jewish faith ("the circumcised") do not trust in outward-based signs, but in an inward faith—so that Jewish believers "walk in the footsteps of the faith that our father Abraham had before he was circumcised."

In other words, Abraham was circumcised as a *sign* that *confirmed* his faith and *confirmed* his acceptance before a holy God; this is the guarantee that the same kind of trusting-fully-in-God faith (without Jewish works of the law) is what makes anyone and everyone (including Gentiles!) acceptable to God. Moreover:

That is why it depends on faith, in order that the promise may rest on grace and be guaranteed to all his offspring—not only to the adherent of the law but also to the one who shares the faith of Abraham, who is the father of us all, as it is written, "I have made you the father of many nations"—in the presence of the God in whom he believed, who gives life to the dead and calls into existence the things that do not exist (Rom 4:16–17).

Through believers—both Jew and Gentile—exercising *faith* in Jesus Christ, God is guaranteeing that his promise to Abraham will be fulfilled. "That is why it depends on faith, *in order that* the promise may rest on grace and be *guaranteed* to all his offspring." (Emphasis mine.)

God is making sure (it is "guaranteed") that all the families/peoples of the earth will be blessed, and that this *family of families*—which owes its existence to God—will be as universally broad and diverse as originally promised. This in turn gives God maximum honor and relational delight, the maximum praise he deserves.

The honor/shame dynamics of Abraham's *faith family* may be summarized as follows:

- **The progenitor honored by God.** Abraham was a pagan man honored by God in being chosen to become the progenitor, the father, of an immense family of offspring that would be multiplied "as the stars of heaven and as the sand that is on the seashore" (Gen 22:17).

- **An honor-giving faith.** "Abraham believed God, and it was counted to him as righteousness" (Rom 4:3). His strong faith greatly honored and glorified the One who made the promise (Rom 4:18–21).

- **The honor of co-benefaction with God.** This Abrahamic kinship group whose origin is *by faith in God* would be so honorable that it would become a co-benefactor with God to bless all the families/kinship groups/nations of the earth (Gen 12:3; 22:18; 26:4).

- **The most-honored Son.** From Abraham's descendants was born Jesus Christ, the most honorable "son of David, the son of Abraham" (Mat 1:1), and Son of God (Mat 3:17)—who is the King of kings and Lord of lords (1 Tim 6:15).

- **The honorable family of families—for the honor of God.** God's family, though begun as a single kinship group (ethnicity), would be extended to all ethnicities in order to prove the integrity of God's original promise to Abraham that all the families of the earth would be blessed. This gives maximum honor and glory to God!

- **The shameful death that glorified God.** The perfect life, substitutionary death, and resurrection of the offspring of Abraham, Jesus Christ (Gal 3:16), became the way for the blessing to go to "all his offspring"—all the Gentile people groups (Rom 4:16). This vindicates God's honor (John 12:27–28) because it shows that he can be trusted for all his promises.

- **Boundless honor and worship to God.** Our faith in the grace of Christ is like Abraham's faith in that it is apart from the cultural demands of the Jewish law (Rom 4:9–11); it is thus ethnically neutral, in order that *all peoples* will be accepted into God's family of families to worship the Lord Jesus Christ.

- **Our destiny—an eternal kingdom.** God's family of families constitutes a kingdom (Rev 5:9–10); all persons in this kingdom have their honor located completely in Christ their King (Rev 22:4) and boast in the glory of God (Rom 5:2). God is the source of every blessing, all honor and glory, every grace (Rom 11:36).

Family-based honor in the New Testament

It is both a deliberate literary choice, and a deliberate spiritual choice, that the Gospel of Matthew begins with *family*—the genealogy of Jesus Christ, a careful description of the Lord's family ancestors:[6]

> The book of the genealogy of Jesus Christ, the son of David, the son of Abraham. Abraham was the father of Isaac, and Isaac the father of Jacob, and Jacob the father of Judah and his brothers (Mat 1:1–2).

The genealogy continues all the way through "Joseph the husband of Mary, of whom Jesus was born, who is called Christ" (v. 16).

That Jesus is called both the son of David and the son of Abraham in the opening verse, Matthew 1:1, indicates the concern Matthew has for naming the Messiah in the most honorable way.

Neyrey's comments are helpful, noting that in Matthew's Gospel, Jesus is called

> (1) *Son of God* (Matt. 2:15; 3:17; 4:3, 6; 8:29; 11:27; 14:33; 16:16; 17:5; 27:40, 43, 54); (2) *Son of Abraham* (1:1); (3) *Son of David* (1:1; 9:27; 12:23; 15:22; 20:30, 31; 21:9, 15) and (4) *Son of Joseph* (13:55). Fully in accord with his culture, Matthew deems it essential for the proper honoring of Jesus that his readers know his "blood," that is, his rootedness in certain ancestral families. If these are noble and honorable, so will the latest offspring be. And who can top the family of Abraham and David, much less that of God?[7]

The significance of the genealogy of Jesus Christ makes little sense to modern people in the West who are future-oriented rather than ancestor-oriented ... who place much more value on the individual than the family ... and who emphasize *achieved* honor over *ascribed* honor.

But to first-century peoples in the Roman Empire, and to Jews in particular who comprised the primary audience of Matthew's Gospel, the genealogy not only made sense, it was vitally important. One's ancestry was the beginning point of one's honor. And if you were making the case for the supreme honor of the Son of God (as Matthew was in his Gospel), then it was *essential* that the honorable ancestry of the Person in question be made known and be entirely trustworthy.

Jesus and "family"

The New Testament makes many additional references to *family* of which I will mention only a few, but they are essential for understanding the unique new dynamics of kinship honor inaugurated through Christ.

---

6. Jerome Neyrey makes a convincing argument that the Gospel of Matthew is a type of literature called *encomium: literature in praise of men.* Most Westerners understand the *encomium* as a eulogy. Neyrey contends that most children attending school in the Roman Empire learned the literary form of *encomium.* They were instructed that every encomium begins with the lineage or ancestors of the person in question. See Neyrey, *Honor and Shame in the Gospel of Matthew,* 70–89.

7. Neyrey, *Honor and Shame in the Gospel of Matthew,* 57.

There are two Christ-inaugurated dynamics concerning family (or kinship), and they form a curiously beautiful paradox. These dynamics consist of (1) a *narrowing* dynamic, and (2) an *expanding* dynamic.

Consider the following account from Matthew's gospel.

> While he was still speaking to the people, behold, his mother and his brothers stood outside, asking to speak to him. But he replied to the man who told him, "Who is my mother, and who are my brothers?" And stretching out his hand toward his disciples, he said, "Here are my mother and my brothers! For whoever does the will of my Father in heaven is my brother and sister and mother" (Mat 12:46–50).

Rather shockingly, Jesus is redefining *family* for the Jews, the people of God. Jerome Neyrey calls it a "new index of honor."[8] No longer is it satisfactory to think that being ethnically Jewish equates with being a part of God's family. Jesus *narrows* the criteria for membership in God's family considerably. Pointing to his disciples, Jesus says, "Here are my mother and my brothers! For whoever does the will of my Father in heaven is my brother and sister and mother." Doing the will of God—*obedience!*—became the deciding criteria; this is the *narrowing* dynamic.

But Jesus *expands* the concept of God's family as well. Being a member of God's family and possessing the corresponding honor of being related to Jesus is now available to *anyone and everyone*; indeed, it is available to *"whoever* does the will of my Father in heaven." This "new index of honor"—this new way of defining who was an "insider"—deeply challenged the status quo understanding of family.[9]

Jesus' teachings turned upside-down the traditional understanding of *people of God, family,* and *father.*

The Apostle Paul elaborates on this new definition of the family of God in his letter to the Galatians.

> Know then that it is those of faith who are the sons of Abraham. ... For in Christ Jesus you are all sons of God, through faith. For as many of you as were baptized into Christ have put on Christ. There is neither Jew nor Greek, there is neither slave nor free, there is no male and female, for you are all one in Christ Jesus. And if you are Christ's, then you are Abraham's offspring, heirs according to promise (Gal 3:7, 26–29).

---

8. Ibid., 54. "'Who is my mother and who are my brothers?' The question reveals a crisis within Jesus' kin group. In such a situation, families tend to paper over their internal problems and thus keep up appearances before others. But here Jesus exacerbates the problem between himself and his family, which threatens their public reputation. Resorting to a comparison, he establishes a non-kinship criteria for family membership. 'Whoever does the will of my Father in heaven is my brother and sister and mother' (12:50). He identifies with a 'family' but not with the empirical group standing outside; he has a 'Father' to whom he is duty bound to show loyalty, the kind of loyalty that is the stuff of later parables (21:28–31, 37). According to this new index of honor he turns away from the blood relatives standing outside and toward the disciples inside: 'And stretching out his hand toward his disciples, he said, "Here are my mother and my brothers! For whoever does the will of my Father in heaven is my brother and sister and mother."'"

9. See Acts 11:1–18. Peter's status quo understanding of what qualifies one for membership in *the people of God* had to be gently smashed by a revelation from God. Peter required a special dream from God in order to extend beyond Jewish cultural boundaries his understanding of the people of God. The *new people of God,* the church, could include Gentiles who followed Jesus—without mandating that they follow Jewish customs. Although this was consistent with the ancient promise of God to Abraham that all the families of the earth would be blessed through Christ, it was nevertheless for Peter a *revelation,* a paradigm shift.

It is a *narrower* definition of the family of God in that only those who "through faith" "in Christ Jesus" are sons (or children) of God. At the same time, it is *broader* in the sense that this kinship group is amazingly egalitarian, *excluding no one* on the basis of ethnicity, gender, or social status. The only thing that matters in *this* family—the *only* qualification necessary for membership in this most honorable kinship group called "Abraham's offspring"—*is faith!* ... faith in "Jesus Christ, the son of David, the son of Abraham" (Mat 1:1).

The glory of membership in God's family

Indeed, Paul makes much of the honor of being in the new family of God. Consider his use of the word *adoption*. Paul uses this word to convey high honor when he lists this as one of the main reasons why Israel has a unique relationship—a special elevated status before God.

> They are Israelites, and to them belong the adoption, the glory, the covenants, the giving of the law, the worship, and the promises (Rom 9:4).

Paul also uses the word *adoption* to amplify the honored status of believers:

> For you did not receive the spirit of slavery to fall back into fear, but you have received the Spirit of adoption as sons, by whom we cry, "Abba! Father!" (Rom 8:15).

Consider the fact that Paul is writing to the church at Rome, capital of the Empire. To people living in the Roman Empire, slavery was common, and the honor and power of fathers over their offspring was considered absolute.[10] Clearly, Paul is highlighting the stark contrast between the shame of slavery—a metaphor for bondage to sin—and the honored status of sons who are in a privileged relationship with their father. This revealed how believers in the new Christian community of faith are to understand their honor-laden relationship with God the Father.[11]

In his first letter, the Apostle Peter expands on the immense, marvelous honor of the new family of God:

> But you are a chosen race, a royal priesthood, a holy nation, a people for his own possession, that you may proclaim the excellencies of him who called you out of darkness into his marvelous light. Once you were not a people, but now you are God's people; once you had not received mercy, but now you have received mercy (1 Pet 2:9–10).

While Jesus and Paul both spoke of the ascribed honor of the new people of God, it is important not to overlook what these new understandings *replaced*. Some

---

10. "In the world of Jesus and Paul, the term *father* included reference not only to one's male blood progenitors and perhaps to one's fathers' fathers but also to the emperor at Rome, the *pater patriae,* the 'father of the fatherland.' ... In Roman culture, this nearly absolute, coercive authority was called *patria potestas,* which in its range included the father's power of life and death over his children, beginning in infancy when a father chose to acknowledge and rear the child or 'expose' it—that is, 'throw the child away.'" From S. Scott Bartchy, "Who Should Be Called 'Father'? Paul of Tarsus between the Jesus Tradition and *Patria Potestas*" in eds. Neyrey and Stewart, 165.

11. See also Rom 8:23; Gal 4:5; Eph 1:5—verses where Paul uses the word *adoption* to describe the relationship of Christians to God.

of the words of Jesus regarding fatherhood and family are indeed perplexing, if not shocking.

> Another of the disciples said to him, "Lord, let me first go and bury my father." And Jesus said to him, "Follow me, and leave the dead to bury their own dead" (Mat 8:21–22).

> For I have come to set a man against his father, and a daughter against her mother, and a daughter-in-law against her mother-in-law. And a person's enemies will be those of his own household. Whoever loves father or mother more than me is not worthy of me, and whoever loves son or daughter more than me is not worthy of me (Mat 10:35–37).

> And call no man your father on earth, for you have one Father, who is in heaven (Mat 23:9).[12]

Jewett states that the father's absolute power over his family, known as *patria potestas,* "was broadly defined as life-long authority over one's family, including even at times the imposition of the death penalty. Such authority was still an important factor in Roman family and political life in the first century."[13] Bartchy writes that Jesus is teaching that "his followers should not, and need not, address anyone but the God of Israel as 'father.'"[14]

God's story—a story of family and honor

Beginning with Abraham in Genesis 12, the whole of God's story demonstrates God's family as the bearer of God's honorific blessing to the rest of the "families" of the earth. God said to Abraham, "And I will make of you a great nation, and I will bless you and make your name great" (v. 2). The promise from God of great honor for Abraham began with his status of *barrenness/shame* to become a *family* with *progeny/honor.* Ultimately, the promise extends magnificently; Abraham's family will become a "great nation"—existing for the God-ordained purpose of blessing all the families/nations of the earth. Abraham is chosen with universal intent.

Therefore, when reading Scripture, we ought to be mindful that most every familial term is saturated with connotations of honor. Words such as: *family ... offspring ... father ... mother ... son ... daughter ... sister and brother ... heir ... lineage ...* and in the New Testament, *adoption ...* these words are all loaded with honorific weight.

Correspondingly, be aware that in ancient Near Eastern cultures, husbands and wives without children carried a burden of shame. This was not abstract but an everyday emotional burden. For example, prior to God's call to Abraham (Gen 12:1–3), the Bible says of Abraham's wife, "Now Sarai was barren; she had no child"

---

12. Bartchy, in eds. Neyrey and Stewart, 169. The article explains each of these perplexing verses with thoroughness for which space does not allow in this book.
13. Jewett, *Romans,* 188.
14. Bartchy, in eds. Neyrey and Stewart, 169.

(Gen 11:30).[15] Every original hearer of this story would have instantly recognized the shame of barrenness being carried by Abraham's wife Sarah, and by Abraham himself.

This serves as a dramatic foil that amplified the magnificent set of honorific blessings—blessings related to *offspring*—which were to accrue to Abraham (Gen 12:1–3), as well as in the promises restated to Isaac and Jacob.

Finally, we observe in Jesus' teachings the reversals of some cultural values in ancient Roman and Jewish societies. According to Bartchy these reversals include:

- the rejection of patriarchal authority and domination of the traditional obligations of filial piety;[16]
- the invitation to become members of a surrogate family not based on blood ties yet expressive of the interpersonal values of sibling kinship;
- the redefinition of the basis for attaining honor by serving rather than competing;
- the demonstration of authentic power that now was characterized by empowerment rather than by control of others.[17]

In our exploration of *name, kinship* and *blood* in the Bible's honor/shame societies, we have looked at both *name* and *kinship.* We turn now to the meaning of *blood.*

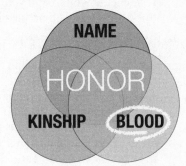

BLOOD AND HONOR

"Blood" can be both the *result* and the *cause* of honor competition and honor-based violence.

Blood as the *result* of honor competition. The Bible's first reference to blood is in Genesis when Cain killed his brother Abel. Cain felt

---

15. Genesis 15:1–8 shows Abraham's intense anxiety about having an heir—as promised by God. Abraham is desperate to know, "Will I be remembered?" He knows that his own legacy is contingent upon God's promise. His honor is at stake! Abraham's honor is totally rooted in whether or not God will be faithful to his word. How does God answer Abraham's questions, doubts, and fears? Through a mysterious covenant ritual (15:9–21) by which Abraham experienced "dreadful and great darkness" (v. 12)—and which profoundly emphasizes God's commitment to his overarching story and his relationship with Abraham. "And he brought him outside and said, 'Look toward heaven, and number the stars, if you are able to number them.' Then he said to him, 'So shall your offspring be'" (v. 5). Abraham at this stage of his life was already eighty or ninety years old; for him to accrue descendants to the extent promised by God would be to accrue honor of an utterly astounding magnitude. This of course would ultimately glorify God immensely because God will be shown faithful to his promise. He will be known ultimately by all families as the ultimate source of every blessing, the progenitor of all honor and glory in the universe.

16. *Filial piety* means "a virtue of respect for one's parents and ancestors." Jesus is teaching that obedience to God the Father trumps all human family obligations. Filial piety is a dominant characteristic of many Majority World societies. "In more general terms, filial piety means to be good to one's parents; to take care of one's parents; to engage in good conduct not just towards parents but also outside the home so as to bring a good name to one's parents and ancestors; to perform the duties of one's job well so as to obtain the material means to support parents as well as carry out sacrifices to the ancestors; not be rebellious; show love, respect and support; display courtesy; ensure male heirs, uphold fraternity among brothers; wisely advise one's parents, including dissuading them from moral unrighteousness; display sorrow for their sickness and death; and carry out sacrifices after their death." See "Filial piety," *Wikipedia*, http://en.wikipedia.org/wiki/Filial_piety, accessed 17 May 2013.

17. Bartchy, in eds. Neyrey and Stewart, 178.

jealous over the fact that "the LORD had regard for Abel and his offering, but for Cain and his offering he had no regard" (Gen 4:4–5). In revenge, Cain killed Abel. The murder of Cain is symbolized by *blood*.

> And the LORD said, "What have you done? The voice of your brother's blood is crying to me from the ground. And now you are cursed from the ground, which has opened its mouth to receive your brother's blood from your hand" (Gen 4:10–11).

What is the meaning of "your brother's blood is crying to me from the ground"? It is *murder*—the injustice of killing an innocent man. The innocent man's murder and honor demanded vindication.

This, of course, has become a pattern for all of humanity: Honor competition results in violence. Blood is the *result* of honor competition.

Blood as the *cause* of honor competition. In 2 Samuel 4, the account is given of two men, Rechab and Baanah, who murdered Ish-bosheth, son of Saul (2 Sam 4:4–6). Rechab and Baanah thought they could cover up their murder of Ish-bosheth by telling David they were doing him a favor:

> And they said to the king, "Here is the head of Ish-bosheth, the son of Saul, your enemy, who sought your life. The LORD has avenged my lord the king this day on Saul and on his offspring" (2 Sam 4:8).

Rechab and Baanah sorely miscalculated.

> But David answered Rechab and Baanah his brother, the sons of Rimmon the Beerothite, "As the LORD lives, who has redeemed my life out of every adversity, when one told me, 'Behold, Saul is dead,' and thought he was bringing good news, I seized him and killed him at Ziklag, which was the reward I gave him for his news. How much more, when wicked men have killed a righteous man in his own house on his bed, shall I not now require his blood at your hand and destroy you from the earth?" (2 Sam 4:9–11).

David immediately commanded that Rechab and Baanah be executed by "his young men." In fact, "They killed them and cut off their hands and feet and hanged them beside the pool at Hebron" (2 Sam 4:12). What a gruesome result to their miscalculation.

The point here is that Rechab and Baanah thought that David would agree with the default culture of ... *avenging the blood of enemies by killing their offspring.* As a man of God, David would have none of it. But it points to the fact that the default culture recognized that *family blood* was a justifiable catalyst for honor-based violence; family-versus-family revenge was indeed culturally acceptable.

Jerome Neyrey writes:

> [R]elatives who press for the advantage of family members are simply doing their duty to the kinship group, which is an honorable thing. Hence solidarity and loyalty among family members go without saying. Blood replicates the honor of the family.[18]

---

18. Neyrey, *Honor and Shame in the Gospel of Matthew*, 53.

"Blood replicates the honor of the family." Yes, and anyone familiar with a *blood feud* will agree.[19] The definition of a *blood feud* is: "a lengthy conflict between families involving a cycle of retaliatory killings or injury." The cycle of violence is fueled by honor competition.[20]

This is why in honor/shame societies, ethics is generally trumped by honor—usually the honor of the family, *family blood.* The rule of law is practically irrelevant:

> In Sicily too, according to the writer Leonardo Sciascia, himself Sicilian, the family is the state, a be-all-and-end-all in itself. To any Sicilian, "the exact definition of his rights and duties will be that of the family." The mafia, the Camorra of Naples, the Corsicans, the people in Provence and in Spain, share with the Arabs self-regulatory group concepts wholly opposed to the workings of the state with norms legally defined and voluntarily obeyed. Equality under the law, that central constitutional pillar, cannot be reconciled with codes of shame and honor.[21]

Violence of family against family, tribe against tribe, nation against nation is rampant throughout the world. An Internet search of "blood and honor" or "blood feud" brings out the ugly prevalence of this global scourge. Whether it is the Hatfields and the McCoys ... or Sunni versus Shiite ... Arian race against Jewish race ... Chinese against Japanese ... white race versus any others, it is, in essence, all honor-based violence fueled by *blood.*

The blood of Christ is different, hallelujah!

There is a huge contrast between the impact of *blood and honor* in the kingdom of this world and the blood of Christ in the kingdom of God. We have noted that *blood* can be both the result and cause of honor competition; we have noted that the cycle of *blood feuds* can be seemingly endless. But consider these verses that show that the blood of Christ is an entirely different kind of catalyst:

> But now in Christ Jesus you who once were far off have been *brought near by the blood of Christ.* For he himself is our peace, who has made us both one and has broken down in his flesh the dividing wall of hostility ... that he might create in himself one new man in place of the two, so making peace, and might reconcile us both to God in one body through the cross, thereby killing the hostility (Eph 2:13–16). (Emphasis mine.)

> Therefore, brothers, since we have confidence to enter the holy places *by the blood of Jesus,* by the new and living way that he opened for us through the curtain, that is, through his flesh, and since we have a great priest over the house of God, let us draw near with a true heart in full assurance of faith, with our *hearts sprinkled clean from an evil conscience* and our bodies washed with pure water (Hebrews 10:19–22). (Emphasis mine.)

---

19. "Blood feud." Definition from *New Oxford American Dictionary 3rd edition* (New York: Oxford University Press, Inc., 2010). Referenced by Mac OSX 10.8.2.

20. "A blood feud is a cycle of retaliatory violence, with the relatives of someone who has been killed or otherwise wronged or dishonored seeking vengeance by killing or otherwise physically punishing the culprits or their relatives. Historically, the word vendetta has been used to mean a blood feud." See "Famous Blood Feuds," *Wikipedia,* https://en.wikipedia.org/wiki/Feud#Famous_blood_feuds, accessed 17 June 2013.

21. Pryce-Jones, 38.

Blood and honor in this world's kingdom fuels family-against-family violence (blood feuds and vendettas)—but the *blood and honor of Christ* brings healing between families and kinship groups. *Blood and honor* in this world's kingdom is a catalyst for ethnic hatred and genocide—but the *blood and honor of Christ* is a catalyst for the acceptance, even the *celebration* of all ethnic groups and peoples. *Blood and honor* in this world's kingdom opens humanity to the life-killing spirit of jealousy, evil, murder, genocide, the devil—whereas the *"blood of Jesus ... opened for us"* access to the conscience-cleansing Holy Spirit and life-giving presence of God—a new and living way!

Taking in the honor of Christ

Jesus gave a perplexing message to the people in the synagogue:

> Truly, truly, I say to you, unless you eat the flesh of the Son of Man and drink his blood, you have no life in you. Whoever feeds on my flesh and drinks my blood has eternal life, and I will raise him up on the last day. For my flesh is true food, and my blood is true drink. Whoever feeds on my flesh and drinks my blood abides in me, and I in him (John 6:53–56).

The standard evangelical perspective of this passage may be represented by the ESV Study Bible comment:

> *"Unless you eat the flesh of the Son of Man and drink his blood"* cannot be intended literally, for no one ever did that. As Jesus has done frequently in this Gospel, he is speaking in terms of physical items in this world to teach about spiritual realities. Here, to "eat" Jesus' flesh has the spiritual meaning of trusting or believing in him, especially in his death for the sins of mankind. ... Similarly, to "drink his blood" means to trust in his atoning death, which is represented by the shedding of his blood.[22]

We must obviously agree that *eating the flesh* and *drinking the blood of Christ* is not to be taken literally. However, if in ancient Hebrew and Roman culture "blood replicates the honor of the family," then I must ask: Could it be that when Jesus told his disciples to "drink his blood," he was saying that his followers should trust and believe in his life and atonement so deeply, so comprehensively, that *his very honor* would be spiritually ingested into their own lives? Isn't it likely that Jesus was pressing for something more than a mere cognitive trust? Doesn't the physicality of Christ's words imply that he was pressing for his disciples to actually *experience* something visceral, perhaps to *feel* the very honor of Jesus? Perhaps this is how Christ's life—his very attitudes and behaviors—were reproduced in the lives of the disciples in the early church.

This brings us to the end of our exploration of the overlapping dynamic of *name, kinship,* and *blood,* and the role these had in the honor/shame societies of the Bible. Let's summarize:

---

22. *ESV Study Bible* (Wheaton, IL: Good News Publishers/Crossway Books, 2009), Kindle edition locations 130664–130669).

A kingdom summary—dark side and bright side

Name/kinship/blood—kingdom of this world vs. kingdom-reign of God		
	Kingdom of this world	Kingdom-reign of God
NAME	NAME • Self-derived honor pursuits ("let us make a name for ourselves"—Gen 11:4) is rebellion against God • Results in God's judgment, confusion, creates honor deficit that fuels honor competition and honor-based violence	NAME • God-derived honor ("I will bless you and make your name great"—Gen 12:2) creates an honor surplus that can overcome honor-based conflict and violence • God's passion to glorify his name is at the crux of Christ's work on the cross —for the healing of the nations
	KINSHIP • The family is basic unit of society • Honor competition sometimes breeds strife and violence • Breeding ground for ethnocentrism • Breeding ground for fathers who abuse power, cause oppression	KINSHIP • God created a kinship group through Abraham; it is through this honored "family" that all the rest of the kinship groups of the world will be blessed • The church is a global family of families or kinship groups • The local church is God's family and is the primary expression of God's kingdom on earth • We have a new Father of authority, love, and grace
	BLOOD • Stimulates hostility, causes violence and war; catalyst for cyclical pathology of violence • Fuels violence out of "honor-deficit" • Generates family-against-family conflict, blood feuds, vendettas • Fuels ethnocentrism, racial hatred, self-protection; kills community • Opens humanity to the life-killing spirit of jealousy, murder, the devil	BLOOD • Kills hostility, absorbs violence, makes peace; catalyst for healing and reconciliation • Creates peace out of "honor-surplus" in Christ • Heals family-against-family conflict • Celebrates all ethnicities, creates a new community, "one new man" • Opens humanity to the conscience-cleansing Holy Spirit and life-giving presence of God

Figure 2.22: Name, kinship, blood—kingdom of this world vs. kingdom-reign of God

Action points

- *Fast-forward:* To explore how the *dynamic of name/kinship/blood* can shape a contextualized presentation of the gospel of Christ, turn to Section 3, Chapter 8.

- *Reflect:* What are you more proud of? Your original family name or your family-in-Christ name—"Christian?" Explain.

- *Bible study:* In the Great Commission, our Lord commanded us to make disciples of all nations, "baptizing them in the name of the Father and of the Son and of the Holy Spirit" (Mat 28:19). How does this study impact your understanding of what it means to be "baptized in the name"? Given that the word "in" is also translated as "into" in the New Testament, consider the implications of being baptized "into the honor of God."

- *Teaching:* Based on Ephesians 2:15, develop a lesson on the power of the blood of Christ to kill hostility, bring peace in the midst of conflict, cleanse from sin, heal racially inflicted wounds, bring together people of differing social status, and create a new community—"one new humanity"—of radical acceptance and grace.
- *Mission:* What can you do in your cross-cultural ministry to create a culture of honor by which people—both believers and seekers—experience the honor of being part of, or touched by, the family of God? How can you help them *experience* the honor and acceptance of Jesus and his kingdom and desire the honor-surplus that comes from knowing Christ?

Honor/Shame Dynamic #9: Purity

Why is this important?

- Describes how *impurity* and *uncleanness* relegated people as low-status social "outsiders" in a condition of shame—whereas *holiness* and *cleanness* signified people as "insiders" with high honor-status.

- Explains how levitical purity codes and the cycle of sanctification—strange to Western sensibilities—are crucial to understanding the radical nature of Jesus' ministry.

- Reviews examples in the Gospels in which Jesus transcends Old Testament laws and boundaries of ritual cleansing—offering his cure for people in shame due to moral failure, disease, disfiguration, or death.

- Explores the importance of communicating that the gospel of Christ offers not only a cure for sin and guilt—*but also for uncleanness and shame.*

Definition

Purity is the condition or perception that one is acceptable before a holy God according to a specific system of codes. These codes define boundaries for what is holy, common, clean, unclean, and

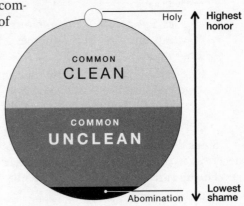

Figure 2.23: From the lowest shame (abomination) to the highest honor (holiness)

161

abomination. Figure 2.23 (on the previous page) is a conceptual diagram showing the range of uncleanness/shame to the purity of holiness/honor.

Jesus heals a leper

Let's consider a passage of Scripture linking both Old and New Testament concepts about purity. It is the account of Jesus healing a leper:

> While he was in one of the cities, there came a man full of leprosy. And when he saw Jesus, he fell on his face and begged him, "Lord, if you will, you can make me clean." And Jesus stretched out his hand and touched him, saying, "I will; be clean." And immediately the leprosy left him. And he charged him to tell no one, but "go and show yourself to the priest, and make an offering for your cleansing, as Moses commanded, for a proof to them" (Luke 5:12–14).

It is impossible to grasp the depth of shame and exclusion of the "man full of leprosy"—and the corresponding power and brilliance of what Jesus does for him—without first reading Leviticus 13 and 14. These long chapters are full of peculiar and practical detail concerning leprosy and other variations of skin disease. God's people are told what they should do when confronting this disease. Here is a summary of how a leper is to live:

> The leprous person who has the disease shall wear torn clothes and let the hair of his head hang loose, and he shall cover his upper lip and cry out, "Unclean, unclean." He shall remain unclean as long as he has the disease. He is unclean. He shall live alone. His dwelling shall be outside the camp (Lev 13:45–46).[1]

Note three things:

- *The leprous person is to make himself unattractive:* He "shall wear torn clothes and let the hair of his head hang loose." The first thing a person in shame wants to do is hide or deny the effects of their problem. But leprous persons were not allowed to cover up their disease or pretend that they were normal.

- *The leprous person is to announce his uncleanness:* "he shall ... cry out, 'Unclean, unclean.'" This is another prohibition against hiding one's disease or shame.

- *The leprous person is to be isolated and segregated:* "He shall live alone. His dwelling shall be outside the camp." The health of the larger community could not be compromised by the disease of the individual; hence, isolation was mandated.

Since the Jews had their identity rooted in their community, the pain and degree of exclusion for *the man full of leprosy* was extreme. Of course, there were good medical reasons for isolating people with this disease. Skin diseases were

---

1. Leviticus 13:1–59 describes the complex laws and process for diagnosing whether a person has leprosy and how he or she should be treated. Leviticus 14:1–57 describes the complex laws and process for cleansing lepers.

often contagious. God was providing clear boundaries that would help them to ensure their own survival.

More than survival ... *holiness!*

But there was more to this than biological survival. The Hebrews had entered into a covenant with the one and only Creator Yahweh—the Almighty holy God, the relational God, who tells them through Moses:

> For I am the LORD your God. Consecrate yourselves therefore, and be holy, for I am holy. You shall not defile yourselves. ... For I am the LORD who brought you up out of the land of Egypt to be your God. You shall therefore be holy, for I am holy (Lev 11:44–45).

And any physical flaw, any disease, would render the person unfit for the presence of God:

> For no one who has a blemish shall draw near, a man blind or lame, or one who has a mutilated face or a limb too long, or a man who has an injured foot or an injured hand, or a hunchback or a dwarf or a man with a defect in his sight or an itching disease or scabs or crushed testicles (Lev 21:18–20).

Leviticus provides the instructions to a fallen people called by an infinite holy God—One who is wholly *other,* wholly *separate* from his creation. Leviticus instructs God's people how to live in relationship with him. *How can this be done? How can dirty, sinful people live in fellowship with a perfectly pure and holy God? Isn't that dangerous?* Leviticus provides detailed instructions for the Hebrew children to relate to this holy and very relational God—through worship and in daily life. These laws are rooted fully in God's relational being and purpose.

Everything in life was categorized in relation to the ultimate standard of holiness. Things not holy were considered *common,* and things *common* were either *clean* or *unclean* (Lev 10:10). God's people could transition from *unclean* to *clean* to *holy*—and transition down from *holy* to *clean* to *unclean*—all in a cycle of sanctification governed by purity codes.[2] God desired relationship, so he instructed his people on how to prepare for and engage with him in worship.

> On the basis of Levitical law, everything in life was either holy or common for the Hebrews. Those things determined common were subdivided into categories of clean and unclean. ... Clean things might become holy through sanctification or unclean through pollution. Holy things could be profaned and become common or even unclean. Unclean things could be cleansed and then consecrated or sanctified to be made holy.

> Common (i.e., clean) things or persons devoted to God become holy through the mutual efforts of human activity and sanctifying (or consecrating) and of the Lord as the sanctifier. Uncleanness maybe caused

---

2. Concerning the levitical priests, Ezekiel was told by God: "They shall teach my people the difference between the holy and the common, and show them how to distinguish between the unclean and the clean" (Eze 44:23).

by disease, contamination, infection, or sin; it could be cleansed only by ritual washing and sacrifice. Hence the importance of the instructions regarding sacrifices in the book of Leviticus. The presence of the holy God resided in the Israelite camp within the tabernacle, and therefore it was imperative to prevent the unclean from coming into contact with the holy. Failure to prevent contamination resulted in death (see Num 19:13, 20).[3]

The actions of people in the cycle of sanctification were of two types, as shown in the diagram below[4]—moving toward honor and inclusion (the holy), or moving toward shame and exclusion (the unclean). This was a most serious issue for God's people Israel.

(1) Actions moving a person toward holiness, toward God (inclusion and honor):

- CLEANSE: People who were *unclean* needed to go through ritual cleansing in order to become *clean*. There were rules for every sort of uncleanness: bodily and sexual discharges including menstruation (Lev 15; 18:19), touching someone with disease (Lev 13), touching a corpse (Lev 22:4–6), eating unclean food (Lev 11), and various diseases of which the worst was leprosy (Lev 13).

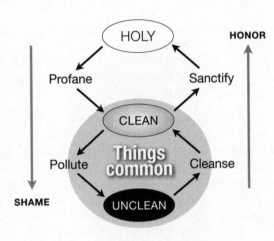

Figure 2.24: The cycle of sanctification

- SANCTIFY: If a person was *clean*, he or she could sanctify himself or herself to become holy (or separate), in order to enter the presence of God. This was necessary for the levitical priests in order for them to serve in the temple.

(2) Actions moving a person away from holiness, away from God (toward exclusion and shame):

- PROFANE: A priest who was holy could become *profaned* by association with anything common (Lev 21). In turn, he would have to be *sanctified*—a ritual done in cooperation with God—in order to regain his "holiness" and the ability to enter the presence of a holy God.

- POLLUTE: A person who was clean could be polluted and thereby become unclean by a variety of things: sexual activity, menstruation, touching a

3. Andrew E. Hill and John F. Walton, *A Survey of the Old Testament* (Grand Rapids, MI: Zondervan, 2009), 133–34.
4. Diagram adapted from Hill and Walton, "The Cycle of Sanctification," 133.

corpse, eating unclean food, or having a disease. The unclean person would then have to follow the appropriate laws of cleansing to once again regain his or her position of cleanness.[5]

Centuries after God gave the law to Moses, God spoke through the prophet Ezekiel that judgment was coming to the priests because, they have "done violence to my law and have profaned my holy things. They have made no distinction between the holy and the common, neither have they taught the difference between the unclean and the clean, and they have disregarded my Sabbaths, so that I am profaned among them" (Eze 22:26).

Uncleanness and shame

With regard to Jesus and the "man full of leprosy," what may we observe?

First, we observe that the man *full of leprosy* had no hope of ever becoming clean again, of ever regaining his honor. He had no hope of ever being reaccepted in his own community. He was relegated to darkness—a life of rejection for the rest of his days. He embodied despair and shame ... *except that Jesus came to town.* And so the man full of leprosy fell on his face and *begged* Jesus to cure him. In full view of his watching world, his desperate last gasp for air in a world of suffocating shame was an act of courage and vulnerability: "Lord, if you will, you can make me clean."

Second, Jesus touched the "man full of leprosy"—and remarkably, Jesus did not become unclean! His personal holiness was untainted. This was unthinkable to the Jewish mind.

Knowing that leprosy was an extreme form of uncleanness, and that uncleanness is easily transferred from one person to another, it is striking to ponder what *other transfer* took place in the interaction between Jesus and the "man full of leprosy." *Was the leprous man's disease and shame absorbed into the compassionate perfection and honor of Jesus? Was the holy purity of Christ somehow transmitted to the man full of leprosy, making him clean?[6] What new reality was Jesus introducing?*

Third, we observe that Jesus was concerned for the man's reintegration and acceptance in his own community: "Go and show yourself to the priest, and make an offering for your cleansing, as Moses commanded, for a proof to them." Jesus wanted the "man full of leprosy" to have his honor restored among his own family, friends, and community. This could only be done if the proper cleansing rituals were observed as prescribed in Leviticus 14.

This short account of Jesus healing the "man full of leprosy" hints at a complex world of boundaries, regulations, and rituals for God's people—all for the purpose of relationship with an infinite God who delights in being known and worshiped. This world was defined by the Mosaic law, and it ensured their survival, brought social order, created culture, and facilitated worship of their holy God.

---

5. See Ezekiel 16:1–62. This chapter describes "The Lord's Faithless Bride" and vividly shows how great uncleanness corresponded to deep shame in ancient Jewish culture.

6. The concept of "transmitting holiness" is contained in Ezekiel: "And he said to me, 'This is the place where the priests shall boil the guilt offering and the sin offering, and where they shall bake the grain offering, in order not to bring them out into the outer court and so *transmit holiness* to the people'" (Eze 46:20; cf. 44:19, emphasis mine).

David deSilva describes in rich detail the mental maps[7] that the Jews had regarding the holy, the clean, and the unclean. They are: *maps of people, maps of space, maps of time, dietary regulations,* and *maps of the body.*

Purity maps

1. Maps of people: Observe the diagram below (Figure 2.25) The spectrum ranged from the *high priest* at the highest level of honor, purity, and acceptance—to the priests, then the Levites, then the lay people of Israel, then the Jews of questionable lineage—down to the *Gentiles* at the lowest level of uncleanness, rejection, shame. In the diagram below, the squares represent the levitical priesthood. The circles represent the people of God, Israel. The squares connote *being inside of, yet separate, from the rest of Israel.* The circular shape represents Israel's being *inside of, yet separate, from the rest of the world*—from the nondescript, amorphous shape of the world around them—the world of non-Jews, the Gentiles.

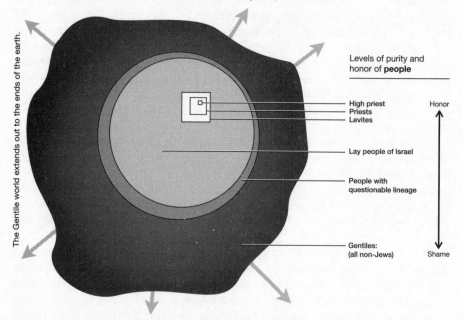

Figure 2.25: A conceptual "map of people" as understood by the ancient Hebrew world [8]

2. Maps of space: The spectrum ranged from the "outside" world of other people and nations, to the "inside" nation of Israel, to the most holy city of Jerusalem (the city of Zion, Ps 48:1), to the temple with its outer court, the inner court, and ultimately to the Holy of Holies—the place of highest honor and greatest danger, for this is where the glory of God appeared.[9]

3. Maps of time: "Remember the Sabbath day, to keep it holy" (Ex 20:8). In a world

---

7. deSilva, 256–69.

8. This diagram is extrapolated from deSilva, 256–57.

9. "Issues of ritual purity dominated the life of ancient Israel, which explains the highly symbolic divisions of the Jerusalem temple into progressively more sacred space as one drew closer to the holy of holies, and as fewer people could enter each successive court." (Klein, Blomberg, and Hubbard, 81).

without weekends,[10] how unusual it was for a society to have a day set apart for God—for worship and rest. One day out of seven was to be holy. In addition, every seventh year, farmers were to forego planting their crops so the land could rest (Lev 25:3–4). Moreover, every fiftieth year was the Year of Jubilee "when each of you shall return to his property and each of you shall return to his clan. That fiftieth year shall be a jubilee for you; in it you shall neither sow nor reap what grows of itself nor gather the grapes from the undressed vines. For it is a jubilee. It shall be holy to you. You may eat the produce of the field" (vv. 10–12).

4. Dietary regulations: Jews were restricted in what they could eat. Food was either clean or unclean. Particularly onerous was the eating of pork, but many other restrictions were given (Lev 11). Given that eating is a daily necessity, the Hebrews were reminded in every gathering around food that they were distinct and separate from the rest of humanity because of their covenant with God. The awareness of who was an *insider (thus, honorable),* and who was an *outsider (thus, shameful),* was reinforced with every meal.

5. Maps of the body: The book of Leviticus gives significant attention to what enters and exits the human body. Maintaining purity relative to blood, sexual fluids, and other discharges was vitally important (Lev 17–18). According to deSilva, "Concern over what enters and exits a body also correlates with the larger concern over what enters and exits the social body and the desire for regulating that flow. ... It comes as no surprise that so much discussion of pollution with regard to the human body focuses on surfaces (clothing and the skin), on fluids that cross through the gates of the body, and on bodies that have crossed the boundary between life and death."[11]

What's the point? Here are the main points thus far concerning *purity codes* and the pivotal cultural value of honor and shame:

- In the social world of God's people, the Jews, in both Old and New Testaments, the laws and practices about purity and uncleanness corresponded to honor and shame. Observe this dynamic in the diagram below.[12]

- The observance of purity codes was required by God in order for his people to remain in fellowship with him—and when they lost fellowship, to regain it through cleansing and sanctification.

- What Jesus introduced in healing the "man full of leprosy"

Figure 2.26: Honor/acceptance vs. shame/exclusion

---

10. deSilva, 260.
11. Ibid., 262.
12. Adapted from a diagram by Jayson Georges, "From Shame to Honor: A Theological Reading of Romans for Honor/Shame Contexts," *Missiology: An International Review,* 38 (2010): 298.

is what David deSilva calls the "rewriting of purity maps."[13] Jesus violated many purity codes by transcending them and introducing a new set of variables for determining what is common or holy, unclean or clean, outside the group or inside the group, shameful or honorable.

Note: The reader is encouraged to examine Appendix 3, "'Jesus stories' involving uncleanness/shame." This chart examines the occurrences in the Gospels which involve Jesus and people with whom he interacted who had the condition of uncleanness. Below we will consider just a few examples:

Jesus cleanses a leper (Mat 8:2-4; Mark 1:40-44; Luke 5:12-14)

- A leper was considered profoundly unclean and defiled. A person would have become unclean by touching the leper; even to be in the same space as the leper would result in uncleanness. (See Lev 14:33-57; a house would be unclean if a person had lived there with leprosy.)

- Radically, Jesus touched the leper. However, Jesus did not become unclean; rather, Jesus' healed the disease and cleansed the leper of his uncleanness. The purity of Jesus was greater than the defilement of the leper.

- The leper was told to show himself to the priest (Luke 5:14), following the laws of Moses (Lev 14:1-32), and thus have his honor restored in the community. The man with leprosy experienced a reversal of his honor-status.

Jesus visits the house of Simon the Leper (Mat 26:6-13; Mark 14:3-9)

- Just before entering his Passion of *Passover meal, betrayal, arrest, flogging, crucifixion, and burial,* Jesus entered the house of Simon the Leper. His house was probably a leper colony.[14] Jesus was anointed there by the woman with the "alabaster flask of very expensive ointment" (Mat 26:7).

- Jesus violated the purity code by going into a leper's house. Jesus entered the intimate space of the shamed and unclean; it is here where he received great affection and honor before enduring the shame of the cross (Heb 12:2). What a paradox!

- Jesus honored Simon the leper by entering his home, his private space. What a privilege for a leper to host the Son of God!

- Jesus profoundly credited the woman who poured the expensive ointment on his feet, raising her honor-status for all time (Mat 26:12-13).

Jesus restores a woman with a discharge of blood (Mat 9:18-26; Mark 5:21-34; Luke 8:40-56)

- A woman with a discharge of blood was considered profoundly unclean (see Lev 15:19-30 for the social implications). The woman in this story had a perpetual discharge of blood and was therefore perpetually unclean, excluded, shamed. In her desperation, she pressed through the crowd

---

13. deSilva, 280.
14. Ibid., 284.

(Mark 5:27), transferring her uncleanness to everyone she touched, and likely incurred everyone's scorn.

- Jesus did not scold the woman. He simply asked, "Who touched my garments?" (Mark 5:30)—as if he didn't know. This challenged the perpetually unclean, perpetually excluded woman, to identify herself. Jesus' question drew her from out of the shadows into the light, affirming her identity, essential dignity, and the honor of her faith—all in the very public presence of the crowd.

- The woman touched the garment of Jesus and was made clean; "the flow of blood dried up" (Mark 5:29), and she was healed.

- Jesus violated the purity code: When he was touched by the perpetually unclean woman, he retained his holiness and purity while she was made clean.

- Jesus eliminated her shame by cleansing her, thus implicitly restoring her to her community. He then further raised her honor-status, saying, "Daughter, your faith has made you well; go in peace, and be healed of your disease" (Mark 5:34). Calling her "daughter" made her part of his kinship group and constituted a rise in her honor-status.

Jesus raises to life a girl who was dead (Mat 9:18–19, 23–26; Mark 5:21–24, 35–43; Luke 8:40–42, 49–56)

- Jairus, a ruler of the synagogue, pleaded with Jesus to come heal his daughter who was at the point of death. By the time Jesus got to his house, the girl was dead (Mark 5:22–23, 35).

- Any corpse was considered unclean. Anyone who would touch the corpse also became unclean (Lev 22:4–6).

- Jesus did not hesitate to touch the corpse, "taking her by the hand" (Mark 5:41). He then spoke to her: "Little girl, I say to you, arise." The little girl was raised to life.

- Jesus was not made unclean by touching the girl. Rather, the girl whose corpse was profoundly unclean (also connoting deep shame) was raised to life. The word spoken to her, "Arise," also symbolized a rise in her honor-status.

Jesus heals a demon-possessed man who lived "among the tombs" (Mat 8:28–34; Mark 5:1–20; Luke 8:26–39)

- The man was unclean in four ways. First, in all likelihood, the man was a Gentile.[15] Second, he was possessed by an unclean spirit (Mark 5:2). Third, he was naked in public (Lev 18). And fourth, he lived not in a house but among

---

15. Matthew's account says, "When he came to the other side" (Mat 8:28). The *ESV Study Bible* says of this verse: "'Other side' often marks the movement from a Jewish to a Gentile territory and vice versa." (Kindle edition location 117709). The fact that there were pigs nearby also strongly suggests this was a Gentile area that Jews avoided. Moreover, when they returned back to the other side, they encountered "a man named Jairus, who was a ruler of the synagogue" (Luke 8:41), obviously a Jew; this only reinforces the contrast that one side of Lake Galilee was dominated by Jews, the other side by Gentiles.

the tombs, among the dead (Luke 8:27; Lev 18). All of these criteria together made this man into an extreme outcast at the lowest level of uncleanness, defilement, and shame. He was in the category of *abomination*.

- The unclean spirit was named Legion, "for many demons had entered him" (Luke 8:30). The "Legion" exercised supernatural power and violence (v. 29).

- Jesus ordered the demons to come out of the man (Luke 8:31). The demons entered a herd of pigs, which in turn, "rushed down the steep bank into the lake and drowned" (v. 33).

- Jesus told the man to "Return to your home" (Luke 8:39)—and Mark adds, "to your friends" (Mark 5:19)—"and declare how much God has done for you." The man was even restored to his community! The Bible says, "And he went away, proclaiming throughout the whole city how much Jesus had done for him." Jesus came to this one who was horribly enslaved, filthy and ugly, and made him clean, beautiful, and productive for the kingdom.

- Jesus had sailed with his disciples to the other side of the Sea of Galilee to "the country of the Garasenes" (Luke 8:26) for one purpose: *to cleanse and set free the man who was possessed by a legion of demons.* Jesus entered a domain of profound uncleanness—the tombs of the dead. He confronts a naked man of ultimate defilement who is possessed by a group of demons, "an unclean spirit." Despite the supernatural power of the Legion, along with the filth, violence and shame imposed on the man, Jesus interacted with the Legion without fear. Jesus was in complete control. His sense of *calm* was evidenced by his "conversation" with the unclean spirit (vv. 26–30). Mark's account says Jesus rebuked the legion, "Come out of the man, you unclean spirit!" (Mark 5:8). Jesus demonstrated his mighty power over every degree of uncleanness, every evil spirit, every darkness.

Jesus has "redrawn the purity maps"

Jesus did the unthinkable when he boldly and compassionately crossed the boundaries between the clean and the unclean, the honored and the shamed— and he did this without himself becoming the least bit polluted or losing honor. David deSilva says it well:

> The Gospels thus present Jesus encountering a stream of the ritually impure and potentially polluting people, but in the encounter, their contagion does not defile Jesus; rather his holiness purges their pollutions, renders them clean and integrates them again into the mainstream of Jewish society where they can reclaim their birthright, as it were, among the people of God.[16]

When Jesus washed the disciples' feet, Peter protested, "You shall never wash my feet" (John 13:8). Jesus replied that he *had* to wash Peter's feet in order for them to share in fellowship. Then, this exchange:

Simon Peter said to him, "Lord, not my feet only but also my hands and

---

16. deSilva, 284–85.

my head!" Jesus said to him, "The one who has bathed does not need to wash, except for his feet, but is completely clean. And you are clean, but not every one of you" (John 13:9–10).

"And you are clean." What a pronouncement! For the Son of God to say this to Peter implied that Peter's *being clean before God* hinged on one thing alone—Peter's abiding submission and devotion to his Lord and Savior. No other ritual cleansing needed.

Redefining the clean, the honorable, the "insiders"

Beyond the Gospels in the New Testament, the language of purity codes—of *clean* and *unclean, sanctified* and *holy*—is retained. After all, it was part of Jewish culture, and to a lesser extent Greco-Roman culture as well.[17] However, the language is repurposed to describe various aspects of the salvation and lifestyle of believers—and of their community, the church.

The rewriting of purity maps was no small revelation for the early church. In Acts 10:1–48 the story is told of how God supernaturally brings about this revelation—through different visions given to two very different people in different locations. The story involved Peter and Cornelius—a God-fearing Gentile, a centurion of "the Italian Cohort" in Caesarea.

Cornelius was the first in this story to receive a vision from God. An angel gave him instructions to "send men to Joppa" and bring back to Caesarea "one Simon who is called Peter" (Acts 10:5). So he sent two servants and a soldier to Joppa. As they were approaching the city, Peter was up on his housetop praying. He got hungry and while waiting for the food, he fell into a trance (v. 10) ...

> and saw the heavens opened and something like a great sheet descending, being let down by its four corners upon the earth. In it were all kinds of animals and reptiles and birds of the air. And there came a voice to him: "Rise, Peter; kill and eat." But Peter said, "By no means, Lord; for I have never eaten anything that is common or unclean." And the voice came to him again a second time, "What God has made clean, do not call common" (vv. 11–15).

Peter protests vigorously three times: "By no means, Lord; for I have never eaten anything that is common or unclean" (v. 14). But the Lord insists: "What God has made clean, do not call common" (v. 15).

God had sovereignly arranged for Peter to violate his purity codes of not eating unclean food nor associating with Gentiles. Escorted by the centurion's two servants and a soldier, Peter traveled to Caesarea to visit the Italian Gentile, Cornelius, who just days before had a vision of sending for a man of God named Peter. When Peter finally got to the home of Cornelius, the whole extended family was there, along with close friends (v. 24). Cornelius and his clan fell down and worshiped Peter (v. 25) but Peter told them, "Stand up, I too am a man."

---

17. "Both in the Greco-Roman world and to a much more rigorous extent in the Jewish world, there is the conviction that the person who would be close to God must be pure and whole like God. Defilement and unholiness separated people from contact with the pure and holy God." Ibid., 247–48.

Peter remarked on the profound awkwardness of the situation. "You yourselves know how unlawful it is for a Jew to associate with or to visit anyone of another nation, but God has shown me that I should not call any person common or unclean" (v. 28). Peter called it "unlawful." It was probably as shocking for Cornelius and his Gentile family and friends—as for Peter—to all be in the same room together.

And what a get-together this must have been! Here was Cornelius and his extended family, plus his friends—amounting to perhaps twenty people. Add to that Peter and "some of the brothers" from Joppa (v. 23), and we can estimate that there were perhaps twenty-five people. It was likely a densely packed gathering. I wonder if everyone had a place to sit down.

Finally, it was story time; everyone listening. Cornelius told of how an angel appeared, telling him to send for a man called Peter. A couple of days had passed to follow through on the angel's instructions. And now, miraculously, the man for whom he had sent was before them.

Intense anticipation

Then, with what I imagine was a collective, breathless anticipation "in the presence of God," Cornelius invited Peter to share all "that you have been commanded by the Lord" (v. 33).

> So Peter opened his mouth and said: "Truly I understand that God shows no partiality, but in every nation anyone who fears him and does what is right is acceptable to him" (vv. 34–35).

Peter continued and shared the gospel story. The blessing of the gospel of peace in Jesus Christ—his perfect life, his sacrificial death and resurrection for salvation, his launching a new community of faith—was now available to *everyone*. "To [Jesus] all the prophets bear witness that everyone who believes in him receives forgiveness of sins through his name" (v. 43). Then:

> While Peter was still saying these things, the Holy Spirit fell on all who heard the word. And the believers from among the circumcised who had come with Peter were amazed, because the gift of the Holy Spirit was poured out even on the Gentiles. For they were hearing them speaking in tongues and extolling God. Then Peter declared, "Can anyone withhold water for baptizing these people, who have received the Holy Spirit just as we have?" And he commanded them to be baptized in the name of Jesus Christ. Then they asked him to remain for some days (vv. 44–48).

God's kingdom of grace, inclusion, and honor in Jesus Christ had broken into Cornelius's home. The breakthrough was made. The barriers, hostilities, and dividing walls were broken down by the atonement of Christ (Eph 2:14). For some two thousand years, Gentiles were considered excluded from the people of God. From the Jewish perspective, Gentiles were lower-status peoples: "alienated from the commonwealth of Israel and strangers to the covenants of promise, having no hope and without God in the world." They "once were far off" from the honor of God's presence, but now have been "brought near by the blood of Christ"

(Eph 2:12–13). Cornelius and his household, along with Peter and his brothers, experienced this intense honor-lifting drama firsthand.

Gentiles could now become full-fledged members of the church. They could be part of the "one new man" (Eph 2:15), the body of Christ. And all this without the ritual of circumcision or having to comply with other Jewish purity codes. The distinction of being part of God's *honorific people* was now available and open to *all peoples.*[18]

This created no small dispute among many of Jesus' disciples and other Jewish believers. Even though Peter went to Jerusalem and explained the situation (Acts 11:2) to the believers there, those of the "circumcision party" criticized Peter, saying, "You went to uncircumcised men and ate with them" (v. 3). The dissension was to be expected, for what Peter introduced to God's people was radical. Dean Flemming rightly asserts, "This was no less than a cultural revolution."[19]

Of course, Peter needed to tell them the long, odd story. The coordinated visions ... the sheets ... the food ... the voice from God ... Peter's protest ... God's insistence ... the knock at his door ... the trip to Caesarea escorted by two servants and a Roman soldier ... the awkward entrance into Cornelius's home ... the invitation to speak God's message ... Peter's sharing the gospel of Jesus Christ ... and finally, the power of the Holy Spirit in the glorious salvation of Cornelius and his household (vv. 5–17).

Stunned into silence

The Jewish believers were completely stunned. "When they heard these things they fell silent" (v. 18). Words failed them. We do not know how long this silence lasted. Was it thirty seconds or thirty minutes? Their silence makes sense. Two thousand years of Jewish culture, tradition, and purity codes were being redefined. The questions—*Who is pure? Who is an "insider"? Who is honorable?*—were being understood in a completely new light.

The new revelation was not easily accepted.[20] The new purity codes were not received by all the believers, and so the Jerusalem Council was called in order to gather the leaders of the church—which by this time included the Apostle Paul—around this issue.

It was the first big dissension in the church (Acts 15:2). Paul and Barnabas were appointed by the church in Antioch to go to Jerusalem and thoroughly discuss the issue with the other church leaders. There they met Peter and the other apostles and elders.

> And after there had been much debate, Peter stood up and said to them, "Brothers, you know that in the early days God made a choice among you, that by my mouth the Gentiles should hear the word of the gospel and believe. And God, who knows the heart, bore witness to them, by giving them the Holy Spirit just as he did to us, and he made no distinction between

---

18. Being part of God's honorific people was not just *available*—it was God's *purpose* that this honor-laden blessing be *intentionally extended* to all peoples. The Lord's church *gets to be in on it!*

19. Flemming, Kindle edition locations 1640–41.

20. Later in Paul's ministry, the threat of Gentiles and Jews being in the same sacred space was, for the unbelieving Jews, a catalyst for violence. This is evident when Paul was arrested in the temple at Jerusalem over the accusation that he had "brought Greeks into the temple and has defiled this holy place" (Acts 21:28). Violent beatings against Paul erupted over this false allegation: "They were seeking to kill him" (v. 31).

us and them, having cleansed their hearts by faith. Now, therefore, why are you putting God to the test by placing a yoke on the neck of the disciples that neither our fathers nor we have been able to bear? But we believe that we will be saved through the grace of the Lord Jesus, just as they will" (vv. 7–11).

Peter retained the levitical concept of cleansing when he explained: "and he made no distinction between us and them [Gentiles], having *cleansed* their hearts by faith" (v. 9). (Emphasis mine.)

"And all the assembly fell silent" (v. 12). The Jewish Christian leaders (they were all Jewish at this time) were stunned once again.

James then contributed to Peter's argument. He quoted the prophet Amos[21] in a passage that both honored the people of Israel and included the Gentiles in God's good purposes.

After this I will return, and I will rebuild the tent of David that has fallen; I will rebuild its ruins, and I will restore it, that the remnant of mankind may seek the Lord, and all the Gentiles who are called by my name, says the Lord, who makes these things known from of old (Acts 15:16–18).

Gentiles were specifically in God's plan and purpose! It was predicated on God's people Israel being rebuilt and restored!

And the conclusion? The church leaders crafted a letter to the church at Antioch (vv. 23–29), with these key sentences:

For it has seemed good to the Holy Spirit and to us to lay on you no greater burden than these requirements: that you abstain from what has been sacrificed to idols, and from blood, and from what has been strangled, and from sexual immorality. If you keep yourselves from these, you will do well. Farewell (vv. 28–29).

No circumcision required!

So being saved *by faith* in Jesus Christ—this is what mattered (nothing more, nothing less). This salvation gave both Jews and Gentiles the *cleansing* they needed to be acceptable to a holy God.

Purity maps re-imagined and redrawn

We have observed that the purity maps of the Old Testament were re-imagined and redrawn, and that purity language was retained by Peter, Paul, and other New Testament authors.

The Apostle John uses similar language to describe how Christians can remain in fellowship with one another and with God. He also explains that it is the blood of Jesus which has the power to *cleanse* God's people from their sins.

But if we walk in the light, as he is in the light, we have fellowship with one another, and the blood of Jesus his Son *cleanses* us from all sin. If we say we have no sin, we deceive ourselves, and the truth is not in us. If we confess our sins, he is faithful and just to forgive us our sins and to *cleanse*

---

21. Amos 9:11–12

us from all unrighteousness (1 John 1:7–9). (Emphasis mine.)

Jesus prayed to the Father (in what is known as his High Priestly Prayer) for those who would believe, "Sanctify them in the truth; your word is truth" (John 17:17). The process of sanctification—to be set apart in order to draw near to Almighty God—was redefined. Sanctification went from being primarily an *external* practice of cleansing rituals to primarily an *internal* cleansing with God's truth.[22] Paul expanded on this concept when he wrote that Christ nurtures his body, the church, by the cleansing power of God's Word:

> that he might *sanctify* her, having *cleansed* her by the *washing* of water with the word (Eph 5:26). (Emphasis mine.)

Similar to Peter, Paul used purity language to describe the core identity of believers.[23]

> To the church of God that is in Corinth, to those *sanctified* in Christ Jesus … (1 Cor 1:2). (Emphasis mine.)

Paul also used purity language to reinforce the extreme importance of moral purity for the people of God:

> Or do you not know that the unrighteous will not inherit the kingdom of God? Do not be deceived: neither the sexually immoral, nor idolaters, nor adulterers, nor men who practice homosexuality, nor thieves, nor the greedy, nor drunkards, nor revilers, nor swindlers will inherit the kingdom of God. And such were some of you. But you were *washed,* you were *sanctified,* you were justified in the name of the Lord Jesus Christ and by the Spirit of our God (1 Cor 6:9–11). (Emphasis mine.)

> For this is the will of God, your *sanctification:* that you abstain from sexual immorality (1 Thes 4:3). (Emphasis mine.)

James uses similar conceptual language, but adds the idea of moving closer to God, as the levitical priests would draw near to God (Lev 9:7). "Draw near to God, and he will draw near to you. Cleanse your hands, you sinners, and purify your hearts, you double-minded" (Jam 4:8).

Other uses of purity language in the New Testament

Paul even gave expression to his calling as an apostle to the Gentiles using purity language—as though he was a temple priest:

> to be a minister of Christ Jesus to the Gentiles in the priestly service of the gospel of God, so that the offering of the Gentiles may be *acceptable, sanctified* by the Holy Spirit (Rom 15:16). (Emphasis mine.)

---

22. The word *primarily* is important here. Even in the Old Testament, God expected that his commandments be followed not only as an external ritual but also as an internal heartfelt devotion. "And now, Israel, what does the LORD your God require of you, but to fear the LORD your God, to walk in all his ways, to love him, to serve the LORD your God with all your heart and with all your soul" (Deu 10:12).

23. See also Acts 20:32 and 26:18 for places where Paul used *sanctified* as a term to describe believers.

Regarding the controversial debate about which foods were "lawful" to eat, Paul makes the radical statement that "everything is indeed clean" (Rom 14:20). He tempers that, however, when he adds, "it is wrong for anyone to make another stumble by what he eats."

Paul makes a parallel between the cleansing of vessels in the Old Testament temple with the cleansing of human vessels; likewise, believers should cleanse themselves to be available for honorable use by their Lord.

> Therefore, if anyone cleanses himself from what is dishonorable, he will be a vessel for honorable use, set apart as holy, useful to the master of the house, ready for every good work (2 Tim 2:21).

Perhaps the most extensive writing concerning the reconfiguring of purity maps is contained in the letter to the Hebrews. Space does not permit an extensive treatment of this.[24] Here is a short list of prominent purity-language truths contained in the letter to the Hebrews:

- Reflecting on the sacrificial system of the Old Testament law, the work of Christ on earth is summarized as the work of "making purification for sins" (1:3).

- The sacrifice of "the blood of goats and bulls" is contrasted with the far superior sacrifice of Jesus Christ as high priest—who offered his own blood to "purify our conscience from dead works to serve the living God" (9:13–14).

- Believers are admonished to "draw near with a true heart in full assurance of faith, with our hearts sprinkled clean from an evil conscience and our bodies washed with pure water" (10:22). Drawing near to the holy presence of God is available *simply by faith.*

- The cleansing power of the atonement of Christ goes way beyond the external. It touches that which is most internal and intimate—our *conscience*—our private thoughts and feelings, our silent ruminations of shame. God cleanses the conscience of all human beings who place their full "assurance of faith" in Jesus.[25]

Cleansing both guilt and shame

It is not just our *guilt* before God which is cancelled; even our *shame* can be healed by the glorious atonement of Christ.

The elaborate system of purity codes and the sacrificial system by which God's people were instructed to live—as described in Exodus, Leviticus, Numbers, Deuteronomy—provides us with a valuable truth: *God is unspeakably high; his holiness causes dread even in the most righteous person; he is gloriously separate from, yet in relation to, humanity.*[26]

---

24. deSilva's *Honor, Patronage, Kinship, Purity* addresses the use of purity language in the book of Hebrews, paralleling the Old and New Covenant. See the chapter: "Purity and the New Testament," 279–315.

25. For another view on the word *conscience* in Hebrews 9:14, Jackson Wu writes, "I think 'conscience' has a more volitional (perception of right/wrong) meaning; yet we are more accustomed to it having a psychological/feelings orientation. Conscience helps us make right decisions, not simply know that we previously did wrong." From personal correspondence with author, 9 April 2014.

26. See Is 6:1–7 as a concise expression of this truth.

Despite the fallenness of humanity—the sinful darkness and shame of people everywhere—God is relational! "God is love" (1 John 4:8), and desires relationship with the world's peoples. This presents a huge problem: *How can the glory and honor of a holy God converge with the defilement, darkness, and shame of humanity?* To do so leads to a terrifying dissonance, an inescapable conflict. Defilement and darkness *must* be vanquished by the overwhelming purity, brilliance, and holiness of God. Through the death and resurrection of Christ, the glory and honor of God will *always* conquer darkness, sin and shame.

The Old Testament helps us grasp that the atonement of Christ is beyond extraordinary.

In the old covenant, entering the Holy of Holies was the supreme honor and glory reserved for just one person (the high priest), and just one time a year (the Day of Atonement).[27] And this in just one tiny location in one small nation—among all the peoples of the earth.

Contrast the new covenant. This privilege of drawing near to God himself, of entering the Holy of Holies, *this honor and glory,* has through the cleansing atonement of Christ been made available literally to anyone *and everyone* who calls on the name of the Lord. Nothing in the universe is more sublime. It is the power of the magnificent Pure One whose name is Jesus Christ!

Three redrawn "purity maps" are described in the chart on the next page.

In Paul's letter to the Ephesians, we can see the dramatic reversal of honor-status for Gentiles who became followers of Christ:

> remember that you [Gentiles] were at that time separated from Christ, alienated from the commonwealth of Israel and strangers to the covenants of promise, having no hope and without God in the world. But now in Christ Jesus you who once were far off have been brought near by the blood of Christ (Eph 2:12–13).

Do you sense the emotion in these verses? Do you grasp the hope to which Paul was so radically committed, the hope which, from Abraham to the time of Christ (some two thousand years of Jewish history)—was not available to Gentiles *until the cross?*[28]

What a drama! Finally, the Gentiles were *included,* finally *honored* as part of the people and purpose of God—all made possible by the cleansing power and purity of Christ.

---

27. And the LORD spoke to Moses, saying, "Now on the tenth day of this seventh month is the Day of Atonement. It shall be for you a time of holy convocation, and you shall afflict yourselves and present a food offering to the LORD. And you shall not do any work on that very day, for it is a Day of Atonement, to make atonement for you before the LORD your God" (Lev 23:26–28).

28. It *was* possible for Gentiles to convert to Judaism in the Old Testament. Ruth, for example is a Moabitess who tells her mother-in-law "Your people shall be my people, and your God my God" (Ruth 1:16). One could not convert, however, without adopting all of the Mosaic law including Jewish food restrictions and other requirements. For men it included circumcision, a significant additional obstacle.

Map type	Old Covenant			New Covenant
MAPS OF PEOPLE *Who* is sacred / pure / honorable?	*Hierarchical community:* High honor-status available to select few, membership in tribe of Levi essential for priesthood			*Egalitarian community:* High honor status available to all, based on: servanthood to others / abiding in Jesus Christ / obedience to God
	Jew or Gentile?			Belief or unbelief in Christ?
	If Jewish, then holy or common?			• No distinction with regard to ethnicity • Sanctification and purity through the blood of Christ and abiding in Christ • Cleansed by truth and the Word of God • Uncleanness is sin/shame produced by internal realities, remedied simply by confession and faith in the work of Christ • Progressive cleansing from recurring sins available by abiding in Christ and his Word • Friendship with God
	If holy, tribe of Levi or other tribe of Jacob?		If common, then clean or unclean?	
	If levitical, priest or high priest?		If unclean, then can the uncleanness be remedied or not?	
MAPS OF SPACE *Where* is sacred / pure / honorable?	*Sacred space is centralized:* Honor is determined by physical proximity to specific sacred land and sacred buildings; presence of God available to select few			*Sacred space is decentralized:* Honor is determined by spiritual proximity to Christ and servanthood in his kingdom; presence of God available to everyone, anywhere, who follows Jesus
	Land of Israel—or rest of the world?			Christ is present wherever believers gather in his name—in honor of Jesus the King • Sacred space anywhere in the world • Sacred space is created by people worshiping Jesus Christ, not by buildings • The presence of Christ is amplified with those going *away* from home—as they go to disciple the nations • Buildings are optional; faith and obedience from the heart is not optional
	If inside Israel, then in Jerusalem (City of Zion)—or rest of Israel?			
	If in Jerusalem, then inside temple—or outside of temple?			
	If in temple, then in the outer court—or inner court?			
	If in inner court, then inside of Holy of Holies—or not?			
MAPS OF TIME *When* is sacred / pure / honorable?	*Worship is periodic:* Separation between sacred and secular			*Worship is continuous:* If all is done to the glory of God, then there is no separation between sacred and secular.
	The Sabbath is the seventh day of the week—a day of worship and rest for the people of God—versus the other six days of the week.			Structured time for worship and rest is healthy but not mandatory: • The Sabbath rest is a lifestyle of worship which God's people enter through faith in Christ—to cease from striving, in part *now*, and ultimately in eternity *future*. • Available anytime and anywhere: Entering into, and abiding in, the holy presence of God through the finished work of Christ.
	Once yearly, entering into the Holy of Holies on the Day of Atonement.			

Figure 2.27: Maps of people, space, and time—redefined in the New Covenant

A kingdom summary—dark side and bright side

Purity—kingdom of this world vs. kingdom-reign of God		
	Kingdom of this world	Kingdom-reign of God
	• Purity codes, when abused, artificially elevate the honor-status of the "insiders" and people in power • Purity codes, when abused, keep people in bondage to external laws • Purity codes, when abused, are obstacles to the mission of the church to cross cultural boundaries and go into all the world • Purity codes, when abused, reinforce ethnocentric bias and attitudes of superiority	• Egalitarian community: Elevated honor status available to all, based on servanthood, abiding in Christ • Sacred space is decentralized: Honor determined by proximity to Christ and serving others • Worship is continuous: If all is done to glorify God, then no separation between sacred and secular • Presence of Christ is amplified with believers going away from home—as they go to disciple the nations

Figure 2.28: Purity—kingdom of this world vs. kingdom-reign of God

Action points

- *Fast-forward:* To explore how the *dynamic of purity* can shape a contextualized presentation of the gospel of Christ, turn to Section 3, Chapter 9.

- *Reflect:* According to Hebrews 10:22, the blood of Christ is powerful enough to cleanse our conscience! Have you experienced this cleansing from both guilt and shame?

- *Bible study:* Read through the book of Leviticus and reacquaint yourself with the purity codes of the Mosaic law. Then read and study the Gospel of Mark in the light of what you've learned.

- *Teaching:* Develop a teaching about Jesus healing the demon-possessed man who lived "among the tombs" (Luke 8:26–39). Invite people to receive the powerful purifying life of Christ to banish their guilt, exclusion, oppression, shame.

- *Mission:* Many unreached or unengaged peoples are part of cultures that include daily ritual cleansing as a part of their religious practice and lifestyle. How would you craft a gospel message that emphasizes both a) the powerful purity of Christ as demonstrated by his miracles, and b) the cleansing power of the cross to remove shame, cleanse the conscience, or lift into God's honor?

This completes our exploration of nine dynamics of honor and shame in the Bible.[29] These dynamics are:

- Love of honor

---

29. These nine dynamics of honor and shame are *basic*. For further study, see deSilva, *Honor, Patronage, Kinship & Purity,* as well as Neyrey, *Honor and Shame in the Gospel of Matthew.*

- Two sources of honor
- Image of limited good
- Challenge and riposte
- Concept of face
- Body language
- Patronage
- Name / kinship / blood
- Purity

When you read and study your Bible with an awareness of these honor/shame principles—all of them in plain sight or just below the surface—you will glean many additional insights and practical applications.[30]

This leads us to the next chapter: We'll discover the master key that opens the door to understand in an integrated way the honor/shame dynamics in the Bible. That master key is: *honor-status reversal*.

Figure 2.29: The honor/shame wheel

---

30. To download a free "Quick Guide to Honor/Shame Dynamics in the Bible," go to: http://globalgospelbook.org/free.

Honor-Status Reversal as a Motif of the Bible

IN MUSIC, "A MOTIF IS A SHORT MUSICAL IDEA, a salient recurring figure, musical fragment or succession of notes that has some special importance in or is characteristic of a composition."[1] Any musician, music teacher, or composer is familiar with the motif. It's what makes any composition "hang together."

A motif in literature "is any recurring element that has symbolic significance in a story. Through its repetition, a motif can help produce other narrative (or literary) aspects such as theme or mood. ... A narrative motif can be created through the use of imagery, structural components, language, and other narrative elements."[2]

This book argues that "honor-status reversal" is a major motif in the Word of God—*God's story.*

Definition

Honor-status reversal is when a person, family, or people have whatever degree of esteem, respect, privilege, power, or authority before a community turned the other way around. One's honor-status can be high or low or in-between, ranging from the lowest honor-status of a leper or a slave—to the immensely powerful high honor-status of a mighty king. Everyone in honor/shame cultures knows their level of honor relative to everyone else in their community.

For this study we classify honor-status reversal according to the end result:

---

1. "Motif," *Wikipedia*, http://en.wikipedia.org/wiki/Motif_(music), accessed 23 May 2013.
2. "Motif," *Wikipedia*, http://en.wikipedia.org/wiki/Motif_(narrative), accessed 20 May 2013.

(1) **End result is honor:** Honor-to-shame-to-honor, or simply, shame-to-honor.

(2) **End result is shame:** Shame-to-honor-to-shame, or simply, honor-to-shame.

These variations may be expressed graphically as shown below:

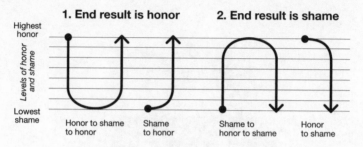

Figure 2.30: Types of honor-status reversal

A classic example in Scripture of honor-status reversal is found in the Apostle Paul's description of our Lord Jesus Christ in Philippians 2:

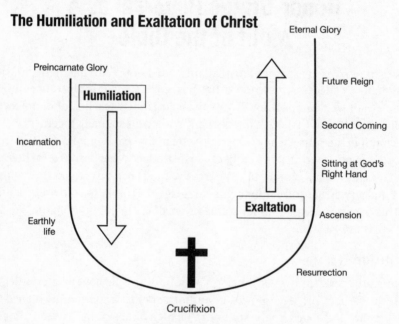

Figure 2.31: Humiliation and exaltation of
Christ as honor-status reversal

Have this mind among yourselves, which is yours in Christ Jesus, who, though he was in the form of God, did not count equality with God a thing to be grasped, but emptied himself, by taking the form of a servant, being born in the likeness of men. And being found in human form, he humbled himself by becoming obedient to the point of death, even death on a cross. Therefore God has highly exalted him and bestowed on him the name that is above every name, so that at the name of Jesus every knee should bow, in heaven and on earth and under the earth, and every tongue confess that Jesus Christ is Lord, to the glory of God the Father (Phil 2:5–11).

Jesus Christ was with the Father in the honor and glory of heaven in eternity past. His honor-status was infinitely high. Christ was in his "pre-incarnate glory."

But Jesus willingly allowed for his honor-status to be reversed. He "emptied himself" ... descending through the incarnation ... born fully human to the virgin Mary ... "taking the form of a servant."

He humbled himself further by dying, "even death on a cross"—the most shameful and ignominious destiny a man could endure.[3] Christ's entire Passion experience was his *humiliation.* However, as Timothy Tennent points out,

> even though Jesus accepted this shame, it did not involve an *actual* loss of honor. Jesus stands up and exhibits control of the situation giving directions to the Roman soldiers (John 18:8), acknowledging that this arrest took place to fulfill Scripture (Matt 26:54, 56), healing the man's ear (Luke 22:51), and even causing the soldiers to draw back and fall to the ground while Jesus remained standing (John 18:5).[4]

Moreover, Jesus' crucifixion-as-destiny on earth was not the end of the story. The pre-incarnate glory and honor he once had in heaven, then willingly laid aside, was to be regained and then magnified as he rose from the dead and sat down at the right hand of the Father. *The honor and glory of Christ was vindicated!* Again, this is an example of honor-status reversal—also known as Christ's exaltation.

The significance of these verses cannot be overstated. As Christians, we believe that the incarnation of Jesus Christ is the crux of human history. That it constitutes the most dramatic account of honor-status reversal has wonderful implications for cross-cultural Christian

Figure 2.32: Honor-status reversal is a major motif in Scripture—the axis of honor/shame dynamics in God's Story

ministry, which we will explore later in this book.

When you read and study the Bible with an awareness of honor/shame dynamics, you'll be a surprised by how frequently you will find that honor-status reversal is *hidden in plain sight.* In fact, the dynamic is so prevalent, I contend that honor-status

---

3. For an overview of the honor/shame dynamics in the arrest, trial, and crucifixion of Jesus, see Tennent, 89–91. Tennent cites Jerome Neyrey, "Despising the Shame of the Cross: Honor and Shame in the Johannine Passion Narrative," *Semeia* 68, (1994): 113–37. Neyrey's full article is available at: http://www3.nd.edu/~jneyrey1/shame.html, accessed 18 December 2013.

4. Tennent, 89.

reversal is a powerful motif in the entire panorama of Scripture. It becomes a powerful key for understanding so many aspects of God's story, Christ's mission, the meaning of the kingdom of God, and the journey of discipleship for believers. Here's another example of honor-status reversal from the words of Jesus:

> Whoever receives this child in my name receives me, and whoever receives me receives him who sent me. For he who is least among you all is the one who is great (Luke 9:48).

Karl Reich explains honor-status reversal this way:

> The very words "least" and "greatest" would automatically call up the thought of the Greco-Roman honor/shame system which was ultimately concerned with greatness. Malina and Rohr argue that this verse cuts at the very heart of the honor/shame system. They write, "A squabble over honor-status would be typical within any ancient Mediterranean grouping. ... Jesus' reversal of the expected order challenges the usual assumptions about what is honorable in a very fundamental way."[5]

Referring to this verse, "And behold, some are last who will be first, and some are first who will be last" (Luke 13:30), Reich continues:

> The pithy comment stays with the audience because of its compact and forceful nature and its enigmatic message. The transformation of polar opposites into their antithesis is unthinkable. The saying of the Lukan Jesus undermines the honor/shame system by proclaiming a reversal of roles.

We have observed the dynamic of honor-status reversal in Paul's description of Christ's incarnation in his letter to the Philippians. We have seen it briefly in one passage in Luke's Gospel. But it must be noted that honor-status reversal is present throughout Scripture. (Otherwise, of course, it cannot be considered a *motif*.) Consider:

 Adam and Eve were "sent ... out from the garden of Eden" (Gen 3:23); they left the glory and honor of perfect fellowship with God and were shamed by their rebellion (Gen 3:10–11) to live apart from the honorable presence of God. The honor of their fellowship with God was reversed to a condition of being a permanent outsider—with shame, guilt, and fear.

 Abraham: The story of Abraham is a story of a wealthy man who is called by God to essentially abandon his identity, to leave the very source of his honor—his father, his kinship, his homeland: "Go from your country and your kindred and your father's house to the land that I will show you" (Gen 12:1). But consider the immense honor he is promised by God: "And I will make of you a great nation, and I will bless you and make your name great, so that you will be a blessing. I will bless

---

5. Karl Reich, *Figuring Jesus: The Power of Rhetorical Figures of Speech in the Gospel of Luke* (The Netherlands: Koninklijke Brill NV, 2011), 156.

those who bless you, and him who dishonors you I will curse, and in you all the families of the earth shall be blessed" (vv. 2–3). Christopher Wright says of God's promise in the call of Abraham: "The word of God that spoke into darkness now speaks into barrenness with good news of *astonishing reversal,* holding before our imaginations vistas of a future that is (almost) beyond belief. God's mission of world redemption begins."[6] (Emphasis mine). It is an honor-status reversal foundational to the entire narrative and revelation of Scripture—including the global mission of God.

Joseph: The story of Joseph takes up a large portion of Scripture (Genesis 37–50), fully fourteen chapters. Joseph was the favorite, most-honored son of Jacob. But his brothers threw him down into a pit to be sold into slavery—a deep shame—from which he eventually rose to become the prime minister of Egypt. It's a classic story of honor-status reversal.

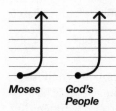

Moses   God's
        People

Moses and The Exodus: The story of Moses in Exodus is also an account of honor-status reversal. A baby born into the oppressed minority society of the Hebrews is found by pharaoh's daughter—and then raised as a prince in the royal palace. Eventually, in a dramatic God-empowered salvation event of epic proportions, Moses led the oppressed Hebrews in the Exodus out of the shame of slavery in Egypt toward the honor of the Promised Land (Ex 6:6–8). The reversal of shame to honor for all God's people is also depicted in Leviticus: "I am the LORD your God, who brought you out of the land of Egypt, that you should not be their slaves. And I have broken the bars of your yoke and made you walk erect" (Lev 26:13). After many generations of oppression, God rescued them. He made them to "walk erect"—their dignity recovered, their honor restored.

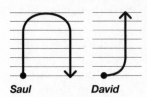

Saul   David

Saul and David: The story of Saul is one of low status to kingly honor—back to low status and shame (1 Sam 9:21; 10:22; 15:17). On the other hand, God took David, a lowly shepherd boy who had faith in the living God, and raised him to become a mighty king whose honor in the eyes of the people permanently exceeded that of the prior king (1 Sam 18:7). The contrast between Saul and David in their honor-status-trajectory is summarized in 1 Samuel: "There was a long war between the house of Saul and the house of David. And David grew stronger and stronger, while the house of Saul became weaker and weaker" (2 Sam 3:1). God honored David even to promising an eternal kingdom to his son (2 Sam 7:11–13), and many saw Jesus as this son.[7]

---

6. Christopher Wright, 200.

7. Ten times in Matthew's gospel, Jesus is referred to as the Son of David, indicating the high honor accorded to David by God in Jewish tradition.

Mephibosheth

A dramatic story of honor-status reversal is recorded in 2 Samuel 9. King David inquired to find if there was "anyone left of the house of Saul" in order to "show him kindness for Jonathan's sake" (2 Sam 9:1). One shameful survivor was found—Mephibosheth—"he is crippled in his feet" (v. 3). With great kindness, David instructed that all of Saul's family land be returned to Mephibosheth, and that Mephibosheth would eat at the king's table (v. 7). *What a reversal*—from the shame of disability and obscurity—to eating every day with the king!

Esther

Esther: The story of Esther is another classic. A beautiful woman (Esther) from the minority culture of the Jews ends up rising in honor as she was chosen to be the wife, the very queen, of the king of Persia. When a plot to kill the Jews was hatched by the evil Haman, Esther's uncle Mordecai asked Esther to courageously intervene with the king on behalf of her people, the Jews. The *ESV Study Bible* says, "The reader is clearly meant to laugh at the way [Haman's] vanity traps him into having to publicly honor the very man he intended to kill (6:6–11), and his death on the gallows he had prepared for Mordecai (7:8–10) is a classic case of a villain falling into his own pit."[8] We see here, again, various examples of honor-status reversal!

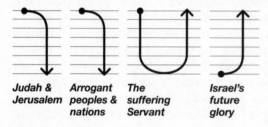

Judah & Jerusalem   **Arrogant peoples & nations**   **The suffering Servant**   **Israel's future glory**

Isaiah: The book of Isaiah is saturated with the dynamic of honor-status reversal. I will mention just a few examples. Judah and Jerusalem will be judged, disgraced, and shamed for their rebellion against God (Is 1:1–8:22). The nations surrounding Judah and Israel will be likewise judged and shamed because of their arrogance; a variety of oracles are spoken against them (various passages in chapters 10–23, 34). In chapter 23, the whole earth undergoes an honor-status reversal, being judged by God for rebellion.

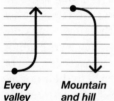

Every valley   **Mountain and hill**

Perhaps the most elegant and poetic example of honor-status reversal is in chapter 40: "Every valley shall be lifted up, and every mountain and hill be made low; the uneven ground shall become level, and the rough places a plain. And the glory of the LORD shall be revealed, and all flesh shall see it together, for the mouth of the LORD has spoken" (40:4–5).

Chapters 52–54 describe the honor-status reversal of the suffering servant. Chapter 52 has status reversals ending in both shame and honor. Chapter 53 deals exclusively with the shame of the Servant who is "pierced for our transgressions ... crushed for our iniquities" (53:5), "because he poured out his soul to death" (v. 12). Chapter 54 deals exclusively with the upward status reversal of God's servant and the surprising, joy-filled honor to come: "'Sing, O barren one, who did not bear; break forth into singing and cry aloud, you who

---

8. *ESV Study Bible*, Kindle edition locations 59670–59671.

have not been in labor! For the children of the desolate one will be more than the children of her who is married,' says the LORD" (54:1).

Finally, chapters 60–66 describe various ways that (following God's judgment in 63:1–19), Israel and even all the nations (66:18–20) will experience a dramatic honor-status reversal through worshiping the one true and living God. This honor in God for all of his people will finally end in *shalom* in "the new heavens and the new earth" (66:10–17, 22).[9]

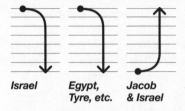

Israel   *Egypt,*   *Jacob*
          Tyre, etc.   *& Israel*

Ezekiel: The book of Ezekiel has numerous examples of honor-status reversal. For example, Israel was *brought low* by God for her idolatries and immorality in chapters 5–6, and 20–24. This dynamic of bringing Israel *down into shame* is seen in these verses: "Moreover, I will make you a desolation and an object of reproach among the nations all around you and in the sight of all who pass by. You shall be a reproach and a taunt, a warning and a horror, to the nations all around you, when I execute judgments on you in anger and fury, and with furious rebukes—I am the LORD; I have spoken" (Eze 5:14–15). God used the nations to judge Israel, but God also *brought down* those same prideful nations—Ammon, Moab, Edom, Philistia, Tyre, Egypt (chapters 25–32)—for their arrogance against God.

The comprehensive theme of honor-status reversal—bringing down the proud while elevating the humble—may be seen in chapter 17. "And all the trees of the field shall know that I am the LORD; I bring low the high tree, and make high the low tree, dry up the green tree, and make the dry tree flourish. I am the LORD; I have spoken, and I will do it" (17:24). The restoration of Israel's honor from a place of degradation and shame is wonderfully represented in chapters 36–37, especially in the passage about the "dry bones" that are *raised up* from graves to become "an exceedingly great army" (37:1–14). God promised that he will "restore the fortunes of Jacob and have mercy on the whole house of Israel" so that "they shall forget their shame" (39:25–26).

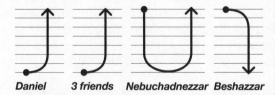

Daniel   *3 friends*   *Nebuchadnezzar*   *Belshazzar*

Daniel: The book of Daniel has a high concentration of stories that contain the dynamic of honor-status reversal. Repeatedly, Daniel and his friends were challenged in their faith, kept their commitment to trust in God, descended into a severe trial, only to rise in vindication and honor. In chapter 1, they were vindicated and promoted for their refusal to compromise their cultural identity as people of the Most High God. In chapter 2, Daniel publicly praised God as the one who "reveals deep and hidden

---

9. Limited space does not permit us to include examples of all Old Testament prophets. But honor-status reversal is a widespread dynamic in all of the OT prophetic books. Examples include Jer 33:1–13; Lam 5:1–22; Hos 10:1–6; 14:4–7; Joel 2:18–29; Amos 2:1–16; 9:11–15; Oba 1–21; Jon 2:1–9; Mic 7:8–17; Nah 2:1–12; Hab 2:6–20; Zeph 2:5–15; 3:14–20; Hag 2:20–22; Zech 3:1–6; 8:1–11:3; Mal 3:11–4:3.

things" (v. 22). Subsequently, Daniel revealed not just *what* King Nebuchadnezzar dreamt, but also its profound meaning (vv. 31–45); as a result Daniel was highly honored and promoted to the position of "ruler over the whole province of Babylon" (v. 48).

In chapter 3, Daniel's three friends refused to worship the huge golden image set up by the king, were thrown into the fiery furnace made seven times hotter than usual—and they survived without their hair being singed. God was literally with them in the fiery trial as "the fourth [who] is like the son of the gods" (v. 25). Again God's people were vindicated and experienced a rise in their honor-status (vv. 29–30).

Chapter 4 reveals the honor-status reversal of King Nebuchadnezzar himself. Because of the king's sin (v. 27) and pride (vv. 28–30), God sovereignly removed him from his throne. Nebuchadnezzar was humiliated as he apparently lost his mind and became like an ox eating grass, ugly and unkempt, isolated in shame (v. 33). Then, Nebuchadnezzar said, "My reason returned to me" (v. 34), and he gave eloquent praise to the Most High (vv. 34–35). It is a dramatic example of honor-status reversal for Nebuchadnezzar: "And for the glory of my kingdom, my majesty and splendor returned to me" (v. 36).

In chapter 5, King Belshazzar threw a party using the vessels from the temple in Jerusalem—and in so doing, dramatically dishonored God (vv. 1–4, 23). A mysterious hand appeared and wrote a message on the banquet wall, causing intense fear and dread (vv. 5–6). Daniel was called in to interpret the message from God (vv. 10–28): *It is the doom and imminent fall of Belshazzar.* The prideful king was killed that same night by the invading army of Darius the Mede (vv. 30–31). It is another classic example of honor-status reversal under the sovereign rule of the Most High God.

The Beatitudes (Mat 5:3–11) begin with: "Blessed are the poor in spirit, for theirs is the kingdom of heaven." In every verse in this most beautiful series, Jesus is teaching that in his kingdom there is a new way of living, a new way of gaining and measuring the honor of a man or woman. This new way of living is not a dismissal of the need for honor—nor a total rejection of the honor/shame values that permeated Greco-Roman culture. It is, rather, a proclamation that a new honor, a higher and permanent honor, is now available to all as they live in God's kingdom in loving submission to the most honorable King of kings.

The Parable of the Prodigal Son (Luke 15:11–32) is considered the best short story ever told.[10] The younger of two sons has turned away from his family and his father. Entering a downward spiral of shame, he ends up in the most degrading condition conceivable—in a famine, feeding swine, wishing to eat what the pigs eat. He comes to his senses and decides to return home to his father. Rather than being rejected and scorned, the father greets him with kisses and weeping.

---

10. See John MacArthur, *The Prodigal Son: An Astonishing Study of the Parable Jesus Told to Unveil God's Grace for You* (Nashville: Thomas Nelson, 2008), 3.

He gives the lost son his prized robe. He provides sandals for his feet and gives him a ring for his finger, signifying the honor and authority of the family. Then the father calls for a huge village celebration to welcome home the lost son. Is there a more powerful parable of honor-status reversal in Scripture?[11]

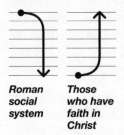

Roman social system

Those who have faith in Christ

Romans: Robert Jewett explains that Roman emperors were worshiped as gods by the people of the Roman Empire. For example, concerning Caesar Augustus:

The imperial cult celebrated "the gospel" of the allegedly divine power of the emperor, viewing him, in the words of an official document from the province of Asia, as a savior ... who put an end to war and will restore order everywhere: Caesar, by his appearance has realized the hopes of our ancestors; not only has he surpassed earlier benefactors of humanity, but he leaves no hope to those of the future that they might surpass him. The god's birthday was for the world the beginning of the gospel that he brought.[12]

Moreover, Nero was lauded as "the saviour and benefactor of the universe."[13] In his commentary on Romans 1:16,[14] Jewett asserts:

The contrast with Roman civic [religion] brings more clearly into focus the implications of Paul's thesis and its correlation with the rest of the *exordium*[15] as well as the subsequent argument of his letter, because this gospel shatters the unrighteous precedence given to the strong over the weak, the free and well-educated over slaves and the ill-educated, the Greeks and Romans over the barbarians. If what the world considers dishonorable has power [Jewett is referring to the gospel of the cross], it will prevail and achieve a new form of honor to those who have not earned it, an honor consistent with divine righteousness. All who place their faith in this gospel will be set right, that is, be placed in the right relation to the most significant arena in which honor is dispensed: divine judgment. Thus the triumph of divine righteousness through the gospel of Christ crucified and resurrected is achieved by transforming the system in which shame and honor are dispensed. *The thesis of Romans therefore effectively turns the social value system of the Roman empire upside down.*[16] (Emphasis mine.)

---

11. See "The Father's Love Gospel Booklet" at http://thefatherslovebooklet.org
12. Jewett, *Romans*, 138. Jewett's citation is "Letter of the Proconsul of Asia, Paulus Fabius Maximus, honoring Augustus in *I. Priene*, 105.35ff cited by Ceslas Spicq *TLNT* 3 (1994) 353."
13. Ibid., 139.
14. "For I am not ashamed of the gospel, for it is the power of God for salvation to everyone who believes, to the Jew first and also to the Greek" (Rom 1:16). Jewett likens Paul's "power of the gospel" with the "word of the cross" in 1 Cor 1:18—"For the word of the cross is folly to those who are perishing, but to us who are being saved it is the power of God." In essence, Paul is saying in Rom 1:16 that he is "not ashamed" of the gospel—the preaching of the *shameful folly of the cross.*
15. *Exordium* means "introduction of a discourse or treatise."
16. Jewett, *Romans*, 138.

Therefore, we assert that Paul's letter to the Romans is a theological treatise shaped in part by the social and cultural situation of the church in Rome—and incorporating at its core the dynamic of honor-status reversal.

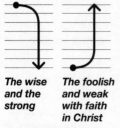

The wise and the strong

The foolish and weak with faith in Christ

1 Corinthians: "But God chose what is foolish in the world to shame the wise; God chose what is weak in the world to shame the strong; God chose what is low and despised in the world, even things that are not, to bring to nothing things that are, so that no human being might boast in the presence of God" (1 Cor 1:27–29). Richard Bauckham asserts that "social status is the issue in much of Paul's debates with the dominant faction in the Corinthian church." The wise are "the powerful elite, or those who aspire to join them. The strong are those whose wealth and social position give them power and influence in society, while the people Paul calls weak are the powerless, the ordinary people with no say and no muscle in this social world."[16] Into this intensely status-conscious faith community, Paul proclaimed the foolishness of "Christ crucified, a stumbling block to Jews and folly to Gentiles" (v. 23).

Lamb of God

Revelation: In God's revelation to John of the cosmic struggle between God's glorious kingdom and the devil's empire of evil, God's final judgment on evil is revealed.

Foundational to God's victory is the resounding conquest of the the Son of God who became the Lamb of God who was slain—and who has through resurrection become the fearless, triumphant Lion of the tribe of Judah (Rev 5:6–7). The honor-status reversal of Jesus Christ—from crucified Lamb to conquering Lion—could not be more clear.

Also contained in Revelation is the honor-status reversal of mighty Babylon.

> And he called out with a mighty voice, "Fallen, fallen is Babylon the great! She has become a dwelling place for demons, a haunt for every unclean spirit, a haunt for every unclean bird, a haunt for every unclean and detestable beast" (Rev 18:2).

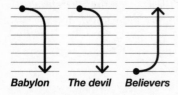

Babylon   The devil   Believers

Numerous other examples of honor-status reversal also appear in Revelation. In chapter 3, the saints at Laodicea are admonished by the Lord, "I counsel you to buy from me gold refined by fire, so that you may be rich, and white garments so that you may clothe yourself and the shame of your nakedness may not be seen" (v. 18), and then a few verses later, in an almost unthinkable expression of elevated honor, the Lord Jesus says, "The one who conquers, I will grant to sit with me on my throne, as I also conquered and sit with my Father on his throne" (v. 21). In addition, the saints who were martyred are honorably clothed in white (6:11) ... the once glorious, evil serpent, the devil, is

---

16. Bauckham, 50.

finally vanquished (20:1–10) ... even the once-inglorious unredeemed peoples of the earth—represented by their kings—bring their glory into the new city (21:22–26). This is but a sampling of the examples in Revelation of honor-status reversal.[17]

Honor-status reversal in less well-known passages, too

I've mentioned some of the big stories of the Bible as examples of honor-status reversal: *Abraham ... Joseph ... Moses ... David ... Esther ... Daniel ... the drama of Christ's incarnation, death and resurrection ... the cosmic drama in Revelation.*

But honor-status reversal shows up in smaller ways, too. A look at the first chapter of Luke's Gospel shows this is true. The chart below and on the next page contains various examples of honor-status reversal:

Basic story / idea	Luke	Beginning status	Honor/shame dynamic	↑ or ↓
Zechariah and Elizabeth—old and childless—become pregnant with John the Baptist	1:5–24	• Advanced in age and childless; barren (1:7)	• Pregnant with son who "will be great before the Lord" (1:15) • "to take away my reproach among people" (1:25)	↑
Mary visited by angel and is given the honorific news that she will bear a son who will be an eternal King	1:26–38	• Teenage girl, virtuous but common • Not shameful, but no honor status	• Visited by angel and told she is the "favored one" (1:28) • Will give birth to a son, Jesus, "called the Son of the Most High," descendant of David (1:32) • Her son will be the King who will reign forever in an eternal kingdom	↑
Elizabeth elevates the honor status of Mary	1:39–45	• Teenage girl, virtuous but common	• "Blessed are you among women, and blessed is the fruit of your womb!" (1:42) • "blessed is she who believed" (1:45) • An amazing pronouncement by Elizabeth (an old woman) about Mary (a young woman) regarding Mary's status compared to all other women	↑
Mary's Song of Praise, The Magnificat	1:46–56	• Humble • Hungry	• "he who is mighty has done great things for me" (1:49) • "mercy is for those who fear him" (1:50) • "exalted those of humble estate" (1:52) • "filled the hungry with good things" (1:53)	↑
		• Proud • Mighty • Rich	• "scattered the proud" (1:51) • "brought down the mighty from their thrones" (1:52) • "the rich he has sent away empty" (1:53)	↓
Birth of John the Baptist, Elizabeth's shame covered and her honor gained	1:57–66	• Zechariah and Elizabeth barren	• "she bore a son. ... Her neighbors and relatives heard that the Lord had shown great mercy to her, and they rejoiced with her" (1:57–58) • Elizabeth gained respect and honor in her community	↑

Figure 2.33: Honor-status reversal in Luke 1 (continued on next page)

---

17. See Appendix 5, "Honor/shame dynamics in the book of Revelation;" this is an extensive chart listing the occurrences of honor/shame dynamics—including honor-status reversal—in the book of Revelation.

Basic story / idea	Luke	Beginning status	Honor/shame dynamic	↑ or ↓
Zechariah's prophecy of the honor-status reversal of the house of David (Israel)	1:67–80	• Needing salvation • Hated by enemies • In darkness • Shadow of death • Constant conflict / oppression	• "the Lord … has raised up a horn of salvation for us in the house of his servant David" (1:68–69) • "that we should be saved from our enemies and from the hand of all who hate us" (1:71) • "the sunrise shall visit us from on high to give light to those who sit in darkness and in the shadow of death, to guide our feet into the way of peace" (1:78–79)	↑

Figure 2.33: Honor-status reversal in Luke 1

And that's just the first chapter in Luke's Gospel! And so it continues—the motif of honor-status reversal shows up in every chapter of Luke.

In fact, in the very next chapter, there is a scene where the parents of Jesus have brought the child Jesus into the temple in Jerusalem (2:22–38). The man Simeon is there, "righteous and devout, waiting for the consolation of Israel" (v. 25). There is deep emotion that permeates this passage of Scripture. Simeon was *longing* for the restoration of Israel's honor among the nations, "waiting for the consolation to Israel." He picks Jesus up in his arms and says:

> Lord, now you are letting your servant depart in peace, according to your word; for my eyes have seen your salvation that you have prepared in the presence of all peoples, a light for revelation to the Gentiles, and for glory to your people Israel (vv. 29–32).

Then something curious happens:

> And his father and his mother marveled at what was said about him. And Simeon blessed them and said to Mary his mother, *"Behold, this child is appointed for the fall and rising of many in Israel,* and for a sign that is opposed (and a sword will pierce through your own soul also), so that thoughts from many hearts may be revealed" (vv. 33–35). (Emphasis mine.)

Simeon was under the anointing of the Holy Spirit (v. 25). He hints at the royal identity of Jesus the Messiah: "Behold, this child is appointed for the fall [↓] and rising [↑] of many in Israel."

Simeon summarized the ministry of Jesus as a ministry of *honor-status reversal!* The shamed will be elevated in honor, and the honorable will be brought low and shamed.

Could it be that with respect to the pivotal cultural value of honor and shame, *honor-status reversal* is the very essence of the gospel?

Richard Bauckham does not use the word *motif,* nor does he use the phrase *honor-status reversal,* but he does use the phrase "consistent divine strategy" in referring to Paul's proclamation of how God works to bring down the high-minded and arrogant—while he elevates the low and humble. Alluding to the opening chapter of Paul's first letter to the Corinthians, Bauckham writes:

> In this passage and its context Paul does something rather remarkable. In the first place, by echoing the Old Testament, he identifies a *consistent divine*

strategy, a characteristic way in which God works, to which the origins of the church at Corinth conform. The God who chose the first Corinthian converts is the God who chose the least significant of all the people (Israel) for his own (Deuteronomy 7:7). This is Hannah's God, who exalts the lonely and humbles the exalted (1 Samuel 2:3–8), just as he is also Mary's God, who feeds the hungry and dismisses the rich (Luke 1:51–53). This is the God who chose the youngest of Jesse's sons, David, the one no one had even thought to summon (1 Sam 16:6–13). This is the God who habitually overturns status, not in order to make the non-élite a new élite, but in order to abolish status, to establish his kingdom in which no one can claim privilege over others and all gladly surrender privilege for the good of others.[18]

This leads us to consider more thoroughly what honor-status reversal means for Christians.

Honor-status reversal for believers

Consider again the diagram at right which illustrates the honor-status reversal of Jesus Christ based on Philippians 2:9–11. Observe this truth again—that after Christ's public humiliation through the crucifixion, he was rewarded and vindicated by supreme, magnificent, comprehensive, highly exalted honor.

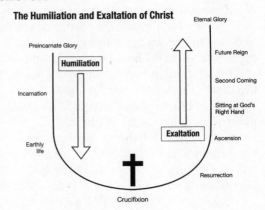

Figure 2.34: Humiliation and exaltation of Christ as honor-status reversal

> Therefore God has highly exalted him and bestowed on him the name that is above every name, so that at the name of Jesus every knee should bow, in heaven and on earth and under the earth, and every tongue confess that Jesus Christ is Lord, to the glory of God the Father (Phil 2:9–11).

So honor-status reversal is clearly represented here in the drama and Person of Christ. Can we also apply this dynamic of honor-status reversal to those who believe Jesus Christ is their Savior? The verses below indicate that, *yes, honor-status reversal applies to believers.*

> Do you not know that all of us who have been baptized into Christ Jesus were baptized into his death? We were buried therefore with him by baptism into death, in order that, just as Christ was raised from the dead by the glory of the Father, we too might walk in newness of life. For if we have been united with him in a death like his, we shall certainly be united with him in a resurrection like his (Rom 6:3–5).

---

18. Bauckham, 51.

Normally, we do not associate the truth of being "baptized into Christ Jesus" and "baptized into his death" as identification with his humiliating shame. It's ugly and assaults our sense of pride. We like to think that Jesus died for our sins in our place, but being "baptized into his death" is harsh and difficult to embrace.

Positional and experiential?

This draws us into the paradox between the believer's *positional* and *experiential* identity in Christ. For some, trusting in Christ as Savior and Lord may include in this life a literal downward status reversal relative to their family or community which involves shame, rejection, or even martyrdom. Thus, being "baptized into his death" is both positional and experiential.

For many others, however, no such shame and rejection is required by their community, so being "baptized into his death" represents more of a *positional* truth, and less an *experiential* truth. The baptism of children comes to mind. I was baptized as a ten-year-old boy. Except for a general sense of dying to self-will, this verse was for me much more of a *positional* rather than an *experiential* reality.

The paradox between the positional and experiential also relates to the truth of being "united with him in a resurrection like his" (v. 5). In order for believers to be included in the honor and exaltation of Christ's resurrection, must we first identify with Christ in the shame of his death? We can answer that for all genuine Christians, this is *positionally* true. This is why the ordinance of *baptism* is given by God for all Christians—symbolizing both a downward death to sin and an upward rise into new life in Christ.

But a caution is in order. We sometimes all too easily ignore the demands of the gospel when, on the one hand, we claim the *positional* truth of our victorious, honored identity in the exalted Christ, but on the other hand refuse the *experience* of obediently relinquishing our status or our rights in the service of our King.

Consider the life of Apostle Paul, for whom there was a genuine merger between *positional* and *experiential* truth. Paul actually *lived* the dynamic of Christ's honor-status reversal. As Michael T. Gorman says, "For Paul, to be in Christ is to be a living exegesis of this narrative of Christ, a new performance of the original drama of exaltation following humiliation, of humiliation as the voluntary renunciation of rights and selfish gain in order to serve and obey."[19]

The Bible says that our *positional* identification with Christ should lead to an *experiential* reality. For example, to be "united with him in his resurrection" is not solely for our eternal life after we die. Otherwise, Paul's emphasis that "we too might walk in newness of life" would not make sense, as this represents living life on earth prior to physical death. "Walking in newness of life" refers to a new lifestyle which both contains and reflects the glory and honor of Jesus Christ. This may lead believers to ask, *is honor-status reversal for us now or for us in the future?* It appears there is a dynamic tension at work. It is similar to the mysterious *already-but-not-yet* nature of the kingdom of God.[20] Therefore, the answer is *yes!*

---

19. Michael T. Gorman, *Cruciformity: Paul's Narrative Spirituality of the Cross* (Grand Rapids, MI: Eerdmans, 2002), 87, as quoted in Dean Flemming: *Contextualization in the New Testament: Patterns for Theology and Mission*, 176, Kindle edition.

20. See Graham Cray, "The Theology of the Kingdom," in eds. Vinay Samuel and Chris Sugden, *Mission as Transformation: A Theology of the Whole Gospel* (Oxford: Regnum Books, 1999), 26–44.

More in Romans 6 and 8. There are other passages in Romans that illustrate honor-status reversal for believers. For example, Romans 6:6–14 elaborates on the reversal that believers experience in Christ:

> We know that our old self was crucified with him in order that the body of sin might be brought to nothing, so that we would no longer be enslaved to sin. For one who has died has been set free from sin. Now if we have died with Christ, we believe that we will also live with him. We know that Christ, being raised from the dead, will never die again; death no longer has dominion over him. For the death he died he died to sin, once for all, but the life he lives he lives to God. So you also must consider yourselves dead to sin and alive to God in Christ Jesus. Let not sin therefore reign in your mortal body, to make you obey its passions. Do not present your members to sin as instruments for unrighteousness, but present yourselves to God as those who have been brought from death to life, and your members to God as instruments for righteousness. For sin will have no dominion over you, since you are not under law but under grace (Rom 6:6–14).

When Paul writes about being set free from slavery to sin (vv. 6–7), and "consider yourselves dead to sin and alive to God in Christ Jesus" (v. 11), we must capture the dynamic of shame associated with slavery to sin. Slaves were low-status people (property, actually) in the Roman Empire.[21] Correspondingly, we must see the dynamic of honor associated with our identifying with the resurrection life of Christ Jesus.

Romans 8:34–38 expresses the dynamic of believers being on the low, shameful end of the spectrum, "being killed ... regarded as sheep to be slaughtered," whereas on the high, honorable end of the spectrum, being "more than conquerors through him who loved us."

Think of the believers at Rome, where the church was an oft-shamed minority group, breathing the air of the honor of the Roman Empire and it's "glorious" conquerors. How much it must have stirred their hearts to hear that, in Christ, they were "more than conquerors"! What a glorious honor-status reversal for the church at Rome—of course, a *positional* truth.

Believers are called to identify with our Lord to such an extent that our relationship with him begins with the willingness to relinquish social status and personal rights (a downward honor-status reversal). At the same time, our being in Christ ultimately leads to a magnificent, upward rise in our honor-status in eternity. Of course, all of these realities are solely *in Christ*.

A steady theme of Paul: Honor-status reversal through Christ

Following are other passages that show the upward honor-status reversal of believers. You will note that these verses show that believers' honor is embedded

---

21. See "Slavery in Ancient Rome": "Slaves were considered property under Roman law and had no legal personhood. Unlike Roman citizens, they could be subjected to corporal punishment, sexual exploitation (prostitutes were often slaves), torture, and summary execution." *Wikipedia*, http://en.wikipedia.org/wiki/ Slavery_in_ancient_Rome, accessed 20 June 2013.

totally in Christ. And you will observe again the *already-but-not-yet* tension between positional and experiential realities (emphases in the quoted verses are mine).

For consider your calling, brothers: not many of you were wise according to worldly standards, not many were powerful, not many were of noble birth. *But God chose what is foolish in the world to shame the wise; God chose what is weak in the world to shame the strong; God chose what is low and despised in the world, even things that are not, to bring to nothing things that are,* so that no human being might boast in the presence of God (1 Cor 1:26–29).

So is it with the resurrection of the dead. *What is sown is perishable; what is raised is imperishable. It is sown in dishonor; it is raised in glory. It is sown in weakness; it is raised in power. It is sown a natural body; it is raised a spiritual body* (1 Cor 15:42–44).

From now on, therefore, we regard no one according to the flesh. Even though we once regarded Christ according to the flesh, we regard him thus no longer. *Therefore, if anyone is in Christ, he is a new creation. The old has passed away; behold, the new has come. All this is from God, who through Christ reconciled us to himself and gave us the ministry of reconciliation. ...* Therefore, *we are ambassadors for Christ,* God making his appeal through us (2 Cor 5:16–20).

I have been crucified with Christ. It is no longer I who live, but Christ who lives in me. And the life I now live in the flesh I live by faith in the Son of God, who loved me and gave himself for me (Gal 2:20).

To redeem those who were under the law, *so that we might receive adoption as sons.* And because you are sons, God has sent the Spirit of his Son into our hearts, crying, "Abba! Father!" *So you are no longer a slave, but a son, and if a son, then an heir through God* (Gal 4:5–7).

A closer look at honor-status reversal in Ephesians 2

Ephesians 2:1–7 gives us a dramatic picture of honor-status reversal from being "dead in the trespasses and sins" to having been "raised ... up with him and seated ... with him in the heavenly places in Christ Jesus." *From death to seated with Christ in exalted honor.* Astounding!

Let's take a closer look at the profound dynamics of honor-status reversal in Ephesians 2 in the charts below and on the next page:

Honor-status reversal—Humanity in relation to God (Ephesians 2:1–7)	
VERTICAL DIMENSION (PERSONAL)	
Our original shameful status in relation to God	Our honor-status reversal by grace through faith in Jesus Christ
• **Spiritually dead:** "dead in . . . trespasses and sins" (2:1) • **Unwittingly following the world's spirit and devil:** "following the course of this world, following the prince of the power of the air" (2:2) • **Victimized by an evil spirit:** "the spirit that is now at work in the sons of disobedience" (2:2)	• **Loving intervention, undeserved, from the powerful, divine Benefactor directed toward us:** "But God, being rich in mercy, because of the great love with which he loved us" (2:4) • **Gave us new life by joining us to the Messiah-King:** "made us alive together with Christ" (2:5)

Our original shameful status in relation to God	Our honor-status reversal by grace through faith in Jesus Christ
• **DNA of an evil, shameful father:** "sons of disobedience" (2:2) • **Enslaved to self:** "lived in the passions of our flesh, carrying out the desires of the body and the mind" (2:3) • **Destined for God's eternal punishment:** "children of wrath" (2:3) • **Unexceptional:** "like the rest of mankind" (2:3)	• **Permanently raised our honor-status in Christ's resurrection:** "and raised us up with him" (2:6) • **Provided us rest and authority in relational co-regency with Christ the King:** "seated us with him in the heavenly places in Christ Jesus" (2:6) • **All to display God's riches to magnify his honor for all eternity:** "so that in the coming ages he might show the immeasurable riches of his grace in kindness toward us in Christ Jesus." (2:7)

Figure 2.35: The vertical dimension of honor-status reversal—humanity in relation to God

Honor-status reversal—Gentiles in relation to God's people (Ephesians 2:11–22)	
HORIZONTAL DIMENSION (SOCIAL / CULTURAL)	
Our original shameful status in relation to God's people	**Our honor-status reversal by grace through faith in Jesus Christ**
• **Unclean, defiled and without hope of being made clean:** "Gentiles in the flesh, called 'the uncircumcision' by what is called the circumcision" (2:11) • **No access to the honor and benefaction of the Messiah-King:** "separated from Christ" (2:12) • **As aliens in relation to God's great people Israel:** "alienated from the commonwealth of Israel" (2:12) • **Unaware of any relational destiny in God:** "strangers to the covenants of promise" (2:12) • **Living in despair without God's presence:** "having no hope and without God in the world" (2:12) • **Disconnected from the most honorable relationship:** "far off" ... "strangers and aliens" (2:13, 19) • **On the other side of** "the dividing wall of hostility" (2:14)	• **From far away in shame to very near through the honor of Christ's blood:** "you who once were far off have been brought near by the blood of Christ" (2:13) • **Messiah-King himself is our new source of honor—dispelling our compulsion for honor competition and hostility:** "For he himself is our peace, who has made us both one and has broken down in his flesh the dividing wall of hostility" (2:14) • **For a completely new kind of kinship group made in peace:** "by abolishing the law of commandments expressed in ordinances, that he might create in himself one new man in place of the two, so making peace" (2:15) • **The shame of Christ's body on the cross absorbed humanity's compulsion for honor competition and hostility—to create a new body among humanity, a community of peace:** "and might reconcile us both to God in one body through the cross, thereby killing the hostility" (2:16) • **Both Jew and Gentile (no superiority for being Jewish) were equally in need of the preaching of this grace and peace:** "And he came and preached peace to you who were far off and peace to those who were near" (2:17) • **The high honor of access to holy God is now available to all peoples— further dispelling honor competition:** "For through him we both have access in one Spirit to the Father" (2:18) • **Shameful state as strange aliens replaced by multi-dimensional honor of citizens, saints, family members:** "So then you are no longer strangers and aliens, but you are fellow citizens with the saints and members of the household of God" (2:19) • **Entering into the honor of God's ancient story, the crux of which is the Messiah-King and Son of God:** "built on the foundation of the apostles and prophets, Christ Jesus himself being the cornerstone" (2:20) • **Brothers and sisters in Christ become the new "sacred space"— wherever they are:** "in whom the whole structure, being joined together, grows into a holy temple in the Lord" (2:21) • **In Christ your new community is the dwelling for the most honorable, holy presence of God:** "In him you also are being built together into a dwelling place for God by the Spirit" (2:22)

Figure 2.36: The horizontal dimension of honor-status reversal— humanity in relation to God's people

The first seven verses in Ephesians 2 speak to all believers—Jew and Gentile—of humanity's relationship with God, from spiritually dead to "made alive with Christ" ... "raised with Christ" ... "seated with him." This is the *vertical dimension*. It refers to our personal, positional, eternity-future in relationship to God.

The last twelve verses of Ephesians 2 speak to Gentile believers and their relationship to God's chosen people. Paul describes it as a profound transformation—a reversal of shame to honor. From separated, alienated, strangers, having no hope—the "uncircumcision" (v. 11)[22]—to citizens, saints, full-fledged family members who together are a dwelling for the presence of God. This is the *horizontal dimension,* the right-now, life-on-earth-with-my-neighbor dimension.

At the crux of two dimensions of honor-status reversal— *there it is—*"salvation by grace through faith."

What is located between these two dramatic expressions of honor-status reversal—between verses 1–7 and 11–22? The often-quoted verses about *salvation by grace through faith:*

For by grace you have been saved through faith. And this is not your own doing; it is the gift of God, not a result of works, so that no one may boast (Eph 2:8–9).

This "salvation verse" sits at the intersection of vertical and horizontal dimensions of honor-status reversal. The vertical dimension refers to a person's relationship with God. The horizontal dimension refers to the Gentiles' relationship with God's people. The epic drama

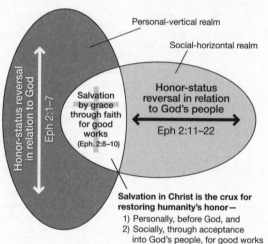

Figure 2.37: Salvation is the crux of two dimensions of honor-status reversal in Ephesians 2

inherent in these dimensions of honor-status reversal—along with the liberation that this brought spiritually, emotionally and socially[23]—is the context for "salvation by grace through faith."

---

22. The intensely shameful status of the "uncircumcised"—in relation to God's people Israel—is depicted by the prophet Habakkuk: "Woe to him who makes his neighbors drink—you pour out your wrath and make them drunk, in order to gaze at their nakedness! You will have your fill of shame instead of glory. Drink, yourself, and show your uncircumcision! The cup in the LORD's right hand will come around to you, and utter shame will come upon your glory!" (Hab 2:15–16).

23. I believe that when Paul wrote in Ephesians 2:4, *"But God, being rich in mercy, because of the great love with which he loved us,"* he intended that his readers—and those listening to the letter being read—experience a kind of deep sense of relief to the anxiety about humanity's predicament created by verses 1 through 3. When Paul wrote in verse 19, *"So then you are no longer strangers and aliens, but you are fellow citizens with the saints and members of the household of God,"* he intended that his readers—and those listening to the letter being read—experience deep relief to the never-ending shame anxiety about levels of honor-status, inclusion or exclusion, acceptance or rejection that they experienced in their honor/shame society.

Timothy Tennent writes: "The New Testament celebrates a salvific transformation that has both vertical and horizontal dimensions. Personal salvation in the New Testament is inextricably linked to becoming a part of the new humanity of Ephesians 2:15."[24] As salvation is *vertical* because sin is *personal,* so also is salvation *horizontal* because sin is *corporate.* According to Hiebert: "There is both personal and corporate sin and personal and corporate dimensions to God's redemption."[25]

The verses, Ephesians 2:8–9, are well known by lay persons in evangelical churches. Not as well known is the verse that immediately follows:

For we are his workmanship, created in Christ Jesus for good works, which God prepared beforehand, that we should walk in them (Eph 2:10).

Why is Ephesians 2:10 referenced less frequently that Ephesians 2:8–9? Would seeing it in the light of honor and shame help us see how the original recipients would have understood it? Let's unpack the meaning of Ephesians 2:8–10 this way:[26]

Honor/shame dynamics of Ephesians 2:8–10	
Ephesians 2:8, 9, 10	Comment
For by grace you have been saved through faith (2:8)	• God is a most-high Benefactor-Savior; he has saved us by grace as we have placed our full trust in him; our honor is embedded in an altogether different King: his name is Jesus Christ.
And this is not your own doing; it is the gift of God, not a result of works, so that no one may boast (2:8–9)	• We claim no self-honor in this; it is not our own doing. • Our self effort has no impact on whether God accepts us; no one can boast (or make a claim to honor) that he or she deserves what God has given.
For we are his workmanship, created in Christ Jesus for good works, which God prepared beforehand, that we should walk in them (2:10)	• Our new lives are created in Christ Jesus, and thus we bear the honor of our King in doing his good works. • Being in Christ, we have the immense honor of being in God's story to do the good works that our King "prepared beforehand"—what a privilege!

Figure 2.38: Honor/shame dynamics in Ephesians 2:8–10

---

24. Timothy C. Tennent: *Invitation to World Missions: A Trinitarian Missiology for the Twenty-first Century* (Grand Rapids, MI: Kregel, 2010), 62.

25. Paul Hiebert, "The Gospel in Human Contexts: Changing Perceptions of Contextualization" in *MissionShift: Global Mission Issues in the Third Millennium,* ed. Ed Stetzer and David Hesselgrave (Nashville, TN: B&H Publishing, 2010), 99, Kindle edition location, 99.

26. The royal nature of Christ as King—emphasized much in this chart—is not *directly* seen in Ephesians 2. I derive this emphasis *indirectly* from three things: (1) The word *Christ* means "Messiah," and Messiah in the Old Testament has many royal, kinglike qualities. For example, Psalm 110:1–7 is a prophecy of Christ; verse 1 is quoted multiple times in the New Testament. It is a vivid expression of Christ as conquering king who saves his people and rules in victory over all his enemies. (2) The passage immediately preceding Ephesians 2 is 1:19–23; it is descriptive of a ruling, reigning king, especially the phrase in verse 20 (referring to Ps 110:1)—"and seated him at his right hand." (3) When Paul was about to leave Ephesus for the last time, he said to the believers, "And now, behold, I know that none of you among whom I have gone about proclaiming the kingdom will see my face again" (Acts 20:25). Paul summarized his communication of the revelation of God in Christ as "proclaiming the kingdom." In the last verse of the book of Acts, Luke writes a similar summary statement about the ministry of Paul while he was under house arrest in Rome, that Paul was "proclaiming the kingdom of God and teaching about the Lord Jesus Christ" (Acts 28:31). Moreover, Paul wrote his letter to the Ephesians from Rome. Therefore, is it too much to say that his entire letter to the Ephesians is an expression of "proclaiming the kingdom"—a kingdom ruled by Jesus Christ the King? To the original readers and hearers of this letter—living as they did under the reign of Caesar—the royal reign of Christ as King was understood.

Remember, because the original recipients of the letter lived in an honor/shame culture, the doing of good works would have been understood as a natural outcome of a great salvation provided by a great Benefactor-King! To return honor to the Great Benefactor by doing his good works would *not* have been seen as incongruous to salvation by grace, but a natural, completely appropriate response. The absence of the expectation to do good works would have been considered deviant from the norm, an anomaly.

Paul's own story of honor-status reversal in Acts 22

Paul recounts the story of his own salvation in Acts 22:6–16 as he defends himself in front of the Jewish leaders in Jerusalem. What he shares is a story of dramatic honor-status reversal.

He begins by describing his original high honor-status. "I am a Jew, born in Tarsus in Cilicia, but brought up in this city, educated at the feet of Gamaliel according to the strict manner of the law of our fathers, being zealous for God as all of you are this day" (Acts 22:3).[27] What a pedigree! Not only that, he also persecuted the early Christians (vv. 4–5) as an attempt to protect the honor of God and Jewish religious standards.

Paul's descent into a shameful state is represented by the following:

- On his way to Damascus, a "great light from heaven" knocked him down! Paul "fell to the ground" (falling is often an indication of loss of honor) (vv. 6–7).

- Paul was challenged by the highest authority in the universe, our Lord Jesus Christ—*"Saul, Saul, why are you persecuting me?"* (v. 7).

- Paul was blinded by the "brightness of that light;" he became abnormally vulnerable so that he had to be "led by the hand" like a child (v. 11).

Paul's rise in honor is represented by the following:

- "And the Lord said to me ..." (v. 10). *God spoke to Paul!* This was an honor claim of an unusually high degree. This would qualify Paul to have roughly equal honor-status with Abraham, Moses, Samuel, David, or Elijah.

- Contrasted with "fell to the ground" (v. 7), the Lord told him to *"Rise,* and go into Damascus" (v. 10). "Rise" indicates an elevation of honor-status.[28]

- "And one Ananias, a devout man according to the law, well spoken of by all the Jews who lived there, came to me, and standing by me said to me, 'Brother Saul, receive your sight.' And at that very hour I received my sight and saw him" (vv. 12–13).

- Paul emphasized that a *most honorable man, Ananias* (v. 12), was used by God to speak to him so that he could regain the normal honor of eyesight after having been blinded. Consider the honor-laden meaning in Paul's account

---

27. "Gamaliel," *Wikipedia,* "Gamaliel holds a reputation in the Mishnah for being one of the greatest teachers in all the annals of Judaism," http://en.wikipedia.org/wiki/Gamaliel, accessed 17 June 2013.

28. Keep in mind that Luke is the author of Acts. And it was Luke who recorded that Jesus was "appointed for the fall and rising of many in Israel" (Luke 2:34), meaning Jesus would have a ministry of honor-status reversal. Paul fits into both categories—*falling* and *rising.*

of what Ananias said: "And he said, 'The God of our fathers appointed you to know his will, to see the Righteous One and to hear a voice from his mouth; for you will be a witness for him to everyone of what you have seen and heard. And now why do you wait? Rise and be baptized and wash away your sins, calling on his name" (vv. 14–16).

- There are massive honor connotations here: *"The God of our fathers"* represents the very honor of their ancestral tradition ... *"appointed you to know his will, to see the Righteous One and to hear a voice from his mouth; for you will be a witness for him to everyone of what you have seen and heard."* This confirms that Paul's honor and authority is to be equated with the great Old Testament prophets. Impressive, indeed!

- *"Rise and be baptized and wash away your sins, calling on his name"*—here the act of baptism is a sign of being cleansed from sin for the honor of entering the presence of God; moreover, he was baptized into the name (honor) of the Lord. This summed up Paul's honor-status reversal. No wonder Ananias told Paul to *"Rise."*

Unquestionably, Paul is making every effort to impress his adversaries, hoping to convince them of the credibility of his story and to authenticate that God had chosen him for a calling, a mission of highest honor.[29] Paul's life was one of dramatic honor-status reversal, mirroring in a significant manner the life, death, and resurrection of Jesus.

From the personal to the communal

Following his personal confession in Philippians 3, Paul changes his "voice" from the first person singular to the first person plural—addressing his faith-family, the body of Christ:

> But our citizenship is in heaven, and from it we await a Savior, the Lord Jesus Christ, who will *transform our lowly body to be like his glorious body,* by the power that enables him even to subject all things to himself (Phil 3:20–21). (Emphasis mine.)

The motif of honor-status reversal applied to believers continues in Paul's letter to the Colossians:

> He has delivered us *from the domain of darkness and transferred us to the kingdom of his beloved Son,* in whom we have redemption, the forgiveness of sins (Col 1:13–14). (Emphasis mine.)

> And you, who once were *alienated and hostile in mind,* doing evil deeds, he has now reconciled in his body of flesh by his death, in order to present you *holy and blameless and above reproach before him* (Col 1:21–22). (Emphasis mine.)

From the shame of being "alienated and hostile" to the honor of "holy and blameless and above reproach before him" ... *honor-status reversal!*

---

29. Paul's attempt to sway his adversaries failed. Acts 22:22–23:15 records the reactions of outrage, violence, chaos, and attempted murder—all in response to the honor claims of Paul.

Moreover, he speaks of believers as:

> having been *buried with him in baptism, in which you were also raised with him through faith in the powerful working of God*, who raised him from the dead. And you, who were dead in your trespasses and the uncircumcision of your flesh, *God made alive together with him, having forgiven us all our trespasses,* by canceling the record of debt that stood against us with its legal demands. This he set aside, nailing it to the cross. *He disarmed the rulers and authorities and put them to open shame, by triumphing over them in him* (Col 2:12–15). (Emphasis mine.)

Healing for shame. The honor-status reversal which Christ himself experienced was not just for his own glorification, but also for the community of believers who follow him as Lord. Honor-status reversal is also for believers—for all who have found life in Jesus Christ! John Forrester writes: "In brief, the ministry of Jesus is this: he sets aside his own honor and glory to identify with human dishonor and shame at its deepest level; but in his own recovery and return to glory, he breaks a path out of shame for all humanity. Each human being is now invited to identify with Christ and to participate vicariously in the depth of his descent and the height of his ascent."[30]

Freedom to serve. "As the Father has sent me, even so I am sending you" (John 20:21). Jesus Christ relinquished his honor in order to serve humanity—an example to believers to live by the same pattern. *How challenging! How honoring!* Jesus sends us to serve in the same pattern that God sent him. Apostle Paul followed Christ's example. He wrote in his first letter to the church at Corinth, "For though I am free from all, I have made myself a servant [slave] to all, that I might win more of them" (1 Cor 9:19). Dean Flemming explains:

> By cloaking himself with the metaphor of slavery, Paul sets his own mission in diametric contrast to the "strong" Corinthians' concern over personal liberty and status. In light of chapter 9 as a whole and the values of Roman culture, Paul's "self-enslavement" could not help but include a social dimension. He has modeled slavish behavior by voluntarily climbing down the ladder of status for the sake of others.[31]

Flemming also says of Paul: "More importantly, his course of downward social mobility becomes an illustration of the gospel itself, an identification with his crucified Lord. The message is embodied by the messenger."[32]

One wonders how many Christian leaders are willing to ignore the importance of "personal liberty and status" and "voluntarily climb down the ladder of success"—in order to embody the message of the gospel for their global neighbors and the unengaged or unreached peoples. I find this a sobering challenge. Undoubtedly, more believers would live in this pattern of honor-status reversal if, like Paul, we also grasped more fully the sublime honor of knowing Jesus Christ! One is compelled to ask: *How much does our own status-seeking culture hinder our walk with God or service in his kingdom?*

---

30. Forrester, 131.
31. Flemming, Kindle edition location, 195.
32. Ibid.

Celebration *and* suffering. Soong-Chan Rah compares the *theology of celebration* focused on the resurrection with the *theology of suffering* focused on the cross. He says that middle-class Christians in America and other wealthy societies tend to identify with the celebration of life located in the resurrection, whereas believers in oppressive minority circumstances will tend to identify with the suffering of Christ on the cross.

> The theology of celebration, which emerges out of the context of affluence and abundance, focuses on the proper management and stewardship of the abundant resources that God has provided. Because there is abundance, the world is viewed as generally good and accommodating to those who are living under the theology of celebration. Life is already healthy, complete and whole. God, therefore, takes on the role of a nurturer and caregiver and takes on more feminine attributes. In the theology of celebration, maintaining and preserving the status quo becomes a central priority. The theology of celebration is a theology of the resurrection.
>
> The theology of suffering, on the other hand, emerges out of the context of scarcity and oppression and therefore focuses on the need for salvation and survival. Because of the reality of oppression, the world is generally considered to be evil and hostile to those who are living under the theology of suffering. Life is precarious, needing a deliverer. God, therefore, takes on the image of a warrior and conqueror and assumes more masculine attributes. In the theology of suffering, fighting injustice becomes the central priority. The theology of suffering is a theology of the cross.[33]

When we look at the dynamic of honor-status reversal, we see both suffering and celebration. If we are to take the words of Jesus seriously—"As the Father has sent me, even so I am sending you" (John 20:21)—then the whole church is called to identify with both the shame of Christ's suffering and the honor of Christ's resurrection.

Jesus shares his glory. In what is known as the High Priestly Prayer of Christ in John 17, Jesus prayed to the Father:

> I do not ask for these only, but also for those who will believe in me through their word, that they may all be one, just as you, Father, are in me, and I in you, that they also may be in us, so that the world may believe that you have sent me. *The glory that you have given me I have given to them,* that they may be one even as we are one (John 17:20–22). (Emphasis mine.)

Why is it so challenging to our Christian sensibilities that Jesus prayed to the Father, "The glory that you have given me I have given to them"? Normally we think that glory belongs exclusively to God. But this is not supported by the overall testimony of Scripture.[34]

---

33. Rah, Kindle edition, locations, 2565–74.

34. Some may counter that God does not share his glory with anyone, citing verses from Isaiah: "I am the LORD; that is my name; my glory I give to no other, nor my praise to carved idols" (Is 42:8), and, "For my own sake, for my own sake, I do it, for how should my name be profaned? My glory I will not give to another" (Is 48:11). However, these verses are in the context of the idolatry of his people, the worship of false gods. Obviously, God will never relinquish his glory to mere idols. But God's Word plainly teaches that God shares some of his infinite honor and glory with those who follow the Lord Jesus Christ. See Is 55:5; John 5:44; 12:43; Rom 2:7; 8:21; 1 Cor 2:7; Eph 2:6; Col 1:27; Jude 1:8; Rev 3:21). In Christ, God's people are glorious. (For more on this, see the Section 2, Chapter 1 on the love of honor.)

I contend that when we as believers *in community* embrace our honor-status reversal *in Christ*—both in his descent of sacrificial service and his ascent unto glory—something miraculous happens by the grace of God and the Holy Spirit. We gladly, freely serve others in humility without regard to our own honor-status because we have no honor deficit; we have apprehended that Jesus has shared with us his divine honor from out of his eternal "riches in glory" (Phil 4:19).

Oh, the love of God!

With all this emphasis on honor for Christ—*and* honor for those who follow him—we dare not forget the vital importance of God's love. "God *so loved* the world that he gave ..."! If the dynamics of honor and shame comprise the wheel—and honor-status reversal is the axle—then let us consider the love of God as the engine that propels and makes motion possible. Imagine a car without an engine—utterly useless! And to take the word picture one step further, we can imagine God's passion for his glory as the *fuel* that powers the engine and *propels it forward*.

Why should sinful and shameful humans be able to experience the glories of honor-status reversal? Why should they be able to experience forgiveness of sins, their shame covered, and their honor restored before God? It ultimately points us to the tapestry of God's abounding love for the world (John 3:16) and God's passion for his glory (John 12:28).

What does this mean for *people* and *peoples* struggling with shame?

- *What does it mean* ... for Christ's gospel being extended to the billions of lost people and thousands of people groups whose pivotal cultural value is honor and shame? What about those peoples who are unreached and unengaged?

- *What does it mean* ... for people who are victims of abuse—whose shame is from no fault of their own?

- *What does it mean* ... for members of minority groups and minority peoples—who suffer humiliation every day of their lives?

- *What does it mean* ... for people whose overwhelming concern is their pursuit of social status, acceptance, and climbing the ladder of success?

- *What does it mean* ... for the ordinary person who lives with a constant low-grade depression because he or she somehow feels unworthy?

It means there is an answer to the perplexing problem of shame for individuals and peoples. Are we up to the task of actually communicating and living out this *global gospel?*

It is clear that knowing and experiencing the honor of Christ is biblical. We head now into the next section of the book to explore various ways that this global gospel of Christ can be understood and communicated in the light of the various dynamics of honor and shame.

SECTION 3

A Global Gospel for Our Multicultural World

A Global Gospel for Our Multicultural World

IN SECTION 1, WE DEMONSTRATED that Western theology has a blind spot concerning honor and shame, and that shame is an extremely serious sinful pathology in our world. In Section 2, we examined nine basic features of honor and shame in the Bible—and one honor/shame motif.

We have been made aware of the unethical dimensions of honor/shame by looking at the dark side of each of the various honor/shame dynamics. But we have also looked at the bright side, in which honor/shame dynamics are clearly a part of the kingdom-reign of God.

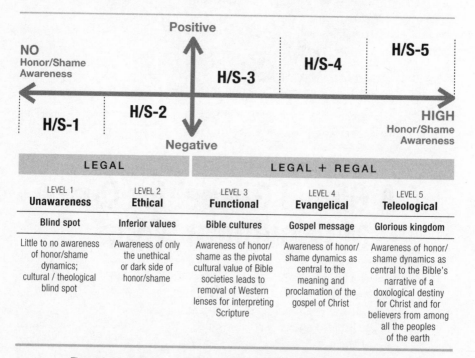

LEGAL		LEGAL + REGAL		
LEVEL 1 **Unawareness**	LEVEL 2 **Ethical**	LEVEL 3 **Functional**	LEVEL 4 **Evangelical**	LEVEL 5 **Teleological**
Blind spot	Inferior values	Bible cultures	Gospel message	Glorious kingdom
Little to no awareness of honor/shame dynamics; cultural / theological blind spot	Awareness of only the unethical or dark side of honor/shame	Awareness of honor/ shame as the pivotal cultural value of Bible societies leads to removal of Western lenses for interpreting Scripture	Awareness of honor/ shame dynamics as central to the meaning and proclamation of the gospel of Christ	Awareness of honor/ shame dynamics as central to the Bible's narrative of a doxological destiny for Christ and for believers from among all the peoples of the earth

Figure 3.01: H/S-1 to H/S-5: Levels of awareness of honor and shame
(for full chart see Appendix 2)

Referring to Figure 3.01, on the previous page, we have thus moved beyond level H/S-1—"Unawareness"—to the "Ethical" level of H/S-2, and onward into level H/S-3, the "Functional" level.

In the "Functional" level we discovered how we can *use* honor/shame dynamics to better interpret the Scriptures. We also learned about another function: knowing about honor/shame dynamics helps us better understand, and thus build relationships, with people from the Majority World.

Moreover, recalling our concern for the unreached and unevangelized peoples of the world, we considered the fact that thousands of Buddhist, Hindu, Muslim, and tribal peoples are collectivistic rather than individualistic. They are therefore much more motivated by honor/shame dynamics than Western peoples.

We posed this question at the end of Section 1: *Considering the pervasive sinful pathology of shame in our world, is the gospel of Jesus Christ robust enough, comprehensive enough, global enough to provide the cure?* We answer, YES!

A related question, however, is whether our witness to this good news actually reflects the comprehensive fullness of what the gospel of Christ can do—not only for the guilt of humanity, but also for its deeply sinful pathology of shame.

Therefore, we now move into Section 3, which is called "A Global Gospel for Our Multicultural World." This section lifts us to level H/S-4. This is the "Evangelical" level. It is at this level that we will discover how the gospel message of Jesus Christ can be articulated using any one or all of the honor/shame dynamics. We will discover the ample scriptural material that shows how the atonement of Jesus Christ overlaps with honor and shame.

We will discover that *honor/shame dynamics are central to the meaning and proclamation of the gospel of Christ.*

Caution—innovation ahead

I believe that the contents in this section represent what, for some, will be innovative and perhaps controversial, so I want to lay a strong foundation. This introduction is therefore rather lengthy in laying that foundation and consists of three parts:

Overview: In this first part, I emphasize the bias which Westerners often carry, referencing seven leading Christian scholars from around the world. The various quotes and comments from these scholars have been selected to pointedly address the issue of Western theological bias and the need for greater contextualization. *Warning:* Many North American and Western readers may feel uncomfortable with this material.

Gospel seed: In the second part, I will explain the concept of the "seed of the gospel"—husk and kernel—for the purpose of contextualizing a *global gospel.*

Conversation: In the third part, I will present an approach to contextualizing the gospel that features a "conversation within Scripture" between *the atonement of Christ* and the Bible's *pivotal cultural value of honor and shame* so that fresh presentations of the gospel can be developed that may better resonate among people in honor/shame cultures.

These three items will form the basis for the following ten chapters of Section 3.

AN OVERVIEW:
Western theological bias and the need for contextualization

David J. Bosch (1929–1992)[1]

Bosch's massive work of scholarship, *Transforming Mission: Paradigm Shifts in Theology of Mission,* has much to contribute to the discussion in this book. In writing about the colonial mission period, Bosch states:

> In chapter 9 of this study, ... I have stressed the decisive influence of Western colonialism, cultural superiority feelings, and "manifest destiny" exercised on the Western missionary enterprise and the extent to which this compromised the gospel. ... By the time the large-scale Western colonial expansion began, Western Christians were unconscious of the fact that their theology was culturally conditioned; they simply assumed that it was supra-cultural and universally valid. And since Western culture was implicitly regarded as Christian, it was equally self-evident that this culture had to be exported together with the Christian faith.[2]

Bosch speaks of the "danger of absolutism of contextualization," which I take to be reflected in the often-assumed principle that, *the Western presentation of the gospel is universally resonant for all cultures.*

This is, in fact, what has happened in Western missionary outreach where theology, contextualized in the West, was in essence elevated to gospel status and exported to other continents as a package deal. Contextualism thus means universalizing one's own theological position, making it applicable to everybody and demanding that others submit to it.[3]

Bosch then argues that the West is not alone in this tendency. It's part of human nature to think ethnocentrically—to be unaware of one's own cultural or theological bias. "If Western theology has not been immune to this tendency, neither are Third-World contextual theologies. A new imperialism in theology then replaces the old."[4]

Could it be that the days of *colonialism in mission methods* may be largely behind us—while *colonialism in theology* is still an issue? The Western Christian academy still dominates, and Western theological approaches are usually considered universally valid by Western mission practitioners and cross-cultural workers. Ponder the many Western organizations that offer theological training for all pastors anywhere—all with an unconscious Western theological bias. For

---

1. David Jacobus Bosch was an influential missiologist and theologian from South Africa. He is widely remembered for his book *Transforming Mission: Paradigm Shifts in Theology of Mission* (Maryknoll, NY: Orbis Books, 1991). This work is regarded as a "magnum opus" of Christian scholarship and one of the most comprehensive, thoroughly researched, and frequently referenced books on the mission of the Christian church. He was a member of the Dutch Reformed Church and fought for many years—courageously and counter-culturally—against apartheid in South Africa. He was Professor of Missiology at the University of South Africa in Pretoria. See "David Bosch," *Wikipedia,* http://en.wikipedia.org/wiki/David_Bosch, accessed 30 December 2013.

2. Bosch, *Transforming Mission,* 448. Bosch's chapter "Mission as Inculturation" (447–57) is an excellent overview about the problem of bias.

3. Ibid., 428.

4. Ibid.

the massive short-term mission movement, this is certainly the case. It's difficult to come to terms with the fact that the "Western air" we breathe actually influences the way we *think-and-do theology*. Moreover, does not theology affect mission practice and methodology? Considering the West's theological blind spot about honor and shame, on this count alone, I contend that the era of colonialism in world missions is not really over.[5]

Samuel Escobar[6]

"As the Father has sent me, even so I am sending you" (John 20:21). In Samuel Escobar's *The New Global Mission: The Gospel from Everywhere to Everyone*, he references John 20:21 as "not only a mandate for mission, but a model for mission style."[7] Reflecting on his participation in the Lausanne global mission consultations, Escobar writes:

> When in the light of biblical imperatives we revised some of the traditional ways of doing mission, we realized to what degree that pattern had become just a human enterprise and was in danger of being merely the religious side of the expansion of one culture and one empire.

> Essentially the shift to the emphasis of John's version of the [Great] Commission *on the way* in which Jesus himself accomplished his mission means the abandonment of the imperial mission mentality. Imperial missiology carried on missionary work from a position of superiority: political, military, financial, technological. While "the cross and the sword" symbolized it at the height of Iberian mission in the 16th century, "commerce and Christianity" symbolized it at the height of Protestant European mission in the 19th century. And in our lifetime "information technology and gospel" has come to symbolize it. In the imperial missiology paradigm, Christianity is thus dependent on the prop and tutelage of another powerful partner. ... The paradigm shift that this understanding requires is still underway, especially among the evangelical missionary establishment.[8]

Later in the book, Escobar reflects on the habit of Western Christians to impose their theology on Christians of the Majority World while being unaware of the "social conditioning" that influences it. Quoting American missionary William Dyrness, "The day is surely past when we simply allow Third World believers to have their say while we Western theologians prepare the definite answers to

---

5. Commenting on theological colonialism as a negative impact of globalization, Darrell L. Whiteman writes: "The bad news is that people are likely to try to dominate the conversation from a position of power, which in turn creates a new form of ecclesiastical and theological hegemony. Once again, it will look like the West is trying to dominate the world, not with economic structural adjustment policies that create poverty but with theological arrogance." From *Globalizing Theology: Belief and Practice in an Era of World Christianity*, eds. Craig Ott and Harold A. Netland (Grand Rapids, MI: Baker Publishing Group, 2006), Kindle edition locations 1184–86.

6. Samuel Escobar is a leading Latin American theologian. A native of Peru, he served as professor of missiology at Eastern Baptist Theological Seminary in Pennsylvania. He was also president of United Bible Societies and International Fellowship of Evangelical Students.

7. Escobar, 25.

8. Ibid., 26.

their questions. For now we recognize that if we listen carefully we find our own assumptions challenged and our thinking sharpened." Escobar continues:

> The acute question of the social conditioning of theological perception is one of the key points at which presuppositions are challenged and theological understanding may be sharpened. ... This also implies the clarification of the historical conditions within which Western theological categories developed, in order to show their limitations as ways of reading Scripture.[9]

For example, if we as North American Christians do not recognize that we have a "socially conditioned" bias that prioritizes the individual over the group, we will be more inclined to read Scripture as though it is always *written to me, the individual,* rather than *written to God's people, the community.* If we as Western Christians do not recognize that we have a "socially conditioned" bias that prioritizes the *legal* over the *regal* aspects of the gospel, we will unwittingly ignore the many references to the gospel of the kingdom in the New Testament.

Escobar is clearly calling for a new humility on the part of Western Christians with regard to our theology—to grapple with the fact that our beliefs are, in part, "socially conditioned" into "Western theological categories."

Lesslie Newbigin (1909–1998)[10]

We referenced Newbigin earlier. "We must start with the basic fact that there is no such thing as a pure gospel if by that is meant something which is not embodied in a culture. ... Every interpretation of the gospel is embodied in some cultural form." Newbigin continues: "The missionary does not come with the pure gospel and then adapt it to the culture where she serves: she comes with a gospel which is already embodied in the culture by which the missionary was formed."[11] Later in his book, he writes about the danger of a *domesticated gospel.*

> The result then is that the world is not challenged at its depth but rather absorbs and domesticates the gospel and uses it to sacralize its own purposes. We have seen that happen in the history of the old churches of Western Christendom. It is the experience of the younger churches of the East and South which has alerted us to this domestication of the gospel in our culture. ... True contextualization accords to the gospel its rightful primacy, its power to penetrate every culture and to speak within each culture, in its own speech and symbol, the word which is both No and Yes, both judgment and grace.[12]

I contend that the Christian West (and we are speaking here of the evangelical church) is exporting and promoting a *domesticated gospel,* one that reinforces its own Western theological biases. Moreover, to the degree that the Christian West

---

9. Ibid., 137.

10. Lesslie Newbigin (1909–1998) "was a British theologian, missiologist, missionary and author. Though originally ordained within the Church of Scotland, Newbigin spent much of his career serving as a missionary in India and became affiliated with the Church of South India and the United Reformed Church, becoming one of the Church of South India's first bishops. A prolific author who wrote on a wide range of theological topics, Newbigin is best known for his contributions to missiology and ecclesiology." See "Lesslie Newbigin," *Wikipedia,* http://en.wikipedia.org/wiki/Lesslie_Newbigin, accessed 30 December 2013.

11. Newbigin, 144.

12. Ibid., 152.

discourages an indigenous Christian community from using its own "speech and symbols" to create its own theology—it thereby hinders the maturing of that indigenous church.

Soong-Chan Rah[13]

Soong-Chan Rah's *The Next Evangelicalism: Freeing the Church from Western Cultural Captivity* addresses the white cultural captivity of the American evangelical church. Rah argues that this cultural captivity has been expressed in a variety of ways, including paternalism in world missions.

> In the history of world missions, one of the most significant concerns is the paternalism and cultural insensitivity that may be a part of the missionary enterprise. Because of an existing imbalance of power, the movement of the gospel message from Western culture to non-western culture yields a system of dependence and results in a cultural hegemony.[14]

Normally, I have thought about paternalism as an attitude problem (that of superiority) rather than a theological problem. Perhaps it is both. I have come to believe that an individualistic, law-oriented gospel that addresses the problem of guilt to the exclusion of the problem of shame is a form of cultural hegemony. Rah would add that there's another problem: A gospel that addresses the problem of *individual personal sins* while ignoring *social, systemic sins* of racism, consumerism, or materialism is likewise seeing the gospel from only one dimension.[15] He recommends that we look at the gospel from a variety of perspectives—like the way we can watch a football game from various vantage points, various "seats," in a stadium:

> It is the arrogance of Western, white captivity to assume that one's own cultural point of view is the *be all* and *end all* of the gospel story. Every seat has its advantages and disadvantages, and it is imperative for the entire global community of believers to learn from one another in order to more fully understand the depth of the character of God.[16]

Tite Tiénou[17]

Tite Tiénou references the dramatic southward shift of the world Christian movement and how this can help rectify the misperception of Christianity as a Western religion.

13. "Rev. Dr. Soong-Chan Rah is Milton B. Engebretson Associate Professor of Church Growth and Evangelism at North Park Theological Seminary in Chicago, Illinois, and the author of *The Next Evangelicalism: Freeing the Church from Western Cultural Captivity* (Downers Grove, IL: InterVarsity Press, 2009). Rah is formerly the founding Senior Pastor of the Cambridge Community Fellowship Church (CCFC), a multi-ethnic, urban ministry-focused church committed to living out the values of racial reconciliation and social justice in the urban context." See *Profrah.com*, http://www.profrah.com/about.html, accessed 30 December 2013.

14. Rah, Kindle edition locations 2178–81.

15. Ibid. Chapter 2 is "Consumerism and Materialism: The Soul of Western, White Cultural Captivity" (Kindle edition locations 679–81). Chapter 3 is "Racism: The Residue of Western, White Cultural Captivity" (Kindle edition locations 1000–1001).

16. Ibid., Kindle edition locations 2301–04.

17. Tite Tiénou is co-provost, senior vice president of education and dean at Trinity Evangelical Divinity School in Deerfield, Illinois. He is also professor of theology of mission. Dr. Tiénou has served as president and dean of Faculté de Théologie Évangélique de l'Alliance Chrétienne in Abidjan, Côte d'Ivoire, West Africa. He also served as a pastor in his native Burkina Faso. See *Trinity Evangelical Divinity School*, http://divinity.tiu.edu/academics/faculty/tite-tienou-phd/, accessed 30 December 2013.

The good news, in this case, is that since people of color now represent the majority of Christians in the world, the perception of Christianity as a Western religion can be corrected. Making the case for Christianity on the basis that it is a worldwide global religion can, especially in Africa, erase the stigma of Christianity as a white man's religion. This will bring about apologetic dividends not only for Christians in Africa but also for those in Asia, Latin America, and the Pacific Islands. In other words, if Christianity is de-Westernized, Christians in Africa, Asia, and Latin America will be able to defend themselves when accused of being agents of Westernization and puppets in the hands of foreigners whose intention is the destruction of local cultures and religions.[18]

However, Tiénou also critiques the reluctance of the Western theological academy to come to terms with the globalizing of the Christian faith.

Acknowledging the fact that the majority of Christians are no longer Westerners is one thing. One may even concede that the demographic future of Christianity belongs to Africa, Asia, and Latin America. Does this also mean that the future of Christian theology and scholarship is being decided on these continents as well? One cannot presume a positive answer to this question in spite of the fact that Andrew Walls affirms that "the primary responsibility for the determinative theological scholarship for the twenty-first century will lie with the Christian communities of Africa, Asia, and Latin America."[19]

Tiénou expands on the challenge of Western theological bias by acknowledging the problem of English as the de facto language of theological conferences and scholarship:

English seems to be the language of global Christianity; it dominates international Christian conferences and international theologizing. ... The present domination of English in international theologizing effectively closes the door to theologians who do not express their thoughts in that language. But can Christian scholarship and theology be truly global with one language in control? The use of English as the de facto language for international theological scholarship can only reinforce the dialogue of the deaf.[20]

Tiénou's usage of the phrase, "the dialog of the deaf," refers to the caricature of Americans as bad listeners. Tiénou applies the phrase to Christian theologians and the academy when he writes, " ... America and the third world are engaged in a dialogue of the deaf. This characterization is applicable to the relationship between Western Christian scholars and those in Africa, Asia, and Latin America." He quotes Ali Mazrui: "Americans are brilliant communicators but bad listeners."[21]

---

18. Tite Tiénou: "Christian Theology in an Era of World Christianity" in *Globalizing Theology: Belief and Practice in an Era of World Christianity,* eds. Ott and Netland (Grand Rapids, MI: Baker Publishing Group, 2006), Kindle edition locations 692–98.

19. Ibid., Kindle edition locations 747–52. Tiénou quotes Andrew Walls: 2002a. "Christian Scholarship in Africa in the Twenty-first Century." *Transformation* 19, no. 4 (October): 217–28.

20. Ibid., Kindle edition locations 848–53.

21. Ibid., Kindle edition locations 840–42. Tiénou quotes Ali Mazrui, *Cultural Forces in World Politics* (Portsmouth, NH: Heinemann, 1990).

Timothy C. Tennent[22]

We have already referenced Tennent's book, *Theology in the Context of World Christianity*.[23] This book is a remarkable overview of a variety of theologies in our world. Tennent grapples with being faithful to the authority of the biblical text, while at the same time learning from various theologies in our incredibly diverse global Christian community.

Tennent has also written *Invitation to World Missions: A Trinitarian Missiology for the Twenty-first Century*. He writes of "Mission by Translation" and examines how the early church sought to "communicate the gospel within the intellectual and linguistic frameworks of their hearers, rather than insisting that the Gentiles discover Jesus within the existing framework of Judaism."[24] Tennent cites three examples of how the early church adapted their message using the "thought forms of their target group."[25] Tennent's three examples are summarized as follows:

- **"Jesus as Messiah—Jesus as Lord."**[26] Consider these two verses that historian Luke records in Acts: "Now those who were scattered because of the persecution that arose over Stephen traveled as far as Phoenicia and Cyprus and Antioch, speaking the word to no one except Jews. But there were some of them, men of Cyprus and Cyrene, who on coming to Antioch spoke to the Hellenists also, preaching the Lord Jesus" (Acts 11:19–20). Tennent says that the church that was scattered was "speaking the word to no one except Jews," but others "spoke to the Hellenists;" these were the Gentile Greeks, the non-Jews. How did they communicate the gospel to them? They could have preached *Christ* Jesus—meaning *Messiah* Jesus, alluding to the hopes and longings of the Jewish people. But, Tennent writes, "The title *Messiah*, as rich as it was, simply did not carry much meaning for a Gentile." Instead, they were "preaching the *Lord* Jesus." Tennent says, "They utilized the title *kurios*, which, although richly used in the biblical tradition, was the word Hellenistic pagans gave to their cult deities."[27]

- **"Jewish Scriptures and Pagan Sources."**[28] Acts 17:16–34 records the account of Paul's visit to Athens. He visited the Areopagus where he preached a message to those who were gathered there. Instead of using Old Testament prophecies of the Messiah as a beginning point of communication, he finds common ground by quoting two Greek poets with whom the Athenians were undoubtedly familiar.

---

22. "Asbury Theological Seminary President Timothy C. Tennent took office on July 1, 2009, and was inaugurated in November of the same year. He previously served 11 years as Professor of World Missions and Indian Studies at Gordon-Conwell Theological Seminary in South Hamilton, Mass. ... He also teaches annually at the Luther W. New Jr. Theological College of Dehra Dun, India, where he has served as an adjunct professor since 1989. He has also ministered and taught in China, Thailand, Nigeria and Eastern Europe. Ordained in the United Methodist Church, he has pastored churches in Georgia, and preached regularly in churches throughout New England and across the country." See *timothytennent.com*, http://timothytennent.com/about/, accessed 30 December 2013.

23. Timothy Tennent, *Theology in the Context of World Christianity* (Grand Rapids, MI: Zondervan, 2007).

24. Tennent, *Invitation to World Missions*, 329.

25. Ibid., 332.

26. Ibid., 328.

27. Ibid.

28. Ibid., 329.

In verse 28, Paul quotes from the seventh-century B.C. Cretan poet Epimenedes, when he declares, "In him we live and move and have our being." In the same verse Paul goes on to say, "As even some of your own poets have said, 'We are indeed his offspring,'" which Tennent adds is "a quotation from the Cilician poet Aratus."[29]

- **"Jesus is the logos of God."**[30] The Apostle John begins his Gospel, "In the beginning was the Word, and the Word was with God, and the Word was God" (John 1:1). The Greek word *logos* is translated *Word* and refers to an impersonal force, the "active reason" or "animating principle"[31] for the creation and sustaining of the universe. "John's contemporaries would have understood *logos* as a philosophical term referring to a rational capacity or generative principle that is present in all of nature."[32] So when John writes, "And the Word became flesh and dwelt among us" (John 1:14), he transformed the usage of the word *logos* as an impersonal force to a usage depicting the deeply personal, relational Jesus—the One who is fully God and fully human.

Jackson Wu[33]

In Section 1, Chapter 2, we explored some of the ideas from Jackson Wu's *Saving God's Face*. His diagram (see pages 49–51) helped us understand why theological blind spots occur. I'll add here one paragraph from his book:

> The aforementioned observations are not an implicit condemnation of Western theology. Rather, it is essential that those seeking to contextualize the gospel plainly recognize the long theological current that moves much Western missiological thinking. If particular Western conceptions of the gospel are assumed and then contextualized for another cultural context, serious questions arise about the viability of a genuinely non-western articulation of the gospel. This is not to say other contextual theologies must contradict historically Western theologies. Susan Baker highlights a danger of contextualization, namely "reductionism." She warns against constricting theology to any one set of themes and texts, cautioning, "In this [reductionism] we find that we have reduced Scripture to only one part of what the Lord has to say to us, and we lose sight of the overall redemptive-historical unfolding of God's complete plan for us." In short, uncritically assuming the gospel can undermine the credibility of contextualization.[34]

Wu's phrase "uncritically assuming the gospel" is key. I contend that a majority of Western pastors and Christian leaders, along with missionaries and short-term

---

29. Ibid.
30. Ibid., 332.
31. Ibid.
32. Ibid.
33. Jackson Wu is a teacher at a seminary in Asia. His degrees include: B.S. (Applied Mathematics), M.A. (Philosophy), M.Div, Ph.D (Applied Theology). His blog is jacksonwu.org.
34. Wu, 20–21. Wu quotes Susan Baker in "The Social Sciences for Urban Ministry," in *The Urban Face of Mission: Ministering the Gospel in a Diverse and Changing World,* eds. Manuel Ortiz and Susan S. Baker (Phillipsburg, NJ: P & R Publishing, 2002), 77.

mission trip-goers, are unwittingly "assuming the gospel" and thereby practicing "reductionism" with their Western ways of thinking.

Western theological bias begets the need for more effective contextualization

In quoting these seven scholars—Bosch, Escobar, Newbigin, Rah, Tiénou, Tennent, and Wu—the point I am trying to make is two-fold.

- First, I am emphasizing that the Western Christian community tends to exert its own theological biases in the global church; this needs to be recognized and mitigated.

- Second, effective contextualization is essential for making the gospel come alive in every culture.

It is wrong to *assume* that the gospel as articulated in one culture is the best way to articulate it in another culture. To "assume the gospel" as Bosch and Wu contend, runs the risk of an imperialist attitude (often unwittingly) that prioritizes Western culture over others.[35]

Moreover, as Timothy Tennent points out, we see from the very authors of Scripture, that the gospel can borrow phrases, words, "thought forms" from the audience—the people to whom the gospel is being presented—in order to more faithfully communicate the richness and depth of the good news of Jesus Christ.[36]

I contend that the "thought forms" of thousands of non-Western, unreached and unengaged people groups consist in large measure of the pivotal cultural value of honor and shame. Plus, many of our neighbors in our cities and communities—whether co-workers, colleagues, immigrants, refugees, students, asylum seekers—have "thought forms" that likewise overlap with the values of honor and shame—*much more* than with the Western values of guilt, innocence and law.

Western-educated Christians must find better ways to communicate the expansive, transforming truths of the gospel of Christ without having to carry the Western baggage with which they are so comfortable.

THE SEED OF THE GOSPEL

David Bosch writes about *the seed of the gospel* having two parts: the *husk* and the *kernel*. The husk refers to *form;* the kernel refers to *function.*[37] Bosch contends that the traditional approach to contextualization by Christian missionaries has been to modify the husk while keeping the kernel the same; in other words, the kernel

---

35. Chris Flanders provides a lucid example from the missionary enterprise in Thailand, referencing a report published back in 1888. The missionaries articulated a "gospel," which although true, was also unwittingly rooted, in part, in Western thought forms. It meant that "Thai people and Thai culture had nothing to contribute to the gospel message." Flanders contends this has resulted in "a deep disconnect with Thai culture, the effects of which the Christian church in Thailand continue to struggle against, even to this present day." See Flanders, 19–20.

36. Dean Flemming has written an entire book on this subject: *Contextualization in the New Testament: Patterns for Theology and Mission.* He identifies how various authors of the New Testament borrowed the ideas and thought forms of their respective audiences—both to articulate the gospel and to help them move toward Christ-centered transformation.

37. Bosch, 449.

is the gospel and it is supra-cultural. He critiques this traditional view as follows:

> The faith as understood and canonized in the Western church ... was the unalloyed *kernel;* [on the other hand] the cultural accoutrements of the people to whom the missionaries went were the expendable *husk.* In the accommodation process, the *kernel* had to remain intact but adapted to the forms of the new culture; at the same time, these cultures had to be adapted to the "kernel." (Emphasis mine.)[38]

Bosch contends that a traditional view of contextualization is inadequate. Jackson Wu agrees:

> [M]any view contextualization as a process that comes after one has already settled on the meaning of the gospel, that is, what

The Seed of the Gospel
(only the "husk" contextualized)

Figure 3.02: Seed of the gospel— traditional view (language and other cultural forms change, but how the gospel is articulated remains unchanged)

The Seed of the Gospel
(both the "husk" and the "kernel" contextualized)

Figure 3.03: Seed of the gospel— modified view

constitutes its content. [Kevin] Vanhoozer, critical of this approach, says, "Contextual theology, according to this view, is a matter of extracting the doctrinal kernel from its original cultural husk and then reinserting it in, or adapting it to, a new cultural husk. The key presupposition of this model is that the essential message is supra-cultural, able to be abstracted from its concrete mode of expression. Contextualization, according to this view, is primarily a matter of communication: decoding and encoding."[39]

What is needed is an approach to contextualization that goes beyond *decoding and encoding*—to contextualize both the *husk and kernel* of the gospel.[40] This way, by the grace of God and the Holy Spirit, the gospel would best resonate with the host culture or people group. The gospel would therefore have a greater likelihood of being received and being transformational.

---

38. Ibid., 449.

39. Wu, 23. Wu quotes Kevin Vanhoozer, "'One Rule to Rule Them All?' Theological Method in an Era of World Christianity," in *Globalizing Theology: Belief and Practice in an Era of World Christianity*, eds. Craig Ott and Harold Netland (Grand Rapids, MI: Baker Academic & Brazos Press, 2006), 100.

40. Chris Flanders uses the concept of "gospel seed" as *husk* and *kernel* to critique the persistent failure of mission efforts in Thailand to effectively contextualize the gospel, "Rarely ... does discussion about the proper content of the [gospel] message exist. Even those who do attempt to formulate a message more in terms of Thai culture ultimately offer only new *husks* within which the essential evangelical *kernel* of remission of sins and relief from guilt may be more effectively wrapped. To this day, it seems that there is little attention to how Thai culture may help frame the message of the gospel" [emphasis mine]. See Flanders, 38.

Summary: Every communication of gospel content, including the very *kernel* of the gospel, contains cultural assumptions and ideas which, first of all, resonate with the culture of the messenger (preacher, missionary, believer). The question is whether it *also resonates* with the people with whom the messenger is communicating.

Could it be that Western believers can do a better job presenting the gospel to Majority World peoples so that the good news truly resonates? Could it be that the key is including biblical "thought forms" *in the very kernel of the gospel*—which include the values of honor and shame?

"CONVERSATION WITHIN SCRIPTURE"
between the atonement of Christ and honor/shame

Jackson Wu recommends a "dialogical approach to contextualization"—a *dialog* or *conversation* between "Scripture, the interpreter, the missionary/messenger, and the recipient of the message."[41] I am doing something like that in this third section of the book.

We will explore several theological "conversations" in Section 3. Each "conversation" consists of a question about the gospel and culture—specifically the cultural value of honor and shame—followed by an exploration from Scripture which, in turn, will provide an answer.

In Section 2, we examined in the Bible nine different dynamics of honor/shame societies—and one honor/shame motif—for a total of ten separate dynamics. In this section, we will devote one chapter to each of these ten dynamics. Here's the question we will be asking in each chapter.

> *Is there enough biblical material to warrant an exploration of how the honor/shame dynamic intersects with the good news of Jesus Christ, so that a fresh presentation of the gospel can be developed to better resonate among people in honor/shame cultures?*

The diagram for this conversation looks like this:

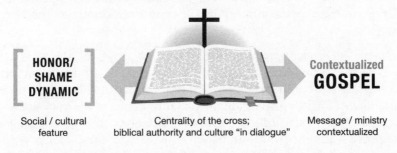

HONOR/ SHAME DYNAMIC		Contextualized **GOSPEL**
Social / cultural feature	Centrality of the cross; biblical authority and culture "in dialogue"	Message / ministry contextualized

Figure 3.04: Conversation between Scripture, honor/shame dynamics, and the gospel

---

41. Wu, 1. For the phrase "dialogical contextualization," Wu references David K. Clark, *To Know and Love God: Method for Theology* (Wheaton, IL: Crossway, 2003).

In each chapter we will explore biblical material about the atonement of Christ—crux of every gospel message—and whether it overlaps with the particular honor/shame dynamic in question.[42] We will be making some exciting discoveries.

Can the culture of Scripture be the primary influence in the way we articulate the gospel?

I propose that this "dialogical" exploration between Christ's atonement and various honor/shame dynamics in Scripture can be helpful to the global church. We live in an increasingly multicultural church in which theological dialog focuses on varying facets of the gospel, informed by various local cultures, traditions, and histories. For example, Western theology, African theology, Chinese theology, Latin American theology—these *all* are shaped in part by values of their respective host cultures.

In contrast, the exploration contained in this section attempts to offer gospel presentation alternatives which are informed by the Bible's *own* culture—the pivotal cultural value of honor and shame. Culturally speaking, we are using the honor/shame culture of Bible societies as a *starting point*. This may be distinguished from starting with cultural signposts in a host culture which, through the creative efforts of a missionary or theologian, may in turn point to the gospel.

Whereas local theologies may be influenced by unique local customs, traditions, or social dynamics, in this exploration we begin with Scripture's own pivotal cultural value of honor and shame and attempt to find valid variations for articulating the gospel message.

Kevin Vanhoozer has written about intercultural theological dialog in a globalized world; he writes forcefully about the challenge and the value of placing primary importance on *Scripture*—over culture, tradition or history.

> The lived experience of this or that culture, along with the history and tradition of the church as a whole, has a legitimate role to play as a *secondary* theological source. The primary source, however, must remain Scripture. The Bible is the formative text with which all Christians, regardless of their cultural context, must ultimately grapple, the authoritative script that all Christians must perform, albeit in a diversity of culturally appropriate ways.[43]

Indeed: *"The primary source, however, must remain Scripture."* This third section of the book shows how each of the honor/shame dynamics (presented in Section 2) overlaps with the atonement of Christ. You will see that these multifaceted explorations of Christ's gospel contained in this section of the book are wholly based on the Bible. You will also see that these variations in expressing the gospel message are different from—and supplementary to—traditional Western approaches.

---

42. See Timothy Tennent's excellent overview of the implications of honor and shame for systematic theology, especially in relation to the atonement, in his *Theology in the Context of World Christianity,* 92–101. Tennent covers "The Public Nature of the Atonement" (94–95), "The Social and Relational Aspect of the Atonement" (95–97), and "Process of Christian Conversion (Application of the Atonement)" (97–99).

43. Vanhoozer, Kindle edition locations 1937–41.

Dean Flemming writes that Paul contextualized his gospel message. He used various ways to articulate the gospel depending on the cultural and social situation.

> Rather than consistently talking about the meaning of salvation in Christ in a few standard terms, [Paul] deploys whatever language will bring out the particular dimension of salvation a given church needs to hear. This observation has implications for our efforts to describe the experience of God's saving work to contemporary people. It surely ought to caution us against exalting any single metaphor or theme—whether "justification by faith" or being "born again" or "Spirit baptism"—to a dominant position. If we follow Paul's lead, we will recognize both the richness of language available to us to describe the church's multidimensional experience of salvation and the variety of situations to which that language must be applied.[44]

Timothy Tennent writes that "honor and shame are among the most important values in the ancient Mediterranean world, and continue to play a vital role in the formation of human identity in much of North Africa, Middle East, and Asia. *A deeper appreciation for how the gospel relates to these values* will be increasingly important as the church continues to expand in the context of cultures that are predominantly shame-based."[45] (Emphasis mine.)

How the gospel relates to honor/shame values is what this section is all about. *You will see:* The church *is able* to articulate the gospel in more than judicial terms. The multifaceted gospel of Jesus Christ does reveal a salvation—not only from the *guilt* of our sinful *behavior*—but also from the *shame* of our sinful *being*.

My intention in this section is that you will more clearly behold our glorious God and Savior by understanding a more multifaceted *global gospel* that may deeply resonate with more individuals, families, and peoples all over the world.

We therefore turn now to Chapter 1 of Section 3 and ask: *Is there a global gospel shaped by the "love of honor"?*

---

44. Flemming, Kindle edition location 107.
45. Tennent, *Theology in the Context of World Christianity*, 101.

A Gospel Shaped by the "Love of Honor"?

Explore a "global gospel." Is there enough biblical material to warrant an exploration of how the dynamic of the **love of honor** intersects with the good news of Jesus Christ, so that a fresh presentation of the gospel can be developed to better resonate among people in honor/shame cultures?

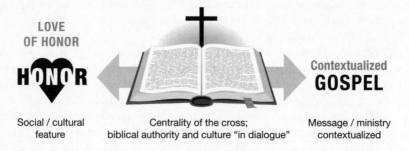

LOVE OF HONOR		Contextualized GOSPEL
Social / cultural feature	Centrality of the cross; biblical authority and culture "in dialogue"	Message / ministry contextualized

Figure 3.05: Can there be a gospel presentation framed by the love of honor?

Yes, there is abundant material in Scripture connecting the "love of honor" with the gospel of Jesus Christ.

Such a presentation of a "global gospel" may be crafted according to this principle: *For peoples living in societies with the pivotal cultural value of honor and shame—the longing for honor and, correspondingly, the alleviation of shame, can be a motivating factor in their journey of believing in Christ and gaining eternal life.*

Most Western presentations of the gospel assume that the primary felt need of *all humanity* is the alleviation of guilt from sin,[1] and that the cross of Christ addresses this need. But this derives from a Western theological bias. Instead, why not begin a "gospel message" with the assumption of humanity's longing for glory and honor, and correspondingly, the alleviation of shame?

---

1. The sin, guilt and shame of all humanity before God is biblically and *objectively* true. The question is not whether this is objectively true. The question is whether a focus on the alleviation of sin and guilt is the best initial message of the gospel to address the *subjective* felt need of peoples for whom honor and shame is a pivotal cultural value.

A gospel message that assumes humanity's longing for glory and honor? Yes! Both Jesus and Paul included these dynamics in their communication. Jesus said to the unbelieving Pharisees, "How can you believe, when you receive glory from one another and do not seek the glory that comes from the only God?" (John 5:44). Paul wrote to the believers at Rome, "To those who by patience in well-doing seek for glory and honor and immortality, he will give eternal life" (Rom 2:7).

One may rightly ask, "But where does the *longing for honor*—and humanity's corresponding need for *the covering of shame*—intersect with the cross of Christ? How does the atonement answer this need?" Below are some options:

Option 1: The Parable of the Prodigal Son as entry point for the gospel. "The Father's Love Gospel Booklet" (see next page) is an example of a "global gospel" presentation that incorporates the longing for honor and the covering of shame. It contains the story of the Prodigal Son, along with artwork that goes along with the story.[2] It is a fitting presentation of the gospel for people who have honor and shame as a vital cultural value.

Shown on the next page are six pages of the twenty-page booklet.[3] The six pages provide a sampling of both the *narrative parts* (pages 1–15)—and *propositional* elements (pages 16–20)—of this gospel presentation.[4]

One of the keys to this "gospel presentation" is the dramatic way that the father in the story endures shame both in relation to the younger son and the older son. Hence, this statement from the booklet: *"Jesus is teaching that God is like a father willing to suffer shame for us."* It points to the verse in Hebrews which says that Jesus, "the founder and perfecter of our faith, who for the joy that was set before him *endured the cross, despising the shame,* and is seated at the right hand of the throne of God" (Heb 12:2). (Emphasis mine.) A key paragraph in the booklet is as follows:

> JESUS DEFEATED SIN, SHAME, DEATH. He died on the cross, suffering shame for all peoples. But in rising from death, Jesus defeated sin and shame for us. And when we believe in Jesus, following Him day by day, we can truly live in victory over sin and shame![5]

"The Father's Love Gospel Booklet" is available in English, Spanish, and Arabic. It is an example of creatively contextualizing both the *husk* and *kernel* of "the seed of the gospel," while retaining fidelity to the Scriptures.

---

2. All of the pages for this booklet may be seen at http://thefatherslovebooklet.org. Designed by Werner Mischke and produced by Mission ONE, 2012. The booklet is available in English and Spanish in the United States. An Arabic version has been produced for distribution in the Middle East. Illustrations are by Robert H. Flores.

3. See http://thefatherslovebooklet.org for the complete pages of The Father's Love Booklet.

4. Jeff Gulleson provided inspiration for the booklet as a resource by which a believer could have a conversation with another person about the nature of the father's suffering love. Mark D. Baker provided significant recommendations for the content of this booklet through personal correspondence. Additional general insights from Kenneth Bailey, *The Cross and the Prodigal: Luke 15 Through the Eyes of Middle Eastern Peasants* (Downers Grove, IL: InterVarsity Press, 2005); Timothy Keller, *The Prodigal God: Recovering the Heart of the Faith* (New York: Penguin, 2008); John MacArthur, *The Prodigal Son: An Astonishing Study of the Parable Jesus Told to Unveil God's Grace for You* (Nashville, TN: Thomas Nelson, 2008).

5. "The Father's Love" booklet, page 18. See http://thefatherslovebooklet.org.

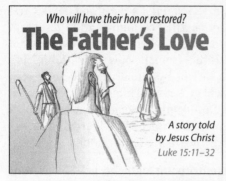

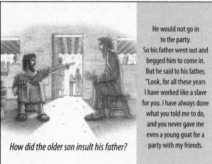
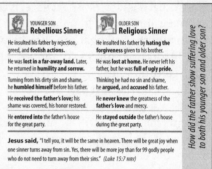
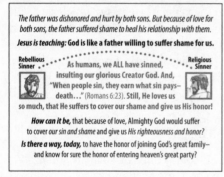
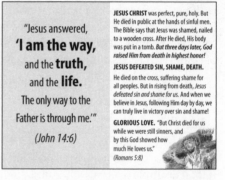

Figure 3.06: Six pages from The Father's Love Booklet (reduced in size to fit on page)

Option 2: Concern for honor and shame in 1 Peter. A second possibility for presenting a gospel message—in which the longing for honor connects with the atonement—would be a booklet, sermon or sermon series from the book of 1 Peter. Here's why:

First, clear references to salvation and the atoning work of Christ on the cross are contained in this epistle (1:3, 18–19; 2:24; 3:18).

Second, the epistle is written to believers who are enduring shame, slander, and hostility because of their faith (1:6; 2:4, 11, 19–21; 3:9, 14–16; 4:1, 12–14, 19; 5:9–10).

Third, Peter places enormous emphasis on the supreme honor of the believer and the prestige of the Christian family (1:6–9, 12, 20–21; 2:4–10; 4:1; 5:4–6, 10–11).

It may be summed up by Peter's declaration "So the honor is for you who believe" (2:7), which is made in the context of a quotation from Isaiah 28:16:

> For it stands in Scripture: "Behold, I am laying in Zion a stone, a cornerstone chosen and precious, and whoever believes in him will not be put to shame." So the honor is for you who believe, but for those who do not believe, "The stone that the builders rejected has become the cornerstone" (1 Pet 2:6–7).

Using the epistle of 1 Peter, every pastor, Bible teacher, or cross-cultural worker should be able to develop a spoken gospel presentation by which the atonement of Jesus Christ intersects with the longing for honor and covering of shame.

Other options for a global gospel highlighting the love of honor:

- *"I will ... make your name great"* (Gen 12:2). This idea is suitable for Muslims, Asian societies, tribal peoples, and others who are devoted to one's ancestors. Present God's purpose with ancient Abraham as an introduction to the gospel of justification by faith (Gen 12:1–3; Gal 3:7–29). Show how Israel is *relativized* because the global gospel is for *all* families and peoples. You can demonstrate how Abraham's story is foundational for the gospel of grace, revealing that Jesus is the offspring of Abraham (Gal 3:16). While this may be a long complicated story, it is likely that people from oral cultures will delight in its complex drama.

- *"Awake, my glory!"* (Ps 57:8). Create a gospel sermon, booklet, or smartphone app with pictures around Psalm 57. Highlight the drama of David's victory over Goliath, the jealousy of Saul and his consequent efforts to kill David, and David's longing for regal honor as expressed in Psalm 57:7–9. Link with Romans 3:23—"for all have sinned and fall short of the glory of God." Show that a relationship with Jesus Christ, who died for our sins, is the means for having one's *glory awakened* for the most glorious purpose on earth: the global mission of God that his glory be declared among all peoples and nations.

What is the significance of a global gospel incorporating the "love of honor"?

Below are some questions that arise from this exploration:

- In what ways is salvation the fulfillment of the longing to have one's shame covered and one's honor restored?

- What can you do with your team to creatively produce resources that highlight a "global gospel" focused on a message of *salvation in Christ as the fulfillment of the longing for honor and the covering of shame?*

- Can we be creative enough to build an expression of a gospel message that extends beyond the cure for guilt and craft a more "global gospel" of Jesus Christ in light of the *longing for honor and alleviation of shame?*

A Gospel Shaped by the "Two Sources of Honor"?

Explore a "global gospel." Is there enough biblical material to warrant an exploration of how the **two sources of honor** intersect with the good news of Jesus Christ, so that a fresh presentation of the gospel can be developed to better resonate among people in honor/shame cultures?

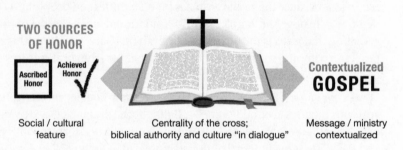

Figure 3.07: Can there be a gospel presentation that incorporates the dynamics of ascribed or achieved honor?

Yes, there is abundant material in Scripture connecting the "two sources of honor" with the gospel of Jesus Christ.

There are two ways that come to mind of how the *two sources of honor, ascribed and achieved,* can be incorporated into a gospel message. The first focuses on Christ. The second focuses on new believers.

Option 1: Focus on the ascribed and achieved honor of Jesus Christ. This is based on the belief that many will be attracted to the suffering servant Jesus Christ who ascended into highest honor and glory. Jesus affirmed this when he said,

> "And I, when I am lifted up from the earth, will draw all people to myself" (John 12:32).[1]

---

1. "[T]he words of Jesus in John 12:32—'When I am *lifted up* from the earth'—have traditionally been interpreted as reference to both his being 'lifted up' on the cross and to his ascension." Bosch, 516.

A gospel presentation that focuses on the ascribed and achieved honor of Christ could appeal to peoples who have—as part of their culture—high honor (even worship) for ancestors. The genealogy of Christ in Matthew 1 takes on a whole new significance for it represents his ascribed kinship-based honor, and thus might be a beginning point for sharing the gospel.

Further expressions of the ascribed and achieved honor of Christ would be represented by:

- The affection of the Father toward the Son at the baptism of Jesus: "And behold, a voice from heaven said, 'This is my beloved Son, with whom I am well pleased'" (Mat 3:17).
- The verses in Paul's letter to the church at Philippi commemorating the incarnation and humiliation of Jesus Christ, followed by his highly exalted reign (Phil 2:5–11).
- Hebrews 1—a most eloquent introduction to this epistle, quoting many Old Testament prophets and describing both the ascribed and achieved honor of Christ.

One wonders whether a simple booklet or video of these verses focusing on the supreme honor of Jesus Christ—perhaps with key stories of his life—would, by the Holy Spirit, capture the hearts of those who are searching for a truly pure and regal King in whom to place their allegiance and derive their honor.

Where does Christ's honor intersect with the atonement? The honor of Christ most plainly intersects with the cross in Philippians 2:5–11. Paul clearly shows that Christ's achieved honor was gained by his infinite humility, virtue, and love. This led him to the most shameful "death on a cross"—the very turning point toward his resurrection and super-exaltation:

> Therefore God has highly exalted him and bestowed on him the name that is above every name, so that at the name of Jesus every knee should bow, in heaven and on earth and under the earth, and every tongue confess that Jesus Christ is Lord, to the glory of God the Father (Phil 2:9–11).

The first chapter of Hebrews places similar emphasis on the achieved honor of Christ as both Creator and Savior:

> through whom also he created the world. ... He upholds the universe by the word of his power. After making purification for sins, he sat down at the right hand of the Majesty on high (Heb 1:2–3).

The key question for readers of such a "global gospel" presentation might be: *Would you like to be known by the most honorable Person in the universe?* Consider Jesus' promise that "he would draw all peoples to himself" as the result of being "lifted up." This represents both his being lifted up on the cross as well as his *exalted ascension*. It is tantalizing to imagine how resonant a message of his honorific ascension might be for people in honor/shame cultures. Isn't it possible that a message focused on the ascribed and achieved honor of Christ would be far more resonant with peoples from honor/shame cultures than it would be in the West?

Let's consider now a second way a global gospel presentation could be conceived focusing on the two sources of honor.

Option 2: Focus on the new source of ascribed honor available to believers. The honor of God himself as the Father of a new family is the same honor in which his children live. This new kinship group of which God is Father is called the church, the body of Christ, the "one new man" (Eph 2:15), the *one new humanity*.

- He predestined us for adoption as sons through Jesus Christ, according to the purpose of his will (Eph 1:5).

- See what kind of love the Father has given to us, that we should be called children of God; and so we are. (1 John 3:1).

- But to all who did receive him, who believed in his name, he gave the right to become children of God (John 1:12).

The word *right* in John 1:12 is from the Greek word *exousia,* which is most often translated *authority* in the New Testament. It has tremendous connotations of honor. In the next verse, John is emphasizing that the essential heredity of those who believe "in his name" is changed forever by Christ. Those who believe in the name/honor of Christ are "born, not of blood nor of the will of the flesh nor of the will of man, but of God" (John 1:13). Ultimately, in the eternal sense, one's spiritual DNA is what matters, not the DNA of one's parents or ancestors. This is why being born again is *vital,* in the truest sense of the word.

> Jesus answered him, "Truly, truly, I say to you, unless one is born again he cannot see the kingdom of God." Nicodemus said to him, "How can a man be born when he is old? Can he enter a second time into his mother's womb and be born?" Jesus answered, "Truly, truly, I say to you, unless one is born of water and the Spirit, he cannot enter the kingdom of God. That which is born of the flesh is flesh, and that which is born of the Spirit is spirit" (John 3:3–6).

Thus, believers have their personal honor completely relocated by God into his family and kingdom. While one's family honor may or may not be great and may vary according to life's good or bad circumstances, the high honor derived from being born again as a child of God is forever settled. For followers of Christ, even death fails to extinguish the honor and vitality of their eternal family identity, for "in him we have obtained an inheritance" (Eph 1:11).

Where does this new honor for believers as children of God—members of a new family, a new reconciling community—intersect with the atonement? The answer is found in Paul's letter to the Ephesians, chapters 1 and 2.

- In love he predestined us for adoption as sons through Jesus Christ, according to the purpose of his will. ... In him we have redemption through his blood, the forgiveness of our trespasses, according to the riches of his grace. ... In him we have obtained an inheritance (Eph 1:4–5, 7, 11).

- And might reconcile us both to God in one body through the cross, thereby killing the hostility. ... So then you are no longer strangers and aliens, but you are fellow citizens with the saints and members of the household of God (Eph 2:16, 19).

The forgiveness of sins "through Jesus Christ," removes both our alienation from God, as well as the alienation between peoples, and forever establishes us as adopted sons and daughters in God's one family, "members of the household of God."

What is the significance of a global gospel incorporating "two sources of honor—ascribed and achieved"?

Below are some questions that arise from this exploration:

- Jesus promised, "And I, when I am lifted up from the earth, will draw all people to myself" (John 12:32). In what way is the worship and exaltation of Jesus Christ *itself* a form of evangelism?

- How would a compilation of key scriptural passages that focus on the ascribed and achieved honor of Jesus Christ (Mat 1:1–17; 3:13–17; Phil 2:5–11; Heb 1:1–13) be a good evangelistic resource?

- What can you do with your team to creatively produce resources that highlight a "global gospel" focused on the honor of being a spiritual child of eternal God the Father?

- What can you do to insure that your church or mission team is not a community that causes shame, but rather is a family that builds shame resilience and helps lead believers to have their shame covered and their honor restored?

- What is the role of the Holy Spirit in giving believers the experiential knowledge that they are honored children of God, adopted into God's family? Paul wrote, "Hope does not put us to shame, because God's love has been poured into our hearts through the Holy Spirit who has been given to us" (Rom 5:5). What can leaders do to create a culture of honor so that believers are experiencing "God's love" being "poured into our hearts through the Holy Spirit"?

A Gospel Shaped by the "Image of Limited Good"?

Explore a "global gospel." Is there enough biblical material to warrant an exploration of how the **"image of limited good"** *intersects with the good news of Jesus Christ, so that a fresh presentation of the gospel can be developed to better resonate among people in honor/shame cultures?*

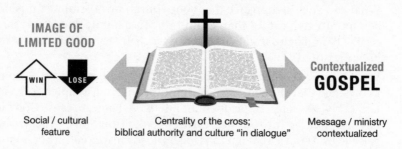

| Social / cultural feature | Centrality of the cross; biblical authority and culture "in dialogue" | Message / ministry contextualized |

Figure 3.08: Can there be a gospel presentation that incorporates the dynamic of the image of limited good?

The gospel of Jesus Christ may be found, not in the "image of limited good," but in its antithesis—"unlimited good."

The honor/shame social dynamic known as the *image of limited good* is inconsistent with the gospel of Christ. This is because Scripture clearly reveals the *unlimited good* of God's glory and grace (John 3:16; Phil 4:19). One could point to the limited good of humanity, that is, the depravity and sinfulness of the human race. But that would not represent an "image" or mere *perception* of sinfulness, but the *actual* fallenness of humanity.

However, in exploring the *image of limited good* as the antithesis to the *"unlimited good"* and glory of God, we do find the good news of Jesus. I will begin this exploration with the passages in the Gospels in which Jesus feeds the multitudes. The key story is that of Jesus feeding the five thousand (Mat 14:13–21; Mark 6:32–44; Luke 9:10–17; John 6:1–13).

In Matthew 14, Jesus had been healing the multitudes. The disciples got weary of it all and asked Jesus to send them back home (v. 15). "But Jesus said, 'They need not go away; you give them something to eat'" (v. 16). The disciples immediately experienced their human limitations and inadequacy in the face of great need. But upon learning that "five loaves ... and two fish" were available, Jesus received what little was offered, and prayed a blessing over the food. The disciples then distributed the food. Miraculously, " ... they all ate and were satisfied. And they took up twelve baskets full of the broken pieces left over. And those who ate were about five thousand men, besides women and children" (v. 20–21). Not only was it enough, it was much more than needed. The disciples discovered that by obeying Jesus, they had participated in a miracle which invalidated the *image of limited good* through a life lived in loving submission to Jesus Christ.

The key phrase is, "And they all ate and were satisfied" (v. 20). In a society in which food was often scarce, people normally would be scrambling to make sure they would get every bit of free food they could, all the while monitoring how they were doing in comparison to their neighbors. It would be a classic opportunity for intense, win-lose competition around the limited resources available.

But this situation was different. Contesting "who would get the most" was unnecessary because, through Jesus, there was more than enough for everyone. *"They all ate and were satisfied"!*

Let's look at each of the versions of this story in the Gospels and explore this condition of surplus, of *more than enough,* and see how the Gospel writers explained this.

> And they all ate and were satisfied. And they took up twelve baskets full of the broken pieces left over" (Mat 14:20).

> And they all ate and were satisfied. And they took up twelve baskets full of broken pieces and of the fish (Mark 6:42–43).

> And they all ate and were satisfied. And what was left over was picked up, twelve baskets of broken pieces (Luke 9:17).

> Jesus then took the loaves, and when he had given thanks, he distributed them to those who were seated. So also the fish, *as much as they wanted.* And when they had *eaten their fill,* he told his disciples, "Gather up the leftover fragments, that nothing may be lost." So they gathered them up and filled twelve baskets with fragments from the five barley loaves left by those who had eaten (John 6:11–13). (Emphasis mine.)

The emphasis which all four of the Gospel writers made is that Jesus lived among those who followed him in such a way that there was *more than enough*—so much so, that *all* could be satisfied.

Jesus had a way of transforming the disciples' limited resources to provide more than enough. The life of following Jesus was demonstrated to be not a life of *limited good and deficit,* but of *unlimited good and surplus.* The effect of this was that honor competition could be marginalized, if not eliminated, because in Jesus Christ there was a new possibility of *surplus*—not just for some, but for all.

Here is a Christ-centered spiritual reality along with a corresponding emotional state that we may describe as an *honor surplus*. There is no *honor deficit* for those who follow Jesus.

Connecting to the atonement. How does this overlap with the atonement? John's Gospel gives us the answer. Jesus said:

> I am the bread of life. Your fathers ate the manna in the wilderness, and they died. This is the bread that comes down from heaven, so that one may eat of it and not die. I am the living bread that came down from heaven. If anyone eats of this bread, he will live forever. And the bread that I will give for the life of the world is my flesh (John 6:48–51).

Jesus taught the spiritual meaning of the miracle of feeding the five thousand. He made it clear that the bread which Jesus miraculously provided to the multitudes was like the manna or bread provided by God in heaven. "I am the living bread that came down from heaven," he said.

And here is the connection to the atonement: "If anyone eats of this bread, he will live forever. And the bread that I will give for the life of the world is my flesh" (John 6:51). Jesus gave his life. Jesus gave his body, his flesh, on the cross for "the life of the world."

"And the bread that I will give for the life of the world is my flesh." This is Jesus' most concise statement about what was to be his forthcoming work on the cross, followed by his resurrection.

This is another example of an honor/shame dynamic (in this case in the form of its antithesis) overlapping with the atonement. The dynamic of *limited good* as it relates to Christ's atonement may be broadly described in the chart on the next page.

"I am the bread of life; whoever comes to me shall not hunger, and whoever believes in me shall never thirst" (John 6:35). The astounding nature of this Jesus-truth is simple: There is a new *possibility of surplus—surplus life, surplus honor and glory, surplus blessings in Christ*—available to those who, by devotion and faith, feast on the life of Jesus Christ.

The gospel is an offering of salvation to all the peoples of the world; it is *in essence* an expression of a God-ordained *unlimited good* available to all. This is, of course, why it is called "good news."

Consider how John 3:16–18 reveals the *unlimited good* of the gospel.

> For God so loved the world, that he gave his only Son, that whoever believes in him should not perish but have eternal life. For God did not send his Son into the world to condemn the world, but in order that the world might be saved through him. Whoever believes in him is not condemned, but whoever does not believe is condemned already, because he has not believed in the name of the only Son of God (John 3:16–18).

First, the singular, only Son was given by God to offer salvation to the whole world, "that the world might be saved through him." And second, salvation from God's condemnation is available to "whoever believes in him"—*whoever!* The offer is unrestricted—an *unlimited good*. (For a more extensive list of verses dealing with salvation and *unlimited good,* see Appendix 4.)

The hierarchical Roman Empire into which Jesus was born was characterized by widespread poverty, injustice, restriction, *limitation*.[1] The struggle for food, for survival ... the competition for patrons willing to provide goods and services ... the unending competition for honor ... all of these dynamics comprised a social environment of *limited good* into which the powerful gospel of *unlimited good in Christ* was proclaimed. The chart below further examines the contrast between the values of a "limited good" mindset and the "unlimited good" available in Christ.

	Limited good	Unlimited good through Christ
Physical reality	• Limited bread, not enough food for all • Deficit	• Unlimited bread; enough food for everyone • Surplus
Physical results	• Competition for limited resources • Conflict: some win, some lose • Many hunger and thirst	• Satisfaction—"they all ate and were satisfied" • Harmony: all who partake of Christ are winners • "Jesus said to them, 'I am the bread of life; whoever comes to me shall not hunger, and whoever believes in me shall never thirst'" (John 6:35)
System	• Closed system • No access to God's intervening grace	• Open system • Jesus, the "living bread that came down from heaven"
Atonement connection	• Reveals the need for a Savior, a Person of transcendent grace who enters the world to offer eternal life to whoever believes	• Jesus is the bread of life, representing unlimited nourishment: "And the bread that I will give for the life of the world is my flesh" (John 6:51) • Jesus gave his life to atone for "the life of the world" (John 6:51). • All peoples have access to the grace of God through the blood of Jesus Christ (Rom 3:21–26; Gal 3:13-14; Eph 2:13–22)
Community factor	• "Your fathers ate the manna in the wilderness, and they died" (John 6:49) • God's provision of manna in the wilderness (Ex 16:13–22) was experienced by individuals *in community*	• Christ's provision of food, feeding the five thousand (John 6:1–13), was experienced by individuals *in community* • Christ's provision as the bread of life "for the life of the world" (John 6:51) is also primarily experienced *in community* by followers of Christ
Spiritual meaning	• Only a limited few in the world—the powerful, the winners—have access to great benefits • Hunger and thirst predominate in the world • Winners prevail over losers • Death is inevitable: "like the bread the fathers ate, and died" (John 6:58) • Feeding on natural "bread" is inherently limiting; one cannot by oneself transcend death	• "This is the bread that came down from heaven, not like the bread the fathers ate, and died. Whoever feeds on this bread will live forever" (John 6:58) • The whole world benefits from the bread of life; *whoever* believes in Jesus • Eternal life through Jesus, the bread of life, is available to all human beings, so that they can transcend death in this life and in the hereafter

Figure 3.09: Limited good vs. unlimited good through Christ, based on Jesus feeding the five thousand

---

1. To review the social dynamics in first-century Palestine, see Section 2, Chapter 7 of this book: "Honor/Shame Dynamic #6: Patronage." See especially pp. 123–125.

"In Adam all die"—and "in Christ shall all be made alive"

The *unlimited good* of Christ is stated by Paul in elegant terms when he wrote, "For as by a man came death, by a man has come also the resurrection of the dead. For as in Adam all die, so also in Christ shall all be made alive" (1 Cor 15:21–22).

The secular Western mind bristles at these words. How can it be that the first man, Adam, imposed spiritual and physical death on all his descendants, on all humanity, over all the earth? The secular mind asks, *Even if the myth was true, why should one man's guilt and separation from God be passed on to all of humanity? Why should I be living with the effects of an ancient person's behavior—someone who lived thousands of years ago? It is unfair to me and reeks of an unjust god.* The secular mind does not allow for a person's individualistic identity to be so deeply linked to a universally shared human affinity. The plausibility structure[2] of the secular mind disallows such thinking.

With regard to Jesus Christ, the secular mind poses a similar question: *How could the death and resurrection of one man, Jesus, have such a positive life-giving impact among all humanity? How is it possible that I directly benefit from believing in the life, death, and resurrection of Christ—someone who lived two thousand years ago?* Again, the secular mind does not allow for the person's individualistic identity to be so deeply linked to a shared corporate human reality. The plausibility structure of the secular mind has no room for such thinking.

Here is where people raised in collectivistic honor/shame societies have an advantage over the individualistic secular mind. Because people in shame-based cultures understand themselves to be embedded in the group, they have an easier time embracing the biblical truth that *we are all* embedded in a sinful human race. We are *together* a depraved humanity in need of a Savior. Timothy Tennent writes:

> Shame-based, dyadistic cultures do not have any serious difficulty accepting our collective condemnation through Adam (Rom 5:12–19). The Scriptures teach that in Adam, as well as through our own willful sinning, the whole human race has dishonored God. We are not merely individually or privately guilty before God. We are also corporate participants in a race that has robbed God of the honor due him. This is why Paul declares such truths as "in Adam all die" (1 Cor 15:22) or "the results of one trespass was condemnation for all men" (Rom 5:18).[3]

It follows that people in honor/shame societies likewise will sometimes have greater openness than secular peoples to this truth of the gospel of Jesus Christ—that "in Christ shall all be made alive." Could this be a contributing factor to the stunning rise of the Christian faith in the Global South over the past century?

---

2. Lesslie Newbigin describes *plausibility structures* as "patterns of belief and practice accepted within a given society, which determine which beliefs are plausible to its members and which are not." He references Peter Berger but does not cite a source. Newbigin's point is that the belief that is held by secular institutions that secular knowledge is objective and without bias is a myth. No one has absolute knowledge; therefore, all knowledge rests on faith commitments. He goes on to say that "the gospel gives rise to a new plausibility structure, a radically different vision of things from those that shape all human cultures apart from the gospel. The Church, therefore, as the bearer of the gospel, inhabits a plausibility structure which is at variance with, and which calls in question, those that govern all human cultures without exception." See Newbigin, 8–9.

3. Tennent, *Theology in the Context of World Christianity,* 96.

A contrasting corollary to this would be that the radical individualism of the secular mind has contributed to the long decline of the Christian faith in the West.

It is a paradox:

- On the one hand, for people in honor/shame societies the *image of limited good* is part of their own cultural values; thus, it may be considered an obstacle to believing the *unlimited good* of the gospel of Christ.

- On the other hand, the dyadistic (group-oriented) nature of honor/shame peoples can make it easier to receive this faith: Jesus Christ is in himself the *unlimited good Savior* who rescues peoples among all humanity from the *unlimited scourge of sin* which all humanity inherited from Adam.

Is this principle becoming clearer—that in grasping the honor/shame dynamics of the Bible and the gospel of Christ, we can grow to be better stewards of God's grace to the multitudes whose pivotal cultural value is honor and shame?

What is the significance of a global gospel which relates to the "image of limited good"?

Below are some questions that arise from this exploration:

- "Blessed be the God and Father of our Lord Jesus Christ, who has blessed us in Christ with every spiritual blessing in the heavenly places" (Eph 1:3). *Moreover:* "And my God will supply every need of yours according to his riches in glory in Christ Jesus" (Phil 4:19). In Jesus Christ, there is a new possibility of *surplus—surplus life, surplus honor and glory, surplus blessings in Christ.* If this is true, then why is it common for believers to live with a persistent sense of deficit and neediness—of rivalry and competition?

- Can your team create resources which highlight a "global gospel"— contrasting the *limited good* of life apart from God with the *unlimited good* of life in Jesus? Can the story of Jesus feeding the five thousand be told in such a way that it is a bridge to understanding the *unlimited good* of the gospel of Christ? How might you contextualize the gospel to show that Jesus is in himself the *unlimited good Savior* who rescues peoples among all humanity—from the *unlimited scourge of sin-which-dishonors-God*—a condition that all humanity has inherited from Adam?

- How can the *unlimited good* of our riches in Christ be understood properly—so that, on the one hand, it does not reflect the excess of consumerism contained in the "prosperity gospel," and, on the other hand, is not limited to a pious spirituality that is divorced from the physical and practical challenges of our life together on earth?

- Christ's provision as the bread of life "for the world" (John 6:51) is experienced primarily by followers of Christ *in community.* In what ways does your church family communicate a spirit of abundant, surplus honor in Christ rather than deficit and neediness? To what extent do your church members experience this *individually* or *in community?*

A Gospel Shaped by "Challenge and Riposte"?

Explore a "global gospel." Is there enough biblical material to warrant an exploration of how the dynamic of **challenge and riposte** *intersects with the good news of Jesus Christ, so that a fresh presentation of the gospel can be developed to better resonate among people in honor/shame cultures?*

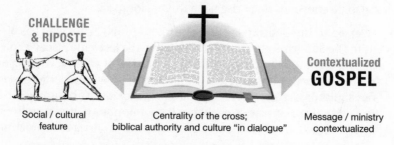

CHALLENGE & RIPOSTE

Contextualized **GOSPEL**

Social / cultural feature
Centrality of the cross; biblical authority and culture "in dialogue"
Message / ministry contextualized

Figure 3.10: Can there be a gospel presentation that incorporates the dynamic of challenge and riposte?

Yes, the gospel powerfully intersects with the dynamic of "challenge and riposte."

Jerome Neyrey refers to "challenge and riposte" as the "game of push and shove."[1] This game may sometimes be nothing more than harmless and humorous competition. But all too often in inter-family conflict, inter-ethnic rivalry, or international gamesmanship, the "game" gets deadly and leads to bloodshed—*honor-based violence.*

The Bible reveals that human games of "push and shove" are but shadows of what exist in the macro and cosmic realm as a conflict between the kingdom of darkness and the kingdom of God. Writing to the church at Ephesus, Paul described the cosmic conflict that the church endures in daily life:

> For we do not wrestle against flesh and blood, but against the rulers, against the authorities, against the cosmic powers over this present darkness, against the spiritual forces of evil in the heavenly places (Eph 6:12).

---

1. Neyrey, *Honor and Shame in the Gospel of Matthew,* 20.

The Bible also reveals that in Christ's atoning work on the cross—followed by his resurrection—God engaged the cosmic powers of darkness and won. John Driver puts it this way:

> A primary way by which the New Testament describes the work of Christ may be called the conflict-triumph motif. Salvation occurs when God pours out righteousness—his own life-giving power—in such a way that both God's people and all creation are delivered from the forces of evil and established in God's kingdom. In a number of New Testament passages the work of Christ is specifically described in terms of victory over evil powers Gal 4:3–9; Eph 1:19–22; 2:14–16; 3:7–13; 6:12; Phil 2:9–11; Col 1:13–14; 2:8–15; 1 Pet 3:18–22).[2]

With regard to Christ's conflict with Satan, Driver adds:

> Satan is pictured as an enemy with power (Luke 10:19) who rules over a kingdom (Luke 11:18), whose soldiers are demons (Mark 5:9). Rather than viewing evil in terms of fortuitous and isolated individual manifestations, Jesus saw it as a unity whose source is "the enemy" (Mark 10:19) who disrupts creation and holds humankind in his grip.[3]

No wonder Apostle John described the purpose of the incarnation as warfare: "The reason the Son of God appeared was to destroy the works of the devil" (1 John 3:8).

How does this victory over God's enemies intersect with Christ's work of redemption on the cross? The better question is: *How can this be understood in any other way?* God's victory over his enemies is one of the crucial dimensions of the atonement. In his letter to the church at Colossae, Paul describes God's triumph over these powers through the cross—and describes it as integral to the work of forgiveness and salvation.

> And you, who were dead in your trespasses and the uncircumcision of your flesh, God made alive together with him, having forgiven us all our trespasses, by canceling the record of debt that stood against us with its legal demands. This he set aside, nailing it to the cross. He disarmed the rulers and authorities and put them to open shame, by triumphing over them in him (Col 2:13–15).[4]

In their book, *Recovering the Scandal of the Cross: Atonement in New Testament and Contemporary Contexts,* Mark Baker and Joel Green describe the conflict-victory motif as a primary way by which the early church understood Christ's work on the cross.

> The writers of the immediate post-apostolic period proclaimed salvation by the cross but offered little explanation on how the cross provided salvation. By the late second century, church leaders like Irenaeus began

---

2. John Driver, *Understanding the Atonement for the Mission of the Church* (Scottdale, PA: Herald Press, 1986), 71.

3. Ibid., 72.

4. It is notable that this passage combines the dynamics of innocence/guilt, honor/shame, and power/fear.

combining proclamation of the saving significance of the cross with explanations of why Jesus had to die on the cross and how that effected our salvation.

Irenaeus and the next few generations of Christians thought about the cross in a context of conflict with the powers of the day. They participated in a Christian church that asserted that Jesus Christ was Lord, and thus they lived in tension with the dominant social structure of the day that declared Caesar was Lord. Both the church and empire solicited ultimate loyalty. At various times throughout the first three centuries of the church's history, Christian believers experienced both local and empire-wide persecution. ... Therefore it is not surprising that Christians framed their discussion of the cross and resurrection in terms of a cosmic conflict between God and the forces of evil, with the resurrection sealing Jesus Christ's victory over sin, the devil and powers of evil.[5]

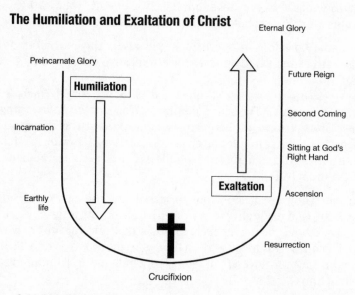

The Humiliation and Exaltation of Christ

Eternal Glory

Preincarnate Glory

Humiliation

Future Reign

Second Coming

Incarnation

Sitting at God's Right Hand

Exaltation

Earthly life

Ascension

Crucifixion

Resurrection

Figure 3.11: Humiliation and exaltation of Christ as cosmic "challenge and riposte"

To human observers at the time of the crucifixion, the cross seemed to be the destruction of Christ, when in fact, the murder of God's Son was ordained by God (Is 53:10; Acts 2:23; Eph 1:7–10) and only led to a cosmic *riposte*, a conquest of eternal and universal proportions.

The death and resurrection of Christ comprised a victory over the ultimate enemy—*sin-and-death-and-hell-and-Satan-and-his-kingdom-of-darkness*, the great adversary of the kingdom of God and all humanity.

---

5. Mark D. Baker and Joel B. Green, *Recovering the Scandal of the Cross: Atonement in New Testament and Contemporary Contexts* (Downers Grove, IL: IVP Academic, 2011), Kindle edition locations 1505–12.

The four steps of challenge and riposte may be understood as follows:

	Four steps of challenge and riposte	Challenge and riposte in Christ's atonement and resurrection
1	Claim of worth or value	• Christ claims divinity and lordship over all creation through his life and teachings
2	Challenge to that claim or refusal to acknowledge the claim	• Jesus tempted by the devil • Frequent honor competition with Pharisees and other leaders • Arrested, interrogated, flogged, tortured, crucified in public, buried
3	Riposte or defense of the claim	• All honor-competition with Jewish leaders won by Jesus • Resurrection, ascension, exaltation as King of kings
4	Public verdict of success awarded to either claimant or challenger	• "Therefore God has highly exalted him and bestowed on him the name that is above every name, so that at the name of Jesus every knee should bow, in heaven and on earth and under the earth, and every tongue confess that Jesus Christ is Lord, to the glory of God the Father" (Phil 2:9–11).

Figure 3.12: Challenge and riposte in Christ's atonement and resurrection

Can this *story of Jesus Christ as suffering servant and conquering King* become a presentation of the gospel? Yes! For people of Majority World cultures—*or Western culture*—for whom shame-anxiety or honor competition is a daily struggle, the story of Christ as servant-conqueror who overcomes the horrible shame of the cross and rises in victory may resonate deeply.

First, I envision this resonance to be due to the fact that the conflict-victory motif of Christ's atonement answers a basic offense held by Muslims. This offense pertains to the public shaming of Christ on the cross. Jesus is the Quran's second most honorable prophet, and Muslims believe that God would never allow "Isa" (Jesus) to be horribly, publicly shamed through death by crucifixion. But as we have seen, the Bible addresses this offense through the vindication of the honor and glory of Christ through all he achieved by his death, resurrection, and his ultimate exaltation.

Second, a carefully crafted presentation of a "global gospel" that conveys the story of Christ, explaining the cosmic *challenge and riposte* of Christ, could resonate deeply because honor competition and honor-based violence is a part of everyday life for many people in the Muslim world.

However, a gospel presentation that majors on the victory of Christ over his enemies must also be balanced with an appeal for personal repentance and forgiveness of sins. Believers are not just giving assent to a cosmic conqueror. Rather, they are relocating their honor under the King of kings, their kind and compassionate Savior to whom they owe their worship, allegiance, and devotion. Therefore, believers must heed the One who says,

The time is fulfilled, and the kingdom of God is at hand; repent and believe in the gospel (Mark 1:15).

To him all the prophets bear witness that everyone who believes in him receives forgiveness of sins through his name (Acts 10:43).

Why? These verses in Colossians 2 explain the awesome good news:

> And you, who were dead in your trespasses ... God made alive together with him, having forgiven us all our trespasses, by canceling the record of debt that stood against us with its legal demands. This he set aside, nailing it to the cross. He disarmed the rulers and authorities and put them to open shame, by triumphing over them in him (Col 2:13–15).

Significance for cross-cultural ministry

A gospel that magnifies the triumph of Christ over all competing powers offers another benefit for cross-cultural ministry. That benefit is in relation to peoples for whom power and fear are critical motivational factors. For many thousands of tribal peoples who practice folk religions, the fear of the spirit world dominates their lives.

In Paul's letter to the church at Colossae, he confronts the problem of syncretism in the church—a syncretism which accommodated the worship of the Roman Caesar, or the Greco-Roman philosophies of the time, or the appeasing of animistic spirits.[6] Dean Flemming, in writing about contextualization in Colossians, affirms the gospel of Christ as a dynamic power that overcomes the enslaving fear of all competing "rulers and authorities"—whether the Roman civil religion, demonic/animistic spirits, or false worldviews.

> We might find a contemporary parallel in the gospel's encounter with worldviews that are burdened with a fear of unseen powers thought to exercise control over practical concerns like crops, flocks, health and family relations. Too often the form of Christian theology that has been imported to these settings from the West has failed to address such issues, giving people the impression that God is powerless to overcome the fears and forces that touch their daily lives. Unless we proclaim Christ as the One who has defeated the powers and is able to free people from fear, they, like the Colossian syncretists, may turn to other answers—amulets, rituals, shamans, occult practices—for protection against the enslaving spirits. A gospel that neglects such worldview issues and their practical outworkings will not only fail to be truly liberating; it may end up actually promoting syncretism rather than preventing it. ... [A] contextualized theology for Asia (and elsewhere in much of the non-western world) must take seriously the demonic and spirit world or it will be evangelistically powerless and pastorally irrelevant.[7]

Paul Hiebert wrote about this in his landmark essay, "The Flaw of the Excluded Middle." He speaks of the "excluded middle level" as an area of worldview belief—in demons, ghosts, evil forces, or matter which is animated by spirits.

It should be apparent why many missionaries trained in the West had no answers to the problems of the middle level—they often did not even

---

6. See Flemming, "Colossians: The Gospel and Syncretism," in *Contextualization in the New Testament*, Kindle edition locations 214–65.

7. Ibid., Kindle edition locations 232–33.

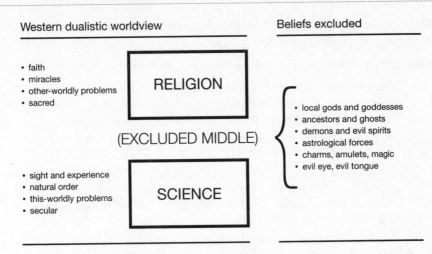

Western dualistic worldview   Beliefs excluded

- faith
- miracles
- other-worldly problems
- sacred

RELIGION

(EXCLUDED MIDDLE)

- local gods and goddesses
- ancestors and ghosts
- demons and evil spirits
- astrological forces
- charms, amulets, magic
- evil eye, evil tongue

- sight and experience
- natural order
- this-worldly problems
- secular

SCIENCE

Figure 3.13: The Flaw of the Excluded Middle (adapted from Hiebert)[8]

see it. When tribal people spoke of fear of evil spirits, they denied the existence of the spirits rather than claim the power of Christ over them.[9]

In the ancient world of the Bible, honor and power were inseparable; this still holds true today among many peoples of the world. This is where the pivotal cultural value of honor/shame overlaps with the dynamic of power/fear—in the honor-claim that Christ is "he who is the blessed and only Sovereign, the King of kings and Lord of lords" (1 Tim 6:15), that he rules over all powers—"visible and invisible, whether thrones or dominions or rulers or authorities" (Col 1:16). Or, as Paul wrote of Jesus Christ in his letter to the Ephesians:

And what is the immeasurable greatness of his power toward us who believe, according to the working of his great might that he worked in Christ when he raised him from the dead and seated him at his right hand in the heavenly places, far above all rule and authority and power and dominion, and above every name that is named, not only in this age but also in the one to come. And he put all things under his feet (Eph 1:19–22).

Therefore, it is also no surprise that Paul wrote of the gospel of Christ as the singular divine dynamic that perfectly answers the profound felt needs of peoples whose motivations are shaped by both honor/shame *and* power/fear:

For I am not *ashamed* of the gospel, for it is the *power* of God for salvation to everyone who believes, to the Jew first and also to the Greek (Rom 1:16). (Emphasis mine.)

---

8. Ibid. Diagram adapted from Hiebert, Kindle edition location 3853–83.
9. Paul Hiebert, "The Flaw of the Excluded Middle" in *Landmark Essays in Mission and World Christianity*, eds. Robert L. Gallagher and Paul Hertig (Maryknoll, NY: Orbis Books, 2013), Kindle edition location 3894–96. Hiebert's article was originally published in *Missiology* 10, no. 1 (January, 1982): 35–47.

What is the significance of a global gospel incorporating the "dynamic of challenge and riposte"?

Below are some questions that arise from this exploration:

- What can you do with your team to creatively produce resources highlighting a "global gospel" that delivers people from fear—a message focused on the honor-laden conquest of Jesus Christ over all spirits, all powers, all rival authorities? Or that presents the vindication of the honor and glory of Christ through his death, resurrection, and his ultimate exaltation?

- Consider the stories in the Gospels that highlight the supernatural power of God by which Jesus *healed, delivered, set free, blessed,* and *provided* for people in need. To what degree is this still a part of the gospel of Christ that we are to proclaim today?

- Muslims, in particular, take offense at the cross of Christ because of the shame that it signifies for the One crucified. What are some creative non-literate ways that the super-exaltation of Jesus Christ as Lord can be communicated as a cosmic *riposte* over shame, over sin, over all of God's enemies?

A Gospel Shaped by the Concept of "Face"?

Explore a "global gospel." Is there enough biblical material to warrant an exploration of how the **concept of "face"** intersects with the good news of Jesus Christ, so that a fresh presentation of the gospel can be developed to better resonate among people in honor/shame cultures?

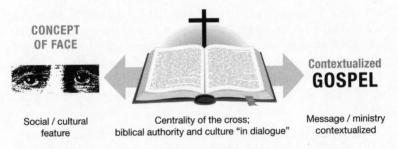

CONCEPT
OF FACE

Contextualized
GOSPEL

Social / cultural
feature

Centrality of the cross;
biblical authority and culture "in dialogue"

Message / ministry
contextualized

Figure 3.14: Can there be a gospel presentation that incorporates the concept of face?

Yes, Christ's work of redemption overlaps with the "concept of face;" a gospel presentation can be adapted accordingly.[1]

To begin, let's examine again the definition of the *concept of face* stated in Section 2, Chapter 6:

> The concept of "face" in Scripture has two parts: First, humanity's shame before God is the result of sin, and is expressed by *turning away* and *hiding from* the face of God. Second, humanity's redemption and healing from shame comes when people *turn to,* and are given peace *before,* the face of God.[2]

We saw that when Adam and Eve sinned they hid from God (Gen 3:8). In the original Hebrew language, this verse reveals that "hiding" is the "withdrawing away from the face (*pānîm*) of God." This is the result of sin. It is deeply *negative*; it is hiding and shame—*the loss of "face."*

---

1. See Flanders, *About Face,* for a comprehensive examination of "face" in Thai culture and how it overlaps with Christian theology and the gospel.
2. This definition is adapted from Stockitt, Kindle edition locations 2679–81.

Scripture, however, also provides *positive* material about "face." Here we see how *"face" is gained* through a saving relationship with God's "face."

> Those who look to him are radiant, and their faces shall never be ashamed (Ps 34:5).

> May God be gracious to us and bless us and make his face to shine upon us, *Selah* (Ps 67:1).

> Restore us, O God; let your face shine, that we may be saved! (Ps 80:3).

In the New Testament, Paul makes the connection between the Old Testament *concept of face* and the light of God that shines into darkened hearts through the *face* of Jesus Christ.

> For God, who said, "Let light shine out of darkness," has shone in our hearts to give the light of the knowledge of the glory of God in the face of Jesus Christ (2 Cor 4:6).

We may infer here a parallel between two "lights." The first "light" arrested and blinded Paul while on the road to Damascus (Acts 9:3); the second "light" appears to be the light that called him, saved him, and shone into his heart. This is a light common to *all believers,* for it is the light that "has shone in *our hearts* to give the light of the knowledge of the glory of God in the face of Jesus Christ."[3]

Therefore, we also see a second parallel, one that links God's "face" with our salvation:

> **To turn to the Lord in salvation is to have one's shame covered**
> **and "face" restored. This happens through the light that**
> **shines into human hearts through the face of Jesus Christ.**
> **Salvation is God's "face" shining upon us and in us.**

We will now go further to find the intersection between the atonement and the *concept of face.*

The atonement and the concept of face

One may rightly ask: *Where does the atonement—the finished work of Christ on the cross, followed by his resurrection—intersect with the concept of face?* It is found in the curious phrase, "saving God's face." I am indebted to Jackson Wu for the contours of this argument (especially points 4 and 5), which is put forward below.[4]

1. *God's glory is ultimate.* All creation is for the display of his glory (Ps 19:1). The honor and glory of God is both the genesis and final reality of the universe.

---

3. It is notable that God's calling of Paul (Acts 9:1–18; cf. Rom 1:1-6; Eph 3:2) constituted both his salvation *and* a summons to mission, specifically "to carry my name before the Gentiles and kings and the children of Israel" (Acts 9:15). This co-mingling of salvation and mission is inherent in the "to give" part of the verse: "God ... has shone in our hearts *to give* the light of the knowledge of the glory of God" (2 Cor 4:6). Although Paul is the pioneer missionary of the Christian church, he is also our example. Could it be that to be called into mission is actually a vital part of our salvation?

4. Wu, 193–220. I am restating his overall thesis below in my own few words, while recognizing that his book is a profound work of scholarship, and I am just wading at the shoreline of an ocean of theological depth.

"For from him and through him and to him are all things. To him be glory forever. Amen" (Rom 11:36).

2. *God's sorrow in humanity's sin.* The world God made was good, but Adam and Eve were tempted by the dark devious destroyer and sinned (Gen 1–3). Thus, the world was cursed under Adam's sin, and God was sorrowful (Gen 6:7). Sin is not only the violation of God's laws. It is ultimately the dishonoring of God's Person (Rom 1:21–26; 2:23). Sin *is* falling short of an ethical standard, but much more than that, sin is falling short of the glory and honor of God (Rom 3:23).

3. *God's promise through God's family to bless all peoples.* God promised Abraham, "I will bless you and make your name great" (Gen 12:2) and "in you all the families of the earth shall be blessed" (Gen 12:3). This constitutes God's plan—to reverse the curse of sin and restore his blessing on all humanity through Abraham's offspring. "Abraham 'believed God, and it was counted to him as righteousness'" (Gal 3:6) apart from the righteous works of the law.

4. *God's Son makes good on God's promise for all peoples.* Jesus Christ is the offspring of Abraham (Gal 3:16). He died on the cross to redeem us from our sins (Gal 3:13). Moreover, Jesus Christ became "a curse for us—for it is written, 'Cursed is everyone who is hanged on a tree'—so that in Christ Jesus the blessing of Abraham might come to the Gentiles, so that we might receive the promised Spirit through faith" (Gal 3:13–14). This opened the "door of faith to the Gentiles" (Acts 14:27) so that all peoples—all tribes and tongues and nations—could receive the honor of joining God's *family-on-mission* and experience eternal life.

5. *God's "face" saved for God's glory in all creation.* In John 12, Jesus was praying to the Father. His soul was filled with fathomless sorrow about enduring the coming events—arrest, mocking, flogging and torture, humiliating crucifixion to bear the sins of the world, separation and rejection from the Father.

    "Now is my soul troubled. And what shall I say? 'Father, save me from this hour'? But for this purpose I have come to this hour. Father, glorify your name." Then a voice came from heaven: "I have glorified it, and I will glorify it again" (John 12:27–28).

When Jesus prays, "Father, glorify your name," he is essentially saying, *Father, vindicate your honor! Save your "face"!*

Why would the death and resurrection of Christ vindicate God's honor? Because it is the only way that God's promise to Abraham to bless all the families of the earth could have come true. God's credibility hinged on a means for all peoples to be blessed and redeemed. Yes, God gave the law to Moses and his people; yes, the law revealed God's righteousness and holiness; *but the law was lifeless in that it was totally unable to save* (Rom 8:2–3).

There was only one way that God's plan to bless all families—to reverse the curse among all peoples—could be guaranteed: *through a heart-captivating faith that individuals and peoples everywhere would place in the name, honor, and finished work of Jesus Christ, a faith that transcends culture.*

With regard to *ethnicity* this faith needed to be *neutral,* accessible to and affirming of all peoples. But with regard to *ethics,* this faith needed to be *superior;* that is, it needed to have the ability to truly transform people from the inside out, conforming them to the righteousness of the Son of God. Therefore, this faith would be a fulfillment of the covenant promise God gave to his people through Abraham (Gen 12:1–3), but the faith would be untethered from the works of the law specific to Jewish ethnicity and culture, such as circumcision. Apostle Paul made this clear:

> That is why it depends on faith, in order that the promise may rest on grace *and be guaranteed to all his offspring*—not only to the adherent of the law but also to the one who shares the faith of Abraham, who is the father of us all (Rom 4:16). (Emphasis mine.)

Jackson Wu explains:

> Christ's atonement centrally concerns the honor of God and the shame of man. Salvation preserves God's honor and takes away human shame. God keeps his promises made in the OT, foremost to Abraham. Jesus' death therefore vindicates God's name. Therefore, God's people will not be put to shame. Christ perfectly honored the Father, who then reckons worthy of honor all who, by faith, are united to Christ. ... Jesus is a substitute in that he pays the honor-debt and the life-debt owed by sinful creatures.[5]

What is the significance of a global gospel incorporating the "concept of face"?

Below are some questions that arise from this exploration:

- What does it mean to be able to present a biblically rich gospel message to peoples for whom the dynamic of honor/shame is vitally important—and to do so in a way that specifically relates to the dynamic of "saving face"? How might a gospel presentation have at its core, that *salvation is God's "face" shining upon us and in us?*

- What does it mean to be able to present the atonement is such a way that it focuses primarily on *vindicating God's honor,* not only *satisfying God's wrath?*

- What does it mean for the church's global missions community to have at its disposal Jackson Wu's paradigm-shifting resource, *Saving God's Face?*

- What can you do with your team to creatively produce resources that highlight a "global gospel" focused on *turning to the Lord in salvation to have one's shame covered and "face" restored*—and to proclaim that the salvation wrought by Jesus Christ *saved God's face?*

---

5. Ibid., 219.

- How can we be courageous and creative enough to contextualize our gospel presentations without a Western cultural bias? How can we expand upon a message focused primarily on the cure for guilt—and craft a more "global gospel" of Jesus Christ in light of the honor/shame *concept of face?*

- Thousands of peoples in and from China, Thailand, Indonesia, Japan, Burma, Korea, Laos, Cambodia, and Vietnam—among others—all have "saving face" as a vital social dynamic in their culture. How valuable would it be to have a gospel presentation to share with them using the language and concepts of *saving face?*

A Gospel Shaped by
the Dynamic of "Body Language"?

Explore a "global gospel." Is there enough biblical material to warrant an exploration of how the dynamic of **"body language"** *intersects with the good news of Jesus Christ, so that a fresh presentation of the gospel can be developed to better resonate among people in honor/shame cultures?*

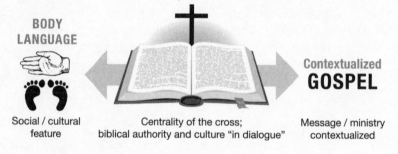

**BODY
LANGUAGE**

**Contextualized
GOSPEL**

Social / cultural
feature

Centrality of the cross;
biblical authority and culture "in dialogue"

Message / ministry
contextualized

*Figure 3.15: Can there be a gospel presentation that incorporates
the dynamic of body language?*

Yes, the dynamic of "body language" in Scripture is used to help describe the gospel of Christ—especially in the "gospel of the kingdom."

Many Christians who say they understand the gospel of Christ overlook what Jesus referred to as "the gospel of the kingdom" (Mat 9:35; 4:23; 24:14; cf. Mark 1:15; Luke 4:18–19, 43; 8:1).[1] For many believers, their understanding of *the gospel* hinges solely on the doctrine of justification by faith found primarily in Romans and Galatians,

---

1. Theologian N.T. Wright says that the evangelical church often overlooks the gospel found in the Gospels: "[I]n many classic Christian circles, including the plethora of movements that go broadly under the label 'evangelical'... there has been the assumption, going back at least as far as the Reformation, that 'the gospel' is what you find in Paul's letters, particularly in Romans and Galatians. This 'gospel' consists, normally, of a precise statement of what Jesus achieved in his saving death ('atonement') and a precise statement of how that achievement could be appropriated by the individual ('justification by faith'). Atonement and justification were assumed to be at the heart of 'the gospel.' But 'the Gospels'—Matthew, Mark, Luke, and John—appear to have almost nothing to say about those subjects." N. T. Wright, *How God Became King: The Forgotten Story of the Gospels* (San Francisco: HarperOne, 2012), Kindle edition locations 223–29.

while at the same time, avoiding the abundant material in the Gospels (and other portions of the New Testament) concerning "the gospel of the kingdom."

So let us explore a few basic features of the kingdom of God. We'll begin with the *body language* used to describe the exclusivity of Christ the King and his kingdom. This simple exploration will inform our understanding of the *gospel of the kingdom.*

1. Exclusive king. Ultimately, Christ harbors no rivals. He is "the blessed and only Sovereign, the King of kings and Lord of lords" (1 Tim 6:15; cf. Rev 17:14; 19:16; Phil 2:9–11). The exclusivity of Christ's reign and kingdom is clear. *Body language* in Scripture is used to amplify the authority and kingship of Jesus. Our key texts are Psalm 8:6 along with Psalm 110:1—perhaps the most-quoted Old Testament verse in the New Testament. Consider these parallel verses to gain insights into the *exclusivity* of Christ's reign in his kingdom.

> You have given him dominion over the works of your hands; you have put *all things* under his feet (Ps 8:6). (Emphasis mine.)

> "The LORD says to my Lord: "'Sit at my right hand, until I make your enemies your footstool'" (Ps 110:1).[2]

The reader will find it helpful to go back to Section 2, Chapter 5, pages 112–117 and reread the many New Testament verses based on Psalm 8:6 and 110:1. The sheer frequency of these New Testament verses cannot be overlooked as a window through which to understand the reign of Christ and his kingdom. In the Gospels of Matthew, Mark, and Luke, Jesus identifies himself (albeit indirectly) as "the Lord" who is to be seated at the right hand of God, seated with his enemies as his "footstool" (Matt 22:43–44; Mark 12:35–37; Luke 20:41–44). Christ reigns in exclusive, overwhelming victory!

2. Kingdom gospel. Second, let us consider a definition of the gospel—one that overlaps with the kingdom of God. John Bright's definition is apt:

> This, then, is the good news which the New Testament with unanimous voice proclaims: that Jesus is indeed the promised Messiah, fulfillment of all the hope of Israel, who has come to set up the kingdom of God among [humanity].[3]

3. Hope of Israel. Third, let us recall how the gospel proclaims that Jesus is the "promised Messiah, fulfillment of all the hope of Israel." We need only to turn to

---

2. The first verse of Psalm 110 clearly articulates the victory of a king over his enemies. But the other six verses of Psalm 110 supplement a multifaceted view of this unusual king. In verse 2, the king rules over his enemies with a "mighty scepter;" in verse 3, the king's subjects are people who "offer themselves freely" in submission under his rule; in verse 4, the king is called a "priest forever after the order of Melchizedek," hearkening back to the superior regal honor of the "king of Salem" who blessed Abraham (Gen 14:18–20); in verse 5 the king is one whose power is on full display when he "will shatter kings on the day of his wrath;" in verse 6 the king is the sovereign just judge over the nations of the earth; in verse 7 the king is not an other-worldly king, but a humble, fully human king who thirsts and drinks water "from the brook by the way; therefore he will lift up his head."

3. John Bright, *The Kingdom of God* (Nashville, TN: Abingdon, 1981), 190. As indicated in the definition of "the gospel," Bright emphasizes that the bridge between Old and New Testaments is the royal reign of Jesus Christ in his kingdom. His argument is thorough and compelling.

the scene in Jesus' home town of Nazareth, recorded only in Luke's Gospel, where he makes a grand and astonishing announcement:

> And the scroll of the prophet Isaiah was given to him. He unrolled the scroll and found the place where it was written, "The Spirit of the Lord is upon me, because he has anointed me to proclaim good news to the poor. He has sent me to proclaim liberty to the captives and recovering of sight to the blind, to set at liberty those who are oppressed, to proclaim the year of the Lord's favor." And he rolled up the scroll and gave it back to the attendant and sat down. And the eyes of all in the synagogue were fixed on him. And he began to say to them, "Today this Scripture has been fulfilled in your hearing" (Luke 4:17–21).

Here is the essence of the gospel of Jesus Christ, the gospel of the kingdom (Luke 4:43), as expressed by Luke. The in-breaking of God's kingdom rule through Jesus is good news to the poor ... liberty to the captives ... sight to the blind ... liberty to the oppressed.

Scot McKnight explores why the first four books of the Bible are called "The Gospel according to ..." and affirms that the gospel is about the fulfillment or completion of Israel's story.

> The earliest Christians called the first four books of the New Testament "the Gospel according to ... " because they declare that very story.
>
> - The Gospels are all about Jesus.
> - They are all about Jesus being the completion of Israel's story.
> - They are all about Jesus' death, burial, resurrection, exaltation, and future coming.
> - They reveal that this Jesus, this Jesus in this very story, saves his people from their sin.[4]

So when Jesus says, "Today this Scripture has been fulfilled in your hearing," he is identifying himself as the embodiment of Israel's Messiah/Savior/King. Jesus is Israel's hope, the *at-long-last-cure* to her centuries of heartsick longing—promised by Israel's prophets (in this case, the prophecy of Isaiah 61).[5]

4. For all humanity. David Bosch points out that the message for *all humanity* that Jesus announced in his hometown synagogue was communicated indirectly. This is due to the fact that, although the message of "good news" was initially received with favor by his Jewish listeners (Luke 4:22), this favor was not sustained. In fact, when Jesus stated that God's blessing was not intended exclusively for the Jews but also for Gentiles, the atmosphere in the synagogue changed from brightness to darkness. Out of nowhere (seemingly), Jesus specifically mentioned the poor

---

4. McKnight, Kindle edition location, 89–90).
5. In addition to Bright's *The Kingdom of God*, other excellent books on the kingdom of God are N.T. Wright, *How God Became King: The Forgotten Story of the Gospels* (New York: Harper Collins, 2011); Scot McKnight, *The King Jesus Gospel: The Original Good News Revisited* (Grand Rapids, MI: Zondervan, 2011), and Vinay Samuel and Chris Sugden, eds., *Mission as Transformation: A Theology of the Whole Gospel* (Oxford: Regnum Books, 1999).

Gentile widow from Zarephath who kept Elijah during three years of famine, and the Syrian general Naaman who was healed of his leprosy (vv. 25–27; both were Gentiles and both were recipients of God's grace and blessing). Suddenly, "when they heard these things, all in the synagogue were filled with wrath" (v. 28), and as a mob, they tried to assassinate Jesus by running him off, trying to throw him "down the cliff" (v. 29). Why?

Interestingly, it all has to do with how *selective* Jesus was in his quotation from Isaiah. The full context of Isaiah 61 contains both a message of salvation *for* Israel—and a message of vengeance *against* Israel's enemies. Isaiah 61:2 reads, "To proclaim the year of the LORD's favor, *and the day of vengeance of our God;* to comfort all who mourn." But Jesus omits the message of vengeance. He simply stops at, "to proclaim the year of the Lord's favor" (Luke 4:19).

The people gathered in the synagogue that day were likely expecting Jesus to include a message of vengeance. Bosch points out:

> [W]hen Jesus read Isaiah 61 in the synagogue, the congregation probably expected him to announce vengeance on their foes, especially the Romans—a vengeance which would be a preliminary step toward the time of liberation. This may explain the initial positive response to Jesus—"and the eyes of all the synagogue were fixed on him" (v 20). They were fervently expecting a sermon with a revolutionary thrust and perhaps Jesus' opening words, "Today this Scripture has been fulfilled in your hearing" (v 21), further fanned these expectations.[6]

But Jesus gave them what they did not expect: A message of *no exclusion* and *no vengeance* toward Gentiles. It was infuriating to them. The contrast between what the Jews *expected* and what Jesus *delivered* was enormous. "In other words," Bosch writes, "blessed is everyone who does not take offense at the fact that the era of salvation differs from what he or she has expected, that God's compassion on the poor, the outcast and the stranger—even on Israel's enemies—has superseded divine vengeance!"[7]

The paradoxical gospel of the kingdom

In the Gospels, Jesus demonstrated his reign over every evil—whether sickness, the demonic, or religious oppression. So on the one hand, the gospel of the kingdom is one of almighty power and rule *already* ... "Repent, for the kingdom of heaven is at hand" (Mat 3:2; 4:17; Mark 1:15). Apostle Paul affirmed that Christ is "the blessed and only Sovereign, the King of kings and Lord of lords" (1 Tim 6:15). Notice the present tense emphasis of the current reign of the King. As David Bosch aptly says, "The hope of deliverance is not a distant song about a far-away future. The future has invaded the present."[8]

On the other hand, the kingdom is also future; it is *not yet* authorized for vengeance against God's enemies to "restore the kingdom to Israel" (Acts 1:6). Yes,

---

6. Bosch, 110.
7. Ibid., 111.
8. Ibid., 32.

this good news of the kingdom (a gospel presentation containing victorious, regal *body language)* has begun with Christ's death and resurrection. *But it has only just begun!* The kingdom awaits a final consummation:

> Then comes the end, when he delivers the kingdom to God the Father after destroying every rule and every authority and power. For he must reign until he has put all his enemies under his feet. The last enemy to be destroyed is death. For "God has put all things in subjection under his feet" (1 Cor 15:24–27).

> Then the seventh angel blew his trumpet, and there were loud voices in heaven, saying, "The kingdom of the world has become the kingdom of our Lord and of his Christ, and he shall reign forever and ever" (Rev 11:15).

Until then, the good news of the kingdom is that through Christ's work as Servant-Savior, God is setting people free—saving them from every form of oppression (Luke 4:18). The present time is when God is blessing, liberating from sin, redeeming *all—everyone, all peoples* who call upon the Lord for salvation—regardless of religion, economic condition, social status, ethnic group, or whether they are friend or enemy of Israel.

The atonement and the gospel of the kingdom

One may rightly ask: *Where does the atonement intersect with the gospel of the kingdom, and the aforementioned victorious body language?* The book of Hebrews provides the answer (emphases mine):

> After making purification for sins, he sat down at the *right hand* of the Majesty on high (Heb 1:3).

> And to which of the angels has he ever said, "Sit at my *right hand* until I make your enemies a *footstool* for your *feet*"? (Heb 1:13).

> Now the point in what we are saying is this: we have such a high priest, one who is seated at the *right hand* of the throne of the Majesty in heaven (Heb 8:1).

> But when Christ had offered for all time a single sacrifice for sins, he sat down at the *right hand* of God (Heb 10:12).

> Looking to Jesus, the founder and perfecter of our faith, who for the joy that was set before him endured the cross, despising the shame, and is seated at the *right hand* of the throne of God (Heb 12:2).

In these verses, there is no specific mention of *king* and *kingdom;* Christ is most often presented in Hebrews as the great High Priest. Nevertheless, all the references to being *seated at the right hand of God* communicates *implicitly* the royal reign of Christ. The phrase "sit at my right hand" refers to Psalm 110:1; thus, there is no choice but to understand this as signifying the reign of the Messiah-King.

A call to repentance is therefore most urgent and reasonable: "The time is fulfilled, and the kingdom of God is at hand; repent and believe in the gospel" (Mark 1:15).

What is the significance of a global gospel incorporating "body language" to convey the gospel of the kingdom of Christ?

Below are some questions that arise from this exploration:

- New Testament references to Psalm 110:1 refer to the exclusive, resounding conquest of Christ as King over his enemies. These verses as a whole unabashedly comprise a message of *conquest,* albeit a conquest through humility, mercy, and love. What kind of people—and what kind of people groups—might respond to such a gospel presentation?

- Most Christians of Western cultural backgrounds consider democratic nations superior to kingdom-states ruled by royalty or countries ruled by dictators. Westerners are suspicious of kings because of their propensity for the abuse of power. How might this unwittingly make Western Christians disinterested in—or biased against—the gospel of the kingdom?[9]

- For people living in poverty or persecution under oppressive rulers, how might the gospel of the kingdom of Christ give them hope?

- Why would a gospel of the kingdom more likely be an offense to those who live with high levels of honor-status or are in places of power? How is the gospel of the kingdom a prophetic message of warning to oppressors?

- Can you think of examples in history (current or past) in which the church reinforced the power of the state or reinforced the power of a particular political party—and thereby compromised the gospel of Christ and lost its prophetic voice? When the church reinforces the status quo, how does this affect the gospel?

- What can you do with your team to creatively produce resources that highlight a "global gospel" focused on the gospel of the kingdom?

---

9. In 1644, the Scottish Presbyterian minister Samuel Rutherford published the book *Lex, Rex: The Law is King.* The book overturned the concept of the divine right of kings ("the king is law"). He argued that the law of God is supreme, and that even kings, therefore, must live under the authority of God's laws. The book was largely embraced by English philosopher John Locke, one of the most influential thinkers of the Enlightenment. For an overview see "Lex, Rex," *Wikipedia,* http://en.wikipedia.org/wiki/Lex,_Rex, accessed 11 September 2013. I believe that the ideas inherent in this title, *Lex, Rex: The Law is King,* contribute to the Western Christian bias against the gospel of the kingdom. It is in the DNA of the West that the *legal* trumps the *regal.* Could this be why Western Christians much prefer a gospel presentation based on laws, such as "The Four Spiritual Laws"? If true that in the West the *legal* always trumps the *regal,* it can be argued that in Scripture, it is the reverse: The *regal* trumps the *legal.* That is, the universe is not ultimately about laws or ethics. The universe is ultimately about a Person of infinite honor—Jesus Christ, King of kings and Lord of lords—from whom the laws of the universe are derived.

A Gospel Shaped by the Dynamic of "Patronage"?

Explore a "global gospel." Is there enough biblical material to warrant an exploration of how the dynamic of **patronage** *intersects with the good news of Jesus Christ, so that a fresh presentation of the gospel can be developed to better resonate among people in honor/shame cultures?*

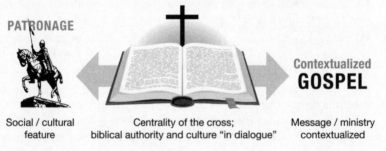

PATRONAGE		Contextualized **GOSPEL**
Social / cultural feature	Centrality of the cross; biblical authority and culture "in dialogue"	Message / ministry contextualized

Figure 3.16: Can there be a gospel presentation that incorporates the dynamic of patronage?

Yes, the dynamic of "patronage" intersects in two ways with the good news of Jesus Christ—the first way is simple; the second, complex.

1. Patronage and the gospel: A simple way. *Let's recall what I wrote earlier in the book:* According to deSilva, first-century believers understood God's grace as a category of patronage. "God's grace (*charis*) would not have been of a different *kind* than the grace with which they were already familiar; it would have been understood as different only in *quality* and *degree*."[1] So the social practice of patronage and benefaction related to the love and grace of God. "For God so loved the world, that he gave his only Son, that whoever believes in him should not perish but have eternal life" (John 3:16). The giving of God's Son would have been seen in the light of *patronage*. A highly honored, magnificent Benefactor is providing a great blessing—*the gift of his own Son* to many people.

---

1. deSilva, *Honor, Patronage, Kinship, Purity*, 122.

This sounds familiar. Because "he so loved the world" the Benefactor *gave;* he "gave his only Son, that whoever believes in him should not perish but have eternal life."

The role of *benefactor* can also be attributed to Jesus. He is the *Benefactor* whose courage and valor is so great that he arranges his own crucifixion for the benefit of others. According to deSilva:

> It is important to [Apostle] John to demonstrate that the crucifixion does not occur because of Jesus' weakness or because his enemies prevail. Indeed, they are continually foiled in their attempts to arrest Jesus until "his hour" arrives (7:30; 8:20; 12:23). John also underscores Jesus' knowledge of the identity of the betrayer in the time of betrayal (6:71; 8:20; 12:23), going so far as to portray Jesus as ordering Judas to perform the deed at a specific time, orchestrating his own sacrifice (13:18–19, 21–30). This heightens the perception of Jesus not as victim but as a willing benefactor who is proactive even in his death.[2]

> His death is a saving death (Jesus entered the world "that the world through him might be saved," 3:17) bringing the benefaction of eternal life on those who believe (3:16, 17).[3]

This means *salvation*—salvation for sinners: "For by grace you have been saved through faith. And this is not your not own doing; it is the gift of God" (Eph 2:8).

So we see that there are two gifts. First, because God gave his Son, and the Son honorably obeys his Father, the gift is Jesus himself. The second gift is being "saved through faith," which "is the gift of God." It is a free gift, "not a result of works, so that no one may boast" (Eph 2:9).

And where do we see the distinct overlap between the Benefactor's gift and the atonement? The answer is found in Romans 5.

Paralleling John 3:16, we see the first gift, the *gift of God's Son*, lavishly given because of his love for sinners in order to save them.

> But God shows his love for us in that while we were still sinners, Christ died for us. Since, therefore, we have now been justified by his blood, much more shall we be saved by him from the wrath of God (Rom 5:8–9).

There it is—*the atonement.* "We have now been justified by his blood, much more shall we be saved by him from the wrath of God."

Then we also see the second gift, the *gift of salvation* itself. In Romans 5:12–21, we behold Paul's expansive treatment of the wonder of the "free gift" (vv. 15–17) of "justification" (vv. 16, 18) leading to eternal life through Jesus Christ our Lord (v. 21). It is all possible because "we have now been justified by his blood" (v. 9).

The word *reign* in this passage is noteworthy. Five times it appears in some form; once in verse 14, twice in verse 17, and twice in verse 21. The word *reign* hints at a kingdom. There is something honorific going on here. What is it? There's an

---

2. David deSilva, *The Hope of Glory: Honor Discourse and New Testament Interpretation* (Eugene, OR: Wipf & Stock, 1999), 78.

3. Ibid., 79.

honor competition between the *reign of death* (v. 14) and the *reign of grace* (v. 21). Robert Jewett explains:

> Since it was the Christ event that brought the overwhelming victory of grace, the reign of sin ended there and the new reign of grace began. In Brandenburger's words, "an all-encompassing change of kingly rule" occurred as a result of the obedience of Christ, and the new reign of grace is incommensurate with the old reign of death and sin … .

> All who are in Christ are granted the ultimate honor of righteousness that assures them both now and in the future access to eternal life … .

> Where God's grace abounds and is received, no further honor is required and the shameful competition that marks the reign of sin should be at an end.[4]

The Benefactor is a King who has given of himself by giving the most costly gift possible—his Son—in order that all peoples might receive the most honorable of gifts: *eternal salvation under the "reign in life" (v 17) of the great Benefactor-King.*

Therefore, we give praise: "Thanks be to God for his inexpressible gift!" (2 Cor 9:15).

We move now to the second, but more complex, way of seeing the gospel in the light of patronage.

2. Patronage and the Gospel: a more complex way—"the Abrahamic gospel."
There are two key biblical texts to which we now turn—the first from Genesis, the second from Galatians.

> Now the LORD said to Abram, "Go from your country and your kindred and your father's house to the land that I will show you. And I will make of you a great nation, and I will bless you and make your name great, so that you will be a blessing. I will bless those who bless you, and him who dishonors you I will curse, and in you all the families of the earth shall be blessed" (Gen 12:1–3).

> Know then that it is those of faith who are the sons of Abraham. And the Scripture, foreseeing that God would justify the Gentiles by faith, preached the gospel beforehand to Abraham, saying, "In you shall all the nations be blessed." So then, those who are of faith are blessed along with Abraham, the man of faith (Gal 3:7–9).

Notice again, Paul summarizes the *gospel preached by God* to Abraham as simply: "In you shall all the nations be blessed."

Recall the question I asked in Section 2, Chapter 7. *When Paul writes that the gospel was preached to Abraham, in what way was this good news to Abraham?* I submit that, based on the concept of patronage woven into the ancient cultural

---

4. Jewett, *Romans*, 389. Jewett cites Egon Brandenburger, *Adam und Christus:, Exegetisch-religionsgeschichtliche Untersuchugen zu Römer 5, 12–21 (1 Kor. 15).* WMANT 29. Neukirchen Verlag, 1962.

context of Bible societies, including the life of Abraham (i.e., his encounter with Melchizedek, Gen 14:17–20), the "gospel to Abraham" is *this truth:*

> God, as the ultimate of source of all honor and glory is sovereignly including Abraham in the honor-laden role of *co-benefactor*—to bless all nations through his family.

Stated another way:

> God will bless all nations. And God will do this through Abraham and his family, to whom the honor is given of being co-patrons and co-benefactors with God, to be a blessing to all the other peoples of the earth.

One may rightly ask again: *Where does the atonement—the finished work of Christ on the cross, followed by his resurrection—intersect with the concept of* patronage *relative to Abraham?* Our answer is found in the final eight verses of Romans 4. Paul is speaking about the dramatic story and faith of Abraham:

> [18] In hope he believed against hope, that he should become the father of many nations, as he had been told, "So shall your offspring be."
>
> [19] He did not weaken in faith when he considered his own body, which was as good as dead (since he was about a hundred years old), or when he considered the barrenness of Sarah's womb.
>
> [20] No unbelief made him waver concerning the promise of God, but he grew strong in his faith as he gave glory to God,
>
> [21] fully convinced that God was able to do what he had promised.
>
> [22] That is why his faith was "counted to him as righteousness."
>
> [23] But the words "it was counted to him" were not written for his sake alone,
>
> [24] but for ours also. It will be counted to us who believe in him who raised from the dead Jesus our Lord,
>
> [25] who was delivered up for our trespasses and raised for our justification.

We may observe the following from these verses:

One, we observe that the atonement of Christ is contained in verse 25: "who was delivered up for our trespasses and raised for our justification."

Two, we see that the subject matter of the passage is how the faith of Abraham (vv. 18–22) is an example for believers in Christ (vv. 22–23), and that it is by this *faith in God* (not by works!)—faith in the death and resurrection of Christ—that believers are forgiven their trespasses and justified toward God (vv. 24–25).

So there is a clear parallel between Abraham's *faith in God's promise* and the believer's *faith in Christ's atonement.* In both cases, a righteous standing before God comes by having unwavering faith in God; works of the Jewish law would be fruitless (vv. 13–15).

Three, we observe an indirect reference to Abraham as co-benefactor with God to the nations. Note that Abraham's faith in God was for God's *global purpose,* for "he believed ... that he should become the father of *many nations"* (v. 18, cf. Gen 17:5, emphasis mine). This is tethered to the original promise of God in Genesis 12:3 that through Abraham "all the families of the earth shall be blessed."

This brings us to a question. We easily see that Abraham's *faith* is an example for believers (vv. 23–24). But the matter at hand in this chapter is the concept of *patronage*. So the question is this:

Is there any sense in which *Abraham's honor*—as co-benefactor or mediator with God in blessing the nations—is also exemplary for believers and the church today?

The answer is a conditional *Yes.*

Let us first examine whether Apostle Paul, the missionary pioneer and example, considered himself a co-benefactor with God to the nations.

Paul wrote to the believers at Corinth, "Therefore, we are ambassadors for Christ, God making his appeal through us. We implore you on behalf of Christ, be reconciled to God" (2 Cor 5:20). We are *ambassadors* for the King of kings! What an honor!

However, while we do see *great honor in being an ambassador in God's mission*, we do not see here the exact concept of patronage. We do see someone who possesses great honor and great authority by speaking in a strong sense of identification with God, who is actually "making his appeal *through us.* We implore you on behalf of Christ, be reconciled to God." Paul is saying that the ambassador for Christ does not just speak *for* God; no, God is actually speaking *through* him that people should "be reconciled to God." So the honor as an ambassador is very great indeed.

This same sense of *honor in God's mission* is also on display in Paul's letter to the Ephesians. He made a bold claim to honor that "the stewardship of God's grace" for the Gentiles had been entrusted to him! It was, Paul says, "given to me for you" (Eph 3:2). Consider these honor claims made by Paul to the church at Ephesus:

- "The mystery was made known to me by revelation" (v. 3). Paul was equating his stature as a man of God with the Old Testament prophets to whom God spoke directly.

- "When you read this, you can perceive my insight into the mystery of Christ" (v. 4). *Wow, Paul, I perceive you are amazing!*

- "And to bring to light for everyone what is the plan of the mystery hidden for ages in God who created all things" (v. 9). Paul was a man with a mission as big as the whole world—he was on mission with the Creator of the universe to enlighten "everyone."

- Near the end of the letter, Paul asked for prayer "that words may be given to me in opening my mouth boldly to proclaim the mystery of the gospel, for which I am an ambassador in chains, that I may declare it boldly, as I ought to speak" (6:19–20). He never wanted to back down from the exalted honor of the immense task given him by God, even in the face of his degrading imprisonment.

Altogether seven times in Ephesians, Paul uses the word *mystery* to describe various aspects of the grace and gospel of God entrusted to him for the Gentile world.

Paul's words near the end of his letter to the Romans are also notable:

But on some points I have written to you very boldly by way of reminder, because of the grace given me by God to be a minister of Christ Jesus to the Gentiles in the priestly service of the gospel of God, so that the offering of the Gentiles may be acceptable, sanctified by the Holy Spirit. In Christ Jesus, then, I have reason to be proud of my work for God (Rom 15:15–17).

Paul clearly saw himself as having the high priestly honor of being a kind of mediator, "because of the grace given me by God to be a minister of Christ Jesus to the Gentiles." His ministry is a "priestly service"—bringing the Gentiles as an offering for God, "sanctified by the Holy Spirit."

The idea here is of bringing Gentiles into the most holy presence of God. Prior to their encounter with Christ, these Gentile believers were not just unclean, they were "strangers to the covenants" (Eph 2:12), "far off" (Eph 2:13), "aliens" (Eph 2:19). *And now they were worshiping in the most holy presence of God?* To the Jewish mind this would have been an outrage. So Paul's ministry is vital, world-changing, powerful, *honorable!* No wonder he says, "I have reason to be proud of my work for God" (Rom 15:17).

Can we begin to appreciate Paul's bold soaring *honor?* Can we begin to sense the deep emotional and intellectual *passion* he had as a bondservant of Jesus Christ—all for the purpose of extending God's blessing to the nations?

Was Paul co-benefactor with God, ambassador for Christ, or high priest for the Gentiles?

Can we say that Paul's passion for proclaiming the gospel of Christ among the Gentiles reflects the dynamic of being a co-benefactor with God? Not exactly. Because of his thoroughly Jewish heritage and training, I believe he saw himself as more of a priestly mediator than a benefactor.

Moreover, when Paul wrote Galatians 3:8—that God "preached the gospel beforehand to Abraham, saying, 'In you shall all the nations be blessed'"—Paul already saw himself in that story of God with Abraham. Paul was *in* that grand overarching narrative. He was called by God, as Abraham was, to be in that same mission to bless all the peoples of the earth. Moreover, Paul would have seen his role in the mission to which God called both Abraham and himself as yes, a "responsibility," but certainly not *mere duty;* instead, Paul's life on mission with God in Jesus Christ was from the beginning (like Abraham's), a supremely high honor.

Therefore, this principle:

The honor of participating with God in his global love story and mission is not just a *result* of the gospel; the honor of being in God's missional story *is itself good news*! It is part of the gospel.

Today, why should *God's call to mission* ... with its adventure, challenging risks and high rewards ... transcendent meaning, privilege and dignity ... and the very presence of Christ himself (Mat 28:20) ... be reserved for a latter step of discipleship? If we ponder the gospel preached to Abraham, that "in you shall all the nations be blessed" ... if we consider that Paul's call from the beginning was to be an ambassador for Christ to the Gentiles ... then this good news, this honor, of joining God on his global mission, is right up front for all believers.

What is the significance of a global gospel incorporating the dynamic of patronage?

Below are some questions that arise from this exploration:

- How can we better communicate the love of the great Benefactor giving so lavishly his only Son? How can we better communicate the honor of being offered the great gift of salvation—the honor of being justified before our great King and holy God?

- Paul was the pioneer missionary of the Christian church, and in this sense he is unique and exceptional; no one will ever replace his contribution to the church. But he also wrote that he is an example to believers (Phil 3:17). Could the call to mission be a more significant part of our salvation than we normally recognize?

- What would a gospel presentation look like that thoroughly explored the story of ancient Abraham—an "Abrahamic gospel"? What if a central thrust was the honor of co-benefaction with God to the nations through Jesus Christ?

- Might the "Abrahamic gospel"—with a focus on ancestor/story/honor—appeal more to oral peoples or more to "postmoderns"?

- How might mission mobilization for Christians in honor/shame cultures be affected by an Abrahamic gospel? Could it be that the *honor* of the mission, the *honor* of being a co-benefactor with God to the nations, should be the crux of all mobilization efforts?

A Gospel Shaped by the Dynamic of "Name/Kinship/Blood"?

Explore a "global gospel." Is there enough biblical material to warrant an exploration of how the dynamic of **"name/kinship/blood"** intersects with the good news of Jesus Christ, so that a fresh presentation of the gospel can be developed to better resonate among people in honor/shame cultures?

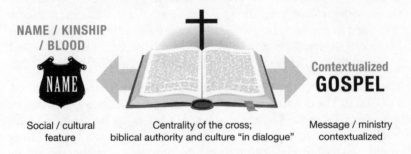

NAME / KINSHIP / BLOOD		Contextualized GOSPEL
Social / cultural feature	Centrality of the cross; biblical authority and culture "in dialogue"	Message / ministry contextualized

Figure 3.17: Can there be a gospel presentation that incorporates the dynamic of name/kinship/blood?

Yes, there is abundant material in Scripture connecting the dynamic of "name/kinship/blood" with the gospel of Christ.

In previous chapters, we have already explored how the dynamics of name, kinship, and blood are included in the message of the gospel of Jesus Christ. For example:

- **Name:** In Chapter 5 of this section, we explored the honor/shame dynamic called the *"concept of face;"* we considered how the atonement of Christ *"saved God's face"* because the honor of God was vindicated. Central to this was Jesus' passionate prayer just before going to the cross, "Father, glorify your *name*" (John 12:28).

- **Kinship:** In Chapter 2 of this section, we explored the *two sources of honor— ascribed and achieved;* we considered the overlap between the atonement and believers gaining the ascribed honor of becoming children of God (John 1:12; 1 John 3:1). Believers are part of God's family—God's *"kinship group."*

- **Blood:** In Chapter 9 we will explore the honor/shame *dynamic of purity* and how the atonement—through Christ's blood (Heb 9:11–12)—is the means by which believers are cleansed from sin and made pure before God (Heb 1:3; 1 John 1:9).

So one could say this dynamic is already covered. However, we must explore an additional dimension of the atonement—and how it may be communicated as part of the gospel. You will see that this expression of a *global gospel* deals with the age-old problem of conflict and bloodshed between *peoples*.

First, let us keep in mind that we are exploring the overlap of name/kinship/blood with the atonement; then let us recall that "blood replicates the honor of the family."[1] What we will observe is that the saving impact of the blood of Christ is applied to individuals and groups on behalf of *a reconciled community-family*.

Paul, in his letter to the Ephesians, sums up the impact of the cross on the two-thousand-year-long division between Jew and Gentile—and by extension, the division between *any peoples*.

> But now in Christ Jesus you [Gentiles] who once were far off have been brought near by the blood of Christ. For he himself is our peace, who has made us [Jews and Gentiles] both one and has broken down in his flesh the dividing wall of hostility by abolishing the law of commandments expressed in ordinances, that he might create in himself one new man in place of the two, so making peace, and might reconcile us both to God in one body through the cross, thereby killing the hostility (Eph 2:13–16).

The "hostility" between Jew and Gentile is resolved through the blood and cross of Christ. The dynamics of the blood and cross of Jesus Christ are world-changing because *in* the blood and cross of Christ, the honor-based violence between *families, bloodlines, ethnic groups, nations* may actually be *killed* by the unlimited love and mercy of God. It is "through the cross, thereby killing the hostility" that reconciliation can arise between peoples in conflict.

Granted, individuals must still personally appropriate by faith the meaning of Christ's redemption. Nevertheless, I believe that these verses in Ephesians 2 stretch our understanding of Christ's atonement and its potential to bring healing and restoration to even groups and peoples in bitter conflict.

A demonstration of reconciliation between warring tribes

One of the classic accounts of transformational Christian mission is *Peace Child* by Don Richardson. He writes in the author's introduction, "*Peace Child* chronicles the agony—and the triumph—of our attempt to probe one of the world's most violent cultures to its foundations and then to communicate meaningfully with members of that culture."[2] What could be the cure for the enduring violence between warring tribes?

---

1. Neyrey, *Honor and Shame in the Gospel of Matthew*, 53.
2. Don Richardson, *Peace Child: An Unforgettable Story of Primitive Jungle Treachery in the 20th Century* (Ventura, CA: Gospel Light, 2005 Kindle edition), Kindle edition location 111.

Below is Richardson's retelling of the moment when he explains the redemptive analogy of the *peace child* to the Sawi tribe. He was trying to help the Sawi understand that the Son of God is *the Peace Child* who is uniquely able to create permanent peace between warring tribes.

> For moons without number your ancestors gave their children to establish peace—not knowing *Myao Kodon* [the greatest Spirit, God] has already provided one perfect Peace Child for all men—His own Son! And because your children were not strong, peace could never last. The children died, and you lapsed back into war again.
>
> That is the reason *Myao Kodon* sent me—to tell you about the Peace Child who is strong—the once-for-all *Tarop* [Peace Child], Yesus! From now on, let Sawi mothers keep their own babies close to their breasts—God has given His Son for you! Lay your hands upon Him in faith and His Spirit will dwell in your hearts to keep you in the way of peace![3]

Look at the passage from Ephesians 2 once again:

> But now in Christ Jesus you who once were far off have been brought near by the *blood* of Christ. *For he himself is our peace,* who has made us both one and has broken down in his flesh the dividing wall of *hostility* ... that he might create in himself one new man in place of the two, *so making peace,* and might reconcile us both to God in one body through the cross, thereby *killing the hostility* (Eph 2:13–16). (Emphasis mine.)

Blood and honor in this world's kingdom is a catalyst for hatred and genocide between warring tribes, ethnicities, and nations. But the *blood and honor* of Christ is a catalyst for the acceptance, even the *celebration* of all ethnic groups and peoples as part of "one new man ... one body" (vv.15–16)—God's forever family!

The reader may recall a diagram in Section 2, Chapter 4 (Figure 2.11: Honor/shame arithmetic which adds up to violence). The diagram indicates that the cause of violence in honor/shame societies is a synergy of dynamics: *love of honor, challenge and riposte,* and the *image of limited good.* The propensity for violence results in either harm toward self or toward others.

In light of the discussion in this chapter concerning Christ's *peacemaking* between peoples through the atonement, a comparison diagram is offered on the next page (Figure 3.18). This diagram compares the kingdom of this world to the kingdom-reign of God.

---

3. Ibid., 171.

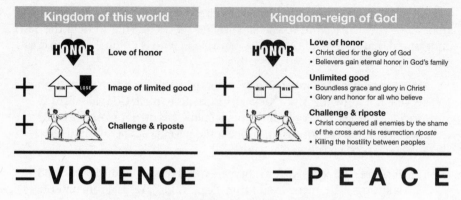

Figure 3.18: A little arithmetic about violence and peace—
kingdom of this world vs. kingdom-reign of God

What is the significance of a global gospel incorporating the concept of "name/kinship/blood"?

Below are some questions that arise from this exploration:

- What does it mean to be able to present Christ's atonement is such a way that its purpose is "killing the hostility" (Eph 2:16) to solve the problem of *violence in humanity among peoples?* Can the gospel of Jesus Christ *actually* be the solution for peoples who are engaged in a seemingly unending cycle of honor competition and bloodshed?

- What can you do with your team to creatively produce resources that highlight a "global gospel" focused on the cross as the one and only place where revenge truly ends? Or a presentation of Jesus as the one and only Son of God who, "through the cross," can kill the hostility among peoples?

- Can we be courageous and creative enough to contextualize our gospel presentations without a Western cultural bias? Can we craft a presentation of a more "global gospel" that *highlights reconciliation and peace between peoples through the blood and cross of Christ*—without minimizing the need for personal, individual repentance?

- Which peoples and nations in the world today are languishing from endless violence? What are the various kinds of messages they may currently be receiving from the "Christian world"? Which messages from the "Christian world" are in sync with the message of peace and reconciliation of the cross? Which messages from the "Christian world" seem to favor violence or revenge?

- To what extent does your church family demonstrate the inter-ethnic and multicultural unity-in-diversity that the blood and cross of Christ make possible?

- What can you do in your church family to develop more of a culture of peace and reconciliation? How can your church demonstrate the power of the blood and cross of Jesus to reconcile people *and peoples* in conflict?

A Gospel Shaped by the Dynamic of "Purity"?

*Explore a "global gospel." Is there enough biblical material to warrant an exploration of how the dynamic of **purity** intersects with the good news of Jesus Christ, so that a fresh presentation of the gospel can be developed to better resonate among people in honor/shame cultures?*

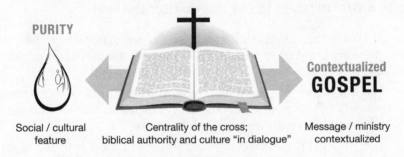

PURITY

Contextualized
GOSPEL

Social / cultural
feature

Centrality of the cross;
biblical authority and culture "in dialogue"

Message / ministry
contextualized

Figure 3.19: Can there be a gospel presentation that incorporates the dynamic of purity?

Yes, there is abundant material in Scripture connecting the dynamic of purity with the gospel of Jesus Christ.

Before exploring the intersection of purity with the gospel of Jesus Christ, I want to highlight this fact: Three major religions of the world other than Christianity are Buddhism, Hinduism, and Islam—and like Judaism and Christianity, each of them has purification rituals as part of their practice. Three paragraphs explaining the importance of purity for Buddhism, Hinduism, and Islam are offered below:

Purity in Buddhism: "Purity (suddha) is an important concept within much of ... Buddhism, although the implications of the resultant moral purification may be viewed differently in the varying traditions. The aim is to purify the personality of the Buddhist practitioner so that all moral and character defilements and defects... such as anger, ignorance and lust are wiped away and Nirvana can be obtained."[1]

---

1. "Purity in Buddhism," *Wikipedia*, http://en.wikipedia.org/wiki/Purity_in_Buddhism, accessed 8 September 2013.

Purity in Hinduism: "An important part of ritual purification in Hinduism is the bathing of the entire body, particularly in rivers considered holy such as the Ganges; it is considered auspicious to perform this form of purification before any festival, and it is also practiced after the death of someone, in order to maintain purity. Although water pollution means that in modern times there is a need for care during bathing in such rivers, the physical impurities within the river do not diminish the attributed power they have to bring ritual purity."[2]

Purity in Islam: The Quran says, "For Allah loves those who turn to Him constantly and He loves those who keep themselves pure and clean" (2:222). "Observing cleanliness of the soul, the clothes, and the surroundings is obligatory upon every Muslim, and this is considered as one of the pillars of Islam. ... Before offering prayers, it is necessary to perform [ritual purification]. The purifying agent is always pure water. However, during times when water is not available or is scarce, [symbolic purification] can be performed with clean dry earth ... If the body or clothes show traces of blood, pus, urine, feces, semen or alcohol, then [purification] becomes essential. ... The Quran says: None shall touch it but those who are clean (56:79)."[3]

Purity: a vital message in our multicultural world

- If it is true that the great majority of unengaged and unreached peoples of the world are Muslim, Hindu, or Buddhist, all of whom have purity codes and practices, ...

- and if it is also true that both the Old and New Testaments have ample material about purity and cleansing, much of it connected with the atonement of Jesus Christ, then it follows that ...

- it is strategic to communicate the gospel of Jesus Christ using *purity concepts and language* from the Bible's stories, parables, principles, and other material.

The following account from Bruce Thomas amplifies the need for such a message, focused less on *forgiveness* from sin-*guilt* and more on *cleansing* from sin-*defilement:*

One day our helper told us that when she was a little girl she had a friend who used to feel her mother's hair in the morning to see if it was damp. Her friend did this so that she could tell if her mother, who was divorced, had been messing around. According to Islam, you are unclean after you have had sex and must take a complete bath, to include washing your hair, in order to be clean again.

When asked why her friend's mother would bother to take the bath if she was already committing adultery, our helper responded that no one

---

2. "Ritual Purification," *Wikipedia,* http://en.wikipedia.org/wiki/Ritual_purification, accessed 8 September 2013.

3. "Ritual Purity in Islam," *Wikipedia,* http://en.wikipedia.org/wiki/Ritual_purity_in_Islam, accessed 8 September 2013.

would dare think of not taking the ritual bath after having had sex. Such a person would be a curse and the ground they walked on would be cursed. In other words, a prolonged state of ritual uncleanness following sexual intercourse was more unthinkable than adultery. ...

In the light of this new perspective, I began to consider that perhaps the greatest need felt by these Muslim people is not for assurance of salvation from sin but for deliverance from the tyranny of being in a near constant state of defilement. Every element of their daily lives is ordered by this insecurity; the direction to face when falling asleep, the Arabic words uttered when beginning a task, speech, or greeting, and even the way to blow your nose or wipe your bottom. Defilements come in various levels and for each level there is an appropriately matched cleansing. Burping and passing gas is one level of defilement. Touching your private parts is another. Touching semen, urine, feces, or menstrual flow is getting pretty serious; serious enough that a woman's prayers will not be heard during her period.[4]

So Bruce Thomas contemplates, "I wonder if there is a more relevant way to present the gospel under these circumstances. Perhaps we could communicate more effectively with a gospel message addressing man's defilement as well as, or as part of, his depravity."[5]

I also ask: Would a gospel presentation using the language and Hebrew concepts of *purity* resonate more deeply with a Muslim than a gospel presentation describing a remedy for guilt and sin? Might this also be true for the Hindu and Buddhist?

Sin as uncleanness

The most foundational passages about sin and uncleanness appear in Leviticus 14 and 16. I will mention this only briefly here; more will be explained a little further on in this chapter. The key verse is from Leviticus 16, describing the Day of Atonement:

> For on this day shall atonement be made for you to cleanse you. You shall be clean before the LORD from all your sins" (Lev 16:30).

Referring to the concepts of sin as uncleanness in the Mosaic law, the prophet Isaiah confirms this Hebrew understanding. I'll offer two examples.

The first example is worded inside of Isaiah's famous vision of God: "I saw the Lord sitting upon a throne, high and lifted up ..." (Isa 6:1). Having seen the Lord, Isaiah is overcome, afraid for his very existence.

> And I said: "Woe is me! For I am lost; for I am a man of unclean lips, and I dwell in the midst of a people of unclean lips; for my eyes have seen the King, the LORD of hosts!" (Isa 6:5).

---

4. Bruce Thomas, "The Gospel for Shame Cultures," *EMQ,* July 1994. EMQ Online at http://www.emisdirect.com/emq/issue-153/750, accessed 8 September 2013.
5. Ibid.

The passage reveals Isaiah's personal sin-identification with the corporate sins of Israel; Isaiah experiences the condition of *uncleanness* as the result of seeing God in his awesome holiness and glory.

The second example is near the end of the book of Isaiah:

> We have all become like one who is unclean, and all our righteous deeds are like a polluted garment. We all fade like a leaf, and our iniquities, like the wind, take us away (Isa 64:6).

The verse reveals Isaiah's personal sin-identification with the corporate sins of Israel; it is the condition of *uncleanness* as the result of *iniquity*.

Who can make us clean?

Is there Someone who is powerful enough, compassionate enough, *pure enough* to make us clean, and to keep us clean?

With this in mind, let us encounter two passages from the Gospels that reveal the purifying, cleansing power of Jesus. The first passage is the account of Jesus cleansing the leper:

> While he was in one of the cities, there came a man full of leprosy. And when he saw Jesus, he fell on his face and begged him, "Lord, if you will, you can make me clean." And Jesus stretched out his hand and touched him, saying, "I will; be clean." And immediately the leprosy left him. And he charged him to tell no one, but "go and show yourself to the priest, and make an offering for your cleansing, as Moses commanded, for a proof to them" (Luke 5:12–14; see also Mat 8:2–4, Mark 1:40–45).

The second passage is the account of Jesus cleansing a woman with a discharge of blood.

> And behold, a woman who had suffered from a discharge of blood for twelve years came up behind him and touched the fringe of his garment, for she said to herself, "If I only touch his garment, I will be made well." Jesus turned, and seeing her he said, "Take heart, daughter; your faith has made you well." And instantly the woman was made well (Mat 9:20–22; see also Mark 5:21–34, Luke 8:40–56).

Lessons from Jesus cleansing a leper

- A leper was considered profoundly unclean and defiled. A person would have become unclean by touching the leper; even to be in the same space as the leper would result in uncleanness. (See Lev 14:33–57; even a house would be unclean if a person had lived there with leprosy.)

- Radically, Jesus touched the leper.[6] However, Jesus did not become unclean; rather Jesus' healed the disease and cleansed the leper of his uncleanness. The purity of Jesus was greater than the defilement of the leper.

- Jesus commanded him to show himself to the priest (Luke 5:14), following

---

6. The radical nature of Jesus touching the leper may be better understood in the light of Lev 22:4–8. The Aaronic priesthood had to be especially vigilant in order to avoid contact with (touch) things or persons unclean.

the laws of Moses (Lev 14:1–32), and thus, the leper was able to have his honor restored in the community. The man with leprosy experienced a reversal of his honor-status.

Lessons from Jesus cleansing the woman with a discharge of blood

- A woman with a discharge of blood was considered unclean (Lev 15:19–30). The woman in this story had a perpetual discharge of blood, and was therefore perpetually unclean, excluded, shamed. In her desperation, she pressed through the crowd (Mark 5:31), transferring her uncleanness to everyone she touched, incurring everyone's scorn.

- The woman touched the garment of Jesus and was made clean; "the flow of blood dried up" (v. 29) and she was healed.

- Jesus violated the purity code: When he was touched by the perpetually unclean woman, he retained his holiness and purity, while she was made clean.

- Jesus eliminated her shame by cleansing her, thus restoring her to her community. He then further raised her honor-status, saying, "Daughter, your faith has made you well; go in peace, and be healed of your disease" (v. 34). Calling her "daughter" made her part of his kinship group and constituted a rise in her honor-status.

We marvel at the compassion and cleansing power of Jesus in the gospels. But was this *power of Jesus to cleanse*—something we merely read about in an ancient book—the result of which is to admire the heroic Jesus? Or is this something more? Believing that Jesus is alive today, we propose:

A gospel presentation of Christ's *cleansing purity* will resonate better with multitudes of peoples than the message of his *forgiving grace*.

So we turn to explore the intersection of (1) the atonement of Jesus Christ—his death on the cross followed by his resurrection—with (2) the concept of *purity* and experience of *cleansing*.

Where does the atonement—the finished work of Christ on the cross followed by his resurrection—intersect with the concept of *purity?* We will explore both Old Testament and New Testament passages.

Purity, cleansing, atonement—in Leviticus 14 and 16

Leviticus 14 begins, "The LORD spoke to Moses, saying, 'This shall be the law of the leprous person for the day of his cleansing. He shall be brought to the priest ...'" (vv. 1–2). Keep in mind that this chapter describes how the leprous person is to be cleansed. (This is in contrast to Leviticus 16, which describes the Day of Atonement as God's provision for cleansing from sin for all Israel.) Below is an overview of the steps toward cleansing for the leprous person revealed in Leviticus 14:

The priest goes outside of the camp to where the lepers are; he looks on the skin condition of the people and sees if anyone has been healed from leprous disease (v. 3). If the priest sees that a person's skin has cleared up, he or she is then allowed to proceed "for the day of his cleansing." Then commences a long complex process.

- To the priest, the leper appears to be healed of his malady. But he is not yet clean. The formerly leprous person begins the process of cleansing by providing two clean birds, one of which is killed by the priest for a sacrifice. A ritual ensues involving fresh running water, along with the sprinkling of blood from the bird that was sacrificed "on him who is to be cleansed." The living bird is let go "into the open field" (vv. 4–7).

- Then, the person being cleansed must shave his hair, wash his clothes, and bathe. Only then will he be able to re-enter the camp. But he must remain outside of his tent for seven days. On the seventh day, he must shave all of his hair again, including beard and eyebrows, wash his clothes again, and bathe again; "he shall be clean" (vv. 8–9).

- On day eight, the person being cleansed gets two male lambs without blemish for a sacrifice, plus a very specific grain offering. He goes to the priest, who in turn, sets the person and all "these things before the LORD." One lamb is killed, representing the sin offering. The other lamb is killed representing the guilt offering (vv. 10–13).

- Of course, the ritual involved blood. "The priest shall take some of the blood of the guilt offering, and the priest shall put it on the lobe of the right ear of him who is to be cleansed and on the thumb of his right hand and on the big toe of his right foot" (v. 14). Then the ritual repeats—right ear, right hand, right big toe[7]—except this time with oil. The priest also takes some of the oil and puts it on the person's head; the priest "shall make atonement for him before the LORD" (vv. 15–18).

- Again—blood atonement: "The priest shall offer the sin offering, to make atonement for him who is to be cleansed from his uncleanness. And afterward he shall kill the burnt offering. And the priest shall offer the burnt offering and the grain offering on the altar. Thus the priest shall make atonement for him, and he shall be clean" (vv. 19–20).

Yes, *"the priest shall make atonement for him, and he shall be clean."* This overlap between the *atonement* and the honor/shame dynamic of *purity* could not be more clear.

Moreover, in Leviticus 16 we read of the once-per-year "Day of Atonement," by which the entire Hebrew people received cleansing for their sins.

For on this day shall atonement be made for you to cleanse you. You shall be clean before the LORD from all your sins" (Lev 16:30).

---

7. What is the meaning of the priest touching both blood and oil to the *ear, hand,* and *big toe?* Might this be an emphasis on cleansing the whole person? Notably, the *right* ear, *right* hand, and *right* big toe implies the *honor restored* of the whole person. Being cleansed from defilement meant that one's honor was restored in *listening* to others in relationship (ear), in *working* in one's vocation (hand), and in *walking* through the journey of life (foot). Moreover, while the *blood* symbolizes the work of Christ, the *oil* can symbolize the vital work of the Holy Spirit, without whom one cannot experience the honor of kinship in God's family nor have power to live in freedom over sin's defilement.

Try reading Leviticus 16 out loud. You will repeatedly hear the language of "atonement." Notable are the frequent occurrences of the words, *blood* (9), *atonement* (15), *sin offering* (11), *burnt offering* (4), *sins* (2), *iniquities* (2). You will also observe frequent occurrences of words signifying "purity language"—*clean* (1), *cleanse* (2), *uncleannesses* (3), *bathe* (4), *water* (4), and *wash* (2).

And now let us recall the numerous times that Jesus touched or interacted with unclean persons—who, in turn, were cleansed and made whole (see Appendix 3). With the added awareness of Leviticus 14 and 16 in our minds, we may solemnly conclude:

> Jesus was able to *touch unclean people* (without himself becoming unclean), and Jesus was able to powerfully *cleanse unclean persons* of their defilement—because Jesus himself was both the perfect High Priest *and* the perfect blood atonement (Lev 14:14; 16:15–19, 30) necessary for eternal cleansing (see Heb 7:26–27; 9:13–14).

Purity, cleansing, atonement in the New Testament

The New Testament has many references to purity, cleansing, and sanctification that plainly intersect with the atonement. The New Testament authors, steeped as they were in the Hebrew Scriptures, drew on their knowledge of the Pentateuch to interpret the work of Christ as the sacrifice for sins. Consider ...

> But if we walk in the light, as he is in the light, we have fellowship with one another, and the blood of Jesus his Son *cleanses us from all sin*. If we say we have no sin, we deceive ourselves, and the truth is not in us. If we confess our sins, he is faithful and just to forgive us our sins and to *cleanse us from all unrighteousness* (1 John 1:7–9). (Emphasis mine.)

> Or do you not know that the unrighteous will not inherit the kingdom of God? Do not be deceived: neither the sexually immoral, nor idolaters, nor adulterers, nor men who practice homosexuality, nor thieves, nor the greedy, nor drunkards, nor revilers, nor swindlers will inherit the kingdom of God. And such were some of you. But you were *washed,* you were *sanctified,* you were *justified* in the name of the Lord Jesus Christ and the Spirit of our God (1 Cor 6:9–11). (Emphasis mine.)

Perhaps the clearest verses about the cleansing power of Christ are from the book of Hebrews. Here is a sampling:

> [Jesus Christ] is the radiance of the glory of God and the exact imprint of his nature, and he upholds the universe by the word of his power. After making *purification for sins,* he sat down at the right hand of the Majesty on high (Heb 1:3). (Emphasis mine.)

> For if the blood of goats and bulls, and the *sprinkling of defiled persons* with the ashes of a heifer, *sanctify for the purification of the flesh,* how much more will the blood of Christ, who through the eternal Spirit offered himself without blemish to God, *purify our conscience* from dead works to serve the living God (Heb 9:13–14). (Emphasis mine.)

Therefore, brothers, since we have confidence to enter the holy places by the blood of Jesus, by the new and living way that he opened for us through the curtain, *that is, through his flesh,* and since we have a great priest over the house of God, let us draw near with a true heart in full assurance of faith, with our *hearts sprinkled clean from an evil conscience* and our *bodies washed with pure water* (Heb 10:19–22). (Emphasis mine.)

Observe the contrasts between Old and New Covenant cleansing in the chart on the facing page, based on verses from the book of Hebrews:

What is the significance of a global gospel incorporating the dynamic and biblical language of "purity"?

Below are some questions that arise from this exploration:

- What does it mean to be able to present the atonement is such a way that its purpose is to *"purify our conscience from dead works to serve the living God"* (Heb 9:14)—in addition to the atonement as the *satisfaction of God's wrath?*

- Gender roles are more clearly divided in Buddhist, Hindu, Muslim, and tribal societies; this is in contrast to the West, where there is much more overlap between male and female roles. Therefore, should the church develop gender-specific presentations of the gospel that center on purity? A gospel presentation for women could begin with the narrative of Jesus cleansing the woman with the issue of blood (Luke 8:43–48); a gospel presentation for men could begin with the narrative of Jesus cleansing the leper (Luke 5:12–14) or the demoniac (Mark 5:1–20). For both men and women, the presentation would be concluded by the atonement of Jesus as the "purification for sins" (Heb 1:3) with an invitation for a person or family to pray, "Jesus, if you will, you can purify our conscience; you can make us clean."

- What can you do with your team to creatively produce resources that highlight a "global gospel" focused on a message of *turning to Jesus for cleansing from defilement* and to proclaim that the salvation wrought by Jesus Christ is for "purification for sins" (Heb 1:3)?

- Can we be courageous and creative enough to contextualize our gospel presentations without a Western cultural bias—and craft a more "global gospel" of Jesus Christ in the light of the *dynamic of purity?*

- Could it be that the books of Leviticus and Hebrews offer a missiological key for the evangelism and discipleship of some Majority World peoples? Westerners avoid teaching and preaching from these books, not only because they are theologically complex, but because religious ritual purification is so *culturally foreign.* However, religious ritual purification, while foreign to Westerners, is commonplace for many Buddhist, Hindu, and Muslim peoples.

	Old Covenant Cleansing	New Covenant Cleansing
Agent of purification	• Human high priest, tribe of Levi "men in their weakness" (7:28) • High priest offers blood of goats and calves (9:12) • Ashes of a roasted heifer	• Son of God, Eternal Creator (1:2), possessing the honor and authority of One who is seated at the right hand of God (1:3) • Jesus Christ is both High Priest and sacrifice; offers his own blood to God (9:11–12) • Eternal Holy Spirit (9:14)
Location of purification	• Tents, tabernacles, temples: "holy places made with hands, which are copies of the true things" (9:24)	• "heaven itself … in the presence of God on our behalf" (9:24)
Frequency of purity ritual	• Annual ritual, unending need (10:1) • Daily ritual: "And every priest stands daily at his service, offering repeatedly the same sacrifices" (10:11)	• Once! One time "for all" (7:27; 10:10–11)
Agent's degree of perfection	• High priest a sinner who will die (7:23) • Animals chosen are least blemished of the herd—based on human observation • Relative purity	• Jesus as "a high priest, holy, innocent, unstained, separated from sinners, and exalted above the heavens" (7:26) • A high priest who never dies but "continues forever" (7:24) • Absolute purity
Recipient of purification	• Human beings: *Jews only* • Primarily external—the flesh of humanity; mostly symbolic, limited permanent change	• Human beings: believers from *all peoples of all the world* • Primarily internal—the heart of humanity, to change human beings from the inside out
Effectiveness	• "For it is impossible for the blood of bulls and goats to take away sins" (10:4) • Human priest "can never take away sins" (10:11) • Relationship with God restored in a symbolic way, and only until the next time a person sins • Sense of honor in community of God's people	• "And by that will we have been sanctified through the offering of the body of Jesus Christ once for all" (10:10) • Purifies the "conscience from dead works to serve the living God" (9:14) • "hearts sprinkled clean from an evil conscience and our bodies washed with pure water" (10:22) • "I will remember their sins and their lawless deeds no more" (10:17) • Human beings enjoy a permanent change because God's laws are placed *inside* human hearts and minds (10:16) • Jesus, the high priest, "is able to save to the uttermost" (7:25) • Relationship with God restored objectively forever; honor restored before the ultimate audience, the audience of One, God himself
Conclusion	• Weak, inferior • Old Covenant is "obsolete … growing old … ready to vanish away" (8:13)	• Powerful, eternal, vastly superior • "Christ has obtained a ministry that is as much more excellent than the old as the covenant he mediates is better, since it is enacted on better promises" (8:6)

Figure 3.20: Contrasts in the power of purification between Old and New Covenants based on the letter to the Hebrews

- Therefore, instead of seeing Leviticus and Hebrews as "advanced books" for "advanced Christians" (being studied at the end of a discipleship journey)—could they rather be seen as books that contain evangelistic *entry points* for the gospel (at the very beginning of a discipleship journey)? Could it be that Buddhists, Hindus, Muslims, and tribal peoples will be—much more than Westerners—attracted to a *"purity gospel"* about *cleansing from defilement?*[8]

---

8. Andrew Walls writes concerning the book of Leviticus: "How many of us, while firm as a rock as to its canonicity, seriously look to the book of Leviticus for sustenance? Yet many an African Independent Church has found it abundantly relevant. (Interestingly, Samuel Ajayi Crowther, the great nineteenth-century Yoruba missionary bishop, thought it should be among the first books of the Bible to be translated.)" Walls' article is "The Gospel as Prisoner and Liberator of Culture: Is There a 'Historic Christian Faith?" in eds. Robert L. Gallagher and Paul Hertig, *Landmark Essays in Mission and World Christianity* (Maryknoll, NY: Orbis Books, 2013), Kindle edition locations 3077–80.

A Gospel Shaped by "Honor-Status Reversal"?

Explore a "global gospel." Is there enough biblical material to warrant an exploration of how the dynamic of honor-status reversal intersects with the good news of Jesus Christ, so that a fresh presentation of the gospel can be developed to better resonate among people in honor/shame cultures?

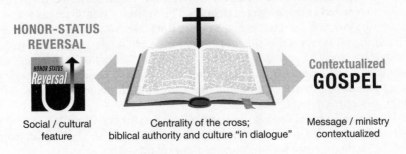

HONOR-STATUS REVERSAL

Contextualized GOSPEL

| Social / cultural feature | Centrality of the cross; biblical authority and culture "in dialogue" | Message / ministry contextualized |

Figure 3.21: Can there be a gospel presentation that incorporates the dynamic of honor-status reversal?

Yes! Honor-status reversal *is the gospel*, signified by four iconic words: Cross, Story, Mission, Kingdom

The diagram, "The Humiliation and Exaltation of Christ," is repeated on the next page for visual reinforcement as we draw our conclusions from four key words.

(1) CROSS: Honor-status reversal is exemplified by Christ's journey, which has the cross as its turning point.

The atonement of Christ on the cross, followed by his resurrection, is the axis of all theology, all mission, all history. Therefore, the global gospel never compromises this truth: "For God so loved the world, that he gave his only Son, that whoever believes in him should not perish but have eternal life" (John 3:16). All theology and all mission endeavors of the church must forever point to the cross of Jesus, where both God's love for the world and God's passion for his glory (John 12:27–28) find ultimate expression. That people "should not perish but have eternal life" is the gift of salvation communicated by the church to all the peoples of the world.

273

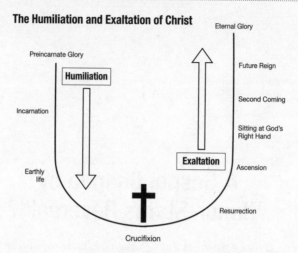

Figure 3.22: Humiliation and exaltation of Christ as honor-status reversal—
a pattern for the mission of the church

(2) STORY: A gospel characterized by honor-status reversal is a powerful narrative for the unreached and unengaged peoples. The drama of honor-status reversal is inherently a journey, a story. It is easy to grasp the Bible as a series of sub-narratives with honor-status reversal as the motif—all inside of a larger grand narrative. The various elements of an epic story are all present in the Bible's stories of honor-status reversal: *plot, setting, journey, family, romance, honor and shame, surprise, suffering, courage, mystery, tragedy, conquest, hero, enemy and villain, blood, crescendo and climax, destination and beatific ending.*

Moreover, in proclaiming the comprehensive story of Christ's honor-status reversal, Christians can avoid preaching a truncated gospel. Theologian Damon So of the Oxford Centre for Mission Studies explains why:

> Regarding the *content* of the Christian gospel, the gospel story of Jesus occupies the central place, but students should be instructed to avoid majoring on one phase of Jesus' earthly life only, as often seen in Western preaching. Often, liberal churches in the West major on the life of Jesus, while conservative churches often major on the death of Jesus. This dichotomy between majoring on the life and majoring on the death of Jesus closely corresponds to the general dichotomy in mission between "social action only" and "proclamation only," neither of which grasp the full gospel story of Jesus and thereby do not practice the holistic gospel in mission.

> By presenting the more complete story of Jesus and his birth, baptism, temptations, public ministry, entry into Jerusalem, death, resurrection, and universal reign, the oral story approach employed in non-Western contexts has presented a more holistic picture of Jesus Christ who thus *in the power of his person* has drawn many people unto himself.[1] (Emphasis in original.)

---

1. Damon So, "How Should a Theological Institution Prepare Students/Leaders Who Will Go Out into the Field to Train Local People (Storytellers) to Tell Bible Stories Effectively," in eds. Samuel E. Chiang and Grant Lovejoy, *Beyond Literate Western Models: Contextualizing Theological Education in Oral Contexts* (International Orality Network, 2013), 33.

I heartily agree with Dr. So and contend there is powerful, inherent missional quality in the *honor-status reversal story of Jesus* for unengaged and unreached peoples.

a. The global gospel is much more than a list of theological propositions about sin and guilt, forgiveness and heaven; it is also a narrative of the conflict of rival kingdoms saturated with the dynamics of honor and shame. This epic story of God is one into which all persons and peoples are invited; this story offers the comprehensive solution to the problem of sin, brokenness, guilt, shame—in humanity, the world, and the cosmos.

b. The global gospel as a *narrative* is especially suited for individuals and peoples for whom an oral style of learning is the dominant way of gathering information and living one's life.

c. If the global gospel as an honor/shame narrative is ideally suited for oral peoples, then it also has superior resonance for the unreached and unengaged peoples of the world (Muslim, Hindu, Buddhist, and tribal)—the majority of whom have honor and shame as a prominent cultural value.

d. All people groups will be represented by those who believe; they are promised glory and honor at the end of the biblical grand narrative (Rev 21:22–27). None are marginalized, because Christ has transformed at least some from every nation and people into a unique reflection of his glory.[2] *What an honor* for all the redeemed to be seated at the marriage supper of the Lamb, the wedding feast of Christ and his bride (Rev 19:6–9). What a hope! What a gospel! What a Savior!

(3) MISSION: Honor-status reversal in the gospel is a pattern for mission; it is inherently *mission-in-motion.* Jesus said, "Peace be with you. As the Father has sent me, even so I am sending you" (John 20:21). As Jesus was sent by the Father *in the incarnational dynamic of honor-status reversal,* even so Jesus is actively sending believers today in the same *incarnational dynamic of honor-status reversal.* Believers and churches are to *get on board,* and enter God's ongoing story in motion. It is the life of the gospel of Jesus in the same mode of mission-in-motion. The life of Jesus, as recorded in the Gospels, was a ministry of honor-status reversal—he was "appointed for the fall and rising of many in Israel" (Luke 2:34). People were and are *moved* as a result of Christ's ministry. Likewise, *the gospel itself* is a powerful multifaceted dynamic that creates upward and downward motion—honor-status reversal—both for those who receive Christ (John 1:12) and for those who reject him.

a. *Salvation power in motion.* The gospel is the very "power of God for salvation" (Rom 1:16) and it is on the move! By the gospel, God lifts individuals, families, and peoples out of sin and shame into the everlasting life, love and honor of the kingdom of Christ. He rescues people from the "domain of darkness" and transfers them into the "kingdom of his beloved Son" (Col 1:13). *Believers take the gospel* to the world—but just as real is the fact that *the gospel takes believers on mission.* Indeed, "the gospel ... is the power of God" that takes believers

---

2. This point is examined thoroughly in Chapter 4.1.

on mission with God across the street and around the world. This dynamic, outward-seeking grace of the gospel may be seen in Paul when he writes to the Ephesians, "assuming that you have heard of the stewardship of God's grace that was given to me for you" (Eph 3:2). The dynamic is: *receiving in order to pass it on.* Is this not the power of the gospel—the power of the Holy Spirit?

b. *Camaraderie, not superiority.* The gospel is indeed "the power of God for salvation to everyone who believes" (Rom 1:16). But believers must share and live the gospel in *camaraderie with* (not in *superiority over)* all peoples— including those of lower status, the poor and oppressed. As members of a global missionary community, Western Christians are still making the shift, as Bosch says, from *padre* to *compadre,* no longer participating "as the ones who have all the answers, but as learners like everyone else."[3] Jesus calls us to an attitude of servanthood in mission: "If I then, your Lord and Teacher, have washed your feet, you also ought to wash one another's feet. For I have given you an example, that you also should do just as I have done to you" (John 13:14–15).

c. *Against the status quo.* The gospel of honor-status reversal does not reinforce the status quo. Rather, believers living by the gospel of honor-status reversal are willing to violate the status quo by stepping down to serve among the poor and the powerless, not only as friends, but also as advocates and fellow sufferers. Jesus blessed the poor and lowly, the hungry, the persecuted (Luke 6:20–23) and pronounced "woes" against the high-status rich, powerful, and comfortable (Luke 6:24–25)—while bringing liberty to the oppressed (Luke 4:18). Likewise, those who represent Christ, and the gospel of honor-status reversal, are willing to speak against the status quo, challenging any social structure—any existing state of affairs—that is in contradiction to the kingdom of Christ. This is the prophetic element of the gospel that may not *necessarily* change the state of oppressive affairs, but which, nevertheless, is good news to the poor by the hope which it brings.

d. *Repentance for the church, not just the lost.* The global gospel of honor-status reversal leads Christians to embrace servanthood and vulnerability as the default mode of mission, and therefore are wary (if not repentant) of mission as an extension of Western power and cultural superiority. This also speaks to pastors everywhere who are seduced by the influence of their leadership, leading to the ugly, sinful abuse of power. The days of mission linked with power and empire are over, or should be. Mission in the twenty-first century must be mission as servanthood, learning by listening, collaboration, and above all *humility*—through the very mind of Christ (Phil 2:5).

e. *Vulnerability is power.* Jesus calls us to live the global gospel as a descent into servanthood and vulnerability (Mark 10:43; 2 Cor 13:4). This kind of ministry is more appealing to secular, postmodern individuals and peoples who are alienated by the misuse of power by the church ... who may have been victimized by people in the church ... or who simply see the hypocrisies

---

3. Bosch, 453.

of Christendom. Many see a controlling church which, over the centuries, has too often reinforced the powerful status quo at the expense of the powerless and marginalized—contradicting the life and teachings of Jesus. Moreover, a gospel that celebrates the acceptance, honor, and community of its members will be much more attractive for the secular multitudes in the West who are often plagued by sin, isolation and shame, fractured families, or a perpetual sense of homelessness.

(4) KINGDOM: Honor-status reversal points to the kingdom reign of Christ. The gospel that embodies honor-status reversal celebrates the already-but-not-yet reign of Christ in his kingdom. The cross was not a morbid pause against which God had to struggle in order to raise Christ from the dead; it was more like an unstoppable, gravitas of glory that catapulted Christ into the highly exalted regal honor and glory of his kingdom. Believers live with the *effect* and the *affect* of this new honor—that honor being in Christ himself, in his family the church, and in his kingdom.

a.   Followers of Jesus have a new source of ascribed honor; it is the honor of God himself as the Father of a new family, a new kinship group called the church, the body of Christ, the "one new man" (Eph 2:15). "But to all who did receive him, who believed in his name, he gave the right to become children of God" (John 1:12; cf. 1 John 3:1). The spiritual DNA of those who follow Christ has been altered because they are "born, not of blood nor of the will of the flesh nor of the will of man, but of God" (John 1:13).

b.   Since God has relocated the Christian's ascribed honor into a new community and kingdom ruled by the beloved Son, Jesus Christ (Col 1:13), believers experience an *honor surplus* saturated with the love of God. This honor surplus is not just an *objective* doctrinal truth with a heavenly destiny (Eph 2:6; cf. Rev 3:21), it is also a *subjective* visceral reality that believers feel today: "And hope does not put us to shame, because God's love has been poured into our hearts through the Holy Spirit who has been given to us" (Rom 5:5). Paul was speaking of an *already,* present-tense *experience* of the Holy Spirit, not a theological concept pointing to the distant future.

c.   Believers have a new unlimited source of honor *today*. Believers have had their honor relocated into Christ and his kingdom: "Blessed are the poor in spirit, for theirs is the kingdom of heaven" (Mat 5:3). Thus, believers can "vacate the playing field"[4] of honor competition and violence, live in the peace of God (Mat 5:9), resist temptation, absorb shame, and even suffer persecution if necessary (Mat 5:10). They are freed from the dark side of honor and shame—rivalry, honor competition, honor-based violence. The demonic dynamic of "honor-trumps-ethics" is replaced by the highest freedom of Christ-empowered righteousness. They have exchanged the binding yoke of "limited good"—for the freedom of the *unlimited good* of Christ, by which they experience the abundance of God's honor and glory, for he "will supply every need of yours according to his riches in glory in Christ Jesus" (Phil 4:19).

---

4. Neyrey, *Honor and Shame in the Gospel of Matthew,* 214.

d. Because Christ is already reigning in power over all his enemies, the global gospel of honor-status reversal compels believers to work for bringing the kingdom of God to earth today. Believers pray, "Your kingdom come, your will be done, on earth as it is in heaven" (Mat 6:10) with authentic faith and corresponding action.

Honor/shame dynamics at the core of the gospel

We have observed that honor-status reversal is a motif of Scripture. We have also seen that honor-status reversal is inherent—that is, *essential, fundamental,* indeed, *basic* to the gospel of Christ. Moreover, we have explored how all of the other honor/shame dynamics (discussed previously in this section) overlap with Christ's atonement, and thus, may be used to articulate the gospel.

What does this mean for contextualizing the gospel in our multicultural neighborhoods? What does it mean for the multitudes of unreached peoples for whom honor and shame is a primary cultural value? What does this mean for the preaching of the gospel?

I agree with Jackson Wu who simply states: "The gospel is already contextualized for honor/shame cultures." And, "honor and shame are built into the framework of the gospel itself."[5]

This means that the global gospel of Jesus Christ has the potential to resonate with the peoples of our multicultural world—and with persons struggling with shame—perhaps far more than we ever realized.

---

5. See Jackson Wu, "Rewriting the Gospel for Oral Cultures: Why Honor and Shame are Essential to the Gospel Story," in the forthcoming book from International Orality Network, *Beyond Literate Western Contexts: Honor & Shame and Assessment of Orality Preference.* Article available at: https://jacksonwu.files.wordpress.com/2014/07/rewriting-the-gospel-for-oral-cultures-why-honor-and-shame-are-essential-to-the-gospel-story-ion-2014-consultation-hbu-jackson-wu.pdf

SECTION 4

Honor/Shame Dynamics in the World Christian Movement

Honor/Shame Dynamics in the World Christian Movement

IN THE PREVIOUS SECTION, we explored the wide-ranging ways that the gospel of Jesus Christ can be articulated by using the Bible's honor/shame dynamics. We explored level H/S-4, the "Evangelical" level, in Figure 2.01. It is all about the "gospel message."

We begin now with Section 4: "Honor/Shame Dynamics in the World Christian Movement." There are four chapters in this final section of the book.

1. Honor/Shame Dynamics in Our Purpose

2. Honor/Shame Dynamics in Our Training

3. Honor/Shame Dynamics in Our Practice

4. Believers Have No Honor Deficit (a summary)

The first chapter, "Honor/Shame Dynamics in our Purpose," explores what may be considered the highest level of awareness of honor and shame in the world Christian movement. Figure 4.01, which is the same as Figure 2.01, is shown on the next page. We see that the final level is called "Teleological." It is so named because the Greek root word *telos* simply means *end*. So we'll be exploring the *end purpose*, the ultimate destination of God's people in God's story. We'll be examining how Scripture's *telos* affects our mission today in the world Christian movement.

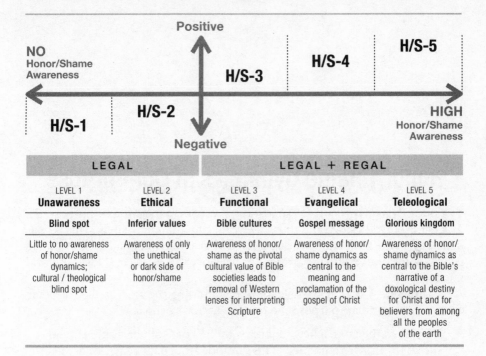

Figure 4.01: H/S-1 to H/S-5: Levels of awareness of honor and shame
(for full chart see Appendix 2)

In chapters 4.2 and 4.3, we will examine some implications for training and practice in the world Christian movement. These two chapters are starting points rather than an attempt at being comprehensive.

A short final chapter offers my summary for the book.

I hope the scripturally rooted truths and ideas in this section will stimulate dialog and creativity in the world Christian community. May believers be helped in bringing the global gospel of Jesus Christ to all the peoples of the earth.

Honor/Shame Dynamics in Our Purpose

HONOR/SHAME DYNAMICS ARE IMPORTANT VALUES in the ultimate purpose, the *telos*,[1] of God's story, and thus, the world Christian movement. This is true, first of all, in the honor and praise that is to be given to God by all nations. "God's penchant for praise" and his passion for his glory is the crux and fuel for world missions.[2]

Psalm 96:1–5 is a key passage for understanding the glory of God as being central to the ultimate purpose and mission of God's people.

> Oh sing to the LORD a new song; sing to the LORD, all the earth! Sing to the LORD, bless his name; tell of his salvation from day to day. Declare his glory among the nations, his marvelous works among all the peoples! For great is the LORD, and greatly to be praised; he is to be feared above all gods. For all the gods of the peoples are worthless idols, but the LORD made the heavens.

The task given to God's people is to "tell of his salvation" and "declare his glory" to all nations and "among all the peoples!" And what is the reason to *tell* and *declare*? *"For great is the Lord, and greatly to be praised."* Simply, God deserves lavish honor and praise. The worship of the one and only true God by all peoples and nations is the ultimate rationale for world missions.

In Steve Hawthorne's article, "The Story of His Glory," the overriding dynamic from Psalm 96 concerning world missions is stated through this elegant principle:

> **God *reveals* his glory *to* all nations in order to *receive* glory *from* all peoples through worship.**[3]

Expanding on this using the language of honor and shame, the principle may be restated like this: *God* reveals *his glory, honor and blessing to persons from among all peoples so they experience salvation from sin and gain abundant blessing. They*

---

1. The meaning of *telos* is simply "an ultimate object or aim; ORIGIN Greek, literally 'end.'" *New Oxford American Dictionary 3rd edition* (New York: Oxford University Press, Inc., 2010).
2. Steve Hawthorne, "The Story of His Glory," *Perspectives on the World Christian Movement, Third Edition* (Pasadena, CA: William Carey Library, 1999). I gratefully acknowledge the influence of Steve Hawthorne's work in this chapter. His article "The Story of His Glory" had a big impact on my life and ministry. His Ph.D. thesis, *Let All the Peoples Praise Him: Toward a Teleological Paradigm of the Missio Dei*, was made available to me in 2013; it is a profound expansion on "The Story of His Glory." The wonderful phrase "God's penchant for praise," is from "The Story of His Glory."
3. Hawthorne, "The Story of His Glory," 50.

have their guilt forgiven, their shame covered and honor elevated in knowing the only true and living God. They are transformed and honored in becoming "conformed to the image of his Son" (Rom 8:29) as God receives from them the glorifying worship he desires and deserves.

Hawthorne explains:

People are indeed saved by the global declaration of God's salvation, but the ultimate value of their salvation is not to be seen in what they are saved *from,* it is what they are saved *for* that really matters. People are saved to serve God in worship. In this respect, we can say that world evangelization is for God. However accustomed we may be to seeing people as being of paramount importance, the Bible is clear: The rationale for mission is the colossal worthiness of God.[4]

This theme is echoed in the opening words in John Piper's book *Let the Nations Be Glad!: The Supremacy of God in Missions.*

Missions is not the ultimate goal of the church. Worship is. Missions exists because worship doesn't. Worship is ultimate, not missions, because God is ultimate, not man. When this age is over, and the countless millions of the redeemed fall on their faces before the throne of God, missions will be no more. It is a temporary necessity. But worship abides forever.[5]

In his letter to the Ephesians, Paul emphasizes three times in chapter 1 the grand purpose of *praise for God and his glory.* Our salvation through Christ's blood and adoption as children of God is "to the praise of his glorious grace" (Eph 1:6); our calling into God's eternal purpose is "to the praise of his glory" (1:12); and our eternal inheritance sealed by the Holy Spirit is "to the praise of his glory" (1:14). Piper writes, "The extraordinary greatness of the praise that the Lord should receive is the ground and impetus of our mission to the nations."[6]

Indeed, the giving of glory and honor to God by humanity's worship and affectionate adoration is at the heart of missions. *For great is the Lord and greatly to be praised!* He is worthy! All of *life,* all of *ministry,* all of *missions* should be to the praise of the glory of God in Jesus Christ.

We become like that which we worship

Psalm 96 offers another crucial reason why the glory of God—the worship of the one and only God—is the ultimate purpose for mission. "For all the gods of the peoples are worthless idols, but the LORD made the heavens" (v. 5). To worship any god but God is to engage in idolatry. And every form of idolatry invariably results in shame, oppression, defilement.[7]

Psalm 135:15–18 makes it plain: "The idols of the nations are silver and gold, the work of human hands. They have mouths, but do not speak; they have eyes, but

---

4. Ibid., 51.

5. John Piper, *Let the Nations Be Glad!: The Supremacy of God in Missions* (Grand Rapids, MI: Baker Publishing Group, 2010), Kindle edition locations 163–66.

6. Ibid., Kindle edition locations 4394–95.

7. Jeremiah 5:5–7 makes clear the profound link between idolatry and oppression. Moreover, when God judges his people for their idolatry, there is inherently a loving, salvific dimension to it.

do not see; they have ears, but do not hear, nor is there any breath in their mouths. *Those who make them become like them, so do all who trust in them."* (Emphasis mine, cf. Ps 115:4–8, Is 44:9–20.)

To worship false gods is to become like them—lifeless. Consider any form of oppression anywhere in the world: You will almost always see underlying that oppression some form of false worship, unholy affection, idolatry.[8] In contrast, in worshiping God through Jesus Christ we become like Jesus—alive, free, vital, yes—*even glorious.* By gazing at Christ, "with unveiled face, beholding the glory of the Lord, [we] are being transformed into the same image from one degree of glory to another" (2 Cor 3:18).

This is why it is in everyone's self-interest—and every *people's* self-interest—to worship the one and only God of all creation. John Piper writes:

> The liberating fact is that the message we take to the frontiers is that people everywhere should seek their own best interest. We are summoning people to God. And those who come say, "In your presence there is fullness of joy; at your right hand are pleasures forevermore" (Ps 16:11). God glorifies himself among the nations with the command, "Delight yourself in the Lord!" (Ps 37:4). His first and great requirement of all men everywhere is that they repent from seeking their joy in other things and begin to seek it only in him.[9]

We want to be glorious *in God* to share the glory *of God*

In the book, *The Changing Face of World Missions: Engaging Contemporary Issues and Trends,* co-authors Pocock, Van Rheenan, and McConnell have a chapter on "Changing Motivations for Missions." They explore the text of 2 Corinthians 3:7–4:18 as one passage that illustrates how God's glory is both the origin and goal of missions.

> As Moses on Mount Sinai reflected God's radiance, Christians under the new covenant begin to reflect the nature of God as they look to Christ. Paul says that they "are being transformed into his likeness with ever increasing glory" (3:18). This transformation, which results from looking upon Christ, who is the image of God, leads to ministry.[10]

It leads to ministry and mission because the glory of Christ is revealed in our hearts. Here's how it works:

> For God, who said, "Let light shine out of darkness," has shone in our hearts to give the light of the knowledge of the glory of God in the face of Jesus Christ (2 Cor 4:6).

---

8. Sadly, there are, in the history of the Christian church, abundant examples of oppression in the name of Christ. This only reinforces the point that, even for Christians, oppression against others is possible when we take our eyes off of Jesus. The sinfulness of Christians—or those who call themselves Christians—may challenge but does not refute the principle: *The knowledge and worship of Jesus Christ by his followers relativizes the desire for revenge, violence, and oppression.* True followers of Jesus Christ are known by their grace and truth, love and compassion.

9. Ibid., Kindle edition locations 969–73.

10. Michael Pocock, Gailyn Van Rheenan, and Douglas McConnell, *The Changing Face of World Missions: Engaging Contemporary Issues and Trends* (Grand Rapids, MI: Baker, 2005), 175.

The glory of God in this verse is compared to something as majestic and powerful as God speaking at creation, "Let there be light" (Gen 1:3). This same powerful God who speaks light and life into existence has shone into our darkened hearts in such a way that this light and life must be given away. Hence, the phrase, "has shone in our hearts to *give* the light." It must be shared! It must be given away! Receiving "the light of the knowledge of the glory of God" in the intimate "face" and honorific personhood of Jesus Christ is so powerful, beautiful, creative, and freeing, that *it must be shared with others.*[11]

Apostle Paul understood the glory of God as the expression of the transcendent Personhood of God revealed in Jesus Christ. In addition, he emphasized that God's glory was not only *transcendent* but also *immanent*—"something existing or operating within."[12] The glory of God is to be *internalized,* something *progressively experienced within* by believers through a life of gazing in wonder at Jesus and living in Christ-directed obedience. This is why Paul wrote, "And we all, with unveiled face, beholding the glory of the Lord, are being transformed into the same image from one degree of glory to another" (2 Cor 3:18).

Believers can become progressively like Jesus, reflecting his glory—itself an astounding honor. Pocock, Van Rheenan, and McConnell write:

> Becoming like God has always been the ultimate motivation for missions. Understandings of hell and lostness are secondary to seeing God's glory and incarnating this glory in Christian ministry. C. S. Lewis says that Christians not only see the beauty of God but also become beautiful: "We want something else which can hardly be put into words—to be united with the beauty we see, to pass into it, to receive it into ourselves, to bathe in it, to become part of it. We are called to taste the *infinite* glory of God and thereby become *finitely* glorious ourselves.[13] (Emphasis mine.)

No wonder Paul wrote, "Therefore, having this ministry by the mercy of God, *we do not lose heart*" (2 Cor 4:1). He repeats the phrase near the end of chapter 4: *"So we do not lose heart"* (v. 16). "Though our outer self is wasting away, our inner self is being renewed day by day. For this light momentary affliction is preparing for us an *eternal weight of glory* beyond all comparison" (vv. 16–17). The inner experience of God's glory in Christ and the ultimate hope of even greater glory in eternity sustained Paul in his calling as an apostle to the Gentiles.

This glory in Christ is to be known *in part* by individual persons. The Bible also reveals that this glory in Christ is to be known in community by people *groups.* It will be known *in fullness* by the singular kingdom community of God's family of

---

11. Some may think this verse is not about sharing the gospel, but rather is about the internal experience of God's glory shining in one's heart. However, consider the previous verses of chapter 4. Paul is writing about the ministry of "the gospel of the glory of Christ" (2 Cor 4:4). Paul is explaining how he ministers; he hides nothing, but rather, "by the open statement of the truth we would commend ourselves to everyone's conscience in the sight of God" (v. 2). Paul is also defending himself from the accusation of self-promotion: "For what we proclaim is not ourselves, but Jesus Christ as Lord, with ourselves as your servants for Jesus' sake" (v. 5). Therefore, I contend that the context of 2 Corinthians 4 recommends that verse 6 is about the *outward purpose* of sharing the gospel—"to give the light of the knowledge of the glory of God in the face of Jesus Christ" (v. 6).

12. "Immanent," *New Oxford American Dictionary 3rd edition* (New York: Oxford University Press, Inc., 2010), referenced by Mac OSX 10.8.2.

13. Pocock, Rheenan, and McConnell, 175–76. They quote C.S. Lewis, *The Weight of Glory and Other Addresses* (Grand Rapids: Eerdmans, 1949), 12–13.

ethnicities. We are also mindful of the fact that the Bible was written by *individuals* with mostly *group-oriented* values.

Therefore, let us briefly focus our attention on the group-oriented aspect of God's revelation.

> And we all [plural], with unveiled face [singular], beholding the glory of the Lord, are being transformed [plural] into the same image from one degree of glory to another (2 Cor 3:18).

> For God, who said, "Let light shine out of darkness," has shone in our hearts [plural] to give the light of the knowledge of the glory of God in the face of Jesus Christ (2 Cor 4:6).

> So we [plural] do not lose heart [singular]. Though our [plural] outer self [singular] is wasting away, our [plural] inner self [singular] is being renewed day by day. For this light momentary affliction is preparing for us [plural] an eternal weight of glory beyond all comparison (2 Cor 4:16–17).

So the glory of God is experienced both individually and *in community*. Other verses that illustrate this collectivistic mindset are found in Hebrews.

> For if the blood of goats and bulls, and the sprinkling of defiled persons with the ashes of a heifer, sanctify for the purification of the flesh, how much more will the blood of Christ, who through the eternal Spirit offered himself without blemish to God, purify *our* [plural] *conscience* [singular] from dead works to serve the living God (Heb 9:13–14).

This indicates that the conscience is not merely experienced individually but in some sense also *in community*—collectively. This is remarkable to me as an individual believer raised in the West because I was trained to believe *I* am only guilty for *my own* sins, and thus bear the consequences of *my own* sins—in *my own* conscience—and *my own* experience.

On the other hand, I understand the concept of "our conscience" when I think about collective German guilt derived from the evils and horrors committed by Germans in the Holocaust of World War II. This collective guilt is suffered by many Germans, even those born after World War II.[14]

Do you see it? *Our* hearts, *our* outer self, *our* inner self, *our* conscience. The point here is that God's revelation in Scripture incorporates a *beautiful balance*—or perhaps a *sparkling tension*—between the individual and the group.[15]

And we will see that in God's ultimate purpose, he lavishly shares his glory with his people comprising both individuals and groups. God does this in such a way that both *individual believers* and *believers comprising people groups* experience redemption. Both individual saints and the distinct people groups of whom they are a part will be elevated to high regal honor through God's kingdom and through the kingdom's King: our Lord Jesus Christ.

---

14. "German collective guilt," *Wikipedia,* http://en.wikipedia.org/wiki/German_collective_guilt, accessed 26 February 2014.

15. It is notable to observe the group dynamic described in the Day of Atonement: "And he shall sprinkle some of the blood on it with his finger seven times, and cleanse it and consecrate it from the uncleannesses of the people of Israel" (Lev 16:19). The Day of Atonement was for the whole "people of Israel."

Mission purpose as God's glory *shared*—with his people, and with his peoples

There is a sense in which all glory and honor belong exclusively to God. Apostle Paul wrote the beautiful summary at the end of Romans 11, "For from him and through him and to him are all things. To him be glory forever. Amen" (Rom 11:36). Because God is creator, all glory originates with God and ultimately is returned to God. Relatedly, Steve Hawthorne writes about God being both the origin and destiny of mission, "God Himself fulfills His mission with His people. God is not merely the origin. He is the *telos*. He cannot be Alpha without also being Omega."[16]

Scripture also teaches that, while all glory and honor belong to God, there is a dominant feature of his character—"God is love" (1 John 4:8)—by which God actually shares his glory and regal honor with his people. God's love is expressed in a relational exchange. God not only saves sinners from judgment and hell, but also elevates their honor by sharing his glory with them.

First, God shares his glory with, and elevates the honor of, individual saints. And second, God shares his glory with, and elevates the honor of, people groups, *panta ta ethne*—all the peoples, nations, and kinship groups.[17] Here's how we can understand this:

- God forgives the sin, covers the shame, and elevates the honor of individual believers.

- All believers are part of their own people group.

- Sin exists both *individually*—and *corporately* (at the level of kinship group, people group, ethnic group, nation).

- The uniqueness and diversity of the peoples are preserved in heaven.

- Because God redeems individual believers who comprise people groups which are preserved in heaven, God also forgives the sin, covers the shame, and elevates the honor of all peoples.

Together, the incredible diversity of individuals and peoples comprise the eternal family of God. This *regal people* is the singular new humanity in Christ

---

16. Hawthorne, *Let All the Peoples Praise Him*, 53.

17. For an excellent overview of the usage of "all the peoples"—*panta ta ethne*—in the Bible, see John Piper's *Let the Nations Be Glad!*, Kindle Locations 3618–4229. Piper's definitive summary about the usage of *panta ta ethne* is as follows: "1. In the New Testament, the singular use of *ethnos* never means Gentile individuals but always people group or nation. 2. The plural *ethne* can mean either Gentile individuals or people groups. Sometimes the context demands that it mean one or the other, but in most instances it could carry either meaning. 3. The phrase *panta ta ethne* occurs eighteen times in the New Testament. Only once must it mean Gentile individuals. Nine times it must mean people groups. The other eight times are ambiguous. 4. Virtually all of the nearly one hundred uses of *panta ta ethne* in the Greek Old Testament refer to nations in distinction from the nation of Israel. ... The promise made to Abraham that in him 'all the families of the earth' would be blessed and that he would be 'the father of many nations' is taken up in the New Testament and gives the mission of the church a people-group focus because of this Old Testament emphasis. 6. The Old Testament missionary hope is expressed repeatedly as exhortations, promises, prayers, and plans for God's glory to be declared among the peoples and his salvation to be known by all the nations. 7. Paul understood his specifically missionary task in terms of this Old Testament hope and made the promises concerning peoples the foundation of his mission. He was devoted to reaching more and more people groups, not simply more and more individuals. He interpreted Christ's commission to him in these terms. 8. The apostle John envisioned the task of missions as the ingathering of 'the children of God' or the 'other sheep' out of 'every tribe, tongue, people, and nation.' 9. The Old Testament context of Jesus' missionary commission in Luke 24:46–47 shows that *panta ta ethne* would most naturally mean all the peoples or nations. 10. Mark 11:17 shows that Jesus probably thinks in terms of people groups when he envisions the worldwide purpose of God" (Kindle edition locations 4210–29).

(Eph 2:15, the "one new man") that has been purchased by his blood and has a sure destiny in Christ.

This is an honor-saturated, group-oriented, ethnicity-focused purpose that is in perfect balance with God's love for individuals. In our exploration below, we'll emphasize beautiful unity amidst breathtaking diversity in the relational love of God. I intend to show that this ultimate *purpose of God* (teleology) has love and honor at its core. I will also show that it bears much significance for our mission purpose, practice and training.

Jesus said it: God shares his glory with believers

First, let us settle the fact that God is actually giving glory to those who follow Jesus Christ. In John 17, Jesus is praying to the Father in what is often called his High Priestly Prayer:

> The glory that you have given me I have given to them, that they may be one even as we are one (John 17:22).

So God gives glory to people who follow Christ as Lord. In John 5, Jesus is speaking to the Pharisees and critiques their unbelief as a failed quest for glory:

> How can you believe, when you receive glory from one another and do not seek the glory that comes from the only God? (John 5:44).

Relatedly, Jesus spoke of the authorities who were afraid to confess Christ: "For they loved the glory that comes from man more than the glory that comes from God" (John 12:43). Clearly, Jesus' own words indicate that God shares his glory with people.

So we may conclude that people can be led to believing faith in Christ by actually *seeking glory promised them by God*. Jesus did not say it is wrong to seek glory. Jesus said it is wrong to seek glory given by people, rather than "the glory that comes from the only God." The Pharisees were only mistaken in *whom* they were seeking glory from, and this mistake undermined their belief in Jesus.

So as astounding as it may seem, God shares his glory with those who love and follow Christ.[18] Hawthorne writes, "God is so rich in glory that He bestows extravagant honors upon His human servants without compromising His own majesty in the slightest."[19]

But the truth of God sharing his glory with his people is not an innovation of the New Testament. The Old Testament also conveys this truth, albeit more indirectly. Let's look again at Psalm 96. Verse 6 reads: "Splendor and majesty are before him; strength and beauty are in his sanctuary." Again, we turn to Hawthorne, who writes of this verse:

> "Splendor and majesty" do not refer to God's self-experience. Rather, along with "strength and beauty" ... they are features of God's presence that are to be the experience of people who approach Him in true worship. There can be nothing more splendid or majestic for humans than to be

---

18. See footnote 34 on p. 203 concerning the verses in Isaiah where God says, "My glory I will not give to another" (Is 48:11).

19. Hawthorne, "The Story of His Glory," 50.

elevated and placed in the gorgeous, heart-stopping grandeur of God's regal presence.

Worship is the way that people glorify God. When looked at from God's point of view, we can see that worship is also God's way of glorifying people—in all the best sense of bringing people into their highest honor. Worship fulfills God's love. He loves people so vastly that He wills to exalt them to something better than greatness; He wants to bring them into an honored nearness to Him.[20]

Exploring the honor/shame dynamics in God's purpose to bless all peoples

We now turn to an exploration of how honor/shame dynamics in God's ultimate purpose (teleology) may be seen in Scripture. Limited space does not permit a comprehensive review of verses with teleological importance relative to missions. Therefore, we will examine here a selective set of Scriptures and consider their significance.[21]

In any study or any perspective of the Bible's teleology, the subject of the *kingdom of God* is front and center. Due to space limitations, we will not explore the many varied ways to interpret the kingdom.

But of this one thing we can be sure: However one understands and experiences the kingdom of God, believers gain a new source of honor by being redeemed by and related to the King, our Lord Jesus Christ.

In this set of Scriptures—primarily from the books of Daniel and Revelation—we will examine the way God shares his glory with persons and people groups.

The kingdom of God is paramount in the story and purposes of God. In Daniel 7 we detect a beautiful merger of honor between God the Father (called "the Ancient of Days"), the Son of Man (Jesus), and the saints of God. Observe, first of all, the verses below concerning God the Father as the Ancient of Days:

As I looked, thrones were placed, and the Ancient of Days took his seat; his clothing was white as snow, and the hair of his head like pure wool; his throne was fiery flames; its wheels were burning fire. A stream of fire issued and came out from before him; a thousand thousands served him, and ten thousand times ten thousand stood before him; the court sat in judgment, and the books were opened (Dan 7:9–10).

God's justice is to be meted out by the Ancient of Days as "the court sat in judgment and the books were opened" (v. 10).

Then, in verse 14, the Son of Man is given the kingdom—with all its glory and diversity.

I saw in the night visions, and behold, with the clouds of heaven there came one like a son of man, and he came to the Ancient of Days and was presented before him. And to him was given dominion and glory and a

---

20. Ibid., 51–52.
21. For a much more exhaustive treatment on God's ultimate purpose or teleology, see Hawthorne: *Let All the Peoples Praise Him.*

kingdom, that all peoples, nations, and languages should serve him; his dominion is an everlasting dominion, which shall not pass away, and his kingdom one that shall not be destroyed (vv. 13–14).

The "son of man" is "given dominion and glory and a kingdom" comprising the diversity of "peoples, nations, and languages"—a vivid vision of Jesus the Son of Man receiving the honor of the Father in the form of the kingdom of God.

Curiously, in 1 Corinthians 15:24 we see another perspective. "Then comes the end, when [Jesus] delivers the kingdom to God the Father after destroying every rule and every authority and power." This is different. Whereas in Daniel 7:13–14, the Father gives the kingdom to the Son, here it is *Christ* who delivers the kingdom to the *Father*.

In Luke's Gospel we find another twist. Scripture reveals God presenting the kingdom to his "little flock." Jesus says, "Fear not, little flock, for it is your Father's good pleasure to give you the kingdom" (Luke 12:32). *Amazing!* The Father gives the kingdom to his "little flock," and does so with *pleasure?* Who are these vulnerable ones, this "little flock"? Is this not the community of the saints of God redeemed by the blood of Christ?

We return to Daniel 7 and find the same sublime truth. Again we find the almost unbelievable bestowal of honor to the saints in Daniel 7:18, 22, and 27.

- In verse 18, it is the saints who *"possess the kingdom* forever, forever and ever."

- In verse 22, "until the Ancient of Days came, and judgment was given for the saints of the Most High, and the time came when *the saints possessed the kingdom."*

- In verse 27, "And the kingdom and the dominion and the greatness of the kingdoms under the whole heaven *shall be given to the people of the saints* of the Most High; his kingdom shall be an everlasting kingdom, and all dominions shall serve and obey him." [22] (Emphasis mine).

We must ask, *To whom is the kingdom of God given?*

Is the kingdom given by Christ to God the Father (1 Cor 15:24)? *Yes.* Is the kingdom given by the Ancient of Days to Jesus, the "son of man" (Dan 7:13–14)? *Yes.* Is the kingdom given by God to the saints (Dan 7:18, 22, 27; Luke 12:32)? *Yes.*

What we observe is nothing less than the relational exchange of honor between God and his people. God the Father, the Lord Jesus, and the saints of God *together* possess and share the kingdom. [23]

It makes sense that God, the Ancient of Days, Creator, Ruler and Judge should possess the kingdom; *he owns it.* It makes sense that Christ as Redeemer, Savior and Lord should possess the kingdom; *he earned it—the peoples who populate it were purchased by his blood* (Rev 5:9).

But how can it be that persons and peoples who were once defiled, inglorious

---

22. Moreover, the *ESV Study Bible* has a footnote on this verse that "obey him" can also be translated "obey them."

23. Could it be that this is what Jesus was hinting at in the Beatitudes? "Blessed are the poor in spirit, for theirs is the kingdom of heaven" (Mat 5:3).

sinners, and enemies of God (Eph 2:1–3) will possess the kingdom? *We are but creatures. We have not earned it!* It stretches human imagination, even the minds of the redeemed, to embrace this ineffable truth.

How do we embrace the totality of honor given to God's people, the community of saints? It is almost too precious to describe.

This is why Peter said, "So the honor is for you who believe" (1 Pet 2:7). This is why Paul considered that "the sufferings of this present time are not worth comparing with the glory that is to be revealed to us" (Rom 8:18).

This is why Paul also described the hope of our salvation as "Christ in you, the hope of glory" (Col 1:27)! And why Paul wrote, that this "hope does not put us to shame, because God's love has been poured into our hearts through the Holy Spirit who has been given to us" (Rom 5:5).

This is why John pondered the mystery: "See what kind of love the Father has given to us, that we should be called children of God" (1 John 3:1).

Honor magnified among the saints and peoples in Revelation

The large chart in Appendix 5 is an overview of the honor/shame dynamics contained in the book of Revelation. The reader is strongly encouraged to at least skim the chart to observe *how abundant* is the honor/shame language. Pay special attention to the center column, which is labeled, *"God gives honor to the saints— individual believers and people groups they comprise."*

The purpose of this chart is to demonstrate the extensive degree to which believers—and the peoples they comprise—are given honor by God. When seen in the light of specific honor/shame dynamics, the inescapable conclusion is this: *The glory and honor that Almighty God shares with the saints gathered from among all peoples is almost beyond imagination.* (And notably, without an understanding of the pivotal cultural value of honor and shame in Bible societies, this conclusion would not be as easily accessible.) One example of Revelation's beatific visions is in chapter 5:

> And they sang a new song, saying, "Worthy are you to take the scroll and to open its seals, for you were slain, and by your blood you ransomed people for God from every tribe and language and people and nation, and you have made them a kingdom and priests to our God, and they shall reign on the earth."
>
> Then I looked, and I heard around the throne and the living creatures and the elders the voice of many angels, numbering myriads of myriads and thousands of thousands, saying with a loud voice, "Worthy is the Lamb who was slain, to receive power and wealth and wisdom and might and honor and glory and blessing!"
>
> And I heard every creature in heaven and on earth and under the earth and in the sea, and all that is in them, saying, "To him who sits on the throne and to the Lamb be blessing and honor and glory and might forever and ever!" (Rev 5:9–13).

The day is coming when every people group will be represented in the magnificent choir worshiping the regal Savior (v. 9). The Lamb is worthy! Christ's honor and glory are supreme. The worship of the slain Lamb of God can never be exhausted. And at the same time we observe that the saints and manifold peoples they comprise are *also honored*—"you have made them a kingdom and priests to our God, and they shall reign on the earth" (v. 10).

Such is the overflowing love and honor of Almighty God. He actually dwells with his people (Rev 21:3). It's incredible that the saints live with God in his house. "Therefore they are before the throne of God ... and he who sits on the throne will shelter them with his presence" (Rev 7:15). What a display of the honor of God's grace and hospitality toward the redeemed.

It is the overflowing love and honor of Christ the King sitting with conquering saints who have joined him on his throne (Rev 3:21). Yes, the saints even gain the honor of sitting enthroned with their Savior. It fulfills God's promise that he "raised us up with him and seated us with him in the heavenly places in Christ Jesus" (Eph 2:6).

It is the overflowing love and honor of the Bridegroom banqueting with his bride (Rev 19:7–9). Banquets are the most celebratory and generous displays of honor and joy! The magnificent mystery of Christ being one with the church (Eph 5:25) will finally become a sacred reality saturated with affection and glory. What a romance!

And finally, it is the overflowing love of Christ receiving the honor of the kings of the earth:

> And I saw no temple in the city, for its temple is the Lord God the Almighty and the Lamb. And the city has no need of sun or moon to shine on it, for the glory of God gives it light, and its lamp is the Lamb. By its light will the nations walk, and the kings of the earth will bring their glory into it, and its gates will never be shut by day—and there will be no night there. They will bring into it the glory and the honor of the nations. But nothing unclean will ever enter it, nor anyone who does what is detestable or false, but only those who are written in the Lamb's book of life (Rev 21:22–27).

In the New Jerusalem (Rev 21:10) again we behold the overflowing love and honor of God as he condescends to receive the glory of the nations. "They will bring into it the glory and the honor of the nations."[24]

At least some from all the peoples are redeemed. All the kinship groups are there. All the nations are represented by their kings as they bring the finest unique works of art and culture, wisdom and science, all the beautiful wonders of their own people. All have been transformed, made clean, holy, unspeakably precious by the purifying atonement of Christ (Heb 1:3).

---

24. Richard Mouw explores the political, cultural, and social dimensions of this passage in Revelation and how it overlaps with Isaiah 60. "In short, ancient kings served as the primary authorities over the broad patterns of the cultural lives of their nations. And when they stood over against other nations, they were the bearers, the representatives, of their respective cultures. To assemble kings together, then, was in an important sense to assemble their national cultures together." Richard J. Mouw, *When the Kings Come Marching In: Isaiah and the New Jerusalem* (Grand Rapids, MI: Wm. B. Eerdmans Publishing Company, 2002), Kindle edition locations 457–58).

Richard Mouw has written of the overlaps between Isaiah 60 and Revelation 21:22–27. He describes how both passages give insights about the eternal city to come. He explores the political, cultural, and social dimensions of these parallel passages of Scripture.

And now these entities are gathered into the renewed Jerusalem. But as they appear in this transformed commercial center, they are no longer signs of pagan cultural strength or displays of alien power. ... Here in the transformed City these vessels and goods serve a very different purpose. Isaiah is very explicit about this new purpose, noting what function each creature and item now performs. Ephah's camels now "proclaim the praise of the Lord" (Is 60:6). Nebaioth's rams "shall minister to you" as acceptable sacrifices on the Lord's altars (Is 60:7). The ships of Tarshish bring precious metals "for the name of the Lord your God" (Is 60:9). And the costly lumber from Lebanon will "beautify the place of my sanctuary" (Is. 60:9). Each of the items mentioned is now to be put to the service of God and his people.[25]

Every regal gift is transformed by Christ. Every gift is received by the King of kings, glorifying God, while at the same time bestowing honor on each and every people.

People group rivalry gone, while every people group's honor is magnified

No peoples will ever be marginalized again. No culture or people will ever again be intimidated by a "market-dominant majority."[26] No ethnic group or race will ever again be discriminated against or fear for its place in the larger community. No one will ever again feel shame because of race or ethnicity. The sense of inferiority that comes from the designations of *upper caste* and *upper class ... middle-class* or *upper-middle class ... lower class* or *lower caste* or *untouchables ...* will be banished forever. No ethnic group or social strata will ever again lord it over another.

Now, because God rewards service and faithfulness, we envision that some peoples or kinship groups will have greater reward than others for their sacrifices to God and their obedience to God's global kingdom purposes. But no people, nation, culture, or kinship group will ever again be *demeaned*. As "the wolf shall dwell with the lamb" (Is 11:6), so also the strong people group will dwell in peace with the less strong; the oppression or hegemony of one nation, culture, kinship, or people group *against* others will be abolished.

And wondrously, the diversity of each people will be preserved. Christopher Wright writes of this passage, "The image we might prefer for the Bible's portrait of the nations is not a melting pot (in which all differences are blended together into a single alloy) but a salad bowl (in which all ingredients preserve their distinctive

---

25. Ibid., Kindle edition locations 218–24.
26. The term is from Amy Chua, *World on Fire: How Exporting Free Market Democracy Breeds Ethnic Hatred and Global Instability* (New York: Random House, 2003).

color, texture, and taste). The new creation will preserve the rich diversity of the original creation, but [be] purged of the sin-laden effects of the Fall."[27]

The nations are both preserved and transformed in Christ from glory to glory, elevated in beauty and honor. The *telos,* the ultimate purpose of God has a multi-ethnic quality. Hawthorne writes: "The peoples endure everlastingly. The city which is heaven on earth will be adorned by Kings of the people continually bringing the treasure and fruit of the peoples to God's throne (Rev 21:22–26)."[28]

The diversity of praise from the variety of peoples and tribes and nations is woven throughout the final book of Revelation. God could have focused his plan on individuals alone, but the glorious heights of his purpose will only be reached with the harmonious worship of all the peoples. It fulfills God's original promise to Abraham to bless all the peoples of the earth (Gen 12:3).

> You ransomed people for God from every tribe and language and people and nation (Rev 5:9).

> After this I looked, and behold, a great multitude that no one could number, from every nation, from all tribes and peoples and languages, standing before the throne and before the Lamb (Rev 7:9).

> Then I saw another angel flying directly overhead, with an eternal gospel to proclaim to those who dwell on earth, to every nation and tribe and language and people. And he said with a loud voice, "Fear God and give him glory ..." (Rev 14:6–7).

> Who will not fear, O Lord, and glorify your name? For you alone are holy. All nations will come and worship you ... (Rev 15:4).

> And threw [Satan] into the pit, and shut it and sealed it over him, so that he might not deceive the nations any longer (Rev 20:3).

> And the city has no need of sun or moon to shine on it, for the glory of God gives it light, and its lamp is the Lamb. By its light will the nations walk, and the kings of the earth will bring their glory into it, and its gates will never be shut by day—and there will be no night there. They will bring into it the glory and the honor of the nations (Rev 21:23–26).

> The leaves of the tree were for the healing of the nations (Rev 22:2).

The tree of life (Rev 22:2) echoing the original garden (Gen 2:9) is now the source of what brings healing to the *ethnōn,* the peoples. I imagine this healing creating a fountain of joy for an ongoing festival of cultural variety amidst the unified worship of Christ. God's global mission "is not merely the salvation of innumerable souls but specifically the healing of the nations."[29] It will be like an ever-growing celebration of manifold, cultural excellencies and wonders for God's joy and the peoples' gladness: "Let the nations be glad and sing for joy, for you judge the peoples with equity and guide the nations upon earth. Let the peoples praise you, O God; let all the peoples praise you!" (Ps 67:4–5).

---

27. Christopher Wright, 456.
28. Hawthorne, "The Story of His Glory," 60.
29. Christopher Wright, 456.

What a gathering this will be! All the saints and the peoples together comprising an immense multitude will boast in the Lord—"Hallelujah! Salvation and glory and power belong to our God. ... Hallelujah! For the Lord our God the Almighty reigns. Let us rejoice and exult and give him the glory" (Rev 19:1, 6–7).

They will have all been redeemed, their sin and shame a faint and distant memory! Their *falling-short-of-the-glory-of-God* (Rom 3:23) will be no more. The honor of every saint and every people will be restored, yes, even elevated before God to its greatest weight and highest value.

> No longer will there be anything accursed, but the throne of God and of the Lamb will be in it, and his servants will worship him. They will see his face, and his name will be on their foreheads. And night will be no more. They will need no light of lamp or sun, for the Lord God will be their light, and they will reign forever and ever (Rev 22:3–5).

At last! The drama of the ages, the vindication of the Lamb of God and the immense honor-status reversal of the nations, is finally complete. No more tears and pain. No more sin. No more guilt. No more shame. No more oppression or curse. Now, only blessing and honor and glory as together the redeemed saints and the peoples dwell before "the throne of God and of the Lamb" (Rev 22:1). And yes, the saints "will reign forever and ever" (v. 5).

"And his servants will worship him" (v. 3). *Of course they will.* The very name of the mighty Lamb of God has been placed "on their foreheads" (v. 4). They will gladly bear Christ's honor on their minds and in their hearts forever—they are the redeemed who serve together as "the wife of the Lamb" (Rev 21:9).

The honorific romance began with Christ the Word (John 1:1–3), continues with Christ the Lamb who was slain and Christ the mighty conqueror over sin, death and hell. It culminates with Christ the Bridegroom. Surely it is a Christ-directed relational *telos*. Steve Hawthorne refers to this as a "Christotelic drama."[30]

> The theodrama is Christotelic in a historic sense, but also in a relational sense. All things come to him. The crescendo of the entire theodrama is not a remembered event or person. Instead, the crescendo is potently anticipated. The climax moves not only forward, but also Christ-ward. All things will eventually come under Him: either to be subdued under His feet as His enemies, or to be perfected under His head as His people.[31]

The origin, the covenantal journey, and the relational destination are all embedded in Christ himself, the Alpha and Omega (Rev 21:6). It is a glory-*sharing* purpose; an honor-*sharing* teleology:

> **God the Father, Son and Holy Spirit are glorified forever and ever while, in mighty love and unending abundance, God *shares his glory with the saints from among all the diverse peoples* in his kingdom for eternity.**

This comprises the *telos* of mission.

---

30. Hawthorne, *Let All the Peoples Praise Him*, 255.
31. Ibid., 256

God-centered or human-centered?

Human perspectives about heaven, the afterlife, God's eternal kingdom, and ultimate purposes tend toward two extremes—the God-centered and the human-centered. Richard Mouw offers helpful comments:

> Carol Zaleski has articulated a nice distinction about the ways in which people think about heaven. "Some depictions of heaven," she writes, "are strongly theocentric, portraying the blessed as caught up in an endless rapture of adoration; others are sociable and anthropocentric. But a more adequate picture would be theocentric and anthropocentric at once."[32]

Mouw then affirms the more anthropocentric elements of *city and culture* in our eternal future:

> [T]he vision of an Eternal City in which the patterns and products of our present cultural lives are transformed, and in which a multitude that no human being can number is gathered from the tribes and nations of the earth to sing the Lamb's praises—this vision still manages to inspire in me a profound sense of wonder and anticipation.[33]

The material below combines God-centered and human-centered purposes for mission. The anthropocentric purposes (both negative and positive) are under an *ultimate* theocentric goal—the glory of God. What follows is an explanation in three segments:

- The *glory of God* is the overarching theocentric motivation for mission.
- *Hell* and *lostness* represent the *need* of humanity—the negative, anthropocentric motivations for mission.
- *Personal honor* and *people group honor* represent the *hope* of humanity—the positive, anthropocentric motivations for mission.

Let's begin with the ultimate—the theocentric purpose of God.

1. The glory of God—overarching theocentric motivation for mission

Pocock, Van Rheenan and McConnell reflect on the trend in mission motivation that has been more God-centered than human-centered. They gratefully acknowledge the movement by which *the glory of God* has infused many believers in North America and around the world as a return to a more God-centered motivation for mission.

> Contemporary trends ... are more positive than negative. Preaching that reflects the glory of God is a return to the core of the gospel. Proclaiming good news is an announcement of God's in-breaking glory, an opening of eyes, a turning from darkness to light, a revolution from "the power of Satan to God" (Acts 26:18) ... .

---

32. Mouw, Kindle edition locations: 31–33. Mouw quotes Carol Zaleski, "Fear of Heaven," *The Christian Century*, March 14, 2001: 24.

33. Ibid., Kindle edition locations 40–42.

The glory of God is the essence of the kingdom of God and therefore can stimulate missions like no other motivation. Rather than complain that lostness is not a part of present theology, mission leaders must seek to *redefine lostness within the broader theological motif of giving glory to God.*[34] (Emphasis mine.)

I heartily agree with these paragraphs above. Indeed, the glory of God is the ultimate purpose of mission because God, who is holy and good, is supreme in all things. God deserves worship and praise from all peoples and nations. The *needs* of humanity—and the *hopes* of humanity—are met in knowing and worshiping Jesus Christ through lifestyles of obedience.

We have, of course, already explored in this chapter various facets of the glory of God as the crux and destiny of Christian mission. So little else needs to be said about this.

We turn now to explore human-centered motivations for mission, the first of which are "negative."

2. Hell and lostness represent the *need* of humanity— the "negative" anthropocentric motivations for mission

When I use the word *negative* here, I do not mean it is *negative and untrue.* I am saying it is *negative and true.* For example, a warning may be given about a very real danger and pending destruction; it is bad news and also true. Negative emotions of fear and foreboding may be the result, but nevertheless the warning is founded on truth. Moreover, if the one being warned heeds the warning and avoids destruction, then the *negative* information has been most valuable![35]

There are two motivations for mission identified as *negative* by Pocock, Van Rheenan, and McConnell. The first is *hell*. The second is *lostness*.[36]

Hell as a "negative" motivation for mission

The problem question answered by this mission purpose is: *How can I avoid eternal judgment from God for my sin?* This foreboding question has motivated untold multitudes throughout church history.

In the Middle Ages of Europe and the period known as Christendom, the church was aligned with the state and often used religion as a means of controlling people. The state and the church mutually reinforced the power of the status quo. Salvation was defined as exclusive to the Catholic church, and the fear of hell fortified this belief for multitudes.

> During the Middle Ages the church used fear of hell to maintain the allegiance of its people. Hell was portrayed as a place of turmoil, chaos, pain, despair, and wretchedness. Dante's *Inferno* graphically described the state of souls after death with sins punished according to their severity. Sinners were traitors who rebelled against God and the church. ... Johann

---

34. Ibid., 178.
35. See Ezekiel 33:1–9 for a vivid expression of this principle.
36. Pocock, Van Rheenan, McConnell, 161–81. Their excellent chapter on this topic is titled "Changing Motivations for Missions: From Fear of Hell to the Glory of God."

Tetzel, using fear of hell to extract money for indulgences during the time of Martin Luther, illustrates how the threat of eternal punishment can induce response.[37]

Unfortunately, spiritual abuse by the church has a long, sordid history. It continues today in some faith communities in which leaders manipulate their members through emotional and other forms of abuse.

However, the fallenness of church leaders does not negate the truth claims of Jesus Christ regarding hell. In the gospels, Jesus clearly taught of the reality of perishing in hell, warning us of coming judgment (John 3:16; Luke 16:19–31; Mat 25:46). Jesus said,

> And if your hand causes you to sin, cut it off. It is better for you to enter life crippled than with two hands to go to hell, to the unquenchable fire. And if your foot causes you to sin, cut it off. It is better for you to enter life lame than with two feet to be thrown into hell. And if your eye causes you to sin, tear it out. It is better for you to enter the kingdom of God with one eye than with two eyes to be thrown into hell, "where their worm does not die and the fire is not quenched" (Mark 9:43–48).

According to the Bible, hell is a reality which is *negative and true.* It remains a compelling and urgent motivation for mission. Eternal punishment is reserved for all who dishonor the glorious, infinite, Almighty God. Gratefully, we serve a God of love who has made provision through Christ to save sinners from judgment.

The Bible teaches that God's judgment in condemning Satan, his fallen angels and unredeemed persons to hell is a horrible eternal destiny to be feared and avoided. Everyone must be given the opportunity to be saved. This need of humanity constitutes a "negative" purpose of mission.

Lostness as a "negative" motivation for mission

The problem question answered by this mission motivation is: *How can I be saved from my sin and hopelessness?*

Jesus said, "For the Son of Man came to seek and to save the lost" (Luke 19:10). Therefore, a powerful purpose for Christian mission is the lostness of individual persons in particular and humanity in general. "If Jesus came to seek and to save the lost, should that not also be our motivation?"[38]

Luke's Gospel includes in chapter 15 three parables—the lost sheep, the lost coin, and the lost son—to emphasize *humanity's need* and the *Father's heart* in seeking the lost. These parables magnify how terrible it is to be lost, living apart from God. "People without God cannot discover their ultimate identity, that they were created to live in a relationship with God. Humans living without God have lost their created identity. They are operating by human initiative or under the varying influences of Satan."[39]

Without salvation from lostness, people worship lifeless idols (whether pagan or secular) and live in varying degrees of hopelessness. They are unable to worship

---

37. Ibid., 164–68.
38. Ibid., 162.
39. Ibid., 173.

God or glorify him as Creator. This need of humanity also constitutes a "negative" purpose of mission.

To summarize point 2 (which concerns *hell* and *lostness*), here is the principle for negative motivations for mission:

Negative anthropocentric motivations for mission—
hell **and** *lostness*—**are under the ultimate**
theocentric purpose of the glory of God.

We turn now to human-centered motivations for mission that are "positive."

3. Personal honor and people-group honor represent the *hope* of humanity—the "positive" anthropocentric motivations for mission

As we explore these two human-centered motivations for mission that are "positive," we see that the *longing for honor* is at the core of both. A cautionary note is in order.

Whenever I speak of the longing for honor, it triggers a related thought: *the problem of human pride.* A caution is in order because the Bible says, "Pride goes before destruction, and a haughty spirit before a fall" (Pro 16:18). We can rightly say that *pride* was a major reason for the Fall of humanity (Gen 3). Therefore, we must proceed circumspectly.

On the one hand, we make note of the perils of overemphasizing the *longing for honor* as a biblically based motivation for mission—because honor and pride are seductive. On the other hand, we cannot ignore the testimony of Scripture concerning the fact that God shares his honor and glory with the saints. So there is a tension here which requires our examination.

How can we resolve this tension? The answer is—*through Jesus.*

Christ our glory. We resolve this tension by emphasizing that all this honor and glory for believers is embedded in our being *in Christ,* "the hope of glory" (Col 1:27).[40] God has adopted us into his family (Eph 1:5; Rom 8:15). Our honor is in our adopted kinship—we are siblings of Jesus our elder brother (Rom 8:29). Our honor is exclusively and totally in what God has done for us in Christ. *It's all by grace, that no one may boast* (Eph 2:9).

Paul is our example. He resolved this tension *by boasting in the Lord.* When Paul wrote "Let the one who boasts, boast in the Lord" (1 Cor 1:31), he was quoting Jeremiah:

> Thus says the LORD: "Let not the wise man boast in his wisdom, let not the mighty man boast in his might, let not the rich man boast in his riches, but let him who boasts boast in this, that he understands and knows me, that I am the LORD who practices steadfast love, justice, and righteousness in the earth" (Jer 9:23–24).

Paul's focus was constantly on Jesus and how Christ had changed his life: "But far be it from me to boast except in the cross of our Lord Jesus Christ, by which

---

40. I am grateful to Steven Hawthorne who has emphasized this point in personal conversations: Our honor as believers is embedded exclusively in Jesus Christ.

the world has been crucified to me, and I to the world" (Gal 6:14). Indeed, we need discipline to keep our eyes on Jesus—and humility to boast in nothing but the cross.

Having briefly addressed this appropriate caution, let us now explore the two human-centered mission motivations which have at their core *the longing for honor.*

The longing for personal honor as a "positive" motivation for mission

The problem question answered by this mission motivation is: *How can my longing for honor be satisfied?*

This is a *positive* human-centered motivation for mission. It is based on the truth demonstrated earlier in this chapter (and throughout this book)—that God, by his infinite grace and the riches of his glory, shares his honor with individuals who believe and follow Jesus Christ.

This *longing for personal honor* is in the heart of every person. Sin is the obstacle that blocks this longing from being fulfilled. The hope of salvation—the hope of *glory* in knowing and serving Christ—is good news that must be shared with everyone. The honor of joining God's eternal family must be proclaimed. This glorious *hope* of humanity (in contrast to a *need* of humanity) constitutes a "positive" purpose of mission.

The longing for people-group honor as a "positive" motivation for mission

The problem question answered by this mission motivation is: *How can our people's longing for honor be satisfied?*

The *longing for people-group honor* is, collectively, in the heart of every tribe, tongue, and nation. Sin is the obstacle that blocks this longing from being fulfilled. The hope of glory in knowing and serving Christ *collectively* must be made known. The honor of joining God's eternal family of ethnicities must be proclaimed.

The sure destiny in Christ's kingdom is that at least some from all peoples will have their own cultures transformed; these peoples and cultures will be elevated to their greatest beauty and highest value. Believers from all peoples will worship and glorify God forever and ever. *And this is good news which must be shared with everyone.*

This glorious *hope* of humanity (in contrast to a *need* of humanity) also constitutes a "positive" purpose of mission.

To summarize point 3 (that concerns *personal honor* and *people-group honor),* here is the principle for human-centered, positive motivations for mission:

> **Positive anthropocentric motivations for mission—**
> *personal honor* and *people-group honor*—**are also under**
> **the ultimate theocentric purpose of the glory of God.**

Seeing these varied mission motivations as a unified whole

The combination of points 1, 2, and 3 (explained above) is represented by Figure 4.02, on the next page.

Figure 4.02: Negative and positive anthropocentric purposes
under the ultimate purpose of the glory of God

The *glory* of God, the *need* of humanity, the *hope* of humanity—all biblical motivations for mission

Jesus Christ is "the Alpha and the Omega" (Rev 1:8) and "the Lamb who was slain" (Rev 5:12), worthy of all honor and glory. God deserves the worship of all creation. "For from him and through him and to him are all things. To him be glory forever. Amen" (Rom 11:36). God's glory is not only the *source* and the *crux* of all creation. God's glory is its very *destiny*. It is the theocentric motivation for mission.

And with regard to anthropocentric motivations for mission ...

The negative: On the one hand Scripture reveals a *hell* reserved for God's judgment on Satan, his fallen angels and all persons who have rebelled against God. The Bible also reveals the utter *lostness* of humanity apart from God. These "negative" truths that motivate people for mission are ultimately reflections of the glory of God. They are expressions of God's righteous judgment—and his compassion in seeking the lost.

The positive: On the other hand, Scripture also reveals a God who promises to elevate the honor of individual *believers* as well as the distinct *peoples* whom they comprise. These "positive" truths that motivate people for mission are centered in the promises of God to cover the shame and elevate the honor of *persons* and *people groups*. This is also placed under the ultimate reality of the glory of God, for it is a most glorious reflection of his generosity and love.

Mission motivation can be purely for *the glory of God*. Mission motivation can also be to save persons from the punishment of *hell* and the despair of *lostness*. Mission motivation can be the elevation of the *honor of persons* or the *honor of people groups*. Practically speaking, isn't our mission motivation and purpose often a blend of all these dynamics?

Whatever the motivation, believers on mission with God are all ultimately gathering worshipers for God. As John Piper says, "God is pursuing with omnipotent passion a worldwide purpose of gathering joyful worshipers for himself from every tribe and tongue and people and nation."[41]

The chart below summarizes this chapter.

Theocentric telos and motivation for mission—Jesus Christ the Alpha and Omega			
Theology of the glory of God			
Eternal punishment for dishonoring the glorious infinite, Almighty God	Those who worship idols become like them—lifeless, hopeless	Redeemed persons—the saints—will worship and glorify God forever and ever	At least some from all peoples will worship and glorify God forever and ever
Anthropocentric motivation—*negative/fear*		Anthropocentric motivation—*positive/hope*	

Theology of	Hell	Lostness	Personal honor	People-group honor
Problem question	How can I avoid eternal judgment by God for my sin?	How can I be saved from my sin, guilt, and hopelessness?	How can my longing for honor be satisfied?	How can our people's longing for honor be satisfied?
God so loved the world	God's love in forgiving sinners—satisfying the wrath of God against sin	God's love in seeking and saving the lost	God's love for persons in forgiving sin, covering shame, receiving their worship, sharing with them his honor	God's love for people groups in forgiving sin, covering shame, receiving their worship, sharing with them his honor
Transformation	• New life in Christ • New eternal destiny	• New life in Christ • New eternal destiny	• New life in Christ • New eternal destiny • New source of honor	• New life in Christ • New eternal destiny • New source of honor • Peoples and their cultures transformed

Figure 4.03: Anthropocentric motivations for mission—positive and negative—under a theocentric telos

Honor/shame dynamics in our mission purpose—final considerations

- **Christ our glory.** Lest we become proud, we must remember that all this honor and glory for the saints and the peoples is embedded in our being "in Christ." God has adopted us into his family (Eph 1:5; Rom 8:15). Our honor is in our adopted kinship—we are siblings of Jesus our elder brother (Rom 8:29). *Our honor, simply, is totally and exclusively in what God has done for us in Christ.* It is by grace, that no one may boast (Eph 2:9). What practices or disciplines would help believers retain their devotion to Christ to avoid the temptation of thinking that their honor is located within themselves?

- **Attracting persons and peoples.** In the history of Christian mission, particularly in the period of colonial missions, many *individual persons* were saved and became believers. Some were extracted from their tribes and people groups and given residence in the mission compounds. This extraction from their community often became a hindrance to further evangelism in their community. Even today, many first-generation believers experience alienation from their communities and families of origin. What might happen if the efforts to evangelize and plant churches were done

41. John Piper, *Let the Nations Be Glad!* Kindle edition locations 1080–81.

with a dual approach, attracting both *persons* and *peoples* to Christ, not only because of their guilt which must be repented of and forgiven, but also because of the honor that both *persons* and *peoples* would gain from being followers of the risen Christ?

- **Blessing the unengaged.** What does this mean for peoples who have honor/shame as a pivotal cultural value and are considered unreached or unengaged? Can questions such as *"How can my longing for honor be satisfied?"* or *"Does Jesus care about our people's longing for honor?"* be entry points for evangelism and church planting efforts? Dream together with your team. What might this look like?

- **Call for creativity.** How might this mission *telos,* which includes a concern for *personal honor* and *people-group honor,* impact evangelism to marginalized or low-status peoples? What can you and your team do to create evangelistic resources and church-planting training that *begin with the end in mind,* that is, that begin with all peoples worshiping the most worthy person in the universe, Jesus Christ, and having their unique shame profile *covered* and unique cultural honor *magnified* through Christ in his kingdom? What immediate actions can you and your team engage in to reveal the love and honor of God for persons and peoples that point to this ultimate reality?

- **Honor-oriented mobilization.** How might this truth that God shares his honor and glory with persons and peoples impact mission mobilization in honor/shame cultures?

- **Shame resilience, honor surplus.** We must not fail to grasp an intention of the Word of God: There is abundant honor available to believers, both now and in eternity, through Christ and his kingdom. Therefore, it is to be normative—not exceptional—that believers know our Lord in such a way that they experience an *honor surplus*—an overflowing of life in Jesus (John 7:38). This honor surplus should correspond to strong shame resilience empowered by the Holy Spirit, so that believers are able to live ethically superior lives, committed to God's mission to bless all the peoples of the earth, willing to suffer for the sake of Christ's name. What behaviors would characterize a believer with strong shame resilience and an honor surplus in Christ? What behaviors would characterize the believer who lacks this honor surplus in Christ?

- **Through the Holy Spirit.** What is the role of the Holy Spirit in making *real* the believer's honor surplus in Christ? What is the role of the church family?

- **Two biblical extremes—hell and heaven.** The letter to the Hebrews warns about the inescapable retribution from God that comes to those who "neglect such a great salvation" (Heb 2:3). When believers embrace the hope of this fullness of honor in Christ that God gives to redeemed persons and peoples, they experience *a positive reality*, an honor surplus, "a great salvation." How might this honor-enhancing reality in Christ provide an effective contrast to the message of the *negative reality* of hell and lostness? Does the positive side somehow make the negative side more real or more believable?

Honor/Shame Dynamics in Our Training

NOTE: The following comments are directed at the academy—the colleges, universities, and seminaries around the world that train Christian leaders. However, it is important to recognize that millions of believers have been trained for cross-cultural ministry outside of formal higher education.

Therefore, it is important to note that the principles below, while directed at the higher education community, may also be transferred to more informal training programs. It is possible to design curriculum fitting the principles below to be appropriate for both formal and informal programs.

I AM PROFOUNDLY GRATEFUL FOR *THE BOOKS* ... the books and articles that are the fruit of academic scholarship and which are the ground of this work. It should not be overlooked that this book you are reading would not have been possible without the academy. I am indebted to the tireless work of countless faithful scholars.

That the work of so many can be preserved and distributed so efficiently on the printed page (or ebook) still amazes me—it is surely a blessing of God. Indeed, only God can measure the influence of the Christian academy—colleges, universities, and seminaries—in training leaders and cross-cultural workers all over the world for the work of blessing the nations.

Let us also recall (from the preface) that the issue we have been exploring in this book is contextualization. The singular issue that this book addresses was defined by posing this question:

> *How can the honor/shame dynamics common to the Bible and many Majority World societies be used to contextualize the Christian faith in order to make it more widely understood and accepted?*

So we begin now by examining one of the most "widely accepted"[1] models for contextualizing the Christian faith. It was developed by the acclaimed scholar and missiologist Paul Hiebert. His approach is called "critical contextualization" and

---

1. Pocock, Van Rheenan, and McConnell, 337.

has four steps. The following summary of Hiebert's model, while not word-for-word, is taken largely from Pocock, Van Rheenan, and McConnell.[2]

Step 1: Exegete the host culture. Cross-cultural workers study the culture phenomenologically. They suspend judgment; they uncritically gather information about beliefs and customs of the host culture.

Step 2: Exegete Scripture. Local leaders and cross-cultural workers together find bridges from Scripture back to the host culture; this is known as the "hermeneutical bridge." Local leaders guide the community in a study of Scripture to address issues at hand.

Step 3: Community evaluates beliefs and customs. The community critically examines its traditional beliefs and customs in light of its new biblical understanding. The community may choose to:

1. retain the old practice, custom, or belief if it is not unbiblical,

2. reject the practice, custom, or belief because it is unbiblical, or

3. retain but modify the practice or belief to give it Christian meaning through appropriate rituals, actions, or symbols.

Step 4: Community develops new contextualized practices. Leaders help the faith community arrange the practices and beliefs they have chosen into a ritual that expresses the Christian meaning of the event.

This process may be diagramed as shown below:

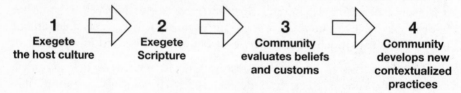

Figure 4.04: Paul Hiebert's four steps of critical contextualization

What this approach does not take into account is the Western blind spot about honor and shame. Remember, the majority of Western missionaries—plus a multitude of non-Western Christians trained by Western leaders—have a blind spot about honor/shame as a pivotal cultural value of Scripture. Many are thus "uncritically assuming the gospel;" this was pointed out earlier with quotes from David Bosch, Jackson Wu, and others (see pages 208–215). So as valuable as Hiebert's model is, could it be that it should be expanded? I believe so.

Therefore, I propose a contextualization process that expands on Paul Hiebert's model. I make this recommendation with the utmost respect and admiration for the work of Hiebert. And in no way am I suggesting that he was unaware of the importance of honor/shame dynamics in cross-cultural ministry. But I have not

---

2. Pocock, Van Rheenan, and McConnell cite Paul E. Hiebert, "Critical Contextualization." *Missiology: An International Review* 12 (July): 287–96.

yet run across any of his writings that address the blind spot about honor and shame in Western theological education.[3]

With these caveats, I make the recommendation below in Figure 4.05, *"Expanding upon Paul Hiebert's four steps of critical contextualization—with foundational Step A: Exegete Bible cultures."*

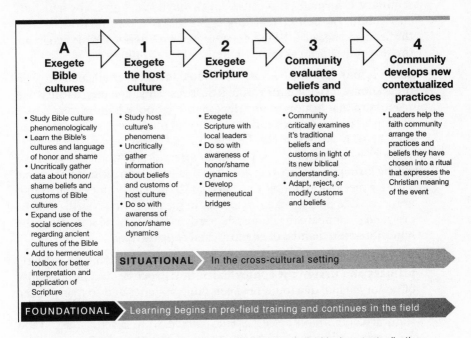

Figure 4.05: Expanding upon Paul Hiebert's four steps of critical contextualization— with foundational Step A: Exegete Bible cultures

In this diagram I have added a step at the beginning—"Step A: Exegete Bible cultures."

One might ask, **Why add Step A?** Would not the average Christian teacher, missions pastor, or cross-cultural worker already understand the cultures of the Bible? Would not the average missionary be able to incorporate the understanding of "Bible cultures" as part of "Step 2—Exegesis of Scripture"? The answer is *only partially,* since there is a blind spot in Western theology about honor/shame. The majority of Christian education is conducted without an awareness of the Bible's pivotal cultural value of honor and shame. Consequently, I propose adding "Step A" at the beginning.

---

3. Here is an example of Hiebert's writings concerning honor/shame dynamics in group-oriented cultures: "Shame plays a more important role in group-oriented communities than does guilt. When people fail, they feel ashamed that they have let down their group, their ancestors, and their gods. They feel less a sense of guilt at having personally broken some universal moral law. In fact, there may be little awareness of such laws. All important norms are group norms. Shame is also tied to success and honor. A group-oriented student is ashamed when the teacher asks her to stand up because she has the best grade in the class. This makes her stand out from the group. Shame is a dynamic that pressures people to conform to their group and so maintains harmony and peace." Paul G. Hiebert, *Transforming Worldviews: An Anthropological Understanding of How People Change* (Grand Rapids, MI: Baker Academic, 2008), Kindle edition locations 2297–2302.

In this model, Step A is foundational. Here's why:

- **Step A is foundational because it is part of pre-field training.** Missionaries, mission pastors, and teachers from the West would learn about the Bible's honor/shame dynamics *before* engaging in cross-cultural ministry. Formally, this can happen through learning at the level of the Bible college and seminary. Informally, this can occur through small-group or self-study curriculum. The point is to do this *before* the cross-cultural workers go to the field. And because the Bible is saturated with honor/shame dynamics, this learning continues throughout the life of the Christian.

- **Step A is foundational because it is rooted in and promulgated through the academy.** It is primarily through the research and writing of Christian academics that honor/shame dynamics have been identified as a part of biblical hermeneutics and cross-cultural ministry. It will be through the Christian academy that the dynamics of honor and shame in Bible societies would be taught as part of an intercultural studies program. It will be through the Christian academy that this could ultimately become *basic* for theological studies. Courses could be developed, for example, that are devoted to honor/shame dynamics in the Bible. Or a course could be designed to compare the honor/shame dynamics of Bible societies to the honor/shame dynamics of an unreached people group.

- **Step A is foundational because it advances the Word of God as being primary and first in the contextualization process.** The commonality of honor/shame dynamics between Bible societies and so many of the world's peoples has profound implications. Step A implies that cross-cultural workers place *at least as much emphasis* on exegeting the Old and New Testament cultures of the Bible as on exegeting the host culture. This has the effect of reinforcing the sufficiency of Scripture relative to more than doctrine and spiritual practice. It also fortifies the belief that ancient biblical cultural values are vitally relevant for Christian cross-cultural ministry and world evangelization today.

I believe there would be four benefits of this model:

1. It intentionally removes the blind spot many have concerning honor/shame in Scripture. Leaders in the academy should evaluate what steps to take in curriculum development to remove the blind spot in Western theology concerning honor and shame. With modified programs, students studying for the ministry in Bible colleges and seminaries would gain the understanding of honor/shame dynamics as a foundation for all of their future ministries. This could mitigate the effects of other Western theological biases, as well.[4]

2. It would make building healthy cross-cultural relationships easier. It would speed up the process of missionary adaptation to the various Majority World cultures in which they serve. Once missionaries become immersed in the honor/shame

---

4. For example, the Western bias toward *individualism* would be balanced by greater appreciation for *community*. And the Western bias toward a *legal* framework of the gospel would be balanced by the *regal* (gospel of the kingdom).

realities of the Bible, they would more easily build relationships cross-culturally, and more effectively communicate as gospel messengers in Majority World societies.

3. It would help mitigate the perception that Christianity is a Western religion. In the learning journey about honor and shame, it becomes more and more apparent to the student of Scripture that the Bible is not a Western book, but an Eastern book. The awareness of honor/shame dynamics will magnify the believer's awareness that Western culture has many values that are different from those of the Bible and of Majority World peoples. Ultimately, this can only help advance the gospel among those who believe Christianity is a foreign religion exported from the West or from America.

4. It would reinforce the primacy of Scripture in matters of culture and contextualization. This approach magnifies the principle of *sola Scriptura*.[5] In this approach, *sola Scriptura* would apply not only to doctrinal truth and spiritual matters. It would also have the effect of bending the attitudes of cross-cultural workers toward greater authority of Scripture regarding *cultural* values. This would apply especially to the pivotal cultural value of honor and shame and what it means for contextualizing the gospel.

Avery Willis offered good counsel about the primacy of Scripture in contextualization. His comments below are from a book edited by Ed Stetzer and David Hasselgrave which addresses, among other things, Paul Hiebert's advocacy for "critical contextualization." Willis recommended:

a. *Begin with the supremacy of Scripture.* We should start where Hiebert ended—with truth (or gospel as Hiebert calls it). God has revealed Himself and truth to us through the general revelation of creation and through His specific revelation of Himself in His Son and Scripture. God's revelation is both personal and relational, and we know Him through our personal relationship with Jesus and through His written record of truth—the Bible. The missionary must start with God's revelation of truth.[6]

b. *Understand the biblical culture.* Although we start with revelation, we must understand the biblical culture and its influence on God's revealed truth in Scripture. The new missionary and the missional church with its short-term volunteers could miss the importance of understanding the role of culture in Scripture.[7]

"We must understand the biblical culture and its influence on God's revealed truth in Scripture." Indeed! I propose, however, that the significance of biblical cultures—especially the Bible's dynamic of honor and shame—applies not just to "the new missionary, and the missional churches with its short-term volunteers." It also applies to seasoned missionaries and cross-cultural workers, teachers and

---

5. See "What Does *Sola Scriptura* Mean?" by John MacArthur. "The Reformation principle of *sola Scriptura* has to do with the sufficiency of Scripture as our supreme authority in all spiritual matters. *Sola Scriptura* simply means that all truth necessary for our salvation and spiritual life is taught either explicitly or implicitly in Scripture. It is not a claim that all truth of every kind is found in Scripture." From *Ligonier Ministries*, http://www.ligonier.org/blog/what-does-sola-scriptura-mean/, accessed 22 March 2014.

6. Avery T. Willis Jr., "Response to Hiebert's Article: 'The Gospel in Human Contexts' and to the Responses of Pocock and Whiteman" in eds. Stetzer and Hesselgrave, Kindle edition location 148.

7. Ibid., 148–49.

leaders who have never learned about the extensive honor/shame dynamics in Scripture.

Reducing or reinforcing biblical authority?

In the same volume in which Willis's article appears, Andreas Köstenberger offers similar advice (with a caveat):

> Reflection on the church's mission should be predicated on the affirmation of the full and sole authority of Scripture. Unless the church's convictions regarding its mission and strategies are committed to the authority of Scripture, the purity of its missionary thought and practice will be compromised. Thinking derived from the social sciences will inevitably leaven the dough of its missiology.[8]

I agree wholeheartedly with Köstenberger's first two sentences above. It is with the third sentence I have an issue. Yes, Köstenberger's concerns are valid about certain aspects of the social sciences diluting the authority of God's Word. But with regard to the dynamic of honor/shame, I would challenge Köstenberger's thought that "the social sciences will inevitably leaven the dough of its missiology."

At this point we need to recall what was stated early on in this book when we explored the role of the social sciences in interpreting Scripture. On page 37, here is what I said, quoting a standard evangelical textbook on biblical interpretation:

> According to Klein, Blomberg, and Hubbard, " ... social-scientific studies fall into two broad categories: 1) research that illuminates the social history of the biblical world and 2) the application of modern theories of human behavior to scriptural texts."[9]

This book is written with the understanding of primarily the first category—"research that illuminates the social history of the biblical world"—thus, a tool for faithful *exegesis* of God's Word. My goal is to interpret the Word of God according to its original cultural context.

Therefore, when it comes to the Bible's honor/shame dynamics, I contend that the effect of knowing the applicable social science would be just the opposite of "leavening the dough of its missiology." For it is through the use of social science that we uncover a major blind spot and gain a more authentic reading of Scripture by which to appreciate its ancient cultural values. Does this not help us convey with greater authority the original meaning of God's Word?

I contend that use of the social sciences for understanding the pivotal cultural value of honor and shame—so pervasive in Scripture—has the effect of *reinforcing the authority of God's Word.*

We moderns need to become better acquainted with the ancients. The prophet Jeremiah had this word for God's people:

---

8. Andreas J. Köstenberger, "Twelve Theses on the Church's Mission in the Twenty-first Century: In Interaction with Charles Van Engen, Keith Eitel, and Enoch Wan," in eds. Stetzer and Hesselgrave, 64.

9. Klein, Blomberg, Hubbard, 78. This is one small part of their extensive treatment of the subject.

Thus says the LORD: "Stand by the roads, and look, and ask for the ancient paths, where the good way is; and walk in it, and find rest for your souls" (Jer 6:16).

I believe that pursuing an understanding of the pivotal cultural value of honor and shame in Scripture is part of our journey down the "ancient paths." It is a paradox but not a contradiction that the *ancient* can lead us to more effective cross-cultural ministry *today*.

It is the academy where an environment of skilled teaching and deep learning will have a major role in expanding literacy about the Bible's cultural value of honor and shame. In turn, this will help cross-cultural workers, pastors and teachers communicate as faithful messengers of the gospel to all the people touched by *their* ministries, across the street and around the world.

Having explored some issues relative to honor/shame and *training* in the world Christian movement, let us now turn to the matter of our *practice*.

Honor/Shame Dynamics in Our Practice

FOR MORE THAN FIVE YEARS, I have studied the dynamics of honor and shame in the Bible, learning from a variety of Christian scholars, many of whom use the social sciences. I have read the Bible more frequently, more seriously, and with greater insight and enjoyment than ever before. Several books of the Old Testament and most of the New Testament in my Bible have become color-coded to bring out the honor/shame dynamics (I like using colored pencils for this).

In the process of this learning journey, I have learned to submit some of my Western theological biases to the higher authority of Scripture. New facets of biblical understanding have opened up to me. I have grown in love and wonder for our Lord Jesus Christ. Learning from scholars who use social science has only reinforced my love for the Bible and my convictions about its authority as the Word of God.

I have had the joy of teaching about honor and shame in numerous interactive workshops and half-day seminars. The material always seems to "make the light bulbs go on;" it seems to resonate with many students of the Bible. If they are involved in cross-cultural ministry, it resonates even more.

Moreover, I've had the joy of teaching collaboratively in Thailand about honor and shame with the indigenous Christian leader of a large ministry in Thailand. In 2013, I taught with him about the Bible's honor/shame dynamics in a three-day conference. On the following Sunday, I preached from Luke 5:12–14. The message was about Jesus healing the leper who had begged, "Lord, if you will, you can make me clean" (Luke 5:12). I brought out the cultural issues of honor/shame and the group dynamics that are in the passage. Our Mission ONE cross-cultural partner translated everything into Thai.

Shortly after returning home, I received an email from our partner:

> Werner, a feedback on the honor/shame conference. We have heard from one of the leaders attending the conference that although this is your first time teaching in Thailand you spoke like one who has known the Thai people all along. The leader said that you spoke like one of them. He further said that he had never seen or heard of any Westerner who so identified with the Thai culture like you. This is a confirmation that we are on the right track with the language of honor/shame.[1]

---

1. Chansamone Saiyasak, personal correspondence, 25 November 2013.

I had never taught in Thailand before. I actually know very little about Buddhism, the official religion of Thailand. I know nothing of the Thai language, and almost nothing of Thailand's king and royal family. But I have seriously studied honor and shame as the pivotal cultural value of the Bible. This one factor—*my understanding about honor/shame dynamics in the Bible*—contributed mightily to my effectiveness in connecting with these southeast Asian Christian leaders. Moreover, this experience strongly reinforced for me this theory:

Communicating with an awareness of the Bible's honor/shame dynamics has the potential of endearing God's Word to persons and peoples in honor/shame cultures in ways that we as Christians are only beginning to understand.

In this chapter, I recommend three practices for the world Christian movement related to honor and shame. These few recommendations are, of course, shaped by my own limited experience. So, this short list should not be considered comprehensive. Rather, think of this list of three as a sampling of suggestions to create dialog and spur additional ideas.

My three recommendations are:

1. Learn the Bible's language of honor and shame in a personal journey.

2. Incorporate the "honor factor" in mission strategy and practice.

3. Shift from high control to high trust.

RECOMMENDATION #1: Learn the Bible's language of honor and shame in a personal journey

I propose that becoming *literate* in the Bible's language of honor and shame is a foundational skill for God's global mission.

No language can be learned in a one-day seminar. But since we do have the Bible in our own language, learning the Bible's language of honor and shame is a fairly simple process. It is however, a lifelong journey of discipline and discovery.

Missionaries go through "language school" when preparing for cross-cultural ministry. But the kind of language school I am thinking of is not a formal educational program of learning a new language like Spanish or Swahili. Rather, it is learning the language of honor and shame informally as we read our own Bibles.

This is for anyone involved in Christian ministry—mission agency leaders, pastors and mission pastors, missionaries, laypersons, and cross-cultural workers of all kinds. This training consists of being on a journey together in learning the Bible's language of honor/shame.

Read the Bible ... read the Bible ... *read the Bible!*

This informal approach can be done alone, but would be enhanced by a small group. All it requires is a Bible and a commitment to learn. And this cannot be emphasized enough: *We must read our Bibles often and extensively.* There is no substitute for reading the Bible! Marking it up as you go is also helpful. I am convinced that modern Christians must recover the simple discipline of reading their Bibles in a focused way—extensively, daily, lovingly. Of course, this kind of discipline is aided when believers in small groups learn together. Below is a simple recommendation for a small group learning journey to *read, speak, walk.*

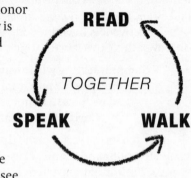

- **READ** God's Word using the lens of honor and shame. Reading the Bible this way is an attempt to know the Word of God the way the original hearers would have heard it or read it. It's an effort to de-Westernize our reading of the Scriptures. Read one book of the Bible at a time. My suggestion is to begin with the Gospel of Luke. (To learn how the author reads the Bible to see the honor/shame dynamics, see Appendix #1.)

- **SPEAK** using the Bible's language of honor and shame, both in conversation and in prayer. Talk with others about what you're learning. Become comfortable using words like *honor* and *glory* relative to our own relationship with Christ. Pray Scripture. Pray together using the honor/shame words found in God's Word.

- **WALK** your own authentic path of shame to honor in the light of Christ. Discover the honor of who we are in Jesus Christ, individually and corporately. Be vulnerable and real about your own shame—the shame dynamics of your own life, whether as an agent or victim of sin—and let the Holy Spirit and Person of Christ deal with that. Personal prayer times and trusting small groups are healthy places for vulnerability.

This journey is more fruitful when we do it *together.* We usually find that transformation occurs in our lives through accountability and encouragement. Small groups can offer this to us.

RECOMMENDATION #2: Incorporate the "honor factor" in mission strategy and practice

A. Sharing the gospel of Jesus Christ is an honor. Bringing the blessing of the gospel to the unreached and unengaged is a greater honor.

What do we hope for? What are the various outcomes of mission activity? *Evangelize the lost?* Yes. *Disciple persons and families in the ways of Jesus Christ and start churches?* Yes. *Transform communities?* Yes. But all of these outcomes should lead to an even higher, more honorable outcome.

Shouldn't the ultimate outcome be to extend the blessing of the gospel to those ethnic groups and peoples who have yet to receive the blessing of knowing and worshiping Jesus Christ? What if more Christians and churches considered this their highest honor?

Apostle Paul is our example in this regard. Let's look at a passage from Romans 15. The chart below unpacks the honor/shame dynamics verse-by-verse.

Verse	Text of Romans 15:15–21	Honor/shame dynamic
15–16a	But on some points I have written to you very boldly by way of reminder, because of the grace given me by God to be a minister of Christ Jesus to the Gentiles in the priestly service of the gospel of God,	• Paul considers "the grace given me by God" a form of benefaction from God, his divine Patron. • Because Paul is engaged in "the priestly service of the gospel of God," he has gained a high honor in the Jewish social system—that of the priest/mediator.
16b	so that the offering of the Gentiles may be acceptable, sanctified by the Holy Spirit.	• Paul's ministry outcome—"that the offering of the Gentiles may be acceptable, sanctified"—results in glory to God and an increase in honor status for the Gentile people groups as they worship God.
17	In Christ Jesus, then, I have reason to be proud of my work for God.	• Paul is proud of his work for God. He has satisfied the principle of reciprocity in patron-client relationships. • Paul has gained "achieved honor" through his apostolic ministry for his divine Patron.
18	For I will not venture to speak of anything except what Christ has accomplished through me to bring the Gentiles to obedience—by word and deed,	• Paul acknowledges that his honor surplus is embedded exclusively in his identity in Christ. • Paul is an honorable co-patron with Christ in blessing the Gentile peoples.
19	by the power of signs and wonders, by the power of the Spirit of God—so that from Jerusalem and all the way around to Illyricum I have fulfilled the ministry of the gospel of Christ;	• In Romans 1:16 the power of the gospel results in not being ashamed; likewise, here in 15:19, the honor of Paul's ministry includes power and covers a large geographic territory. • Parallels the overlap between honor and power in the Roman Empire.
20	and thus I make it my ambition to preach the gospel, not where Christ has already been named, lest I build on someone else's foundation,	• Paul's intention is to go to the barbarian peoples of Spain (15:24, 28; cf. 1:14). Paul's "ambition" is to bring greater honor to the name of Christ. • Paul would thus gain more achieved honor for himself as the gospel messenger.
21	but as it is written, "Those who have never been told of him will see, and those who have never heard will understand."	• Paul quotes Isaiah 52:15 which immediately precedes Isaiah 53—signifying the atoning work of Christ. • Christ's work of redemption will be seen and understood! This brings salvation to the Gentile peoples—along with honor and glory to God.

Figure 4.06: Dynamics of honor/shame in Romans 15:15–21

Is there a more honorable pursuit in the world Christian community than to bring the gospel of Jesus Christ to the unengaged or unreached peoples? Is there an "honor factor" in mission practice that is greater than reaching the unreached?

B. Greater self-sustainability for indigenous Christian ministries means greater honor for their community and greater credibility for the gospel.

Let's consider another verse involving Paul. This is from Luke's account on the occasion of Paul's departure from Ephesus. Luke writes that Paul says:

315

In all things I have shown you that by working hard in this way we must help the weak and remember the words of the Lord Jesus, how he himself said, "It is more blessed to give than to receive" (Acts 20:35).

In essence, Paul is saying this: Jesus taught us that it is more *honorable* to give than to receive. This has a bearing on the work of Christian world missions.

Giving financially may be considered more honorable than *receiving financially*. If this is so, should not more Western mission agencies and churches involved in cross-cultural partnership help their indigenous partners move toward greater sustainability?

The organization with which I serve, Mission ONE, is engaged in a long-term plan to help our cross-cultural partners achieve greater financial sustainability. This way, they ultimately will be able to operate their ministries out of their own home-grown resources. This process may require great faith, persistence, and the learning of new skills over a period of time. But it has at least two major benefits.

First, it is a blessing for an indigenous missions organization to be able to generate their own funds locally in order to support their own workers and ministries. Of course, this enhances the dignity and honor of the indigenous Christian leaders, workers, and their families.

Second, when the financial support for a Christian mission is locally resourced, it adds legitimacy to the gospel. The director of an indigenous mission organization in Thailand told me that the more they are able to generate funds locally, the greater honor and credibility it gives to the Christian faith. When the gospel is being planted in and grown "out of Asian soil,"[2] it is not being imported from, nor funded by, the West. In a nation like Thailand, where the Christian faith has long been considered inimical to Buddhist and Thai identity, this is a strategic issue. The Thai people are but one among thousands of peoples for whom this issue is vital.

RECOMMENDATION #3: Shift from high control to high trust

Honor is at stake when it comes to control. Those with control in a situation usually assume the greater honor. Those with less control assume less honor.

In the world Christian movement, *control* is an increasingly important issue. Who controls the agenda? Who controls the funds? How do we steer the ship?

Leaders are grappling with cross-cultural partnerships and interagency collaboration across international borders. Organizations such as The Lausanne Movement[3] are helping mission leaders from all over the world work together more effectively.

One thing is clear: The world Christian movement needs more and more leaders with the skills to navigate the often stormy waters of cross-cultural collaboration.

Alex Araujo has developed a metaphor for Christian cross-cultural partnerships

---

2. See Chansamone Saiyasak, "The Adaptation of Buddhism and Christianity to Asian Soils," in eds. David Hartono and Greg Young Paek, *Discern What Is Right: Seoul Strategic Forum 2011* (Pasadena, CA: East-West Center for Missions Research & Development, 2012), 218–39.

3. The Lausanne Movement, http://www.lausanne.org.

that helps believers make the shift from *high control* to *high trust*. It is called the "sailing paradigm."[4]

Cross-cultural workers from the West should be trained to recognize their Western "powerboat mindset" of *high control*. They should transition to a more vulnerable "sailboat mindset" of *high trust*. This will help them to (1) better cooperate with the wind of God, the Holy Spirit, (2) better navigate the currents, waves, and storms of cross-cultural ministry and partnerships, (3) serve more effectively in their host communities, and (4) honorably collaborate with their cross-cultural partners.

Figure 4.07 captures the essence of this paradigm.[5]

	POWERBOAT	ROWBOAT	SAILBOAT
Mindset	Western	Majority World	Biblical
Power source	Human effort + management methods + high technology	Human effort	The Wind: Holy Spirit / God's Word
Speed	Usually fast	Often slow	Sometimes fast, sometimes slow
Trust factor	High control / low trust	High vulnerability / low trust	High trust
Orientation	Task	Relationship	Relationship and task in balance

Figure 4.07: Alex Araujo's comparison of powerboat, rowboat, and sailboat mindsets[6]

Araujo's article (written collaboratively with Mary Lederleitner and this author) uses a simple metaphor—*sailing*. It offers insight for why and how Christians with economic power from the West can modify their mindset for healthier cross-cultural partnership.

As the world gets smaller and the world Christian movement grows ever more diverse, it will be more and more needful for Christians across great economic and cultural divides to work together as one. *This is not easy.*

How will the big and strong, the wealthy and economically stable (the so-called *honorable)* work collaboratively with the small and weak, the poor and economically vulnerable (the so-called *less honorable*)? How can the body of Christ work together with all its amazing diversity?

Honor in the body of Christ

In chapter 12 of Paul's first letter to the Corinthians, we find some answers. He wrote about how a healthy body of Christ is to function. Paul employs honor/shame dynamics to make his case.

---

4. See Araujo, Lederleitner, and Mischke, "To Catch the Wind," http://sailingfriends.files.wordpress.com/2009/10/to-catch-the-wind-short-final.pdf, accessed 25 March 2014.

5. Roger Parrott made a presentation with the same sailboat theme at the 2004 Lausanne Conference. See http://www.lausanne.org/2004-forum/opening-address.html. Accessed 25 March 2014.

6. Werner Mischke, *The Beauty of Partnership* (Scottsdale, AZ: Mission ONE, 2010), 71.

The eye cannot say to the hand, "I have no need of you," nor again the head to the feet, "I have no need of you." On the contrary, the parts of the body that seem to be weaker are indispensable, and on those parts of the body that we think less honorable we bestow the greater honor, and our unpresentable parts are treated with greater modesty, which our more presentable parts do not require. But God has so composed the body, giving greater honor to the part that lacked it, that there may be no division in the body, but that the members may have the same care for one another. If one member suffers, all suffer together; if one member is honored, all rejoice together (1 Cor 12:21–26).

Paul's prescription for solving the problem of division is a function of honor/shame dynamics. The principle may be stated like this:

Unity in the body of Christ happens in proportion to the way the so-called *strong and honorable* demonstrate honor and respect toward the so-called *weak and less honorable*.

Let us now consider how this passage may speak to the world Christian community at the beginning of the twenty-first century.

This passage speaks to me in the light of the American church's economic, cultural, and theological leadership relative to the rest of the world. Generally, American Christians have attitudes in the global Christian community reflecting their national position of leadership. Consequently, Americans often unwittingly assume the role of the strong and honorable. This can lead to what some refer negatively to as *hegemony*—"leadership or dominance, especially by one country or social group over others."[7]

In his popular book, *Civilization: The West and the Rest*, author Niall Ferguson speaks of Western influence—in which America plays a dominant role: "With every passing year, more and more human beings shop like us, study like us, stay healthy (or unhealthy) like us and pray (or don't pray) like us. Burgers, Bunsen burners, Band-Aids, baseball caps, and Bibles: you cannot easily get away from them wherever you may go."[8]

Let's take a look at American hegemony in the broader global economic and political realm. Consider how Yale professor Amy Chua describes American hegemony in the international community.

America today has become the world's market-dominant minority. Like the Chinese in the Philippines or the Lebanese in West Africa, Americans have attained heights of wealth and economic power wildly disproportionate to our tiny numbers. Just 4% of the world's population, America dominates every aspect—financial, cultural, technological—of the global free markets we have come to symbolize. From the Islamic world to China, from our NATO allies to the southern hemisphere, America is seen not incorrectly as the engine and principal beneficiary of global marketization. For this—for our extraordinary market dominance, our seeming global

7. "Hegemony," *New Oxford American Dictionary*, 3rd ed. (New York: Oxford University Press, Inc., 2010).
8. Niall Ferguson, *Civilization: The West and the Rest* (New York: Penguin Books, 2011), 8.

(value) in both the material and spiritual areas of the missionaries' life and culture."[12]

A powerboat mindset for mission implies reliance on expensive structures, technology, and "missions machinery." Money makes "mission" *go fast*. And there is tremendous pressure on people for results and the measurement of outcomes in order to maintain funding. This shapes ministry strategy and reporting protocol.

In an honor/shame culture, honor is a more important "currency" than money. Honor is the social capital by which things get done. There is nothing more important than your honor, your family name, your reputation in the community to which you belong. Consequently, Western believers who prioritize *money* or *task* over *relationship* in their mission efforts will often find themselves misunderstood or frustrated.

The sailboat formula. Consider now the "sailboat formula for Christian mission" in which the primary catalyst is listening to God and to people.

$$\text{👂} \times \left(\text{🎓} + \text{✈} + \text{🙏} + \text{\$} \right) = \textbf{Faithfulness}$$

Figure 4.09: Sailboat mindset—listening as the primary catalyst for mission

In this paradigm, we have the "sailboat formula for Christian mission." Listening replaces money as *the* catalyst for global missions. Listening comes first; money is sometimes optional and in balance with other priorities. The primary emphasis is on listening to God—catching the wind of the Holy Spirit. It implies a quantum leap by Christian mission leaders from the West in listening to Christian brothers and sisters in the Majority World. It means adopting more of a servant role in the world Christian movement.

Moreover, ministry can go forward without excessive reliance on funding. It is sometimes fast, sometimes slow; it depends on the wind of the Holy Spirit. The results are up to God and can greatly exceed our plans ... or not. Either one is okay, because God is in control. What is required is that God's people be found faithful and diligent in their work and obedience to God.

What is the impact of this "sailboat mindset" in an honor/shame culture? Since listening contributes so much to healthy relationships, honor is naturally accrued by the believer who spends a lot of time listening. Since honor is the currency of the culture, honor is the social capital by which things get done. Western believers who prioritize listening and relationship enjoy simply being together, being with people. One result of this is an increase in their honor-status. They discover they have influence. They find themselves better understood. They are joyful in being faithful. And if God "adds the increase," they are joyful about the fruitfulness of their ministries.

---

12. Christopher R. Little: "Business as Mission under Scrutiny," *EMQ*, April 2014. Little quotes Jacob Loewen, *Culture and Human Values: Christian Intervention in Anthropological Perspective* (Pasadena, CA: William Carey Library, 1975), xi, xii. http://www.emqonline.com/emq/issue-327/2940, accessed 5 May 2014.

Let's return now to the principle articulated above. Paul's prescription for resolving division in the body is a function of honor/shame dynamics. The principle was stated like this:

Unity in the body of Christ happens in proportion to the way the so-called *strong and honorable* demonstrate honor and respect toward the so-called *weak and less honorable*.

There is no greater way to honor our brothers and sisters in Christ around the world than by *listening deeply.* Empathic listening will lead to more understanding, more informed prayer, better collaboration, more passion for the mission, and sometimes even more funding.

It started in Lebanon by listening

Pastor Issam is a dear friend in Lebanon who leads a ministry to bless various Muslim peoples in the name of Jesus. His organization is one of our Mission ONE partners. What a privilege to have often been with this joy-filled brother riding in his car as we drove the curvy roads through ancient cities, towns, hills, and valleys of Lebanon. The memory makes me glad.

Once while driving together, just the two of us, we talked and shared about our personal lives and the work of the ministry. Some things we shared were happy, some troubling. A few times he spoke about challenging situations that troubled him, and he would say, "It's a big shame."

This stuck with me: "It's a big shame." I began to thirst for an understanding of what that meant in his culture. This thirst has carried me on a long journey to discover the commonality of honor/shame dynamics in Scripture and Majority World peoples. I am grateful to say—my thirst has been quenched.

And so this book about honor/shame and the global gospel of Jesus ends on the theme of *listening*—listening as a catalyst for world missions. It is a long journey for anyone to better understand the honor/shame dynamics in Scripture, culture, and mission. The journey began for me by *simply hearing the simple things* Pastor Issam shared with me in Lebanon, several years ago.

SUMMARY:
Believers Have No Honor Deficit

WHAT ARE WE TO MAKE OF OUR JOURNEY to gain awareness about honor/shame dynamics? Here's how I summarize what this journey means to me.

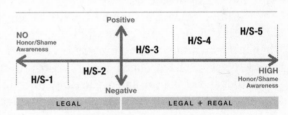

Figure 4.10: H/S-1 to H/S-5:
Levels of awareness of honor and shame

There is an answer to the perplexing problem of sin for individuals and peoples. The answer is found in Jesus Christ. This is profoundly good news.

There is a kingdom with an infinitely mighty King who, because of his own honor and compassion, shares his glory with people while absorbing their sin, guilt, and shame. Those who follow this King are sometimes called Christians, or simply *believers*. Believers have no honor deficit. They are not ashamed. They are children of God, siblings of the King. They are full and they are free, on mission with God to bless all the peoples of the earth.

King Jesus is the One whose glory and honor is of such magnitude that he gives and shares his glory (John 17:22) with those who "believed in his name" so that they literally become "children of God" (John 1:12; 1 John 3:1). Believers experience a dramatic elevation of their honor before God—an honor-status reversal. Although the King gives and shares his glory lavishly, in doing so, the King's own honor is not diminished whatsoever. More and more people worship him—so the worshipful glory given to our King increases (John 12:32; 2 Cor 4:15) as he shares his life and glory with those who follow him.

Believers who love and obey the King are his siblings (Mat 12:48–50). They have been born again into a new family—a new kinship group. They have been born, "not of blood nor of the will of the flesh nor of the will of man, but of God" (John 1:13). They have a new spiritual DNA out of which springs forth a life-transforming honor that sets them free. By the grace of God believers enjoy a divinely imparted ascribed honor (not achieved honor), so that no one may boast (Eph 2:9), and God receives all the glory he deserves (Rom 11:36). How offensive this is to self-exalting, self-sufficient human pride!

Believers have no honor deficit.
They are children of God, siblings of the King.
They are not ashamed.
They are full and they are free,
    on mission with God to bless all the peoples of the earth.

For persons debilitated by sin and shame ... for peoples who are oppressed, victims of a majority people obsessed by their own power ... for those who consider themselves outsiders and aliens ... there is a new source of honor that heals and covers their shame. It is experienced through the gospel (good news) of the kingdom (Luke 4:43; 8:1; 16:16; Acts 8:12; cf. Acts 19:8; 20:25; 28:23, 31). It is located in the King and kingdom of Jesus.

The honor that issues forth from this kingdom is embedded exclusively in Christ. This honor in Jesus creates for believers a visceral experience that conquers shame. It is an honor surplus provided to followers of Jesus the moment they are saved. It is symbolized when believers are baptized, immersed into "the name of the Father and of the Son and of the Holy Spirit" (Mat 28:19). This honor surplus is a fullness of life that overflows. It is thirst-quenching, thoroughly satisfying (John 7:38). This honor surplus is maintained experientially by being filled with the Holy Spirit, growing in the knowledge of the Word of God, and sharing in the life of Christ's nurturing body-community (1 Cor 12:21–26), the church.

Believers have no honor deficit.
They are children of God, siblings of the King.
They are not ashamed.
They are full and they are free,
    on mission with God to bless all the peoples of the earth.

One might think that the pursuit of knowing Christ and experiencing his glorious honor is somehow selfish. But this pursuit is the practice that Jesus commanded: "Seek first the kingdom of God and his righteousness" (Mat 6:33). It was embodied by the life of Apostle Paul (Phil 3:7–11). Paul wrote about this pursuit—*this seeking for glory and honor*—to the church at Rome: "To those who by patience in well-doing seek for glory and honor and immortality, he will give eternal life" (Rom 2:7). This pursuit is, in reality, the very antithesis of selfishness or sinful pride.

It is by their kingdom-infused, Christ-embedded, Spirit-breathed, Word-informed, church-supported honor surplus that believers are set free from sin (Rom 6:7–8, 17–18). True believers love and give sacrificially. When insulted, true believers are free, if necessary, to absorb the shame of others. Believers are ministers of reconciliation. Believers can stop being defensive or violent, because in Jesus Christ they are peacemakers.

On the one hand, believers can, like Jesus, humbly challenge the status quo and speak truth to power. On the other hand, they freely can stoop down and wash one another's feet because, like Jesus, they have no honor deficit (John 13:14–15).

All of these freedoms are expressions of selflessness. These freedoms reveal the very life of Jesus.

Believers have no honor deficit.
They are children of God, siblings of the King.
They are not ashamed.
They are full and they are free,
    on mission with God to bless all the peoples of the earth.

Many believers live in a consumerist society in which things are worshiped, but because of their honor surplus, they are free to avoid, or even relinquish, things that signify social status. They may possess the latest technology devices, fashionable cars and clothes, stylish houses, or impressive job titles. But while these things may all be considered gifts from God, believers, nevertheless, consider them optional because believers are content (Phil 4:11). They are content because they are satisfied in knowing and serving their King. Their honor is located in the King and his kingdom, not the kingdom of this world.

Because of their honor surplus in Jesus, they rejoice in suffering and being "counted worthy to suffer dishonor for the name" (Acts 5:41). They joyously live with an ethical righteousness that rises above depraved cultural values that are insulting to God. Believers know that sin is more than the breaking of a legal code; it is the very dishonoring of Almighty God (Rom 1:21–26; 2:23–24).

Believers have no honor deficit.
They are children of God, siblings of the King.
They are not ashamed.
They are full and they are free,
    on mission with God to bless all the peoples of the earth.

Believers saturated with the King's honor gladly serve him. They know it is by the King's saving blood and cross and resurrection that they are spared condemnation (Rom 8:1), and are adopted (Eph 1:5) into the honorific eternal family of God (1 Pet 2:6–10).

They embrace with all their hearts the honor of extending the blessing of salvation in Christ to "all the families of the earth" (Gen 12:3; cf. Gal 3:29). They can join the King and his family on mission to bless all peoples with his great salvation. This honor thrills them because it gives them so much purpose and joy.

Their experience of Christ's kingdom and his shame-conquering love brings healing now (Mat 5:3; Rom 5:5). It will be experienced in fullness and perfection for all believers in eternity.

Believers have no honor deficit.
They are children of God, siblings of the King.
They are not ashamed.
They are full and they are free,
    on mission with God to bless all the peoples of the earth.

This is the global gospel.

APPENDICES

How this author reads the Bible
to see the honor/shame dynamics

Anyone can read his or her Bible and see the honor/shame dynamics. Here's how I do it. I refer to the spectrum of **honor/shame** words (see Figure A1.01 below), and I sometimes underline or circle the words in my Bible using a **fine-point black pen**. I also use colored pencils as follows:

- When I see examples of **honor-status reversal,** I underline or circle these verses in **yellow.** This can include individual verses, lengthy passages, or even long stories. (Having read much of my Bible using this highlighting technique, I am amazed at how extensive are the yellow highlights!)

- Special attention is given to verses related to **kings** and **kingdoms.** This includes both human kingdoms and the kingdom of God. I highlight these words and verses in **orange.** Words like *king, kingdom, majesty, crown, scepter, reign,* and *throne* all have rich connotations of regal honor.

- Verses relative to **salvation** I underline in **red.** Words such as *saved, ransom, redeem, atonement, propitiation,* and *blood* are noted.

- **Blue** is used to highlight verses having to do with the **glory** or **holiness** of God.

- **Green** is used to highlight verses dealing with God's global **all-peoples mission.** Verses with words such as *earth, nations, peoples, Gentiles,* and *world* are underlined.

When these words and verses are highlighted and you see the interaction of the various colors, it offers added insight. It helps me recognize more quickly and see more clearly how honor/shame dynamics overlap with God's global purpose in blessing the nations through salvation in Jesus Christ.

Figure A1.01: A taxonomy of honor/shame words in the Bible

H/S-1 to H/S-5: Levels of awareness about honor/shame dynamics in cross-cultural ministry

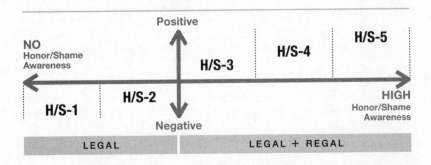

	LEVEL 1 **Unawareness**	LEVEL 2 **Ethical**	LEVEL 3 **Functional**	LEVEL 4 **Evangelical**	LEVEL 5 **Teleological**
Key words	Blind spot	Inferior values	Bible cultures	Gospel message	Glorious kingdom
Level of awareness of honor/ shame (HS)	Little to no awareness of honor/shame dynamics; cultural / theological blind spot	Awareness of only the unethical or dark side of honor/ shame	Awareness of honor/shame as pivotal cultural value of Bible societies leads to removal of Western lenses for interpreting Scripture	Awareness of honor/shame dynamics as central to the meaning and proclamation of the gospel of Christ	Awareness of honor/shame dynamics as central to the Bible's narrative of a doxological destiny for Christ and for the peoples of the earth
Honor/ shame as negative	No awareness	Honor/shame viewed as an unethical value system; it is morally and culturally inferior; it is to be merely understood and then eclipsed by a superior (Western) value system	Dark side of honor/ shame is result of the Fall, leading to sinful pathology that permeates personal life, family life, and social, global, and universal arenas	Dark side of honor/ shame is transcended by having shame covered and honor restored through the gospel of Jesus Christ in one's person, family, and community	Dark forces of honor/shame will be conquered by King Jesus to reclaim the universe from his enemies; all enemies of Christ will be shamed and put under his feet
Honor/ shame as positive	No awareness	Little to no awareness of positive aspects of honor/shame dynamics	Awareness of honor/shame as pivotal cultural value of Bible societies; thus, the lens of the authors and original hearers of Scripture; thus, an essential, normative hermeneutic to interpret the Bible today	Honor/shame dynamics are central to the gospel of the kingdom of God; honor/shame dynamics are vital to contextualize the gospel of Christ and are vital for personal spiritual transformation	Honor/shame dynamics are at the crux of God's ultimate purpose; "not yet" (teleological) aspect of the kingdom of God is primary: Christ will be worshiped by all peoples while honoring them in the process

	LEVEL 1 **Unawareness**	LEVEL 2 **Ethical**	LEVEL 3 **Functional**	LEVEL 4 **Evangelical**	LEVEL 5 **Teleological**
Legal or regal view of the atonement and resurrection	Exclusively legal understanding of the atonement; the cross is for sin/guilt	Primarily legal understanding of the atonement; the cross is for sin/guilt	Gospel of the kingdom embraces both legal and regal aspects of the atonement; the cross is for sin/guilt and sin/shame, for personal and social transformation	Gospel of the kingdom embraces both legal and regal aspects of the atonement; the cross is for sin/guilt and sin/shame; Christ's ascension is the victory of King Jesus over all rivals, all enemies	Gospel of the kingdom points to ultimate purpose of the atonement / ascension—to glorify Christ while also glorifying the redeemed among all the peoples, tribes and nations of the world
Ethical or doxological	No awareness	Ethical only	Ethical and doxological	Primarily doxological	Doxology as goal-destiny of all creation
Strategic issues	In the history of Christian mission, missionaries have sometimes violated honor/shame principles—"Pay to all what is owed to them: ... respect to whom respect is owed, honor to whom honor is owed" (Rom 13:7). When this has happened in honor/shame cultures it sometimes created a long shadow of animosity against the gospel. In light of this, strategic activities are: Learning the honor/shame culture of the Bible ... deep listening ... apology and relationship repair.		Honor/shame dynamics are incorporated into theology, hermeneutics, discipleship, missiology; Western theological bias of legal over regal (ignoring honor/shame) is recognized as a remnant of colonialism	Honor/shame dynamics offer contextualized gospel for unengaged and unreached peoples; legal and guilt-oriented gospel is relativized to be in balance with honor/shame and regal-based gospel of the kingdom	Honor/shame dynamics facilitate culture of honor in global church collaboration; strong partners relativized to work in unity with weak; creative worship arts for ethnolinguistic harmony honors Christ as King and honors value of all peoples
Book	Section 1	Sections 1, 2	Section 2	Section 3	Section 4

"Jesus stories"
involving uncleanness/shame

Below is an explanation of the nomenclature of the chart concerning "No. of Occurrences"

- **NO. OF OCCURRENCES:** Refers to the number of times the story or account occurs in the Gospels.

- **MALE OR FEMALE:** The number of occurrences of stories involving men and/or women is differentiated because there were purity regulations for women which differed from men due to conditions such as childbirth and menstruation.

- **TOUCH:** The number of stories in which Jesus is touched by, or touches, someone unclean is measured because uncleanness was often transferred by touch. The word touch or touches occurs 27 times in Leviticus; each time it refers to the condition of being unclean versus clean.

- **PRIMARY:** Refers to uncleanness that would apply to all Jews according to the Pentateuch.

- **SECONDARY:** Refers to Levitical priests according to Lev 21:16–23. God told Moses that priests could not enter the temple if they had physical deformities because they would "profane my sanctuaries" (v 23). Jews with diseases or deformities knew they were of lesser "cleanness" (and correspondingly, lower honor-status) than someone of the priesthood.

PURITY STORIES INVOLVING JESUS	SCRIPTURE REFERENCE	MALE OR FEMALE M	F	TOUCH	PRIMARY	SECONDARY	Leprosy	Gentile	Demonic	Death	Sexual sin	Other
							TYPE OF UNCLEANNESS / SHAME					
Scripture passages about Jesus interacting with people who are unclean/shamed												
Jesus cleanses a leper	• Mat 8:2–4 • Mark 1:40–44 • Luke 5:12–14	3	3		3	3	✓					
Jesus heals a man with an unclean spirit	• Mark 1:21–28 • Luke 4:31–37	2	2			2			✓			
Jesus raises a widow's son from the dead	• Luke 7:1–17	1	1	1	1	1				✓		
Jesus forgives a sinful woman	• Luke 7:36–50	1		1	1	1					✓	
Jesus calls Levi and eats in a home with sinners	• Mat 9:9–17 • Mark 2:13–17 • Luke 5:27–32	3	3			3						✓ In a home with sinners
Jesus restores a woman with a discharge of blood	• Mat 9:18–26 • Mark 5:21–34 • Luke 8:40–56	3		3	3	3						✓ Blood

PURITY STORIES INVOLVING JESUS	SCRIPTURE REFERENCE	NO. OF OCCURRENCES					TYPE OF UNCLEANNESS / SHAME					
		M	F	TOUCH	PRIMARY	SECONDARY	Leprosy	Gentile	Demonic	Death	Sexual sin	Other
Jesus heals a demon-possessed Gentile	• Mat 8:28–34 • Mark 5:1–20 • Luke 8:26–39	3				3		✓ "Other side" near pigs	✓ Legion: unclean spirit	✓ Lived among the tombs		✓ Naked
Jesus raises to life a girl who was dead	• Mat 9:18–26 • Mark 5:21–43 • Luke 8:40–56	3		3	3	3				✓		
Jesus and the woman of Samaria	• John 4:1–45	1		1		1		✓ Gentile blood			✓	
Jesus and the woman caught in adultery	• John 7:53–8:11	1		1		1					✓	
Jesus heals a paralytic	• Luke 5:17–26	1	1			1						✓ Paralyzed
Jesus heals a man with the withered hand	• Mat 12:9–14 • Mark 3:1–6 • Luke 6:6–11	3	3			1						✓ Withered hand
Jesus heals daughter of a Canaanite	• Mat 15:21–28 • Mark 7:24–30	2		2		1		✓	✓			
Jesus heals a deaf man	• Mark 7:31–37	1	1		1	1						✓ Deafness
Jesus heals a blind man	• Mark 8:22–26	1	1		1	1						✓ Blindness
Jesus heals a boy with an unclean spirit	• Mat 17:14–19 • Mark 9:14–29 • Luke 9:37–44	3	3		3	3			✓ Unclean spirit	✓ Seemed dead		✓ Deaf/mute
Jesus casts out a demon	• Luke 11:14–26	1	1			1			✓ Unclean spirit			✓ Mute
Jesus heals a woman with a disabling spirit	• Luke 13:10–17	1		1	1	1			✓			
Jesus heals a man on the Sabbath	• Luke 14:1–6	1	1		1	1						✓ Dropsy
Jesus cleanses ten lepers	• Luke 17:11–19	1	1		1		✓	✓ One Samaritan				
Jesus heals two blind men	• Mat 20:29–34 • Mark 10:46–52 • Luke 18:35–43	3	3		3	3						✓ Blindness
Jesus visits home of Simon the Leper	• Mat 26:6–13 • Mark 14:3–9	2	2	2	2	2	✓					

PURITY STORIES INVOLVING JESUS	SCRIPTURE REFERENCE	NO. OF OCCURRENCES					TYPE OF UNCLEANNESS / SHAME					
		M	F	TOUCH	PRIMARY	SECONDARY	Leprosy	Gentile	Demonic	Death	Sexual sin	Other
Other Scripture passages involving Jesus and the subject of uncleanness/shame												
Jesus tells the parable of the Prodigal Son	• Luke 15:11–32	1	1		1	1		✓ Pigs part of the story			✓	✓ Dishonor against father
Jesus teaches on what defiles a person	• Mat 15:10-20 • Mark 7:14-23	2	✱	✱	✱	✱						✓ Food vs. heart
Jesus' passion and crucifixion	• Mat 27:32–50 • Mark 15:16–37 • Luke 23:26–48 • John 19:16–30	4	4		4	4	✓ Atoning for all effects of the Fall (including disease)	✓ Interaction with Gentile soldiers, officials	✓ Confronts, conquers the world of the demonic	✓ Death in public setting, outside of city	✓ Atoning for effects of the Fall (including sex sins)	✓ Naked suffering in public
TOTALS 48		34	15	28	28	15						

SUMMARY AND NOTES

Totals: There are 48 stories in the Gospels involving Jesus and the condition of uncleanness/shame. Of these:

- 28 stories are examples of Primary Uncleanness
- 15 stories are examples of Secondary Uncleanness.
- 2 story occurrences—as represented by the asterisks (✱) in the chart above—are examples of propositional teaching about uncleanness: "what defiles a man" (Mat 15:10–20; Mark 7:14–3).

Gender:

- 34 stories deal with men; 15 stories deal with women
- Deviations: 1) The story of Jesus visiting the house of Simon the Leper (Mat 26:6–13; Mark 14:3–9) includes both men and women, so the occurrence of "2" is counted for both male and female. 2) Jesus' teaching on what defiles a person (Mat 15:10–20; Mark 7:14–23) is gender neutral; thus, it is not counted.

Touch: 28 stories involve Jesus touching, or being touched by, someone unclean. Apparently, Jesus himself did not become unclean through touch. Rather, Jesus' healing purity was transferred to the ones who were previously unclean. Jesus made them whole.

Christ the Shamed One: The uncleanness/shame that Jesus endured in his crucifixion is represented in this chart quantitatively as an occurrence in the Gospels. It is not represented qualitatively. The uncleanness/shame that Christ endured is of an infinite magnitude to atone for the sins of the world. An extensive further study could be done on the many ways Christ overcame uncleanness and shame through his incarnation and crucifixion.

Verses about salvation or the atonement of Christ in which we observe the dynamic of "unlimited good"

Atonement / salvation verse	How unlimited good is expressed
And they were exceedingly astonished, and said to him, "Then who can be saved?" Jesus looked at them and said, "With man it is impossible, but not with God. For all things are possible with God" (Mark 10:26–27).	• Anyone can be saved. • All things are possible with God because of God's unlimited power and grace.
And taking the twelve again, he began to tell them what was to happen to him, saying, "See, we are going up to Jerusalem, and the Son of Man will be delivered over to the chief priests and the scribes, and they will condemn him to death and deliver him over to the Gentiles. And they will mock him and spit on him, and flog him and kill him. And after three days he will rise" (Mark 10:32–34).	• The most shameful, ignominious death was inflicted on the most glorious and honorable King; in a closed system of limited good, this could only be viewed as a final tragic episode. • "And after three days he will rise." Jesus foretold his resurrection, his conquest over death and hell. • The open system of God intervening on earth to bless humanity for his own glorious purposes is the new pattern for life that reflects God's unlimited good.
For God so loved the world, that he gave his only Son, that whoever believes in him should not perish but have eternal life. For God did not send his Son into the world to condemn the world, but in order that the world might be saved through him. Whoever believes in him is not condemned, but whoever does not believe is condemned already, because he has not believed in the name of the only Son of God (John 3:16–18).	• The singular Son was given by God to offer salvation to the whole world, "that the world might be saved through him." • Salvation from God's condemnation is available to "whoever believes in him"—WHOEVER! • The offer is unrestricted—an unlimited good.
I am the living bread that came down from heaven. If anyone eats of this bread, he will live forever. And the bread that I will give for the life of the world is my flesh (John 6:51).	• "If anyone eats of this bread ..." This bread of eternal life in Christ is available to anyone and everyone. • Christ's sacrifice is "for the life of the world." The gift is not restricted by ethnicity, geography, time, social status: it is global, unlimited. • The offer is unrestricted—an unlimited good.
And it shall come to pass that everyone who calls upon the name of the Lord shall be saved (Acts 2:21).	• Salvation in Christ is available without restriction to "everyone who calls upon the name of the Lord." • The offer is unrestricted—an unlimited good.
To him all the prophets bear witness that everyone who believes in him receives forgiveness of sins through his name (Acts 10:43).	• "Everyone who believes in him receives forgiveness." • The offer is unrestricted—an unlimited good.
Let it be known to you therefore, brothers, that through this man forgiveness of sins is proclaimed to you, and by him everyone who believes is freed from everything from which you could not be freed by the law of Moses (Acts 13:38–39).	• "Everyone who believes is freed." • "From everything from which you could not be freed by the law of Moses." • The words "everyone" and "everything" point to an unrestricted offer—an unlimited good.
But now the righteousness of God has been manifested apart from the law, although the Law and the Prophets bear witness to it—the righteousness of God through faith in Jesus Christ for all who believe. For there is no distinction: for all have sinned and fall short of the glory of God, and are justified by his grace as a gift, through the redemption that is in Christ Jesus (Rom 3:21–24).	• "For all who believe ... for all have sinned ... and are justified by his grace as a gift." • The offer is unrestricted—an unlimited good for all who, by faith believe in Jesus Christ.

Atonement / salvation verse	How unlimited good is expressed
For the Scripture says, "Everyone who believes in him will not be put to shame." For there is no distinction between Jew and Greek; for the same Lord is Lord of all, bestowing his riches on all who call on him. For "everyone who calls on the name of the Lord will be saved" (Rom 10:11–13).	• The offer of being blameless and shameless before God is unrestricted—and it is unaffected by cultural, social, or ethnic superiority; it is exclusively based on belief in Christ. • The offer is unrestricted—an unlimited good; God is "bestowing his riches on all who call on him."
For in him all the fullness of God was pleased to dwell, and through him to reconcile to himself all things, whether on earth or in heaven, making peace by the blood of his cross (Col 1:19–20).	• God is reconciling to himself "all things." • God's work of reconciliation is unrestricted—an unlimited good.
For there is one God, and there is one mediator between God and men, the man Christ Jesus, who gave himself as a ransom for all, which is the testimony given at the proper time (1 Tim 2:5–6).	• The one mediator "Christ Jesus" ransomed his life "for all"—an unlimited good.
And being made perfect, he became the source of eternal salvation to all who obey him (Heb 5:9).	• The offer of salvation is unrestricted, to anyone and everyone, "to all who obey him"—an unlimited good.
He has no need, like those high priests, to offer sacrifices daily, first for his own sins and then for those of the people, since he did this once for all when he offered up himself (Heb 7:27).	• Jesus' sacrifice was "once for all when he offered up himself." • The offer is unrestricted—an unlimited good.

A sampling of honor/shame dynamics in the book of Revelation

Honor/shame dynamic	God gives honor to the saints—individual believers and people groups they comprise	Other honor/shame dynamics
HONOR **Love of honor**	• God has "made us a kingdom" (1:6). • God has "made them a kingdom and priests to our God, and they shall reign on the earth" (5:10). • God provides to the saints an honor surplus embedded in Jesus Christ by which they gain the kingdom and the regal authority to reign—satisfying their longing for honor. • The love of, or longing for, honor by humans is fulfilled by God sharing his honor with them, and by giving them possession of the kingdom (cf. Dan 7:18, 21, 27). • The honor of every people is magnified when God receives "the glory and the honor of the nations" from their regal representatives, "the kings of the earth" (21:22–25).	• God receives glory and honor forever and ever through the praise of angelic beings (4:8–11), the adoring affection of the saints, and the worship of the nations (5:7–9; 7:9–12, 11:16–18; 15:3–4; 19:1–2, 6–8; 22:3).
Ascribed Honor **Achieved Honor** ✓ **Two sources of honor**	ASCRIBED HONOR • The saints of God possess ascribed honor by being dressed in white: 3:4–5, 18; 6:11; 7:9, 13–14; 19:8, 14. • "The one who conquers will have this heritage, and I will be his God and he will be my son" (21:7). Conquering saints will gain the astounding honor of being children of God for eternity—a reward of ascribed honor. ACHIEVED HONOR • The saints of God achieve honor by conquering, maintaining their integrity in the face of temptation and adversity as followers of Christ. "To the one who conquers, I will grant to eat of the tree of life" (2:7, cf. 2:11, 17, 26; 3:5, 12, 21).	ASCRIBED HONOR • Almighty God possesses ascribed honor: "Holy, holy, holy, is the Lord God Almighty, who was and is and is to come!" (4:8). • Jesus possesses ascribed honor: "I am the Alpha and the Omega, the first and the last, the beginning and the end" (22:13; cf. 1:8; 21:6). ACHIEVED HONOR • God possesses achieved honor as creator: "Worthy are you, our Lord and God, to receive glory and honor and power, for you created all things, and by your will they existed and were created" (4:11). • Jesus Christ possesses achieved honor as redeemer: "Worthy are you to take the scroll and to open its seals, for you were slain, and by your blood you ransomed people for God from every tribe and language and people and nation" (5:9).
Challenge and riposte	• In chapter 12, the dragon, representing Satan, and the angels of God engage in a battle for power, honor, and authority—a conflict between the kingdom of darkness and the kingdom of God. • The battle is won by God and the saints who "conquered him by the blood of the Lamb and by the word of their testimony" (12:11).	• "They will make war on the Lamb, and the Lamb will conquer them, for he is Lord of lords and King of kings, and those with him are called and chosen and faithful" (17:14).

Honor/shame dynamic	God gives honor to the saints—individual believers and people groups they comprise	Other honor/shame dynamics
Body language	• "When I saw him, I fell at his feet as though dead. But he laid his right hand on me, saying, 'Fear not, I am the first and the last'" (1:17). The honor of God's right hand on John conveys honor and courage. • Regarding feet: "Behold, I will make those of the synagogue of Satan who say that they are Jews and are not, but lie—behold, I will make them come and bow down before your feet, and they will learn that I have loved you" (3:9).	• The honor and authority of God is symbolized by the "right hand" at least five times in Revelation. • "As for the mystery of the seven stars that you saw in my right hand …" (1:20, cf. 2:1; 5:1, 7; 10:5).
Concept of face	• "They will see his face, and his name will be on their foreheads" (22:4). The saints will gain the very honor of God as they experience the intimacy of seeing the face of God and the name of God is placed on their foreheads. • The honor of God is represented by the name or seal of God on the foreheads of the saints in 7:3; 9:4; 14:1. • High honor and reward is given by God to those who refuse the mark of the beast on their foreheads (20:4).	• The mark of the beast on the forehead (13:16; 14:9) signifies allegiance/honor to the beast. • The impure idolatrous "woman" has the mark on her forehead: "Babylon the great, mother of prostitutes and of earth's abominations" (17:5).
Name / kinship / blood	**NAME** • "The one who conquers, I will make him a pillar in the temple of my God. Never shall he go out of it, and I will write on him the name of my God, and the name of the city of my God, the new Jerusalem, which comes down from my God out of heaven, and my own new name" (3:12). • "Then I looked, and behold, on Mount Zion stood the Lamb, and with him 144,000 who had his name and his Father's name written on their foreheads" (14:1). The honor of the name of both God the Father and God the Son is given to each of the 144,000 saints. **KINSHIP** • "The one who conquers will have this heritage, and I will be his God and he will be my son" (21:7). Conquering saints will gain the astounding honor of being sons of God for eternity. • Believers martyred are called "brothers" (6:11). **BLOOD** • The blood of saints as martyrs is referenced in 6:10; 16:6; 17:6; 18:24; 19:2. • Saints conquer the great deceiver "by the blood of the Lamb" (12:11).	**NAME** • Commerce—buying and selling—only if one has the name of the beast (13:17). • Saints are "enduring" and "bearing up" for the sake of God's name (2:3; cf. 2:13, 17; 3:8). • The "rider's name was Death" (6:8); Abaddon is the name of the angel in the bottomless pit (9:11). • God's name is blasphemed in 13:6; "cursed" in 16:9. • The unrighteous do not have their name in the book of life (13:8). • Jesus Christ has "a name … no one knows but himself" (19:12). **KINSHIP** • A loud voice in heaven calls saints our brothers: "the accuser of our brothers has been thrown down" (12:10). **BLOOD** • Christ "has freed us from our sins by his blood" (1:5; cf. 5:9; 7:14). • Jesus Christ wears "a robe dipped in blood" (19:13)—his mantle of honor has been immersed in the honor of his blood. • Bloodshed and death result from God's judgment on the unrighteous (6:12–17; 8:7–8; 11:6; 14:20; 16:3).

Honor/shame dynamic	God gives honor to the saints—individual believers and people groups they comprise	Other honor/shame dynamics
Purity	**POSITIVE PURITY LANGUAGE** • The saints wear white robes depicting their purity/honor in Christ: "Yet you have still a few names in Sardis, people who have not soiled their garments, and they will walk with me in white, for they are worthy" (3:4–5). The saints' honor is located in their lifestyle of purity, walking with Christ. • See also other verses in which saints are clothed in white: 3:18; 6:11; 7:9, 13–14; 19:8, 14. • Those who have "washed their robes and made them white in the blood of the Lamb" (7:14) are allowed to enter the New Jerusalem (22:14).	**POSITIVE PURITY LANGUAGE** • God is worshiped as holy (4:8; 15:4; 16:5) and described as holy (3:7; 6:10). • Christ has white hair (1:14), a white horse (6:2; 19:11), and is seated on a white cloud (14:14). • Almighty God judges the world from a white throne (20:11). • The city of God is called holy in 11:2; 21:2, 10; 22:19. • Angels are holy in 14:10. **NEGATIVE PURITY LANGUAGE** • Coming out of the dragon are "three unclean spirits like frogs" (16:13). • Babylon is referred to as the sexually immoral woman of impurities and abominations (17:4–5). • Babylon is a "haunt for every unclean spirit … unclean bird … unclean and detestable beast" (18:2). • Evildoers are "filthy" (22:11). • Uncleanness of "sexual immorality" in 2:14, 20–21; 9:21; 14:8; 17:2; 18:3, 9; 19:2. • Nothing unclean will ever enter the New Jerusalem (21:27).
Honor-status reversal	**HONOR-STATUS REVERSAL OF THE SAINTS** • The honor-status reversal of the saints is typified in these verses: "To him who loves us and has freed us from our sins by his blood and made us a kingdom, priests to his God and Father" (1:5–6). Freed from the shame of sin, gaining the kingdom and honor of the priesthood. • A rise in honor-status is awarded to all the ones who conquer in their fight against sin and the forces of darkness (2:11). These rewards include, for example: "the crown of life" (2:10); to be given "authority over the nations" (2:26); to be made "a pillar in the temple of my God" (3:12); to sit on the throne with God (3:21); to become God's son (21:7).	**HONOR-STATUS REVERSAL OF JESUS CHRIST** • Jesus said, "I died, and behold I am alive forevermore, and I have the keys of Death and Hades" (1:18). Jesus died by the ultimate shame of crucifixion, but he is now alive forevermore with power and authority over death and hell. **HONOR-STATUS REVERSAL AS GOD'S JUDGMENT** • "The kings of the earth and the great ones" hide in the caves from God's judgment (6:15). • The great deceiver Satan is "thrown down" (12:9–10). • Babylon the Great is "fallen" (chapter 18). A wealthy and mighty city saturated by evil, uncleanness, and pride is cast down: honor-status reversal. • Death and Hades, and anyone whose "name was not found written in the book of life" are "thrown into the lake of fire" (20:14–15).

Works Cited

Alexander, T. Desmond, Brian S. Rosner, D. A. Carson, and Graeme Goldsworthy, eds. *New Dictionary of Biblical Theology, Exploring the Unity and Diversity of Scripture*. Downers Grove, IL: InterVarsity Press, 2000.

Angeles, Peter A. *Dictionary of Christian Theology*. San Francisco: Harper, 1985.

Araujo, Alex, Mary Lederleitner, and Werner Mischke. "To Catch the Wind: A New Metaphor for Cross-Cultural Partnership." In *The Beauty of Partnership: Gain the skills to achieve successful cross-cultural partnerships around the world*. Edited by Werner Mischke. Scottsdale, AZ: Mission ONE, 2010.

Araujo, Alex, and Werner Mischke. "A report on 'Catching the Wind of God—A Sailing Retreat' (Contrasting the "Powerboat" and "Sailboat" mindset for leadership)." Accessed 25 March 2014. http://sailingfriends.files.wordpress.com/2009/10/sailboat_retreat_report_15oct20092.pdf.

Arnold, Dean. Foreword to *The Fall of Patriarchy: Its Broken Legacy Judged by Jesus and the Apostolic House Church Communities*. Edited by Dell Birkey. Tucson, AZ: Fenestra Books, 2005.

Aronson, Marc. *Unsettled: The Problem of Loving Israel*. New York: Atheneum, 2008.

Bailey, Kenneth. *The Cross and the Prodigal: Luke 15 Through the Eyes of Middle Eastern Peasants*. Downers Grove, IL: InterVarsity Press, 2005.

Baker, Mark D., and Joel B Green. *Recovering the Scandal of the Cross: Atonement in New Testament and Contemporary Contexts*. Downers Grove, IL: IVP Academic, 2011. Kindle edition.

Baker, Susan. "The Social Sciences for Urban Ministry." In *The Urban Face of Mission: Ministering the Gospel in a Diverse and Changing World*. Edited by Manuel Ortiz and Susan S. Baker. Phillipsburg, NJ: P & R Publishing, 2002.

Barrett, Alicia. "God in the Letter of James: Patron or Benefactor?" in *The Social World of the New Testament: Insights and Models*. Edited by Jerome H. Neyrey and Eric C. Stewart. Peabody, MA: Hendrickson, 2008.

Bartchy, S. Scott. "Who Should Be Called 'Father'? Paul of Tarsus between the Jesus Tradition and Patria Potestas." In *The Social World of the New Testament*. Edited by Jerome H. Neyrey and Eric C. Stewart. Peabody: MA: Hendrickson, 2008.

Bauckham, Richard. *Bible and Mission: Christian Witness in a Postmodern World*. Grand Rapids, MI: Baker Academic, 2004.

Berkhof, L. *Systematic Theology*. Grand Rapids, MI: Eerdmans, 1941.

bin Laden, Osama. "Full text: bin Laden's 'Letter to America.'" *The Guardian*. Sunday 24 November 2002. Accessed 15 September 2013.

Borthwick, Paul. *Western Christians in Global Mission: What's the Role of the North American Church?* Downers Grove, IL: InterVarsity Press, 2012. Kindle edition.

Bosch, David J. *Transforming Mission: Paradigm Shifts in Theology of Mission*. Maryknoll, NY: Orbis, 1991.

Brandenburger, Egon. *Adam und Christus:, Exegetisch-religions-geschichtliche Untersuchugen zu Römer 5, 12–21 (1 Kor. 15)*. WMANT 29. Neukirchen Verlag, 1962.

Bright, John. *The Kingdom of God*. Nashville: Abingdon, 1981.

Brown, Brené. *Daring Greatly: How the Courage to Be Vulnerable Transforms the Way We Live, Love, Parent, and Lead*. New York: Gotham, 2012.

———. *The Gifts of Imperfection: Let Go of Who You Think You're Supposed to be and Embrace Who You Are*. Center City, MN: Hazelden, 2010.

Campbell, Donald K., Wendell Johnson, John Walvoord, and John Witmer. *The Theological Wordbook: The 200 Most Important Theological Terms and Their Relevance for Today*. Nashville: Word Publishing, 2000.

Chapman, Colin. "Christian responses to Islam, Islamism and 'Islamic terrorism.'" *Jubilee Centre,* Cambridge Papers 16, no 2, (June 2007). Accessed 16 September 2013. http://www.jubilee-centre.org/document.php?id=55.

Cheng, Yongtao. "The Concept of Face and Its Confucian Roots." In *American Anthropologist* 46, no. 1 (March 1994).

Chin, Hsien Hu. "The Chinese Concepts of 'Face'." In *American Anthropologist* 46, no. 1 (March 1994): 45, 61.

Chua, Amy. *World on Fire: How Exporting Free Market Democracy Breeds Ethnic Hatred and Global Instability.* New York: Random House, 2003.

Clark, David K. *To Know and Love God: Method for Theology.* Wheaton, IL: Crossway, 2003.

Cray, Graham. "The Theology of the Kingdom." In *Mission as Transformation: A Theology of the Whole Gospel.* Edited by Vinay Samuel and Chris Sugden. Oxford: Regnum Books, 1999.

Crook, Zeba A. *Reconceptualizing Conversion: Patronage, Loyalty, and Conversion in the Religions of the Ancient Mediterranean.* Berlin: Walter de Gruyter, 2004.

deSilva, David A. *Honor, Patronage, Kinship, & Purity: Unlocking New Testament Culture.* Downers Grove, IL: InterVarsity Press, 2000.

———. *The Hope of Glory: Honor Discourse and New Testament Interpretation.* Eugene, OR: Wipf & Stock. 1999.

———. "Turning Shame into Honor: The Pastoral Strategy of 1 Peter" in *The Shame Factor: How Shame Shapes Society.* Edited by Robert Jewett, et al. Eugene, OR: Cascade Books, 2011.

Driver, John. *Understanding the Atonement for the Mission of the Church.* Scottdale, PA: Herald Press, 1986.

Duling, Dennis. *The New Testament: An Introduction.* New York: Harcourt, Brace, Jovanovich, 1994.

Dyrness, William A., and Veli-Matti Kärkkäinen, eds. *Global Dictionary of Theology.* Downers Grove, IL: InterVarsity Press, 2008.

Echevarria, Daniel. "Top Multilingual U. S. Cities." Beyond Words—Language Blog. 3 March 2010. Accessed 18 September 2013. http://www.altalang.com/beyond-words/2010/03/03/top-multilingual-u-s-cities/.

Elwell, Walter A., ed. *Baker Theological Dictionary of the Bible.* Grand Rapids, MI: Baker Book House, 1996.

———. *Evangelical Dictionary of Theology.* Grand Rapids, MI: Baker Book House, 1984.

Erickson, Millard J. *Christian Theology.* 2nd ed. Grand Rapids, MI: Baker, 1998.

Escobar, Samuel. *The New Global Mission: The Gospel from Everywhere to Everyone.* Downers Grove, IL: InterVarsity Press, 2003.

ESV Study Bible. Wheaton, IL: Good News Publishers/Crossway Books, 2009.

Ferguson, Niall. *Civilization: The West and the Rest.* New York: Penguin Books, 2011.

Flanders, Christopher L. *About Face: Rethinking Face for 21st Century Mission.* Eugene, OR: Wipf and Stock, 2011.

Flemming, Dean. *Contextualization in the New Testament: Patterns for Theology and Mission.* Downers Grove, IL: IVP Academic. 2009. Kindle edition.

Forrester, John A. *Grace for Shame: The Forgotten Gospel.* Toronto: Pastor's Attic Press, 2010.

Frey, William H. "America's Diverse Future: Initial Glimpses at the U.S. Child Population from the 2010 Census." The Brookings Institution. 6 April 2011. Accessed 18 September 2013. http://www.brookings.edu/research/papers/2011/04/06-census-diversity-frey.

Garrett Jr., James Leo. *Systematic Theology: Biblical, Historical and Evangelical.* 2 vols. Grand Rapids, MI: Eerdmans, 1990–1995.

Georges, Jayson. "From Shame to Honor: A Theological Reading of Romans for Honor-Shame Contexts." *Missiology: An International Review* 38 (2010): 298.

Giesler, Norman. *Systematic Theology.* Minneapolis: Bethany, 2002.

Gomes, Alan, ed. *Dogmatic Theology by William T. Shedd.* 3rd ed. Phillipsburg, NJ: Presbyterian & Reformed, 2003.

Gorman, Michael T. *Cruciformity: Paul's Narrative Spirituality of the Cross.* Grand Rapids, MI: Eerdmans, 2002.

Green, Joel B., and Lee Martin McDonald, eds. *The World of the New Testament: Cultural, Social, and Historical Contexts.* Grand Rapids, MI: Baker, 2013.

Grudem, Wayne. *Systematic Theology.* Grand Rapids, MI: Zondervan, 1994.

Grudem, Wayne, and Barry Asmus. *The Poverty of Nations: A Sustainable Solution.* Wheaton, IL: Crossway, 2013.

Hawthorne, Steve. *Let All the Peoples Praise Him: Toward a Teleological Paradigm of the Missio Dei.* Ph.D. Thesis. Ann Arbor, MI: ProQuest, 2013.

———. "The Story of His Glory." In *Perspectives on the World Christian Movement.* Edited by Ralph Winter and Steve Hawthorne. Pasadena, CA: William Carey Library Publishers, 1999.

Heschel, Susannah. *The Aryan Jesus: Christian Theologians and the Bible in Nazi Germany.* Princeton, NJ: Princeton University Press, 2008.

Hiebert, Paul E. "Critical Contextualization." In *Missiology: An International Review* 12 (July): 287–96.

———. "The Flaw of the Excluded Middle." In *Landmark Essays in Mission and World Christianity.* Edited by Robert L. Gallagher and Paul Hertig. Maryknoll, NY: Orbis Books, 2013. Kindle edition. Originally published in Missiology 10, no. 1 (January, 1982): 35–47."

———. "The Gospel in Human Contexts: Changing Perceptions of Contextualization." In *MissionShift: Global Mission Issues in the Third Millennium.* Edited by Ed Stetzer and David Hesselgrave. Nashville, TN: B&H Publishing, 2010.

———. *Transforming Worldviews: An Anthropological Understanding of How People Change.* Grand Rapids, MI: Baker Academic, 2008. Kindle edition.

Hill, Andrew E., and John F. Walton. *A Survey of the Old Testament.* Grand Rapids, MI: Zondervan, 2009.

Jenkins, Philip. *The Next Christendom: The Coming of Global Christianity.* New York: Oxford University Press, 2002, 2011.

Jewett, Robert. *Romans: A Commentary.* Minneapolis: Fortress Press, 2007.

Jewett, Robert, Wayne L. Alloway, and John G. Lacey, eds. *The Shame Factor: How Shame Shapes Society.* Eugene, OR: Cascade Books, 2011.

Johnson, Todd M., and Kenneth R. Ross, eds. *Atlas of Global Christianity.* Edinburgh: Edinburgh University Press, 2009.

Johnstone, Patrick. *The Future of the Global Church: History, Trends and Possibilities.* Downers Grove, IL: InterVarsity Press, 2011.

Jones, James W. "Shame, Humiliation, and Religious Violence: A Self-Psychological Investigation." In *The Shame Factor: How Shame Shapes Society.* Edited by Robert Jewett, et al. Eugene, OR: Cascade Books, 2011.

Keller, Timothy. *The Prodigal God: Recovering the Heart of the Faith.* New York: Penguin, 2008.

Klein, William W., Craig L. Blomberg, and Robert I. Hubbard Jr. *Introduction to Biblical Interpretation.* Rev. ed. Nashville, TN: Thomas Nelson, 2004.

Köstenberger, Andreas J. "Twelve Theses on the Church's Mission in the Twenty-first Century: In Interaction with Charles Van Engen, Keith Eitel, and Enoch Wan." In *MissionShift: Global Mission Issues in the Third Millennium.* Edited by Ed Stetzer and David Hesselgrave. Nashville, TN: B&H Publishing, 2010. Kindle edition.

Landes, David S. *The Wealth and Poverty of Nations: Why Some Are So Rich and Some So Poor.* New York: W. W. Norton, 1999.

Latsko, Mike. "The Most Abominable Word." In *Mission Frontiers* 35, no. 1 (Jan/Feb 2013): 12.

Lendon, J. E. *Empire of Honour: The Art of Government in the Roman World.* New York: Oxford University Press, 1997. Kindle edition.

Lewis, C. S. *The Weight of Glory and Other Addresses.* Grand Rapids, MI: Eerdmans, 1949.

Little, Christopher R. "Business as Mission under Scrutiny." In *EMQ,* April 2014. Accessed 5 May 2014. http://www.emqonline.com/emq/issue-327/2940

Loewen, Jacob. *Culture and Human Values: Christian Intervention in Anthropological Perspective.* Pasadena, CA: William Carey Library, 1975.

MacArthur, John. *The Prodigal Son: An Astonishing Study of the Parable Jesus Told to Unveil God's Grace for You.* Nashville, TN: Thomas Nelson, 2008.

———. "What Does Sola Scriptura Mean?" *Ligonier Ministries.* 24 September 2012. Accessed 22 March 2014. http://www.ligonier.org/blog/what-does-sola-scriptura-mean/.

Malina, Bruce J. *The New Testament World: Insights from Cultural Anthropology.* Rev. ed. Louisville, KY: Westminster/John Knox Press, 1993.

———. "Anachronism, Ethnocentrism, and Shame: The Envy of the Chief Priests." In *The Shame Factor: How Shame Shapes Society.* Edited by Robert Jewett, et.al. Eugene, OR: Cascade, 2011.

Malina, Bruce J., and Jerome H. Neyrey, SJ. "Ancient Mediterranean Persons in Cultural Perspective: Portrait of Paul." *In The Social World of the New Testament: Insights and Models.* Edited by Bruce J. Malina and Jerome H. Neyrey, SJ. Peabody, MA: Hendrickson, 2008.

Mazrui, Ali. *Cultural Forces in World Politics*. Portsmouth, NH: Heinemann, 1990.

Mbuvi, Andrew M. "African Theology from the Perspective of Honor and Shame." In *The Urban Face of Mission: Ministering the Gospel in a Diverse and Changing World*. Edited by Manuel Ortiz and Susan S. Baker. Phillipsburg, NJ: P & R Publishing, 2002.

McKnight, Scot. *The King Jesus Gospel: The Original Good News Revisited*. Grand Rapids, MI: Zondervan, 2011. Kindle edition.

Miller, Darrow, and Stan Guthrie. *Discipling Nations: The Power of Truth to Transform Cultures*. Seattle, WA: YWAM Publishing, 1998.

Mischke, Werner. *The Beauty of Partnership*. Scottsdale, AZ: Mission ONE, 2010.

———. "The Father's Love Gospel Booklet." Scottsdale, AZ: Mission ONE. http://thefatherslovebooklet.org.

———. "Knowing and sharing the gospel of Christ in the language of honor and shame." Accessed 26 Sept 2013. http://www.slideshare.net/WernerMischke/contextualization-acmi.

Mouw, Richard J. *When the Kings Come Marching In: Isaiah and the New Jerusalem*. Grand Rapids, MI: Eerdmans, 2002. Kindle edition.

Muller, Roland. *Honor & Shame: Unlocking the Door*. Bloomington, IN: Xlibris Corporation, 2000.

———. *The Messenger, The Message, The Community: Three Critical Issues for the Cross-Cultural Church Planter*. Saskatchewan, Canada: CanBooks, 2013.

Nathansan, Donald. *The Many Faces of Shame*. New York: Guilford Press, 1987.

Newbigin, Lesslie. *The Gospel in a Pluralistic Society*. Grand Rapids, MI: Eerdmans, 1989.

Neyrey, Jerome H. *Honor and Shame in the Gospel of Matthew*. Louisville, KY: Westminster John Knox Press, 1998.

———. "Despising the Shame of the Cross: Honor and Shame in the Johannine Passion Narrative." In *Semeia* 68 (1994): 113–37.

Neyrey, Jerome H., and Eric C. Stewart, eds. *The Social World of the New Testament: Insights and Models*. Peabody, MA: Hendrickson, 2008.

Nicholls, Bruce. "The Role of Shame and Guilt in a Theology of Cross-Cultural Mission." In *Evangelical Review of Theology* 25, no. 3 (2001): 232.

Noll, Mark: *The New Shape of World Christianity: How American Experience Reflects Global Faith*. Downers Grove, IL: InterVarsity Press, 2009. Kindle edition.

Pannenberg, Wolfhart. *Systematic Theology*. Vols. 1–3. Grand Rapids, MI: Eerdmans, 1991–1997.

Pattison, Stephen. "Shame and the Unwanted Self." In *The Shame Factor: How Shame Shapes Society*. Edited by Robert Jewett, Wayne L. Alloway, and John G. Lacey. Eugene, OR: Wipf & Stock Publishers, 201o.

Payne, J. D. *Strangers Next Door: Immigration, Migration and Mission*. Downers Grove, IL: InterVarsity Press, 2012. Kindle edition.

Peterson, Brooks. *Cultural Intelligence: A Guide to Working with People from Other Cultures*. Boston: Intercultural Press, 2004.

Piper, John. *God's Passion for His Glory: Living the Vision of Jonathan Edwards (With the Complete Text of The End for Which God Created the World)*. Wheaton, IL: Crossway Books, 1996.

———. *Let the Nations Be Glad!: The Supremacy of God in Missions*. Grand Rapids, MI: Baker Publishing Group, 2010. Kindle edition.

———. *The Pleasures of God: Meditations on God's Delight in Being God*. Sisters, OR: Multnomah, 1991, 2000.

Pitt-Rivers, Julian. "Honor and Shame." In *Honor and Shame: The Values of Mediterranean Society*. Edited by J. G. Peristiany. London: Weidenfeld & Nocholson, 1966.

Pocock, Michael, Gailyn Van Rheenan, and Douglas McConnell. *The Changing Face of World Missions: Engaging Contemporary Issues and Trends*. Grand Rapids, MI: Baker, 2005.

Pryce-Jones, David. *The Closed Circle: An Interpretation of the Arabs*. Chicago: Ivan R. Dee, 1989, 2009.

Radosh, Allis, and Ronald Radosh. *A Safe Haven: Harry S. Truman and the Founding of Israel*. New York: HarperCollins, 2009.

Rah, Soong-Chan. *The Next Evangelicalism: Freeing the Church from Western Cultural Captivity*. Downers Grove, IL: InterVarsity Press, 2009. Kindle edition.

Redles, David. "Ordering Chaos: Nazi Millennialism and the Quest for Meaning." In *The Fundamentalist Mindset: Psychological Perspectives on Religion, Violence, and History*. Edited by Charles B. Strozier, David M. Terman, James W. Jones, and Katherine A. Boyd. New York: Oxford University Press, 2010.

Reich, Karl. *Figuring Jesus: The Power of Rhetorical Figures of Speech in the Gospel of Luke*. The Netherlands: Koninklijke Brill NV, 2011.

Richards, E. Randolph. "Reading, Writing, and Manuscripts." In *The World of the New Testament: Cultural, Social, and Historical Contexts*. Edited by Joel B. Green and Lee Martin McDonald. Grand Rapids, MI: Baker, 2013.

Richards, E. Randolph, and Brandon J. O'Brien. *Misreading Scripture with Western Eyes: Removing Cultural Blinders to Better Understand the Bible*. Downers Grove, IL: InterVarsity Press, 2012. Kindle edition.

Richardson, Alan, and John Bowden, eds. *The Westminster Dictionary of Christian Theology*. Philadelphia: The Westminster Press, 1983.

Richardson, Don. *Peace Child: An Unforgettable Story of Primitive Jungle Treachery in the 20th Century*. Ventura, CA: Gospel Light, 2005. Kindle edition.

Roberts, Sam. "Listening to (and Saving) the World's Languages." *The New York Times*. 28 April 2010. Accessed 18 September 2013. http://www.nytimes.com/2010/04/29/nyregion/29lost.html?_r=0.

Rohrbaugh, Richard. "The Social Location of the Markan Audience." In *The Social World of the New Testament: Insights and Models*. Peabody, MA: Hendrickson, 2008.

Rutherford, Samuel. *Lex, Rex: The Law is King*. Public domain, 1644.

Saiyasak, Chansamone. "The Adaptation of Buddhism and Christianity to Asian Soils." In *Discern What Is Right: Seoul Strategic Forum 2011*. Edited by David Hartono and Greg Young Paek. Pasadena, CA: East-West Center for Missions Research & Development, 2012.

Samuel, Vinay, and Chris Sugden, eds. *Mission as Transformation: A Theology of the Whole Gospel*. Oxford: Regnum Books, 1999.

Schreiter, Robert J. "Reconciliation as a Model of Mission." In *Landmark Essays in Mission and World Christianity*. Edited by Robert L. Gallagher and Paul Hertig. Maryknoll, NY: Orbis Books, 2013. Kindle edition.

Smedes, Lewis B. *Shame and Grace: Healing the Shame We Don't Deserve*. New York: HarperCollins, 1993.

So, Damon. "How Should a Theological Institution Prepare Students/Leaders Who Will Go Out into the Field to Train Local People (Storytellers) to Tell Bible Stories Effectively?" In *Beyond Literate Western Models: Contextualizing Theological Education in Oral Contexts*. Edited by Samuel E. Chiang and Grant Lovejoy. International Orality Network, 2013.

Stetzer, Ed, and David Hesselgrave. *MissionShift: Global Mission Issues in the Third Millennium*. Nashville, TN: B&H Publishing, 2010. Kindle Edition.

Stockitt, Robin. *Restoring the Shamed: Towards a Theology of Shame*. Eugene, OR: Cascade Books, 2012. Kindle edition.

Tangney, June, and Ronda Dearing. *Shame and Guilt*. New York: Guilford Press, 2002.

Tennent, Timothy C. *Invitation to World Missions: A Trinitarian Missiology for the Twenty-first Century*. Grand Rapids, MI: Kregel, 2010.

———. *Theology in the Context of World Christianity: How the Global Church Is Influencing the Way We Think about and Discuss Theology*. Grand Rapids, MI: Zondervan, 2007.

"The Four Spiritual Laws," renamed "How to Know God Personally." Cru. Accessed 14 September 2013. http://www.cru.org/how-to-know-god/would-you-like-to-know-god-personally/index.htm.

Thielicke, Helmut. *The Evangelical Faith*. Grand Rapids, MI: Eerdmans, 1974.

Thiessen, Henry. *Lectures in Systematic Theology*. Rev. ed. Grand Rapids, MI: Eerdmans, 1977.

Thomas, Bruce. "The Gospel for Shame Cultures." In *EMQ. July 1994. Accessed 8 September 2013*. http://www.emisdirect.com/emq/issue-153/750.

Tiénou, Tite. "Christian Theology in an Era of World Christianity." In *Globalizing Theology: Belief and Practice in an Era of World Christianity*. Edited by Craig Ott and Harold Netland. Grand Rapids, MI: Baker Publishing Group, 2006. Kindle edition.

Ting-Toomey, Stella. "Face and Facework: An Introduction." In *The Challenge of Facework: Cross-Cultural and Interpersonal Issues*. Edited by Stella Ting-Toomey. Albany, NY: State University of New York Press, 1994.

Tira, Sadiri. "Diaspora Missiology." The Lausanne Movement (blog). 6 October 2010. Accessed 20 September 2013. http://conversation.lausanne.org/en/conversations/detail/11103#.UjuI9hbM7o4.

Triandis, Henry C. "Cross-Cultural Studies of Individualism and Collectivism." In *Nebraska Symposium on Motivation 1989: Cross-Cultural Perspectives*. Edited by Richard A. Diensbar and John J. Berman. Lincoln, NE: University of Nebraska Press, 1989.

Vanhoozer, Kevin. "'One Rule to Rule Them All?' Theological Method in an Era of World Christianity." In *Globalizing Theology: Belief Practice in an Era of World Christianity*. Edited by Craig Ott and Harold Netland. Grand Rapids, MI: Baker Academic & Brazos Press, 2006. Kindle edition.

Walls, Andrew. "Christian Scholarship in Africa in the Twenty-first Century." In *Transformation* 19, no. 4 (October 2002): 217–28.

———. "Globalization and the Study of Christian History." In *Globalizing Theology: Belief and Practice in an Era of World Christianity*. Edited by Craig Ott and Harold Netland. Grand Rapids, MI: Baker Academic & Brazos Press, 2006. Kindle edition.

———. "The Gospel as Prisoner and Liberator of Culture: Is There a 'Historic Christian Faith'?" In *Landmark Essays in Mission and World Christianity*. Edited by Robert L. Gallagher and Paul Hertig. Maryknoll, NY: Orbis Books, 2013. Kindle edition.

Welch, Edward T. *Shame Interrupted: How God Lifts the Pain of Worthlessness and Rejection*. Greensboro, NC: New Growth Press, 2012.

Whiteman, Darrell L. "Anthropological Reflections on Contextualizing Theology in a Globalizing World." In *Globalizing Theology: Belief and Practice in an Era of World Christianity*. Edited by Craig Ott, Harold Netland, and Wilbert Shenk. Grand Rapids, MI: Baker Academic, 2006. Kindle edition.

Willis, Jr., Avery T. "Response to Hiebert's Article: 'The Gospel in Human Contexts' and to the Responses of Pocock and Whiteman." In *MissionShift: Global Mission Issues in the Third Millennium*. Edited by Ed Stetzer and David Hesselgrave. Nashville, TN: B&H Publishing, 2010. Kindle Edition.

Wright, Christopher J. H. *The Mission of God: Unlocking the Bible's Grand Narrative*. Downers Grove, IL: InterVarsity Press, 2006.

Wright, N. T. *How God Became King: The Forgotten Story of the Gospels*. San Francisco: HarperCollins, 2012. Kindle edition.

Wu, Jackson. "Rewriting the Gospel for Oral Cultures: Why Honor and Shame Are Essential to the Gospel Story," in the forthcoming book from International Orality Network, *Beyond Literate Western Contexts: Honor & Shame and Assessment of Orality Preference*. Article available at: https://jacksonwu.files.wordpress.com/2014/07/rewriting-the-gospel-for-oral-cultures-why-honor-and-shame-are-essential-to-the-gospel-story-ion-2014-consultation-hbu-jackson-wu.pdf.

———. *Saving God's Face: A Chinese Contextualization of Salvation through Honor and Shame*. EMS Dissertation Series. Pasadena, CA: William Carey International University Press, 2012.

Yang, Lawrence Hsin, and Arthur Kleinman. "'Face' and the Embodiment of Stigma in China—The Cases of Schizophrenia and AIDS." *Social Science and Medicine* 30, (2008): 1–11.

Zaleski, Carol. "Fear of Heaven." In *The Christian Century* (March 14, 2001): 24.

Index of Scriptural References

Additional resources concerning honor/shame and Christian ministry

globalgospelbook.org
- Access free resources related to this book
- Order additional copies of *The Global Gospel;* bulk quantities available at a significant discount

wernermischke.org
- Werner Mischke's blog
- Variety of free resources to learn about honor/shame

jacksonwu.org
- Blog by "Jackson Wu" explores the intersection of "doing theology" and "thinking mission"
- Wu is the author of *Saving God's Face: A Chinese Contextualization of Salvation through Honor and Shame*, and *One Gospel for All Nations: A Practical Approach to Biblical Contextualization*

honorshame.com
- Weekly blog by "Jayson Georges," missionary and author
- Comprehensive site about honor and shame in Christian ministry
- Website contains a variety of learning resources
- Training options available
- Jayson is the author of *The 3D Gospel: Ministry in Guilt, Shame and Fear Cultures*

Mission ONE:
Helping you and your church connect with God's global mission through healthy cross-cultural partnerships

Mission ONE trains and mobilizes the Church, focusing on cross-cultural partnerships to engage the unreached and serve the poor and oppressed.

A bridge to outstanding indigenous leaders and their ministries

Founded by evangelist Bob Schindler in 1991, Mission ONE partners with key leaders and teams of national (indigenous) evangelists and church planters in Africa, Asia, and the Middle East. These teams conduct evangelism, church planting and holistic ministry among unreached peoples—who have little or no access to hearing the gospel of Christ.

- **Healthy partnerships.** Mission ONE serves as a bridge between the church in the United States and indigenous ministries in "the hard places." Mission ONE helps you engage in healthy, multi-faceted cross-cultural partnerships with proven, highly effective ministries.

- **Unreached peoples.** Most of the ministries with whom Mission ONE partners serve among Hindu, Muslim, Buddhist, or tribal peoples. More than 80% of their workers labor in the "10-40 Window Region," where the vast majority of unreached peoples live.

- **Business for transformation.** Mission ONE is empowering its national partners with business for transformation strategies toward long-term sustainability. These kingdom businesses take a holistic approach—emphasizing 1) spiritual awakening, 2) economic viability, 3) social justice, and 4) environmental stewardship.

What distinguishes Mission ONE? One feature is the depth and duration of relationship between Mission ONE leaders and it's international partners. Another feature is the quality of its training resources to help you equip your church or mission team.

**Mission ONE is your bridge to fruitful, proven indigenous Christian leaders and their ministries— *your due diligence is already done.*
Enter into an already successful partnership with Mission ONE.**

Mission ONE®
Partnership with nationals. It just makes sense.^{SM}

mission1.org

Mission ONE / PO Box 5960 / Scottsdale, AZ 85261 / USA / 480-951-0900

Operation WorldView:
Explore your destiny in God's global story

Inspired by Perspectives™—eight easy one-hour missions education sessions for churches, small groups, students, mission teams

Inspired by the life-changing course, *Perspectives on the World Christian Movement,* Operation WorldView introduces the Biblical, Historical, Cultural, and Strategic aspects of world missions. Eight lessons are presented primarily by Mission ONE's Bob Schindler and Werner Mischke— through a DVD curriculum that serves the missions training needs of local churches. It's perfect for small groups, church-wide studies, Sunday School classes, Christian schools, and home-schoolers.

The "Why" of missions in an easy-to-use small group format

Featuring powerful missions training lessons based on classics such as "The Story of His Glory" and "The Kingdom Strikes Back," Operation WorldView helps students, small groups and mission teams explore profound truths in Scripture, history and culture—which together explain in a compelling way the powerful "why" of missions. Each component explores one key question:

- **Biblical:** What is the story above all stories?
- **Historical:** What does it mean, the kingdom strikes back?
- **Cultural:** What is the romance of the universe?
- **Strategic:** What is your destiny in God's story?

Operation WorldView is your missions curriculum for small groups. It centers on the surpassing magnitude of the Person of Jesus—and invites participation in his global "Love Story."

mission1.org/**equip**

Operation WorldView is designed and produced by Werner Mischke/Mission ONE

The Beauty of Partnership:
Lead your team to gain the skills for healthy cross-cultural partnerships

In just six weeks, The Beauty of Partnership *equips individuals, small groups and mission teams for healthy cross-cultural partnerships.*

The Beauty of Partnership equips individuals, church groups, and mission teams to develop effective cross-cultural relationships—while reducing misunderstanding, confusion, and wasted money.

With *The Beauty of Partnership* you'll discover how godly character, cultural intelligence, and organizational competence work together beautifully for ministry success. You'll learn vital skills such as empathic listening and how to navigate different culture styles.

1 Godly Character

2 Cultural Intelligence

Organizational Competence *3*

LEADER'S EDITION

Includes Discussion Guide DVD

The Beauty of Partnership

Lead your team to gain the skills to achieve successful cross-cultural partnerships

Werner M

The Beauty of Partnership™

Discussion Guide DVD

Equipping followers of Jesus Christ for healthy cross-cultural partnerships to bring hope to the peoples of the world

The Beauty of Partnership is a ministry of Mission ONE PO Box 5960 Scottsdale, AZ 85261 USA • 480-951-0900 info@mission1.org

The Beauty of Partnership™

The Beauty of Partnership is designed on the basis of adult learning theory, incorporating four types of learning tasks— *inductive, input, implementation,* and *integration.* The study is very personal and highly interactive— perfect as a learning journey for your mission team or small group.

mission1.org/**equip**

The Beauty of Partnership is edited and produced by Werner Mischke/Mission ONE

The Father's Love Booklet:
Helping you know and share
the gospel of Jesus Christ
in the language of honor and shame

The Father's Love Booklet is designed for believers to share the gospel of Christ with people for whom honor and shame is vitally important.

This pocket-size booklet tells the good news of Jesus Christ through what is commonly known as "The Story of the Prodigal Son." With this booklet you can help people find hope, salvation, and honor in following Jesus Christ.

- Contains the story of The Prodigal Son— Luke 15:11–32

- Incorporates ideas from cross-cultural workers laboring in honor/shame contexts

- 20 pages, 3.1 x 4.1 inches; compact size fits into a shirt pocket

- The English edition uses the Easy-To-Read Version of the Bible (ERV)—this makes it easier to read and understand by people for whom English is a second language

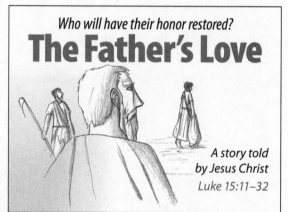

Who will have their honor restored?
The Father's Love
A story told by Jesus Christ
Luke 15:11–32

- Suitable as a teaching tool—believers can memorize the parable so that they bring out the story's honor/shame dynamics

- Designed for interaction and easy conversation

- Helps people from societies with honor/shame cultures to understand the basic message of Jesus Christ

- Available in English, Spanish and Arabic

To inquire about investing resources to translate The Father's Love Booklet into other languages, contact Mission ONE.

mission1.org/equip

The Father's Love Booklet is produced by Werner Mischke/Mission ONE